ENCOUNTER BETWEEN EASTERN ORTHODOXY AND RADICAL ORTHODOXY

This excellent collection surprises at many turns. It offers not only a unique perspective onto a theological dialogue so far unheard, it also opens up new avenues in theological conversation for both participants – the Radically Orthodox and members of the Eastern Orthodox family. Radical Orthodoxy is pushed to articulate a theology of tradition and to locate its own theology of participation within the Patristic patrimony far more deeply than before; the Eastern Orthodox are pushed toward a re-engagement with Bulgakov and the theosophical tradition so attractive to the Radically Orthodox. There is much here for all interested in the future of serious theological dialogue.

Lewis Ayres, Candler School of Theology, Emory University

This is a stimulating and fruitful exchange between Eastern Orthodoxy and Radical Orthodoxy by leading scholars of each that both draws upon tradition and opens horizons for the future. Addressing the problems of modernity from their different starting points, the collection offers profound material for reflecting upon our own situation. It deserves a wide readership and will amply repay serious engagement.

John Behr, Dean, St Vladimir's Orthodox Theological Seminary

This book presents the first debate between the Anglo-Catholic movement Radical Orthodoxy and Eastern Orthodox theologians. Leading international scholars offer new insights and reflections on a wide range of contemporary issues from a specifically theological and philosophical perspective. The ancient notion of divine Wisdom (Sophia) serves as a common point of reference in this encounter. Both Radical and Eastern Orthodoxy agree that the transfiguration of the world through the Word is at the very centre of the Christian faith. The book explores how this process of transformation can be envisaged with regard to epistemological, ontological, aesthetical, ecclesiological and political questions. Contributors to this volume include Rowan Williams, John Milbank, Antoine Arjakovsky, Michael Northcott, Nicholas Loudovikos, Andrew Louth and Catherine Pickstock.

Encounter Between Eastern Orthodoxy and Radical Orthodoxy

Transfiguring the World Through the Word

Edited by

ADRIAN PABST
University of Nottingham, UK

and

CHRISTOPH SCHNEIDER
University of Zurich, Switzerland

ASHGATE

Published by
Ashgate Publishing Limited
Wey Court East
Union Road
Farnham
Surrey, GU9 7PT
England

Ashgate Publishing Company
Suite 420
101 Cherry Street
Burlington
VT 05401-4405
USA

www.ashgate.com

British Library Cataloguing in Publication Data
Encounter between Eastern Orthodoxy and radical orthodoxy:
    transfiguring the world through the Word
    1. Orthodox Eastern Church – Theology 2. Philosophical theology
    I. Pabst, Adrian II. Schneider, Christoph
    230'.046

Library of Congress Cataloging-in-Publication Data
Encounter between eastern orthodoxy and radical orthodoxy: transfiguring the world through the Word / edited by Adrian Pabst and Christoph Schneider.
    p. cm.
ISBN 978-0-7546-6091-0 (hardcover : alk. paper) 1. Philosophical theology. 2. Orthodox Eastern Church–Relations. 3. Anglo-Catholicism. 4. Radicalism – Religious aspects – Christianity. I. Pabst, Adrian. II. Schneider, Christoph.

BT40.E58 2008
280'.042 – dc22

2008023031

ISBN 978-0-7546-6091-0

Mixed Sources
Product group from well-managed forests and other controlled sources
www.fsc.org Cert no. SGS-COC-2482
© 1996 Forest Stewardship Council
FSC

Printed and bound in Great Britain by
TJ International Ltd, Padstow, Cornwall

Contents

Notes on Contributors   *vii*

Foreword by David Bentley Hart   *xi*

Acknowledgements   *xv*

Introduction: Transfiguring the World through the Word   1
Adrian Pabst and Christoph Schneider

PART I   SOPHIA, THEOLOGY AND PHILOSOPHY

1   Glorification of the Name and Grammar of Wisdom
     (Sergii Bulgakov and Jean-Marc Ferry)   29
     Antoine Arjakovsky
          Commentary   40
          Rowan Williams

2   Sophiology and Theurgy: The New Theological Horizon   45
     John Milbank
          Commentary   86
          Antoine Arjakovsky (translated by Adrian Pabst)

PART II   SOPHIA, POLITICS AND ECCLESIOLOGY

3   The Metaphysics of Hope and the Transfiguration of Making in the
     Market Empire   93
     Michael Northcott

4   Wisdom and the Art of Politics   109
     Adrian Pabst

PART III   ONTOLOGY, EAST AND WEST

5   Ontology Celebrated: Remarks of an Orthodox on Radical Orthodoxy   141
     Nicholas Loudovikos
          Commentary: Ecumenical Orthodoxy – A Response to Nicholas
          Loudovikos   156
          John Milbank

6   *Kenosis*, *Poiesis* and *Genesis*: Or the Theological Aesthetics of
     Suffering   165
     Graham Ward
          Commentary: Silence, Intellect and Discourse in the Quest for the
          True Teaching – Reflections on Hermes Trismegistos' 'Definitions'   176
          Igor Dorfmann-Lazarev

7   The Beatific Vision of St Thomas Aquinas   185
     Phillip Blond

PART IV   ORTHODOXY AND TRANSFIGURATION

8   Space, Time and the Liturgy   215
     Andrew Louth
          Commentary: Liturgical Twilight – A Footnote to Andrew Louth   232
          Catherine Pickstock

9   Wisdom in the Fathers: An (Eastern) Orthodox Perspective   239
     Marcus Plested

10   The Theologico-Political Constitution of Monastic Liturgy   249
     Mihail Neamţu

11   The Transformation of Eros: Reflections on Desire in Jacques Lacan   271
     Christoph Schneider

Index   *291*

Notes on Contributors

Antoine Arjakovsky is Professor and Director of the Institute of Ecumenical Studies at the Ukrainian Catholic University (Lviv) and Guest Professor at the Centre Sèvres (Paris). His publications include *Histoire de la pensée orthodoxe contemporaine: La génération des penseurs religieux de l'émigration russe* (2002) and *Entretiens avec le cardinal Lubomyr Husar: Vers un christianisme post-confessionel* (2005), as well as numerous articles.

Phillip Blond is Senior Lecturer in Philosophy and Theology at the University of Cumbria. He is the editor of *Post-Secular Philosophy: Between Philosophy and Theology* (1997), and was a contributor to the collection *Radical Orthodoxy. A new theology* (1998). He has published academic articles in a number of journals, including in *Modern Theology* and *Studies in Christian Ethics*.

Igor Dorfmann-Lazarev is a research fellow at the *Istituto per le ricerche di storia sociale e religiosa*, Vicenza. Previously he taught at the universities of Roma I and Roma II, Montpellier and Durham. In 2007, he received an award from the French Academy for the monograph based on his doctoral thesis, *Arméniens et Byzantins à l'époque de Photius* (2004). He has published book chapters as well as articles in a number of international journals, including *Australian Slavonic and East European Studies* and *Istina*.

David Bentley Hart, an Eastern Orthodox scholar, is a visiting professor at Providence College, where he occupied the Randall Chair from 2006 to 2007, and has also taught at the University of Virginia and Duke Divinity School. Among his publications are *The Beauty of the Infinite: The Aesthetics of Christian Truth* (2003), *The Doors of the Sea: Where Was God in the Tsunami?* (2005), *In the Aftermath: Provocations and Laments* (2008), and the forthcoming *Christian Revolution* (2009).

Nicholas Loudovikos is Professor of Systematic Theology at the Theological Department of the Higher Ecclesiastical Academy of Thessaloniki, Visiting Lecturer at the Institute for Orthodox Christian Studies in Cambridge and Adjunct Professor at the University of Wales. He is the author of *Theopoiia: the postmodern theological aporia* (2007); *The Apophatic Ecclesiology of Consubstantiality. The Primitive Church Today* (2002); *Closed Spirituality and the Meaning of the Self. The Mysticism of Power and the Truth of Nature and Personhood* (1999); *Theological History of Ancient Greek Philosophy* (2003); *A Eucharistic Ontology. Maximus the Confessor's eschatological ontology of being as gift* (1992, English translation forthcoming); *Science in the Destiny of Theology* (2009); *Orthodoxy and Modernization: Byzantine Individualization, State and History in the perspective of the European Future* (2006).

Andrew Louth is Professor of Patristic and Byzantine Studies at the University of Durham. He taught at the University of Oxford from 1970 to 1985 and at the University of London from 1985 to 1995. His most recent publications include *St John Damascene: Tradition and Originality in Byzantine Theology* (2002). He translated St John of Damascus' *Three Treatises on the Divine Images* (2003) and is co-editor and contributor to *The Cambridge History of Early Christian Literature* (2004).

John Milbank is Research Professor of Religion, Politics, and Ethics and Director of the Centre of Theology and Philosophy at the University of Nottingham. Previously he was the Frances Myers Ball Professor of Philosophical Theology at the University of Virginia, Reader in Philosophical Theology and Fellow of Peterhouse in the University of Cambridge. He is the author of *Theology and Social Theory: Beyond Secular Reason* (1990), *The Word Made Strange: Theology, Language, Culture* (1997), *Truth in Aquinas* (with Catherine Pickstock) (2000), *Being Reconciled. Ontology and Pardon* (2003) and *The Suspended Middle: Henri de Lubac and the Debate concerning the Supernatural* (2005). He is also the co-editor of *Radical Orthodoxy. A new theology* (1998).

Mihail Neamțu received his Ph.D. in theology and religious studies from King's College London. From 2005 to 2007, he was a Research Fellow at the New Europe College in Bucharest. He has published articles in philosophical theology and has translated a number of contemporary authors (Jean-Luc Marion, H. Tristan Engelhardt Jr., John Behr, Andrew Louth, and David Bentley Hart). He is also the author of two books: *The Owl Among Ruins. Theological Insomnia in Post-Communist Romania* (2005, 2nd revised edition) and *The Grammar of Orthodoxy. Tradition after Modernity* (2007).

Michael Northcott is Professor of Ethics in the School of Divinity at the University of Edinburgh. He has published widely in the field of theological ethics. His most recent publications include *The Environment and Christian Ethics* (1996), *Life after Debt: Christianity and Global Justice* (1999), *An Angel Directs the Storm: Apocalyptic Religion and America* (2004) and *A Moral Climate: The Ethics of Global Warming* (2007).

Adrian Pabst is a Leverhulme Research Fellow at the Department of Theology and Religious Studies in the University of Nottingham and a member of the Centre of Theology and Philosophy. He has published articles on philosophical and political theology in *Telos*, *Revue des sciences philosophique et théologiques*, *New Blackfriars* and *American Catholic Philosophical Quarterly*. He is the co-author (with Olivier-Thomas Venard) of *Radical Orthodoxy. Pour une révolution théologique* (2004). His first monograph, *Metaphysics: The Creation of Hierarchy* will be published by Eerdmans in 2009–10.

Marcus Plested is Vice-Principal and Academic Director of the Institute for Orthodox Christian Studies in Cambridge. He read History then Theology at Merton College, Oxford and completed his doctorate with a thesis on the Macarian Homilies. He has published widely in the field of Orthodox Christian studies. His most recent book is *The Macarian Legacy: The Place of Macarius-Symeon in the Eastern Christian Tradition* (2004).

Catherine Pickstock is Reader in Philosophy of Religion at the Faculty of Divinity in the University of Cambridge. Her publications include *After Writing: On the Liturgical Consummation of Philosophy* (1997), *Truth in Aquinas* (with John Milbank) (2000) and *Theory, Religion and Idiom in Platonic Philosophy* (forthcoming). She is also the co-editor of *Radical Orthodoxy. A new theology* (1998).

Christoph Schneider is a temporary Research Assistant at the University of Bern. He studied theology at the University of Zürich, gained a Masters in Systematic Theology and Philosophy of Religion at King's College London and completed his doctoral studies at the University of Zürich. He was also a visiting scholar at the Faculty of Divinity in the University of Cambridge. In October 2005, he organized the conference 'Transfiguring the World Through the Word' that led to the present collection of essays.

Graham Ward is currently the Head of the School of Arts, Histories and Cultures at the University of Manchester and also Professor of Contextual Theology and Ethics. He is the author of several books, including *Cities of God* (2000), *True Religion* (2002), *Cultural Transformation and Religious Practice* (2005), *Christ and Culture* (2006), *Religion and Political Thought* (with Michael Hoelzl, 2006) and *The New Visibility of Religion* (with Michael Hoelzl, 2008). He is the editor of *The Postmodern God* (1997), *The Certeau Reader* (1998) and *The Blackwell Companion of Postmodern Theology* (2001). He is also the co-editor of *Radical Orthodoxy. A new theology* (1998).

Rowan Williams is the Archbishop of Canterbury. He was previously the Lady Margaret Professor of Divinity at Oxford University, before becoming the Bishop of Monmouth and subsequently the Archbishop of Wales. He is the author of many books, including *After Silent Centuries* (1994), *On Christian Theology* (2000), *Lost Icons: Reflections on Cultural Bereavement* (2000), *Arius: Heresy and Tradition* (2001), *Tokens of Trust*: *An Introduction to Christian Belief* (2007) and *Dostoevsky: Language, Faith, and Fiction* (2008). He is also the editor of *Sergii Bulgakov: Towards a Russian Political Theology* (1999).

Foreword

David Bentley Hart

Apart from an obvious and largely accidental homonymy, and perhaps something of a shared tendency towards combativeness, there seems little uniting Eastern Orthodoxy and the Radical Orthodoxy movement. The former is chiefly marked – or so it often seems – by its historically fated conservatism, its broad indifference to any but the Eastern Church Fathers, its diffidence in regard to philosophical schools and debates outside its own tradition, and its at times admirable and at times deplorable insularity; the latter by its *frissons* of theological and political radicalism, its militantly 'Latin' and 'Augustinian' approaches to theology, its fascination with everything *au courant* in the world of continental thought, and its cheerful openness to an endless variety of influences (the unwholesome on some occasions along with the wholesome). More to the point, perhaps, the former is an ancient Church, comprising (at least, on optimistic estimates) a quarter billion souls, and carrying within itself some two millennia of traditions and memories, while the latter is a theological movement of recent vintage, the adherents of which can be numbered (at most) in the hundreds, and the purpose of which is to influence the development of speculative theology in all Christian communions. It is, needless to say, difficult fruitfully to compare creatures of such disparate species.

That said, there is – it seems to me – a natural affinity between the two, and a sphere of interests common to them. Both are, if nothing else, expressions of a single metaphysical and theological tradition. One is a more organic, continuous, ramifying, and floriferous expression, with all the strengths and weaknesses of any purely natural phenomenon, and the other a more reflective and critical expression, nurtured under the conservatory conditions of the academy, with all the security and fragility that entails. But both subsist in an element of what should be described – honestly and proudly – as the Christian Platonist tradition. (Some among the Orthodox take exception to this designation, principally because it is so obviously correct, but it is a fact that Orthodoxy is never more Platonist than when denouncing 'Platonism'). Everything the Orthodox treasure in the eastern patristic tradition – its emphasis upon the metaphysics of participation, the deification of the creature in Christ, the ascent of the soul to the vision of God, the spiritual reality of the divine image in the soul, the mystical co-inherence of the Body of Christ, and the real will of God to save all human beings, as well as its salutary ignorance of any real partition, conceptual or ontological, between nature and grace – constitutes the native atmosphere in which Radical Orthodoxy has evolved. Even the latter's 'Augustinianism' is devoid of any of those special features of the late Augustine's catastrophic misreading of Paul that are so profoundly distasteful to Eastern Christians: the doctrine of predilective predestination *ante praevisa merita*, the morbidly forensic understanding of original sin, the thrashing legions of unbaptized babies descending to their perpetual and condign combustion, and so on. The radically orthodox Augustine is the saner, more Platonist soul of the earlier theology, rather than the author of *De correptione*, the *Retractiones*, and the *Enchiridion*.

All of that, however, amounts to little more than saying that Eastern Orthodox tradition and the theology of Radical Orthodoxy reflect many of the same broad currents of Catholic tradition. The more crucial rationale, though, for the sort of serious engagement between the two parties this volume represents is that they are already involved in a sort of tacit alliance against a single enemy. Each is, in its distinctive way, a kind of evasion of or rebellion against modernity. Granted, in the case of the Orthodox Church, the 'evasion' has been more a matter of omission and of historical circumstance than of a conscious resistance to the pathologies of modern thought and culture, and so the 'rebellion' sometimes degenerates into a depressingly imprecise hostility towards 'the West' as a whole. And granted, also, in the case of Radical Orthodoxy, both the evasion and the rebellion at times seem almost utopian in their abstraction from the concrete particularities of communities and nations and ecclesial traditions. But, in both cases, one encounters an ethos naturally antagonistic to post-Christian understandings of the self, of freedom, and of society, and to the dehumanizing and ultimately nihilistic consequences towards which they lead. And, in both cases also, one encounters an awareness that the most destructive forces within modernity were in some sense incubated within theology (though again, in the case of some Eastern Christians, this awareness is sometimes diffused into a more general, and somewhat vacuous, distrust of 'Latin' theology as a whole).

It is a commonplace (though, happily, a sound one) to observe that much of the modern vision of reality – the 'mechanical philosophy', the reduction of the concept of freedom to that of pure spontaneity of will, the politics of the absolutist state, and so on – was to some extent obscurely born in the late mediaeval collapse of the Christian metaphysical tradition as it had developed over more than a millennium, and especially in the rise of nominalism and voluntarism. The original impulse guiding these developments, of course, was a desire upon the part of certain theologians to affirm as radically as possible the sovereign transcendence of God; but the image of God thus produced – as hardly needs to be said – was ultimately of a super-rational and even super-moral God, whose divinity consisted entirely in the omnipotence and arbitrariness of his will, and who was not truly transcendent of his creation, but merely the supreme power within it. In detaching God's freedom from God's nature as Goodness, Truth, and Charity – as this theology necessarily, if not always intentionally, did – Christian thought laid the foundations for many of those later revolutions in philosophy and morality that would help to produce the post-Christian order. It was inevitable, after all, that the object of the voluntarist model of freedom would migrate from the divine to the human will, and that a world evacuated of its ontological continuity with God's goodness would ultimately find no place for God within itself. And, in early modernity, when the new God of infinite and absolute will had to a very great degree displaced the true God from men's minds, the new technology of print assured that all Christians would make the acquaintance of this impostor, and through him come to understand true liberty as a personal sovereignty transcending even the dictates and constraints of nature.

Moreover – more crucially – the God thus produced was monstrous: an abyss of pure, predestining omnipotence, whose majesty was revealed at once in his unmerited mercy towards the elect and his righteous wrath against the derelict. And he was to be found in the theologies of almost every school: not only Jansenism, Lutheranism, and Calvinism, but also the theology of the Dominican Thomists, such as Bañez and Alvarez (though the Dominicans, through their superior faculty for specious reasoning, did a better job of convincing themselves that their God was a good God). That modern Western humanity came in large measure to refuse to believe in or worship such a God was ineluctable, and in some sense extremely commendable (no one, after all, can be faulted for preferring atheism to Calvinism or the old 'two-tiered' Thomism).

In any event, these are old arguments and there is no need to rehearse them here. All I wish to point out is that Eastern Orthodoxy – through its innocence of these theological deformations – and Radical Orthodoxy – through its rejection and abhorrence of them – are already in some way bound together in a single destiny; and, as the community of believing European Christians continues to dwindle away (as it certainly will, far into the foreseeable future), they should not hesitate to lend their strengths each to the other, and to mend their own infirmities thereby. What such an interaction might produce is difficult to say, but one might venture a few guesses. Perhaps certain Eastern Orthodox theologians might be moved to reconsider the Eastern hostility towards Augustine that has become such a vogue among the Orthodox in the past five decades, and that has made many of them insensible to the brilliance even of works such as *De Trinitate*, and that continues to produce offensively silly caricatures of Augustine's theology in Orthodox scholarship. Perhaps, by the same token, certain of the radically orthodox could be weaned from their preposterous refusal to acknowledge that Augustine's late theology of nature and grace, sin and election, must be accounted the chief cause within the Latin tradition of that tradition's susceptibility to the appeal of voluntarism. Some Eastern theologians might be emboldened partly to abandon the Neo-Palamite theology that has become so dominant in their Church since the middle of the last century, and frankly acknowledge its incoherence, and come to recognize that in many ways Augustine or Thomas was closer to the Greek Fathers in his understanding of divine transcendence than was Palamas (at least, Palamas as he has come to be understood); these theologians might even feel freer to avail themselves of many of the riches of their own tradition that have been forgotten as a result of the triumph of the Neo-Palamite synthesis. And perhaps some of the radically orthodox, taking the example of modern Eastern theology more to heart, might learn better to integrate the mystical and spiritual dimensions of the faith into their expositions of doctrine and into their theological speculations. Most importantly, perhaps, the Eastern Orthodox might be reminded by their encounters with Radical Orthodoxy that a true defiance of the more nihilistic currents of modernity should take the form not simply of a retreat into liturgical and spiritual tradition, but of a social and political philosophy as well. And perhaps the radically orthodox might profit from an exposure to the sheer obduracy of Eastern Christianity – the effect of decades and centuries of misfortune and oppression – and learn to fortify themselves against the almost certain failure of their project as a social and political force.

One could go on, of course, but the endless addition of one 'perhaps' to another leads nowhere, except in the direction of an ever more random association of ideas. Suffice it to say that the time is ripe for a collection of this sort and – both for the conversation it comprises and for the further conversations it portends – this book is a worthy object of celebration.

Acknowledgements

This collection is partly based on a conference held under the same title in Cambridge from 30 September to 2 October 2005. We are grateful to the Institute for Orthodox Christian Studies (IOCS), in particular its former principal Dr Grant White and his successor Professor David Frost for their support. We would also like to thank Wesley House and the Faculty of Divinity in the University of Cambridge for providing facilities and hosting the conference. We acknowledge with gratitude a conference grant from the British Academy that made this event possible.

We are grateful to all the speakers for making their papers available for publication. We would like to thank those who did not participate in the conference for their contributions to this collection.

We owe a special debt of gratitude to our publishers Ashgate, in particular Sarah Lloyd, Anne Keirby and Rosie Phillips, for their patience and flexibility in relation to the delivery of the manuscript. Finally, we would like to thank Anthony Paul Smith for compiling the index.

Feast of St John Chrysostom, Archbishop of Constantinople
13 November 2008
Adrian Pabst and Christoph Schneider

Introduction
Transfiguring the World through the Word

Adrian Pabst and Christoph Schneider

This collection of essays is in large part based on the proceedings of the conference 'Transfiguring the World through the Word: an encounter between Radical Orthodoxy and Eastern Orthodoxy', which took place from 30 September to 2 October 2005 at Wesley House and the Divinity Faculty in the University of Cambridge. Yet it has been significantly extended to include essays written by authors who were invited but unable to attend the conference, or who attended but could not give a paper. While Catholic and Reformed theologians have already responded to the Radical Orthodoxy movement,[1] no extensive encounter with Eastern Orthodoxy had taken place prior to this conference. The publication of these essays seeks to fill this gap in the existing literature. More importantly, it also hopes to pave the way for further shared reflection on the common Christian theological tradition and the future of the Christian Churches.

Any genuine ecumenical conversation in which the partners honestly consider the possibility that they could learn something from each other has to replace false compromise and self-righteous denominational pride with a true passion for truth. False compromise is surely a sign of a community's lack of identity; and self-righteous denominational pride can only be interpreted as the expression of a tradition's self-enclosure. Both attitudes thwart the continuous reception of grace and prevent the dynamical unfolding of the Christian tradition. While Anglicanism has been routinely accused of lacking a distinct identity, Eastern Orthodoxy is often viewed as stubbornly uncompromising in the ecumenical dialogue. Although Radical Orthodoxy is (primarily) an Anglo-Catholic movement, it does definitely not conform to the aforementioned Anglican stereotypes. Right from the beginning it rejected the 'idolization of academic 'politeness' ...'.[2] At least within the Anglican context, Radical Orthodoxy is perceived as too confrontational and polemical in its relentless criticism of secularism and liberal theology. As far as Eastern Orthodoxy is concerned, it at times confuses its role as the guardian of genuine Christianity

---

[1]   Laurence Paul Hemming (ed.), *Radical Orthodoxy? – A Catholic Enquiry* (Aldershot, 2000); James K.A. Smith and James H. Olthius (eds), *Radical Orthodoxy and the Reformed Tradition: Creation, Covenant, and Participation* (Grand Rapids, MI, 2005); cf. Adrian Pabst and Olivier-Thomas Venard, *Radical orthodoxy: Pour une révolution théologique* (Geneva, 2004); James K.A. Smith, *Introducing Radical Orthodoxy. Mapping a Post-secular Theology* (Grand Rapids, MI, 2004).

[2]   *Radical Orthodoxy Manifesto*, Thesis 23.

with a fiercely anti-Western and anti-ecumenical attitude that contributes nothing to a constructive theological debate. However, in some cases the critique of the West is theologically motivated and based on a profound knowledge of the Christian tradition. Georges Florovsky falls into this category. For him, 'Christian reunion is simply universal conversion to Orthodoxy'.[3]

Insofar as Radical Orthodoxy and the best traditions of Eastern Orthodoxy seek to recover and extend an overarching theological vision, separately and together they represent a robust challenge to the secular liberal approach that has tended to dictate ecumenical dialogue for the last 50 years or so. Thus the most fruitful approach to ecumenism in the twenty-first century is to begin by emphasizing that all Christian denominations face the common threat of secularism.[4] Alexander Schmemann defined it as

> a world view and consequently a way of life in which the basic aspects of human existence – such as family, education, science, profession, art, etc. – not only are not rooted in or related to religious faith, but in which the very necessity or possibility of such a connection is denied. The secular areas of life are thought of as *autonomous*, i.e. governed by their own values, principles, and motivations, different from the religious ones.[5]

To recognize that the secularized world concerns all Christians does not mean that doctrinal differences become irrelevant and that confessional boundaries should be blurred or even prematurely abandoned. Rather, the challenge of secularism puts the different embodiments of Christian faith to the test. It helps us see which Churches possess the spiritual and theological resources to safeguard a faithful but also dynamic continuation of the Christian tradition that is able to embrace and transform all aspects of human life. An inattentive Church will ceaselessly oscillate between a shallow universalism that embraces uncritically every intellectual fashion and a fideistic sectarianism whose identity is constituted by *re*acting against either other denominations or secular worldviews. In both cases we are dealing with distortions of Christian faith that will not provide us with a positive orientation of human life to its first principle and final end in God.

Radical Orthodoxy has clearly stated how it believes both these pitfalls can be avoided. There is no need to give an account here of their creative reinterpretation of pre-Scotist Christianity, which rejects the dichotomy between nature and grace, and reason and revelation. What is at stake is a *re-enchantment* (*Wiederverzauberung*) of the world in Christ. This term was used to characterize the work of the Russian

---

[3]   Georges Florovsky, *Collected Works: Ecumenism I. A Doctrinal Approach*, ed. R.S. Haugh (14 vols, Vaduz, 1972–89), vol. 13, p. 134.

[4]   Cf. John Meyendorff, *Living Tradition. Orthodox Witness in the Contemporary World* (Crestwood, NY, 1978), p. 167.

[5]   Alexander Schmemann, 'Problems of Orthodoxy in America: III. The Spiritual Problem', *St. Vladimir's Seminary Quarterly*, 9/4 (1965): 173.

philosopher Pavel Florenksy, but it may nicely sum up the theological intentions of the Radical Orthodoxy project as well.[6] The essays included in this collection will address this issue in some detail with respect to the sophiological tradition, the idea of participation, politics, liturgy, language, (theo-)poietics and desire.

This introduction will not summarize or assess each contribution but instead reflect more broadly on the notion of transformation and re-enchantment. The subtitle of this collection is *transfiguring the world through the Word*. That is to say, the transfiguration of the world is brought about by God through Christ in the Spirit, but mediated by human beings. The first part tries to elucidate this process (I). It will then be asked in what way Radical Orthodoxy constitutes a challenge for Eastern Orthodoxy with respect to the question of transformation (II). In the last part the same question is addressed to Radical Orthodoxy: what can it learn from the Eastern tradition as regards the notion of transformation? (III).

It goes without saying that there is an asymmetry in the dialogue between Radical Orthodoxy and Eastern Orthodoxy insofar as the former is a recent academic and intellectual movement and the latter a Church with a history of two thousand years. As far as Eastern Orthodoxy is concerned, the focus will be mainly on the Russian tradition.

Transformation and Synergy

The Christian re-enchanting and transfiguring of the world has its ground in the incarnate *Logos*, Jesus Christ. According to the well-known patristic formula this means: 'the unassumed is the unhealed, only that which is united to the Godhead is saved'.[7] Anthropologically and theologically, this process of assumption takes place in such a fashion that the divine attributes correspond to the human virtues in the same way as Incarnation corresponds to deification (*theosis*). These correlations follow the logic of *tantum-quantum*: 'As much as God is humanized to man through love for mankind, so much is man able to deify himself [ἑαυτὸν] to God through love'.[8] Since there is no separation between nature and grace, there cannot be a dichotomy between divine action and human passivity either. As John Milbank points out, 'that which is wholly done for us by God, namely deification by grace, is yet also our highest act and as such properly our own – even that which is most properly our own'. On the other hand, 'the most active human action is passive in relation to God'.[9]

---

[6]   Michael Hagemeister, 'Wiederverzauberung der Welt: Pavel Florenskijs Neues Mittelalter', in Norbert Franz, Michael Hagemeister, Frank Haney (eds), *Pavel Florenskij – Tradition und Moderne* (Frankfurt a.M., 2001), pp. 21–41.

[7]   Gregory of Nazianzus, *Epistle* 101, 32 (SC 208, p. 50).

[8]   Maximus Confessor, *Ambiguum* 10 (PG 91: 1113B).

[9]   John Milbank, *The Suspended Middle. Henri de Lubac and the Debate concerning the Supernatural* (Grand Rapids, MI/Cambridge, UK, 2005), pp. ix, 105.

The deification of man is closely connected with the view of man as *microcosmos* and the world as *macroanthropos*. Anthropology and cosmology are here inextricably intertwined. This idea, aspects of which can be traced back to pre-Socratic times, is taken up by the Church Fathers and plays a particularly important role in the writings of Nemesius of Emesa (c. 390) and Maximus the Confessor (c. 580–662). All the divisions of the cosmos are reflected in man, who – as 'natural bond' – mediates between the extremes of creation. This mediating function consists in perceiving and apprehending the created world in all its variety and in unifying the cosmos by referring it to its centre, the *Logos* – Christ. The accomplishment of this task requires spiritual purification and excludes what Maximus calls the misuse of creation. But even if human beings are actively involved in this process, in patristic theology the creative transformation of creation – in the sense of cultural activity – remains limited. As a thinker of the seventh century Maximus did not formulate a theory of culture.

This is exactly the concern of Sergii Bulgakov (1871–1944). Aware of the need for Orthodoxy to engage with the contemporary world, he develops a Christian theory of cultural activity. In *Philosophy of Economy*, it is *economy* that serves as the basic paradigm for his philosophy of culture. Economic activity is understood in terms of effort and labour that is goal-directed.[10] What is required is 'a theory of action based on knowledge, a *praxeology rather than an epistemology*'.[11] Under the conditions of the Fall, nature and the world are experienced as a constant threat, and labour struggles with the elemental forces of nature in order to conquer and humanize them. Yet despite the fragmented and chaotic character of the empirical world, creation remains in its essence a unified and coherent whole, even if we can only catch glimpses of this sophic ground. It is the task of historical humanity to raise the world to a higher level, to transform nature, to bring the divine Wisdom in creation to its full realization. According to Bulgakov, Sophia is the unifying principle of this cultural process, that which holds together the different fields of human activity such as economics, art, science and politics.

Bulgakov's theory of economic activity goes beyond ancient philosophy and medieval Christian thought in two important respects. First, he tries to make modernity's heightened awareness for human creativity and the 'plasticity' of the world fruitful for Christian theology. Both of these aspects have become manifest in modern science, art, economy and so forth, and Bulgakov tries to reinterpret them within an explicitly Christian framework: 'Christian humanism, which presumes the development of all creative capacities of man, may be understood as a new

---

[10] The Russian word *koziaistvo* (хозяйство) which is translated as 'economy' does not only denote the system of trade and industry but also means 'household'. It does refer to all activity in society. 'National economy' thus 'has connotations of the life of a giant household', Catherine Evtuhov, *The Cross and the Sickle: Sergei Bulgakov and the Fate of Russian Religious Philosophy* (Ithaca/London, 1997), p. 146.

[11] Sergei Bulgakov, *Philosophy of Economy. The World as Household*, trans., ed. and intro. C. Evtuhov (New Haven/London, 2000), p. 178.

comprehension, a new revelation of Christianity. It is no new Christianity, it is only its new comprehension'.[12] Secondly, he emphasizes the historical character of this cultural process. Sophia is viewed as the organizing force that leads the world to truth and is defined as '*truthfulness*, Truth as a process, as becoming'.[13] At the same time, he refrains from idolizing human creativity by pointing out that human beings cannot produce anything '*metaphysically new*'.[14] Only God can create *ex nihilo*. Human activity is always a recreation and replication of something already given. In spite of the historical and changing character of human existence and culture, self-determination as well as the transformation of the world mediated by human beings must follow the ideal model of Sophia. To ignore the pre-given character of the sophic nature of creation will amount to generating a satanic world of shadow and darkness.

Genuine Christian creativity follows the above-cited patristic formula that only 'the assumed is the healed' – and that 'the unassumed is the unhealed'. In and through the Incarnation, God has restored the cosmic role of human beings so that they are re-enabled to fulfil their mediating function between God and creation. Deification of human beings and the cosmos is based on a Chalcedonian Christology which confesses Christ as one person (ἕν πρόσωπον) and one hypostasis (μία ὑπόστασις) in two natures (δύο φύσεις). On the one hand, the Council of Chalcedon decided that the natures remain without confusion, without change, without division and without separation. On the other hand, the tradition declared that they are perichoretically intertwined (περιχώρησις) in the sense of a real reciprocity.[15] This is the only way to safeguard both God's full kenotic presence in creation and the full deification of human beings according to grace. Yet the divine assumption of the human nature does only renew the *tropos* of the human nature but not its *logos*, since communion with the *Logos* in fact *is* the natural state of true humanity.

Any imbalance in the relationship between the two natures will inevitably disfigure the specifically Christian understanding of the divine-human relationship.

---

[12] Sergii Bulgakov, 'Social Teaching in Modern Russian Orthodox Theology' in Sergii Bulgakov, *Towards a Russian Political Theology*, ed. and intro. Rowan Williams (Edinburgh, 1999), p. 282.

[13] Bulgakov, *Philosophy of Economy*, p. 176. The historical dimension of human life and culture is not developed in Maximus the Confessor and Greek patristic thought; see Hans Urs von Balthasar, *Kosmische Liturgie. Das Weltbild Maximus' des Bekenners* (2nd ed., Einsiedeln, 1961), pp. 176–7.

[14] Ibid., p. 145; Sergius Bulgakov, *The Bride of the Lamb* (Grand Rapids, MI, 2002), p. 321.

[15] Maximus Confessor, *Ambiguum* 5 (PG 91:1045D–1060D); John Damascene, *De fide orthodoxa* II, 3 and 4 (PG 49:993–1000); Lars Thunberg, *Microcosm and Mediator. The Theological Anthropology of Maximus the Confessor* (2nd edn, Chicago, Ill, 1995), pp. 21–36; Jean-Claude Larchet, *La divinisation de l'homme selon saint Maxime le Confesseur* (Paris, 1996), pp. 333–46.

On the one hand, this can result in immanentism, in a false autonomy, self-assertion and self-deification of the created order, which remains separated from the Godhead. Human freedom and creativity flourish and human beings produce culture in all its facets, yet this process is not an actualization of creation's God-given potency but a deviation from their real *telos*. In some cases, the function of the divine is reduced to formally sanctioning cultural practices that are completely devoid of Christian content. That is to say, Christianity is instrumentalized, it is used to bestow (additional) authority on a non-Christian worldview or ideology. The catastrophic marriage between nationalism and Christian faith falls into this category, instances of which can be found in East and West alike.

On the other hand, monophysite tendencies can lead to a voluntarist conception of divine revelation and its concomitant, a deficient anthropology. This will inevitably result in a dichotomy between divine action and human passivity. Revelation is thought of in terms of actualistic thought-categories and divine presence is reduced to a series of punctual events. The freely evoked human response to God, properly conceived as a divine-human synergy, gives way to 'revelatory positivism' and passive obedience. Since the response to God – insofar as it is theologically reflected upon at all – is considered to be merely human, it cannot take on a sacramental character. Accordingly, the idea of Christian creative activity and Christian culture is excluded *a priori*. Monophysitism, too, will in the end come to accept the existence of a secular world.

Radical Orthodoxy: A Challenge for Eastern Orthodoxy

As one of the central dogmas of Christian faith, the doctrine of the two natures of Christ is an appropriate tool to identify where in a particular tradition aspects of reality 'have not been assumed by the divine Word'. The process of assumption must embrace the whole of human reality in its diachronic and synchronic dimension. Diachrony here refers to the diachronic indwelling of God in the Church and synchrony stands for the ideal that all of reality at a given time is to be assumed by the divine Word. To be sure, the Christological dogma of the two natures of Christ cannot be separated from the doctrine of the Trinity, and the diachronic and synchronic presence of God is inconceivable without reference to Pneumatology.

As far as the diachronic dimension of divine presence is concerned, Radical Orthodoxy aims at a 'non-identical repetition of the past'. This idea shall serve as the guiding paradigm for the present section. The diachronic presence of God is manifest in tradition with its two poles: *sedimentation* and *innovation*. The term 'sedimentation' refers to the accumulated experiences of a tradition in the form of texts, rituals, practices and so forth. Our attitude to sedimentation leads either to *faithfulness* to past experiences or to *ossification*. Appropriate innovation is informed by *eschatological vision*; if it is distorted, it becomes *utopianism*. The Church faces the extremely demanding task to keep a balance between these two poles. The synchronic presence of God means that theology has to be *mediating* but not *accommodating*. As Radical Orthodoxy has pointed out, while 'theology must speak *also* of something else [than God], it seeks always to recognize a theological *difference* in such speaking'.[16] If theology loses its mediating function, it becomes automatically accommodating, at least with respect to those aspects of reality that it (wrongly) believes to fall without its sphere. It thus implicitly succumbs to secularism, even if this is not intended. Needless to say that the diachronic and the synchronic aspect are closely intertwined.

Diachrony: Tradition as Sedimentation and Innovation

Sedimentation: ossification or faithfulness to tradition? If the Church aims at an 'identical repetition of the past', sedimentation is overemphasized at the expense of innovation and the tradition becomes ossified. This is the constant danger of the Eastern tradition. The dialogue with Radical Orthodoxy should remind it that 'orthodoxy is an always unfinished task'[17] and that an identical repetition of the past is neither desirable nor possible. As Berdyaev notices, to place the stress too much on asceticism – understood as obedience, humility and meekness – can be as dangerous as overemphasizing creativeness and inspiration. Obedience can turn into servitude and abdication from responsibility, particularly socio-political responsibility. It can prevent us from developing our full creative potential and it can become an instrument of evil if it is misused by the authority to which this obedience is due. (False) humility and (false) meekness may in fact be expressions of pride, hypocrisy and resentment.[18] An exclusive orientation towards obedience and humility gives Christian faith a quasi-buddhistic character. World-renunciation, spiritual slavery and legalism become predominant and manifest themselves outwardly as institutionalism, ritualism and hierarchism. External organization and the visible aspect of the Church no longer inspire and shape, but suppress true spiritual life and human creativeness.[19] The Church thus becomes ossified.

As regards theological work, the question about the appropriate relationship between continuity and discontinuity within the Orthodox tradition needs to be raised again. Most of today's Orthodox theologians operate within a theological framework that is close to the 'Neopatristic synthesis' advocated by Vladimir Lossky, Georges Florovsky and others. Very few theologians try to work along the lines of the circle around Sergii Bulgakov, which developed a more sophisticated

---

[16]   See John Milbank, Graham Ward, Catherine Pickstock, 'Suspending the material: the turn of radical orthodoxy', in John Milbank, Graham Ward, Catherine Pickstock (eds), *Radical Orthodoxy. A New Theology* (London/New York, 1999), p. 2.

[17]   John Milbank, *Sophiology and Theurgy: the New Theological Horizon*.

[18]   Cf. Nicolas Berdyaev, *Spirit and Reality*, trans. G. Reavey (London, 1939), pp. 88–9.

[19]   Sergius Bulgakov, *The Comforter*, trans. B. Jakim (Grand Rapids, MI/Cambridge, UK, 2004), p. 308.

understanding of a 'living tradition' and which was much better equipped for a constructive *and* critical engagement with other denominations and contemporary thought.[20] What is at stake here is not a comprehensive defence of the controversial sophiological tradition. Like all theology, it is work in progress, as Bulgakov himself admitted. Contrary to many Orthodox voices, only an active and rigorous engagement with the contemporary intellectual world, as carried out by Radical Orthodoxy, enables us to avoid being secretly influenced by secular thought that is opposed to Christian faith. Some contemporary theology that at first glance reads like exegesis of the Church Fathers is in fact at the mercy of contemporary intellectual fashions and thus not a faithful continuation of the tradition. However, it is also imperative for theology to discern which new insights in the history of ideas *must* be embraced by Christian theology. Bulgakov's reclaiming of human creative activity for Christian faith is a case in point. Modernity's discovery of man's immense creative capacity to transform the world more or less coincided with the secularization of the Western world. Yet this creative potential is in itself something good and was always intimated in the Christian tradition. As Bulgakov puts it:

> Our epoch is characterized by a broad development of creativity 'in its own name,' by a deluge of anthropotheism, in the form of a luciferian creative intoxication, and by an immersion in dull sensual paganism. *These developments cannot be overcome by mere rejection; they can be overcome only by the unfolding of a positive Christian doctrine of the world and creative activity, and by manifestation of its power* ... This is only a further unfolding of the Chalcedonian and ditheletic dogma, according to which the fullness of the human nature and the entire power of human creative will and energy in Christ are united with the divine nature, are co-manifested with it and are deified by it.[21]

Generally speaking, this is not the current intellectual strategy in contemporary Orthodox theology and Bulgakov's works therefore remain a challenge. It often even constitutes a stumbling block. In this respect the Eastern tradition has to learn a lot from Radical Orthodoxy. As their writings reveal, all aspects of human life need to be reconsidered from a Christian viewpoint since there is nothing that falls outside God's creation apart from sin – which is not part of creation but privation of the Good. A Christian notion of human innovation, creativity and imagination is of particular importance and needs to be further developed since it forms the basis of all cultural processes.

Any theologian who (wrongly) aims at an identical repetition of the past must be aware that creativity is a permanent task for the Church. It is not possible

---

[20]   For an overview of the debates between these two groups see Paul Valliere, *Modern Russian Theology. Bukharev, Soloviev, Bulgakov. Orthodox Theology in a New Key* (Edinburgh, 2000), pp. 373–403.

[21]   Bulgakov, *The Bride of the Lamb*, p. 332 (emphasis added).

to minimize human involvement 'quantitatively' (in the process of setting out the teaching of the Church) by confining oneself to historical research or the systematization of the thought of the Church Fathers. Human beings are always wholly and actively involved in transmission, whatever method or approach they choose to elucidate the sedimentation of their tradition. The real question is about the quality of this involvement and how it can be shaped theologically. The view that there was a closed period of time within which revelation was actively received, followed by another period during which it is passively handed on, is just a variant of 'revelatory positivism' and, Christologically-speaking, Monophysitism. As Bulgakov has indefatigably pointed out, an appropriate understanding of Chalcedon leads to the notion of history as synergism between God and man.[22] Human creativity is not abandoned but transformed by divine presence. This is not to say that human creativity and the resulting innovation cannot deviate from tradition in a destructive way. This will be discussed in the following section.

Innovation: utopianism or eschatological vision?   If innovation flourishes without being sufficiently constrained by a tradition's sedimentation, the result is *utopianism*. According to Bulgakov, the revolutionary movement in Russia fell prey to this temptation and sought to realize a deformed, secularized eschatology. But he also notices that – despite the atheistic orientation of the intelligentsia – some of its inspiration and aspiration was derived from Orthodoxy.[23] What they created was a conception of 'innovation' that put the revolutionary in the place of God or his providence, not just with respect to the *telos* of the revolutionary movement but also regarding the methods by means of which this *telos* was sought to be achieved.

According to Dostoevsky, the attempt to refute the existence of God scientifically and philosophically had already been abandoned by the 1870s. Rather, 'practical socialism' emerged by correcting God's creation. The notion of '*historical reality* as the unfolding of God's will in time'[24] is declared meaningless and absurd. God's diachronic presence in history and his synergistic co-operation with human beings is replaced by an atheist 'man-godhood' and human autonomy. For Bulgakov, it is neither socialism nor economic materialism that constitutes the essence of Marxism but Ludwig Feuerbach's atheist humanism.

---

[22]   Ibid., p. 343.

[23]   Sergii Bulgakov, 'Heroism and the Spiritual Struggle' in Bulgakov, *Towards a Russian Political Theology*, pp. 69–112, see particularly p. 74, where he writes: 'How often in the Second Duma have I heard in the passionate speeches of the atheistic left – strange to say! – resonances of Orthodox psychology, suddenly revealing the influence of its spiritual formation and implantation.'

[24]   Richard Peaver, in Fyodor Dostoevsky, *Demons*, trans. R. Pevear and L. Volokhonsky (London, 1994), p. xx (italics added).

The intelligentsia's attitude to time and history is utopian. The revolutionary intellectual is not satisfied with fulfilling the role of a humble worker since he has committed himself completely to maximalism. He is not willing to sacrifice his high principles, even if under the present circumstances, it is obvious that there is no way to realize them. Accordingly, he shies away from 'studying the mediating connections that bring the goal nearer', and 'makes a leap of historical imagination ... with little interest in the path he has leapt over ...'.[25] For the intelligentsia, socialism 'is not a cumulative concept meaning progressive socio-economic transformation ... not a 'historical movement', but a transhistorical 'ultimate goal'...'.[26]

Utopianism can be characterized as a disregard for the diachronic dimension of human existence in its socio-political as well as personal dimension. In order to transform a given order, it is imperative to examine the sedimentations of one's tradition, which determines the range of possible changes that can be carried out at given time. Bulgakov notices the same tendency as regards the personal level. For the intelligentsia 'the idea of *personal* morality, *personal* self-development, the attainment of *personality* itself are extremely unpopular (and conversely, the word 'social' has a peculiar, sacramental character)'.[27] Heroic maximalism applies all the energy to improving the external environment but ignores the personal requirements to successfully accomplish transformation of the socio-political realm.

What counterbalances the distorted view of innovation – utopia – is the right attitude to sedimentation: faithfulness to tradition. Only thus can appropriate innovation, governed by eschatological vision, be realized. Bulgakov sets the heroic intellectual against the Christian saint. Humility, obedience and patience now come into focus as central Christian virtues. The Christian saint trusts in God's providence with respect to world history as well as individual lives, but plays an active role in it. There is neither absolute freedom nor complete determinism. For the saint, maximalism is a demand he makes first and foremost on himself and not on the external world. He is always focused on the next small step he can take, on the complete fulfilment of the tasks at hand. At the same time he believes that all this is part of a greater whole, although he cannot fully grasp, let alone determine it. The discipline of obedience 'teaches us how to endure the burdens of history, the yoke of obedience in history; it creates a certain "earthiness", a sense of connectedness with the past and grateful indebtedness to it – something which is now so easily forgotten for the sake of the future'.[28]

The focus on interiority and ascetic struggle for purity and integrity is not to be interpreted in terms of quietism, servility and compliance with unjust social conditions at the external level. What is required is rather an *active passivity*,

---

[25]   Bulgakov, 'Heroism and the Spiritual Struggle', pp. 84, 87.

[26]   Ibid., p. 86.

[27]   Ibid., p. 92.

[28]   Ibid., p. 99.

for 'ascetic humility and creative audacity, obedience and the acceptance of responsibility – are antinomically harmonized in spiritual life'.[29] Any dichotomy between sedimentation and innovation must be overcome by avoiding both ossification and utopianism. The Eastern tradition possesses an immensely rich treasure of ascetic literature, an accumulation and systematization of experiences full of deep insights into the pathology of human sinfulness and its therapy.[30] On this level of sedimentation, instruction and guidance, which follows a relatively fixed pattern, is possible and indispensable. Asceticism is characterized by a certain law-like regularity that changes only insignificantly over the centuries – even if an identical repetition is excluded here too. Without self-renunciation, the gradual acquisition of the virtue of humility, without continuous repentance and obedience to tradition, Christian existence is unthinkable. Otherwise human creative activity degenerates into self-assertion and even assumes demonic features – as so masterly depicted in Dostoevsky's *Demons*. Innovation, in the sense of intellectual development of socio-political visions and their implementation, turns out to be an all too human utopia. Furthermore, a one-sided emphasis on creativity, prophecy and personal audacity provokes individualism and sectarian fragmentation. It incites anti-hierarchical tendencies and anarchism.[31]

On the other hand, the taking up of one's cross is not just a passive carrying but also active taking. Renunciation of one's will, understood in the Christian sense, requires the greatest effort of will-power. Originality, freedom, personal appropriation of the Christian tradition and responsibility for the world all form part of an anthropology that is consistently informed by Chalcedon. Obedience (to a human intermediary) should not be considered an end in itself but often has the function of a method, of a spiritual exercise. For the ultimate goal of ascetic life is the sanctification of one's will, its conformity with the divine will, rather than its eradication and this can only be accomplished by a free consent to every act of obedience. Unlike sedimentation, innovation and creative audacity are always new, unique and individual and therefore do not conform to any law; they cannot be repeated. Innovation inevitably entails risks and only the test of time can show whether a move that went beyond the familiar can be viewed an embodiment of an eschatological vision.[32]

Bulgakov's insistence that ascetic humility and creative audacity need to be in a state of mutual equilibrium is in line with Radical Orthodoxy's use of the middle-voice.[33] The middle voice is the diathesis, or third voice between active

---

[29]   Bulgakov, *The Comforter*, p. 308.

[30]   See Jean-Claude Larchet, *Thérapeutique des maladies spirituelles. Une introduction à la tradition ascétique de l'Église orthodoxe* (Paris, 2000).

[31]   Bulgakov, *The Comforter*, pp. 298–313.

[32]   Ibid.

[33]   Cf. Catherine Pickstock, *After Writing. On the Liturgical Consummation of Philosophy* (Oxford, 1998), pp. 35, 105, 112.

and passive. It is the locality, not the affectedness of the subject that matters.[34] To put this in theological language: 'Grace is the *milieu* in which man is wholly free.'[35] The middle voice is thus an apt linguistic tool to describe the 'non-competitive' relationship between divine and human action. Human beings act at the same time as they are subject to divine action. We are located in a tradition but this locatedness cannot be separated from our active appropriation of tradition. There are no dichotomies between sedimentation and innovation, obedience and freedom, active and passive, or faith and works. When Eastern Orthodoxy is at its best, it keeps this middle position.

Synchrony: Mediation without Accommodation

Doctrine in world history   Radial Orthodoxy has described its theological agenda as follows: (compared to Barthian Neo-orthodoxy) it wants to be 'more mediating, but less accommodating – since, while it assumes that theology must speak also of something else, it seeks always to recognise a theological difference in such speaking'.[36] This means, first, that theology is not a discipline confined to a partial sphere of reality but rather embraces the whole of reality. Secondly, theology is not supposed to accommodate itself to secular thought; a comprehensive reframing of reality must be consistently theological. As far as the 'non-accommodating' character of theology is concerned, it is not difficult to find Orthodox theologians in the twentieth century who support such a view. Georges Florovsky, for instance, writes that

> the task of theology lies not so much in translating the Tradition of faith into contemporary language, into the terms of the most recent philosophy, but lies rather in discovering the ancient patristic tradition in the perennial principles of Christian philosophy; this task lies not in controlling dogma by means of contemporary philosophy but rather in re-shaping philosophy on the experience of faith itself so that the experience of faith would become the source and measure of philosophical views.[37]

The problem in Eastern Orthodoxy lies rather with the question of mediation. The point is that mediation and non-accommodation are closely intertwined. Unless the work of mediation is really carried out, the non-accommodating attitude toward the world is lost too, for the 'unassumed is the unhealed'. To be sure, the basic theological categories of the Eastern Church, as developed in the first centuries,

---

[34] Cf. Philippe Eberhard, *The Middle Voice in Gadamer's Hermeneutics. A Basic Interpretation with Some Theological Implications* (Tübingen, 2004), pp. 9, 16, 133.

[35] Meyendorff, *Living Tradition*, p. 176.

[36] Milbank *et al.*, 'Suspending the Material', p. 2; cf. John Milbank, *Being Reconciled. Ontology and Pardon* (London/New York, 2003), p. 109.

[37] Florovsky, *Collected Works: Aspects of Church History*, vol. 4, p. 168.

constitute an all-encompassing, truly cosmic Christian ontology. But only few Orthodox theologians have really thought through what it means in the modern and post-modern era that human creative activity includes 'the entire domain of culture and civilization'.[38] Furthermore, since non-accommodating mediation is a divine-human enterprise that is synergistically performed by the Church throughout the centuries, the synchronic cannot be separated from the diachronic.[39]

For this reason, Florovsky's statement is misleading or at least incomplete. Although theology is not dependent on any philosophy, it is neither in possession of a timeless 'essence' of Christian faith, articulated in eternally fixed dogmas that can be 'applied' in ever new circumstances. Rather, this 'essence' is only present and accessible in the series of historical manifestations successively generated by the tradition. As regards doctrine, this means that there is a history of dogma in the sense that newer dogmas can be understood as further elucidations of older ones. Bulgakov puts this well:

> The fullness of Revelation and the fullness of life are built into the Divine foundation of the Church – *divinely*. But in the *divine-human* mind of the Church, to the extent that this involves temporality and relativity, this fullness enters in only gradually and partially, for which reason the *history* of dogmas can and does exist, as we can in fact observe. New dogmas arise, and in this sense dogmatic development, too, exists.[40]

As a result of the synergistic character of the Church, human beings are always actively involved in its history. The wish to safeguard doctrinal (as well as epistemic and existential) security by introducing the notion of passive reception, 'uncontaminated' by human involvement, is misplaced and misses the mystery of the Incarnation. Christian faith is the most perfect 'humanism' in the sense that grace actualizes the full potential in human beings. The development of Christian doctrine is a permanent task, even if creativity – as outlined above – is always constrained by past insights, which cannot be ignored.

The same question can also be addressed from the synchronic perspective. On the one hand, the doctrines of the Trinity and the Incarnation are the criteria on the basis of which theology construes and evaluates the world. On the other hand, the full depth of meaning of these doctrines only emerges *in* and *through* this engagement with the world. We do not approach the world with fixed categories; rather, these categories are themselves modified and refined in the process of

---

[38]   Bulgakov, *The Bride of the Lamb*, p. 323. There are well known historical reasons for this deficit that need not be spelled out here.

[39]   For this see John Milbank, *Theology and Social Theory. Beyond Secular Reason* (Oxford/Malden, MA., 1990), pp. 382–8.

[40]   Sergii Bulgakov, 'Dogma and Dogmatics', in *Living Tradition. Orthodoxy in the Modern World* (Paris, 1937), p. 20 (in Russian). The translation is taken from Valliere, *Modern Russian Theology*, p. 387.

construing the world from a Christian viewpoint. Good examples include modern 'theologies of language', as for instance developed by John Milbank or some of the Russian religious philosophers.[41] Ancient and medieval Christian thinkers did not develop a satisfactory account of language. But this has certainly become a desideratum in the twentieth century, due to the central place which philosophy of language occupies in the analytical and continental tradition alike. Milbank takes eighteenth-century thinkers such as Berkley, Hamann, Herder and Vico as a starting point and argues that the 'post-modern embracing of a radical linguisticality … has always been secretly promoted' by traditional Christianity.[42] He also points to the differences between the Christian and the sceptical post-modern notion of unlimited semiosis. The theologies of language developed by the Russian philosophers Pavel Florensky, Sergii Bulgakov and Aleksei Losev, by contrast, draw on specifically Eastern Orthodox doctrines such as the theology of icons or the essence-energy distinction.

In all of these thinkers, a theology of language is only conceivable as an elaboration on the doctrines of the Trinity and the Incarnation. This is the 'hermeneutic strategy' which aims at mediation without accommodation and which allows for controlled innovation and doctrinal development. It is certainly not foreign to Eastern Orthodoxy; rather, it is more faithful to the heritage of the Church Fathers.[43]

Sacerdotium and Imperium   According to Radical Orthodoxy, the quest for 'mediation without accommodation' cannot be reduced to doctrine or separated from the cultural and socio-political dimension of Christian life. The Orthodox Church shares this view and believes that its task is to embrace the whole human culture.[44] A Manichean withdrawal from the world is unacceptable, as is the belief in a Pelagianzing eschatology, where a secular and immanentist understanding of history replaces the Christian one. As far as the Eastern tradition is concerned, the relationship between sacerdotium and imperium was modelled according to the hypostatic union between the divine and the

---

[41]   John Milbank, *The Word Made Strange. Theology, Language, Culture* (Oxford/ Malden, 1997), esp. pp. 84–120; Naftali Prat, 'Orthodox Philosophy of Language in Russia', *Studies in Soviet Thought* 20 (1979): 1–21; Thomas Seifrid, *The Word Made Self: Russian Writings on Language, 1860–1930* (Ithaca, 2005); Steven Cassedy, *Flight from Eden. The Origins of Modern Literary Criticism and Theory* (Berkely, 1990), ch. 5: 'Icon and Logos, or Why Russian Philosophy Is Always Theology'.

[42]   Milbank, *The Word Made Strange*, p. 85.

[43]   Meyendorff, *Living Tradition*, p. 168.

[44]   Cf. *Die Grundlagen der Sozialdoktrin der Russisch-Orthodoxen Kirche*, trans. C. Christova (Sankt Augustin, 2001), I/2; Metropolitan Anthony of Sourozh, *Encounter* (London, 2005), pp. 21–6; Alexander Schmeeman, *For the Life of the World* (Crestwood, NY, 2002), p. 13; Bulgakov, *The Bride of the Lamb*, pp. 332–3.

human nature of Christ. The common eschatological goal of empire and priesthood, the realization of the Christian humanum, did not lead to a clear-cut differentiation of jurisdiction. The ideal was a 'harmony' or 'symphony' for the benefit of human society.[45]

Already in John Chrysostom and Eusebius we find two tendencies, which become characteristic of Eastern political thought. On the one hand there is complete trust in the empire. On the other hand an attempt is made to safeguard ecclesial autonomy and, if necessary, to educate and hold accountable the emperor. Neither individuals nor legally defined institutions were considered infallible. Throughout Byzantine history, eminent figures such as St John Chrysostom, St Maximus the Confessor, St John of Damascus and St Theodore of Studite repeatedly criticized both emperors and ecclesiastical authorities. As pointed out by John Meyendorff, these critical voices should not be considered exceptions to an otherwise more accommodating practice; rather, they were an integral part of the Eastern tradition. To them, it was clear that the Council of Chalcedon had political implications and that the political system of 'symphonia' was its correct implementation. For Meyendorff, the lasting legacy of Byzantium consists in the insight that

> just as man, individually, is destined to 'deification' and is fully himself when he is in communion with God, a communion which was realized by Jesus Christ and in Him made accessible to all in the faith, so human society is called to conform itself to God's presence and become the Kingdom of God.[46]

This is not to say that the *symphonia* between empire and Church was without problems. In the West, the medieval Church became more and more powerful. Through the investiture controversy it successfully withstood the emperor's concentration of power. But it could only achieve this at the price of a far-reaching inner-theological paradigm shift. From the eleventh century onwards, authority and particularly the authority of the Pope, was ideologically and terminologically influenced by the legalism of the imperial court.[47] In the West, there was a tendency for ecclesiastical power to claim worldly dignity. In the East, by contrast, worldly power sought to claim spiritual dignity. Consequently, this development led to a *secularization* of power in the West, including ecclesiastical power, and to a *sacralization* of power, in the East, including worldly power.[48] The secularization of authority in the West, in theology, philosophy and political theory, has been

---

[45] Francis Dvornik, *Early Christian and Byzantine Political Philosophy: Origins and Background* (2 vols, Washington, 1966); Dimiter Angelov, *Imperial Ideology and Political Thought in Byzantium, 1204–1330* (Cambridge, 2007).

[46] Meyendorff, *Living Tradition*, pp. 193–4, 196.

[47] Yves Congar, 'The Historical Development of Authority. Points for Reflection' in John M. Todd (ed.), *Problems of Authority* (London/Baltimore, 1962), pp. 136–44.

[48] Konstantin Kostjuk, *Der Begriff des Politischen in der Russisch-orthodoxen Tradition* (Paderborn, 2005), p. 66.

extensively analysed and criticized by Radical Orthodoxy. What about the history of authority in the East? It goes without saying that the relationship between Church and empire/state in the history of Russia is immensely complex and cannot be grasped by means of a simple formula.[49] In a nutshell, the sacralization of worldly power can mean, positively, the shaping of power according to theological criteria. But it may also amount to a merely formal legitimization of a given political order, while leaving its content untouched or without transforming it satisfactorily. In the latter case, sacralization of worldly power can be equated with secularization – even if the secular character remains deceptively hidden by the use of a sacral and theological terminology. The same applies to the secularization of ecclesiastical power in the West.

As regards the situation of the Orthodox Church in Eastern Europe, Orthodoxy succumbed to secularism by forming national Churches.[50] In the early Church, the emerging patriarchates were named after cities, not peoples, such as Rome, Alexandria, Antioch, and later Constantinople and Jerusalem. The term *ethnos* (ἔθνος), which was for instance used in the thirty-fourth Apostolic Canon and in the ninth Canon of the Synod of Antioch in the fourth century, had in the late Roman Empire also the meaning of province. It cannot be associated with the modern idea of a nation or a nation-state. In Orthodox ecclesiology there is in principle no room for the nation. The *symphonia* between Church and the Byzantine Empire was not based upon ethnic identity. Up to the eighteenth century, Orthodox parishes in the diaspora (outside the Ottoman Empire) usually had a multi-ethnic character. Thereafter conflicts based on ethnic differences became more and more frequent. In 1872 the Synod of Constantinople declared *ethnophyletismos*, the term used for nationalism, a heresy. But this could not stop the development of national Churches, which had already started in the 1830s. In Greece, an autocephalous Church was established in 1833, shortly after the foundation of a new Greek state, which followed the uprising against Ottoman rule. Bulgaria and Romania, too, adopted the model of 'national autocephaly' and in the twentieth century Albania and Macedonia followed suit.

The situation in Russia is rather different. The Orthodox Church in Russia already gained autocephaly in the sixteenth century. However, it has been argued that the development of a national consciousness was inhibited by the fact that Russia remained an empire up to the twentieth century – first in the form of the Russian

---

[49]   It is possible to distinguish five different political models: the Kievan Rus', the Moscow State, the Petersburg period, the Communist era and the post-Communist era. All five have constituted different challenges for the Church (ibid., p. 50). See also Peter Hauptman and Gerd Stricker, *Die Orthodoxe Kirche in Russland: Dokumente ihrer Geschichte* (860–1890) (Göttingen, 1988).

[50]   Ekkehard Kraft, 'Nationalkirchen auf dem Balkan', *Jahrbücher für Geschichte Osteuropas* 51 (2003): 392–408.

Empire under the tsars and then in the form of the Soviet Empire.[51] In any case, Russian 'nationalism' is often interlinked with universalism and messianism and is therefore not primarily an ethnic phenomenon. The term 'messianism' is used here in the sense of a people's conviction that they have been chosen by God to fulfil a specific task that often goes beyond national interests. Peter Duncan distinguishes between two poles of Russian messianism. Either it is state-oriented and based on the idea of Moscow's rule over other people (nationalist messianism), or it regards the Russian people as an example for other nations to follow (universalist messianism).[52] Like Duncan, Geoffrey Hosking also argues that these two versions are in reality inseparable. In his recent book *Rulers and Victims*, Hosking has documented that messianism is a pervasive feature of modern Russian history, both during the times of Tsarism and Bolshevism.[53] The specificity of Russia's messianic vision can be summarized as a variant of missionary nationalism, a nationalist project that, based on divine election, promotes and extends the supposed benefits of a country's rule and civilization to other people.

On this basis, some traditions within the Russian Orthodox Church have promulgated the view that Eastern Russian Orthodoxy differs fundamentally from Western Christianity and that Moscow as the Third Rome is the last Christian bastion against the coming of the Anti-Christ and Armageddon. Such and similar apocalyptic accounts claim that Russia was always a non-Western civilization with long–established indigenous traditions until Peter the Great imported the corrupting ideologies of rationalism and the Enlightenment. The ensuing process of modernization, so the argument goes, undermined and destroyed traditional religion and thus deprived the country of fulfilling its historical destiny as a bulwark against all Western forms of secularism, including Bolshevism and free-market capitalism. In part, this explains why some in Russian Orthodoxy tend to blame the West for moral relativism and are bitterly opposed to any initiatives that might favour reunification with Rome. As will be argued in the next section, Radical Orthodoxy's theological analyses of the history of modernity can help to distinguish between secular nationalism or imperialism and the justified determination that Christianity positions and transforms ethics, politics and culture.

---

[51] Geoffrey Hosking, *Russia*: *People and Empire, 1552–1917* (London, 1997), pp. xix–xxi.

[52] Peter J.S. Duncan, *Russian Messianism. Third Rome, Revolution, Communism and After* (London/New York, 2000), pp. 3, 34–41; cf. Orlando Figes, *Natasha's Dance. A Cultural History of Russia* (London, 2002), pp. 292–354.

[53] Geoffrey Hosking, *Rulers and Victims. The Russians in the Soviet Union* (Cambridge, MA, 2006), pp. 3–35.

Eastern Orthodoxy: A Challenge for Radical Orthodoxy

Radical Orthodoxy has variously been accused of elevating philosophy over theology and reason over faith in a dubious attempt to resurrect the medieval project of natural theology and knowledge of God by reason alone. This, so the argument goes, has led the 'radical orthodox' movement to privilege ancient philosophy at the expense of biblical revelation and to dismiss the important legacy of Protestant theologians in favour of Catholic thought, especially the works of *nouvelle théologie*. As such, it is excessively concerned with recent and current secular thinkers and lacks a clear ecclesiology that is firmly embedded in the Christian tradition. In short, Radical Orthodoxy appears to be at once too pre-modern and too post-modern, desperately trying to apply patristic and medieval theology to the contemporary world in order to create a theological utopia, thus failing to engage with the real problems of the present day. The implication is that this movement shares with Eastern Orthodoxy a rejection of modernity and thus has little, if anything, to learn from it. Even a cursory reading of the works that fall within the 'radical orthodox' imperative refutes this charge, but it is nevertheless instructive because it raises the question as to the kind of challenge the Eastern Orthodox tradition presents to a theological movement such as Radical Orthodoxy. In what follows, it will be argued that a closer engagement with Eastern Orthodoxy could help Radical Orthodox theology to correct and to develop its account of the relation between philosophy and theology as well as ecclesiology, politics and the economy.

Theology and Philosophy: Ontology or Metaphysics?

Already in John Milbank's seminal book *Theology and Social Theory*, the precursor to Radical Orthodoxy, the focus was on capturing the discourse on ontology from post-modern philosophy and to reconfigure it within the theological tradition stretching from Augustine to Aquinas. As Milbank makes clear, the concept of ontology is not foreign to the biblical tradition but instead derives from Christ's life and teaching testified to by the Apostles and transmitted by the Gospel narrative. As such, the divine gift of participation in God's love and peace is open to all those who follow Christ and who in some sense inhabit and live out this narrative.[54] Crucially, for Milbank, the 'Christian story' is not merely one among many possible narratives but is and ought to be the meta-narrative. For it uniquely constitutes 'a master-discourse of non-mastery' and as such involves and calls forth a 'speculative ontology'.[55] In other words, the unicity of Christian *praxis* as exemplified by Christ entails a speculation about the universal participation of the

---

[54]   John Milbank, 'Between Purgation and Illumination', in Kenneth Surin (ed.), *Christ, Ethics and Tragedy: Essays in Honour of Donald MacKinnon* (Cambridge, 1989), p. 189 et seq.

[55]   Milbank, *Theology and Social Theory*, pp. 6, 359, 385, 389, 422–32.

finite human in the divine infinite and the particular social practices that embody this participatory vision. According to Milbank, the ontology that emerges from this kind of 'speculation' is best described as an ontology of the gift and, more specifically, a Trinitarian ontology of peace.[56] In *Radical Orthodoxy* and later publications, the 'radical orthodox' movement argues that ontology – so configured – makes participation the central framework of Christian theology.

While there is much to celebrate from an Eastern Orthodox perspective, it is not clear that the language and conceptuality of ontology is fully consonant with the Christian theological tradition in the East or, for that matter, the West. Not only is the term ontology a modern Western invention – first coined by Johannes Clauberg in 1647, but more importantly, it is associated with a certain strand in theology that prepares the ground for transcendental philosophy. Long before Heidegger, it was Vladimir Solovyov who in his 1873 book *The Crisis of Western Philosophy* traced the lineage of positivism to the transcendental turn of theology (even if he was mistaken in portraying John Scotus Eriugena as the founder of western rationalism).[57] Nor is it certain that Christian theology based on a 'fully Christianized' ontology is best equipped to expose the nihilistic logic of much of post-modern secular philosophy and to offer a compelling alternative to the pure ontology of phenomenology. Ontology as the science of being *qua* being implies one of two things. Either it divides general from highest being and therefore posits an unwarranted separation of ontology from theology. Or else it conflates general and highest being and therefore commits the idolatry of onto-theology – a univocal account of being that forgets and denies the ontological difference between Creator and creation. Moreover, does not ontology, already in its original Aristotelian guise, suggest an excessive focus on causality at the expense of gift and givenness – crucial insights which the Christian tradition owes largely to Dionysius the Areopagite? As such, Eastern Orthodox theology can provide a corrective to the early radical orthodox talk about ontology by replacing it with metaphysics.

Interestingly, in more recent work, Radical Orthodoxy seems to have taken this onboard by arguing that 'radical orthodox' theology recovers and extends metaphysics beyond ontology. Milbank's chapter with the title 'Only Theology saves Metaphysics'[58] inverts that of an earlier essay 'Only theology overcomes metaphysics'.[59] As he explains, the 'metaphysics' that is overcome in the

---

[56] John Milbank, 'Can a Gift Be Given? Prolegomena to a Future Trinitarian Metaphysic', *Modern Theology* 11/1 (1995), esp. 130–61.

[57] Unlike contemporary Orthodox theologians such as John Zizioulas, Solovyov did not incriminate Augustine but instead celebrated the shared metaphysics of theological realism in both East and West.

[58] John Milbank, 'Only Theology saves Metaphysics: on the Modalities of Terror', in Peter M. Candler Jr and Conor Cunningham (eds), *Belief and Metaphysics* (London, 2007), pp. 452–500.

[59] Milbank, *The Word Made Strange*, pp. 36–55.

earlier piece is the onto-theological science of transcendental ontology that has prevailed at least since Suárez and is present in much of contemporary philosophy (the concomitant relegation of theology to the supernatural defines much of contemporary theology). The 'metaphysics' that is saved in the recent piece is the perennial 'realism' that stretched from Plato to Aquinas and was later reworked by Meister Eckhart and Nicolas of Cusa. Here, characteristically, being is not a transcendental framework that includes even the divine; rather being and God are identified as the transcendent source in which all else participates.

Moreover, as already indicated in the preface to *Being Reconciled*, John Milbank's growing interest in Eastern Orthodoxy has led him to develop his account of ontology in the direction of a metaphysical-theological *methexis* of donation which draws on the Eastern Orthodox thematic of energy (*energeia*) and wisdom (*sophia*). In his contribution to the present collection of essays,[60] he argues that the sophiological tradition of Pavel Florensky and Sergii Bulgakov is crucial in refining and extending the key concepts of Radical Orthodoxy, that is participation, mediation and deification. Milbank shows how sophiology conceives mediation between the persons of the Trinity in terms of substantive relations (following a tradition successively elaborated across East and West by the Cappadocians, Augustine and Aquinas). There can thus be no third terms between Father and Son or between Father plus Son and the Spirit. Likewise, there cannot be any third term between the essence of the Godhead and the persons of the Trinity themselves. For there is nothing more general or fundamental than the three divine persons and the Trinitarian relations that pertain between them, and the whole of creation comes from and returns to the one triune God who is the highest being and the supreme good.

The same 'sophio-logic' which we find in certain strands of Eastern Orthodoxy can elucidate some core Christological problems and questions that are at the heart of the 'radical orthodox' project. Again, for Milbank, there can be no third term between the two natures of Christ, nor between both the natures and the divine hypostasis. Nor is there any third term between the Holy Spirit and the Catholic Church. Equally, there is no third term between manhood in general and Godhead, nor between God who is able to become man and humanity which is destined to be deified. Key to this more orthodox and more radical theology is the participation of all that is in divine *Sophia*. The specificity of sophiology is that *Sophia* names a relation or *metaxu* (a term central to Bulgakov's work) which is not situated between two poles but rather remains – simultaneously and paradoxically – at both poles at once. Thus, it does not subsist before the two poles, but it co-arises with them such that they can only exist according to a mediated communication which remains purely occult, a matter of utterly inscrutable affinity. Sophia so configured is of course not a fourth divine person, but is equally (though also differently) of the Father, the Son and the Holy Spirit, a kind of energy that both unifies and

---

[60]   John Milbank, 'Sophiology and Theurgy: the New Theological Horizon', *infra*, chapter 2.

differentiates the One triune God and infuses his glorious creation with the wisdom of knowing him as the Creator. In short, as Milbank writes, 'Sophia rests in the Godhead and in the pond: there lies nothing between the two, but – as 'the true intermediary *metaxu*' [quoting here from Bulgakov's *The Bride of the Lamb*] – she brings them most intimately together'.[61] This underscores the extent to which an ever closer engagement with some Eastern Orthodox theological traditions has led Radical Orthodoxy to revise the question of ontology and to develop a more rigorous metaphysics in the direction of relationality. The challenge is to take forward this project by drawing on the entire Christian tradition of theological realism from the Church Fathers via medieval theologians to modern and contemporary figures in East and West alike. As will be argued in the final section of this introduction, developing an ecumenical theology is an integral part of fusing the promotion of Church unity with a more direct Christian intervention in politics and the economy – in Europe, America and elsewhere.

Ecclesiology, Politics and Economics

As a primarily academic and intellectual movement, Radical Orthodoxy has been criticized for failing to relate debates in the academy to reflections and practices in Church and society. Insofar as the 'radical orthodox' movement has portrayed itself as trans-confessional (bringing together Roman Catholics, Anglicans and some other Reformed traditions), it has also been accused of lacking a coherent ecclesiology capable of providing a proper ecclesial context, not least for Radical Orthodoxy's own reception. Unsurprisingly, the protagonists of the 'radical orthodox' movement have rejected this criticism from the beginning,[62] pointing for instance to the centrality of the Eucharist in the writings of Radical Orthodoxy and the doxological turn of theology that the work of Catherine Pickstock has produced.[63] However, the encounter with the Eastern Orthodox tradition raises a number of new questions and challenges. First, Radical Orthodoxy agrees with Alasdair MacIntyre's argument about tradition-dependent reason, but it has sometimes tended to privilege metaphysical realism at the expense of the ecclesial traditions which embody it. Another way of highlighting the same problem is by asking whether Radical Orthodoxy is a theological movement that attempts to correct and enrich certain Churches like Eastern Orthodoxy, without being an actually existing tradition itself. This is all the more problematic in the light of 'radical orthodox' appeals to authentic practices that have either disappeared

---

[61] Ibid.

[62] John Milbank, 'Enclaves or Where is the Church?', *New Blackfriars*, 73 (1992): 341–52.

[63] See, *inter alia*, William T. Cavanaugh, *Torture and the Eucharist. Theology, Politics and the Body of Christ* (Oxford, 1997); in addition to *After Writing*, see Catherine Pickstock, 'Thomas Aquinas and the Quest for the Eucharist', *Modern Theology*, 15/2 (1999): 159–80; 'Liturgy, Art and Politics', *Modern Theology*, 16/2 (2000): 160–80.

in certain Christian denominations or in the Church as a whole, in particular Eucharistic celebrations and a number of closely associated social practices such as processions, guilds and fraternities. Radical Orthodoxy has a tendency to talk about *the* Church but it is not always evident whether this is a vision of an eschatologically reunified Church that cannot be realized in this world. By embodying an account of tradition that is futural, the Eastern Orthodox Churches in all their diversity and difference combine faithfulness to the apostolic testimony with a creative practice of Christian ministry, in an attempt to transform the contemporary world in line with an alternative future that Jesus Christ has already disclosed to us. As such, the task for Radical Orthodoxy is to uncover ecclesial practices in both East and West that embody theological realism and to reflect on how such practices can be recovered and extended.

Moreover, Eastern Orthodox Church traditions can also guard against any tendency to posit something like an Enlightenment ideal of a universal, atemporal and public reason, which can be applied to 'contingent' Christian traditions in space and time. Such an approach risks detaching theological reason from its ecclesial framework, thus inviting a 'critique of pure Christian reason'. The 'radical orthodox' commitment to the specificity of the Christian *Logos* marks a clear difference with the disembodied rationality of modern philosophy, but its account of reason and faith risks lacking embeddedness in ecclesial traditions. Here it is instructive to draw on the theology of Pavel Florensky. In his chapter on Sophiology in *The Pillar and Ground of the Truth*, he tells a story about *starets* Isidor: 'Full of grace and made beautiful by grace, he gave me the most solid, the most undeniable, the purest perception of a spiritual person I have had in my entire life.'[64] It is worth quoting this passage here because it illustrates clearly how in Orthodoxy theology the most abstract and general (Sophia as a *cosmic* principle) becomes manifest and is embodied in the most concrete and particular. This is by no means a return to an understanding of Christianity that is merely concerned with the interpersonal, and which neglects the cosmic and socio-political dimension of human life. Rather, there is some kind of reciprocity between these two realms, within the higher unity of the Church as the living Body of Christ.

Moreover, the political notion of *Sobornost* is inconceivable without personal *asceticism*, that is to say the practice of obedience, discipline and conversion – notions that resonate strongly with the Benedictine and other Western traditions. The challenge for the 'radical orthodox' movement is to integrate specifically Eastern Orthodox traditions into a wider Christian framework and thereby to shape reflection on how to promote unity among the episcopally-based Churches. Church division is a theological anomaly and the source of political division between East and West. The reunification of Europe and the reversal of Western cultural and political decline will remain a utopia unless the Churches come

---

[64] Pavel Florensky, *The Pillar and Ground of the Truth. An Essay in Orthodox Theodicy in Twelve Letters* trans. Boris Jakim (Princeton/Oxford, 1997), p. 233.

together and form a pan-Christian Episcopal polity. The starting point for Radical Orthodoxy in this respect is to integrate the Eastern Orthodox experience of the 'Byzantine Commonwealth' (Dimitri Obolensky) into its analysis of the rise and fall of Christendom and to devise ways of restoring an overarching ecclesial order. In this respect, one particular issue to consider is how to unite the principle of Petrine primacy with that of conciliarity.

In relation to ecclesiology, the other fundamental question for Radical Orthodoxy that emerges in the encounter with Eastern Orthodoxy is about the translation of theological ideas into political and economic practices that can set limits to state and market power and transform the prevailing system in the direction of global Christian governance. The 'radical orthodox' movement has already provided a theological critique of the dominant ideologies, and exposed them as deeply secular. In addition, Radical Orthodoxy has put forward ideas about an alternative Christian order centred on the Church as the universal polity and based upon Catholic and Anglican social teaching on subsidiarity, intermediary institutions and organic pluralism. Here the Eastern Orthodox tradition can make a number of contributions to a shared theology. First, the history of Byzantium is indispensable for a better understanding of the limits of medieval Christendom, in particular the failure of the Churches to mediate between the trans-national, the national and the local, especially in the struggle with emperors and kings. The challenge for Radical Orthodoxy is not only to help provide a revisionist account of how Church division foreshadowed the political split between East and West and how the demise of Christendom created the conditions for the rise of the modern state and free-market capitalism, but also what insights from this history can be applied to the current global constellation. More specifically, Churches in East and West face the problem of how to relate the local Church to the universal Church and how to offer an alternative polity. If Radical Orthodoxy can offer an account that binds together universal ecclesial principles with particular political arrangements, the project of restoring some traditions of Christendom will no longer appear utopian but instead provide a robust alternative to the ongoing process of secular globalization that enhances the power of some states and trans-national global elites at the expense of local autonomy and cultural diversity. Moreover, in the West the ongoing process of secularization has led to a revival of atheism and the advance of de-christianization. The 'radical orthodox' project of a post-secular theology and politics can learn from the contemporary Orthodox attempt to overcome a post-Christian society after the historical reality of atheist Bolshevism.

Second, in its pursuit of a Christian political and economic alternative, Radical Orthodoxy would benefit from Eastern Orthodox economic theory and social teaching. Bulgakov's Christian re-interpretation of *homo economicus* in his book of 1912 *Philosophy of Economic Activity* (*Filosofiya Khozyaistva*) is already well-known, but the works of Vladimir Solovyov are no less important, especially the way he relates the idea of a 'free theocracy' in economics, social and political philosophy to the idea of a 'free theosophy' in metaphysics and the idea of a 'free theurgy' in aesthetics. Solovyov's critique of transcendental philosophy and positivism and his creative recovery of a theological metaphysics pave the way for a theological-political economy. Coupled with his and Bulgakov's work on the nature of personhood, Eastern Orthodox theology has developed a tradition of personalism spanning the metaphysical, political, social and economic. The task for Radical Orthodoxy is to formulate a synthesis of Western and Eastern accounts of personalism and to reclaim from liberalism the discourse on human dignity and human fulfilment. In this, the 'radical orthodox' movement could learn from Orthodox social teaching which is in some respects more radical than Roman Catholic social teaching, for example on the limits of the western secular human rights discourse and the critique of moral relativism. A necessary extension of the ecumenical theology that Radical Orthodoxy seeks to develop and promote is to highlight the convergence of social teaching in the Catholic, Orthodox and Anglican traditions as well as to show how Christian accounts of the person, society and the economy not only outwits both liberalism and Marxism but also actualizes the ideals of freedom, prosperity, solidarity and equality.

Concluding Remarks

The encounter between Radical Orthodoxy and Eastern Orthodoxy has already produced a number of profound insights in some key areas of theology, as evinced by the depth and breadth of theological thinking in the present collection. Considering the questions that arise from debates in this publication and elsewhere, there can be little doubt that the Eastern Orthodox tradition and the 'radical orthodox' movement have much to learn from a critical and constructive engagement with each other. How best to take this forward? Ecclesiologically and politically, the shared imperative is to combine the pursuit of Church unity with the promotion of Christian ideas and practices in politics, the economy and culture. Like the Roman Catholic Church under Pope Benedict XVI, the Eastern Orthodox Church in general and the Russian Orthodox Church in particular have come to recognize the threat posed to Christianity by both secular extremism and religious fundamentalism and the need to preserve and reinvigorate the Christian identity of Europe. As a result, both Churches are facing the increasing clamour of atheism, the aggressive de-christianization of society and the growing militancy of religious fanatics (in Islam, Christianity and Judaism), all of which undermine the Christian foundation of European culture and thus threaten the cohesion of society.

As an intellectual movement that is already trans-confessional, Radical Orthodoxy is uniquely positioned to promote ecumenical dialogue between the episcopally-based Churches by providing theological concepts to reflect anew on the core of Christian tradition and to take concrete steps towards ecclesial reunification. As a repository of the Christian theological tradition and an embodiment of medieval Christendom, Eastern Orthodoxy has an integral part to play in the overcoming of the East-West split. Radical Orthodoxy and Eastern Orthodoxy have the shared task of working together towards renewing Christian Europe as the most European Europe and to envision a global Christendom that can confront secularism and fundamentalism and promote Christian ideals based on the promise of God's Kingdom on earth.

PART I
Sophia, Theology and Philosophy

Chapter 1

Glorification of the Name
and Grammar of Wisdom
(Sergii Bulgakov and Jean-Marc Ferry)

Antoine Arjakovsky

Monde renversé je t'aime
J'aime à monde renversé[1]

Having read with much interest, or rather I should say with passion, the work of Archbishop Rowan Williams on Father Sergii Bulgakov, the works of John Milbank and Catherine Pickstock, as well as the presentation of Radical Orthodoxy in French by Adrian Pabst and Olivier-Thomas Venard, I share in the desire of Radical Orthodoxy to rediscover the living origins of orthodox Christianity and to promote an engagement between an intellectual movement, that of Radical Orthodoxy, and an ecclesiastical tradition, that of Eastern Orthodoxy. I do not believe that these terms are equivalent. But it seems to me that on both sides are those who have become aware of the end of an era, and of these modern times characterized in particular by assertion of denominational identity. However, at the origin of the ecumenical realization are found those whose lives have been radically changed by friendship – the friendship that was shared by Lord Halifax and Abbey Portal, and also that between Bishop Walter Frere and Father Sergii Bulgakov.

The transfiguration of the world by the Word is at the heart of *The Philosophy of the Word and the Name* by Sergii Bulgakov. His idea was that the worship of the Name of God was like the river of flowing water, shining like crystal, of the new Jerusalem, 'The throne of God and of the Lamb shall be in it; and his servants shall serve him / And they shall see his face; and his name shall be on their foreheads' (Rev 22:3–4). After briefly introducing *The Philosophy of the Word and the Name* by Sergii Bulgakov, I will then compare it with the communicational philosophy of the French thinker Jean-Marc Ferry, a professor at the Free University of Brussels and a close friend of Jürgen Habermas. My aim, in fact, is to demonstrate that from our ultra-modernity comes an idea that suggests the secret presence of the *Logos* at the heart of human intelligence. However, this philosophy still hesitates to pronounce the Name of God, perhaps because Christians themselves still owe a clear answer to the following question: is God's name God himself?

---

[1]   Dominique Fourcade, 'Same player shoot again, ornithologie', in Hadrien France-Lanord *et al.* (eds), *La fête de la pensée: hommage à François Fédier* (Paris, 2001), p. 467.

The Philosophy of the Word and the Name

Sergii Bulgakov, dean of the St Serge Institute in Paris in the 1930s, drafted in the Crimea at the beginning of the 1920s two works that took him the rest of his life to complete. The first is called *The Tragedy of Philosophy* and the second *The Philosophy of the Word and the Name*. During his lifetime, only the first work and one chapter of the second *What is the Word?* were translated in 1927 and 1930 respectively, both into German. In these two papers, Bulgakov's aim was above all to give an argued response to the debate before the First World War in Russia on the subject of the glorification of the Name of God.

It all started in 1907 with the publication of a book entitled *In the Caucasus Mountains* by a monk called Ilarion. In Moscow the book was supported by another monk, Antoni Boulatovitch, but it divided the Russian monasteries of Mount Athos on the subject of whether or not God's name is God himself, to the point that the Archbishop of Constantinople Joachim III was forced to intervene on 12 September 1912 to condemn Ilarion's book. The monks worshipping the Name of God did not back down and on 30 March 1913, the new Archbishop Germain V also strongly condemned those who he considered to be heretics, with the support of teachers from the Halki seminary. Finally, on 18 May 1913, the Holy Synod of Petrograd sent Bishop Nikon to dislodge about 600 rebel monks by force, a sign of the growing tensions between Moscow and Constantinople on the eve of the First World War. Numerous intellectuals moved in favour of the Onomatodox monks, among them Nicolai Berdyaev and Pavel Florensky. The latter explained that the Name of God, like the image of the icon, represents the divinity present in its energy – not in a substantialist sense but in 'its flow of meaning'. The meaning of this was not generally understood and the outbreak of the war in 1914 temporarily closed the debate. During the Council of the Russian Church in 1917, Archbishop Tikhon joined in celebration with the Onomatodox monks as a gesture of reconciliation. However, the conciliatory commission, in which Sergii Bulgakov participated in the role of speaker, did not have time to make the assembly adopt any resolution relating to the decision of 1913. Since then, no decision has been made in the Orthodox Church on the subject of the veneration of the Name of God.

In his two treatises, Bulgakov sought to deepen the thinking on this question which had so far been confined to a simple opposition between the Onomatomdox – the enemies of the veneration of the Name – and the Palamite apophatic teaching on the distinction between essence and energies. Bulgakov saw, first of all, that only the symbolic philosophy of the world was able better to understand the foundations of the Name veneration. Thus, from this point of view, words are not conventional signs, but living and symbolic realities. Bulgakov even agreed with the Cabbalists for whom speech and hearing exist not because of themselves but because sounds exist. The word speaks within us. The word belongs to conscience but also to being. This is contrary to the nominalism of modernity for which words are only signatures of things, which lead to the divorce between things and words, as shown by Michel Foucault. Bulgakov's view was that words are 'things as much as they are meaning'. For him, people do not speak 'with words' but they are the theatre and the leading player: 'from the birth of these by symbolisation of meanings, as much as for particular words as for speech in general'.[2]

This is why Bulgakov drafted a grammatical philosophy in which he distinguished three elements within the word: the phonetic aspect (*phonème*), the 'envelope' (*morphème*) and finally the meaning (*synème*). For Bulgakov, knowledge as 'denomination-judgement' is an artificial process by which a link is established between an object (a noun) and an idea (a predicate).[3] This symbolic philosophy constitutes Bulgakov's 'linguistic turn'. Thus, if reason is inseparable from the verbal expression of a person, if language is energy, and if the essential purpose of language is to give a name, that is to say, to distinguish the field of the subject from that of the predicate, then human judgement itself must be learned in the same way as grammar. It is at this point that Bulgakov discovered in the fundamental structure of the subject-verb-object clause, the 'tri-hypostatic dimension of the being'. This can be formulated as follows: the subject and the object are characterized, first, by the predication of one by the other, secondly, by the transformation of the object by the word of the subject, and thirdly, by the recognition of this transformation in terms of the verb 'to be' – as a result of which the subject and the object are recognized as the same. Grammatically, this means that the sole subject exists as itself in the noun, through itself in the object, and as and through itself in the verb 'to be'. In other words, the subject is the pure hypostasis, the object is the nature of the hypostasis revealed in itself and before itself, so that the verb is the act of self-realization in its own nature.

Bulgakov went a step further in affirming in *La tragédie de la philosophie* that the whole history of modern philosophy and its derivations can be explained by this method of judgement. Indeed for him, the grammatical subject-verb-object clause is the foundation of the consciousness of the self. The mind is a living clause that constantly realizes itself. This means that, for Bulgakov, hypostasis is primary to *ousia*. Modern philosophy however, in equating *ousia* with nature, understands substance as a non-hypostatic nature and thus deprives it of all personal life. For Kant, substance is an abstract hypostasis for which only the subject exists. For Hegel, substance is the thought which self-generates, a philosophical version of Sabellianism. For Schelling, substance is identical with being, but in itself is no more than a relational function.

The overshadowing of nominalism by personalist ontologism thus allows Bulgakov to answer the questions of the Onomatodox. Bulgakov drew a parallel between the Name and the icon: 'the *phonème* corresponds to the colours and the form of an icon, the *morphème* to the hieroglyphic character of the "original" that provides the design for the representation. The *synème* is the name itself, the

---

[2]   Sergii Bulgakov, *La philosophie du verbe et du nom* (Paris, 1991), p. 29.

[3]   Ibid., p. 126.

energy of the representation'.[4] According to Bulgakov, the only basis which allows the resolution of the question of icon worship is thus that of the nature of the Name of God: 'The doctrine of divine energy and of the incarnation of the word-noun, justified by the image and the resemblance of God to mankind.'[5]

The Onomatodox denied the worship of the name of Jesus because of its variation according to language (Issus, Jesus, Ieshoua). The differentiation between the *phonème* and the *synème* (which relates to the speaker) resolves this problem. Moreover, the Onomatodox did not agree that God could freely reveal himself to men solely by the invocation of his name, and they considered that the power of the Name depended solely on the fervour of the prayer. Bulgakov's response was thus:

> They believe that the virtue of God's name is conveyed accordingly to whether or not the prayer is heard, as if the Lord has to be convinced. God hears whoever calls him, but those who call him do not all do so from their hearts, and neither do they always hear God listening to them. Just as the Eucharist is everlastingly the Body and the Blood of Christ, whether it be in 'salvation' for some or 'judgement and condemnation' for others, so the Name of God is a divine energy, regardless of whether our attitude towards it is pious or sacrilegious. Given that the Name of God contains divine energy and that it offers the presence of God, it can be said that from the point of view of practice, energetics, even though it may be very imprecise, that God's name is God himself. More precisely, that the divine power which is present in the Name, and which is indivisible from the Divine Being is, in this sense, God himself.[6]

Possible Comparisons with the Philosophy of Jean-Marc Ferry

I would like to interrupt my presentation of Bulgakov's grammatical philosophy here, in order to highlight some similarities with ideas in contemporary philosophy, despite the fact that, for reasons that I have shown, very few contemporary philosophers or linguists are familiar with Sergii Bulgakov.[7] I will concentrate on the work of Jean-Marc Ferry entitled *Les grammaires de l'intelligence*, published in 2004. Less well known than his brother Luc Ferry who was Minister for Education in the government of the former Prime Minister Jean-Pierre Raffarin, Jean-Marc Ferry is nevertheless regarded by thinkers, among them the late Paul Ricœur, as one of the most shining contemporary French philosophers.

---

[4]   Ibid., p. 184.

[5]   Ibid., p. 174.

[6]   Ibid., p. 202.

[7]   This is what Claude Hagège, Professor of Linguistics at the Collège de France, told me in 1997.

Although Jean-Marc Ferry seems not to have heard of Bulgakov, a similar strand of thinking can be noted between him and the Russian philosopher. First, Ferry rejects, like Bulgakov, modern philosophies of representation. He prefers a communicative ontology, in the same way that Bulgakov advocates *sobornost* ('conciliarity') as the basis of knowledge. Ferry writes that

> It is not from the substance of my own representation that I can conclude my own existence, it is rather by reducing my own representation to an act. What I recognize is thus an 'I', which can be understood as the representation of the self. 'I am' is the product of a positioning, which places me as an opposite.[8]

The same is true for Bulgakov, for whom the revelation of God's name to Moses, 'I am who I am' (Ex 3:14), testifies to a supreme freedom. At this point, Ferry, like Bulgakov, gives precedence to the ideas of self-position and self-revelation above those of adequacy and conformity. This is because in the self-referential as well as in the communicational relationship, the interrogator is also the interrogated.

This means that Ferry, to the same degree as Bulgakov, contradicts the philosophy of Kant. For Kant, the explanation of comprehension, like the relationship between the image, which is viewed, and the concept which it represents, is seen as too theoretical. For Ferry, this idea is fundamentally flawed because of the reality that, in practice, the object is recognized even before the introduction of the idea. For Ferry, philosophy must thus be symbolic and rely on, as with Bulgakov, clauses and judgements: 'The Grammar of propositions only consecrates the power of the symbol by integrating the moment of the icon and the index. It consecrates above all the power of the verb, the conjugated verb which involves in particular the tenses, the pronouns and the modes.'[9] Thus in *Les grammaires de l'intelligence* can be found the same inversion as in *La tragédie de la philosophie*: 'The transcendent rules become grammatical rules. This is the human discourse, it consists of a reference to something, an address to a person and the engagement of the self, which allows not the command of, but the participation in the realities of the world.'

However, Jean-Marc Ferry does not ignore modern linguistic theories in his work. For him, the linguistic paradigm is over-emphasized, as much by the phenomenological hermeneutics of Heidegger as by the analytic philosophy of Wittgenstein. This is because the limits of our language are not the limits of our universe. This is why, in the name of his vision of mankind, Ferry claims a double transcendence in relation to the linguistic world: 'Transcendence of the objective world, in order to base the proposition of a contact with the real; and transcendence of the prescriptive world, in order to base the idealisation of an access to the universal.'[10] It is this double transcendence that allows him to define

---

[8]   Jean-Marc Ferry, *Les grammaires de l'intelligence* (Paris, 2004), p. 112.

[9]   Ibid., p. 116.

[10]   Ibid., p. 138.

the very *logos* of human language. 'The principle of relevance corresponds to the reference to something, the principle of recognition to the address of someone; the principle of responsibility to the engagement of the self.'[11] In this we can recognize Bulgakov's idea that language makes hypostasis appear primary to substance.

In the same way in which Bulgakov furthered the idea of the tri-hypostatic nature of human language, Ferry, for his part, talks of the triangular nature of human discourse. Over and above the pre-symbolic grammars which are the associative and imputative grammars, Ferry defines what he calls a propositional grammar which symbolically structures the tendency to communicate in tertial mode. This is to say, the communication of something to another on the subject of something. This is why our relations with the world follow the plan of three pronominal subjects (I, you, he/she/it), in using the three basic time tenses (past, present, future) whilst relating them to the three modes. (The indicative, that which is, the subjunctive, that which is possible, and the imperative, that which must be.)

This claim of a double transcendence allows Ferry to return to one of Bulgakov's deepest intuitions about God's creation of the world. Ferry holds that at the moment of creation existed chaos or *tohu wa bohu*. From that he concludes that

> God as Spirit did not create the matter but the world as we see it. By the Word, he made the reality of existence be born, so that later it could be acknowledged by man from which he derives an honour, in Hegel's words, his 'right to majesty'. If God is the creator, this is to say that he is the first author of the reality, who reveals the being, rather than giving birth to it himself. His supreme power is no more than grammatical, as is that of mankind, on his own scale. Man's creative imagination, has not, it dares to be said, himself witnessed the six days of time needed for the evolution of grammar, and at the initiation, on the seventh day, of the landscape which his discursive understanding can thus recognise and update during his lifetime of scrutiny.[12]

Bulgakov does not contradict this in *The Philosophy of the Word and the Name*:

> Everything was created non from non-being, but from the *archè*, being brought to its current state from the darkness of *ouk* on, from nothingness, but not yet risen to distinct being, to light. All remains in chaotic disorder, *apeiron*. This potential being was named by word and thought. The same idea can be found in the book of Genesis.[13]

---

11   Ibid., p. 139.

12   Ibid., p. 61.

13   Bulgakov, *La philosophie du verbe et du nom*, p. 119.

Christian Orthodoxy and Sophianic Grammar

Let me now return to the link between Radical Orthodoxy and the Eastern Orthodox tradition. I would like to examine the work of Jean-Marc Ferry in the light of the philosophy of the Name formulated by Sergii Bulgakov. In this way I hope to show that Bulgakov's 1932 redefinition of Orthodoxy as 'Life in Christ within the Spirit', and subsequently upheld by a range of Orthodox thinkers such as Paul Evdokimov, Christos Yannaras and Olivier Clément, is a genuinely radical thought. It is radical in the view of modernity, in the sense that modernity views freedom solely as an independent choice, whilst 'Life in Christ within the Spirit' presents freedom as personal love and inter-dependence. But it is also radical to Eastern Orthodoxy itself which historically no longer regards the true glorification of God as anything other than loyalty to tradition beyond all reason. This is just an overview of some of the consequences of this Orthodox radicalism as much for contemporary linguistics as for Eastern Orthodoxy.

Jean-Marc Ferry concludes his book by placing critical intelligence at the summit of all human intelligence, capable of defining the truth by a process of discursive validation. Whilst animals cannot respond to messages, human beings are able to question them according to a logic of truth and falseness. This is the source of human power, what Ferry calls the concept of self-referential consultation. In this grammar, by responding man becomes responsible for what he says. This is why discursive grammar is based on the orders of validity (the precision of statements, the accuracy of recommendations, the sincerity of declarations and the truth of affirmations).[14] The reconstructed discourse is, according to Ferry, what protects public opinion from the disordered mixture of the modern media.

At this point we should make a distinction between Ferry and Bulgakov. In following Charles Taylor's brilliant analysis of modern disenchantment, Ferry confuses the self-referentiality of behaviour, which is justified by the authenticity which it allows, with the self-referentiality of matter, which serves to place the desires of the human subject in opposition to that which is higher. Taylor however, wrote that 'we find a genuine fulfilment only in relation to a superior reality holding a meaning independent of our desires and ourselves'.[15]

By contrast, Bulgakov starts from the idea that the roots of the human *logos* are found not in the order of communicational validity, but in the divine *Logos*, who in turn reveals itself as the Way, and the Truth and the Life. Bulgakov distinguished two ideas about the *Logos* from the prologue of John: 'One concerns the *Logos* in himself, the divine hypostasis, God; the other the Word who acts in the world but who is orientated towards God, the energy of the *Logos* in the Cosmos, the

---

[14]   Ferry, *Les grammaires de l'intelligence*, p. 200.

[15]   Charles Taylor, *Le malaise de la modernité* (Paris, 1992), p. 88.

Sophie.'[16] This sophianic and thus Trinitarian energy of the *Logos*[17] found its accomplishment in the realization by Christ of the Trinity of the divine name. 'Before Abraham was born, I was' said Christ to the Jews unable to hear his word (Jn 8:31–59). Marie-Joseph Le Guillou, one of the Catholic heirs to Bulgakov's thought, writes that

> in the Trinitarian evidence of the Passover, the revealed divine Name is exactly that which metaphysically founds the world. But it reveals itself at the heart of a mystery of dispossession, that of the father and of the son which leads St. John to say, 'God is love' (Jn, 4:16). If he allows himself to be brought into 'the abode of love of the Son' by the spirit of filiation, man will reach the heart of the Being Himself, and his hermeneutic place will be the Name of the Father.[18]

On the contrary, Jean-Marc Ferry founds the human *logos* on the category of truth held in a legal process formed by the 'orders of validity'. Whilst for Ferry, the true doctrine is the result of a differentiation within the *doxa*, the public opinion, between the existential constative order and the ethical regulative order. For Bulgakov, orthodoxy is the life in Christ within the Spirit. In the philocalic spirituality that glorifies the Name of Jesus incessantly, the ability to justify what is said and done is the sole source of the unification of intelligence to the spirit. This means that to the constantive, regulative and expressive orders should be added equally the orders of faith, hope and love.

In asking whether 'the project can replace the destiny', both the conjunctive and syntaxic propositional grammars allow man to free himself of the illusion, present in associative grammar, that a mechanical binding holds together, for example, the letter A and the colour black. From where though does man find his ability to use his inner freedom from these bindings? The iconic grammar is only completely defeated by the imperative mood, namely the mode of prayer. However, Ferry confines the imperative mode to the magic thought according to which the spoken word has to be law.[19]

It is thus not rational acceptance that constitutes the distinguishing feature of human intelligence in the philosophy of the Name, but the ability to identify the interior verb in each thing and, in naming it to transfigure it. This is why Christ said to his disciples who were chasing demons in his name 'rejoice not that the spirits are subject unto you; but rather rejoice because your names are written in heaven' (Lk 10:20). In the order of the faith, man believes that he will receive on the last day 'a new name' engraved on a white stone. At the Apocalypse, the

---

[16]   Bulgakov, *La philosophie du verbe et du nom*, p. 119.

[17]   Bulgakov writes that 'The Name of God and the Name of Jesus, which express the hypostatic being of the Godhead, are at the same time sophianic', Bulgakov, *La philosophie du verbe et du nom*, p. 213.

[18]   Marie-Joseph Le Guillou, *Le mystère du Père* (Paris, 1973), p. 229.

[19]   Ferry, *Les grammaires de l'intelligence*, p. 126.

Son of man tells the angel of the Church of Sardes that in the last hours 'He that overcometh, the same shall be clothed in white raiment; and I will not blot out his name from the book of life, but I will confess his name before my Father, and before his angels' (Rev 3.5). However, when we talk about the last day, we get the eschatological rather than a passive vision of the temporality. Charles Taylor is fond of quoting the following words of Shelly: 'in more subtle language, a thing defines and creates itself at the same time that it manifests itself'.

Ferry notes accurately that animism opens man to an understanding of nature by looking at plants and animals as persons and not merely things, as they are to modernists. In the same way, scenarios like the personification of Christ by medieval emperor is evidence of an evocative and ascriptive mimesis and not of a proportional logic distinguishing reality from fiction. Ferry also shows that syntaxic-propositional grammar is closed to the energies of the world if it only seeks to establish the inter-subjectivity of people across illocutions and to assure the objectivity of states of fact across predications. Instead, he supports a graded grammar. For Ferry, something encountered does not only indicate one state of possible things but also 'a world of meaning'. By itself it signifies something of itself.

However, Ferry stops mid-flow, and does not dare affirm that the only way past the aberrations of animism (the treatment of plants as human beings) as in the case of propositional grammar (use of the plant as an object) is to open oneself to the revelation of the personal creation by the *Logos* of all *logoi*. The microcosm of man, in discovering from within their sophianic reality, can also name them. In the same way the creation of man in the image of God is the foundation of the mimesis of the world. This is what allows us to understand the history of the world as a divine and human drama. And this is what makes the psalmist say that 'all the creation praises the Lord' (Ps 148). So it is fitting to pass not from evocative-ascriptive mimesis to the refusal of all mimesis, since that would lead to the formation of unconscious destructive mimesis, but to participate in metaphysical, pious, transfigurative and eschatological mimesis.

For Bulgakov, it is the Name of God that is also found at the heart of the divine-human liturgy. He writes:

> Between a representation and the reality of ritual symbolics, there is a rift same as between the Being and non-being as between 'the real' and 'the allegoric'. And the principle or the foundation that constitutes the reality of the liturgical rite is undoubtedly the Name of God whose power acts and sanctifies the congregation who having been sanctified becomes fully authentic and efficient.[20]

---

[20] Bulgakov, *La philosophie du verbe et du nom*, p. 204.

Conclusion

For Jean-Marc Ferry, human intelligence, which is focused on the rational search of consensus by discussion, is thus reduced to the conditions of the communicational experience. These conditions are continually threatened by the subversion of public reason by the media, which leads to 'the mechanical functioning of our buried grammar, subliminal grammar of image association and imputation of functions'. For Bulgakov, on the contrary, human intelligence, when it is rooted in Divine Wisdom, is the light that transfigures all darkness, because God cannot be subjected to the conditions of subjective experience.

Here is where those who are conscious of their unity in Christ also understand that they form a body. Louis-Marie Chauvet, a contemporary Catholic theologian, presented, along the same lines of the Russian theologian, the necessary reconstruction of the subject through the means of language and ecclesiological body:

> The personal subject-body itself is not the scene of '*sacramentum*', the sacrament, since it hosts the announcing triple body: the social body of Church that through the permanent 'us' of the liturgical prayer, positions itself as 'the integral subject of the liturgical action' (Congar); the ancestral or traditional body of the same Church that expresses Herself through words and duly prescribed and institutionally ordered gestures; and finally the cosmic body of the universe, avowed as God's creation, which is fully metonymically represented through some symbolic fragments, such as bread, wine, water and light.[21]

The consequences of this Orthodox radicalism are significant for the Church of the East. The traditions of the Eastern Orthodox Church are known for mysticism, philocalic spirituality and icon worship. However, apophatic theology must not become the refuge of the Oonomatodox heresy. Although I could equally mention Antoine Blum or Oliver Clément here, it is Bishop Kallistos Ware who writes in his work on the power of the Name that 'the apophatic position of reason only has meaning if it allows man to be quiet himself and because of this silence put himself in a position to listen'. In his book *The Inner Kingdom*, Bishop Kallistos Ware also quotes these words of Saint Ignatius of Antioch, '... Jesus Christ, the Word that has risen from silence'.[22] Since the controversy over the book *In the Caucasus Mountains*, we know that on the ascetic path lie many pitfalls. Would we not count among them the refusal of positive knowledge, the refusal of love beyond all reason, the refusal to share the same temporality, the absolute refusal of the divine image that is found at the heart of the simplest human word?

---

[21]   Louis-Marie Chauvet, 'Quand la théologie rencontre les sciences humaines', in *Mélanges offerts à Mgr Joseph Doré, La responsabilité des théologiens* (Paris, 2002), p. 224.

[22]   Kallistos Ware, *The Inner Kingdom* (New York, 2001), p. 89.

Jean-Marc Ferry, like all our contemporaries, fears to speak the Name of God and refuses to see the many Pentecosts of our daily life. It is clear that there was a lack of conceptual creativity at the dawn of modern times, an overshadowing of theandric mystery at the same time as the great rift between Christians. Thus have Christians perhaps spoken the Name of the Father too often in vain whilst forgetting the brotherhood that unites them? By way of an answer I propose to conclude by these magnificent and tremendous words of Sergii Bulgakov: 'The Name of God always puts us in the presence of fire, whether we be aware of it or not.'[23]

---

[23]   Bulgakov, *La philosophie du verbe et du nom*, p. 202.

COMMENTARY

Rowan Williams

Professor Arjakovsky's excellent essay on Bulgakov and Ferry suggests that a central aspect of the conversation between Radical Orthodoxy and the Eastern Christian tradition needs to be in the area of theories of language. John Milbank's essays in *The Word Made Strange* already indicate the importance for Radical Orthodoxy of this subject: Milbank argues that it is precisely Christian theology that makes possible the 'linguistic turn' – but also exposes the error and risk of the way it has been understood in modernity and postmodernity. We cannot have a viable theory of language that supposes there to be a primitive gulf between substantive reality and verbal representation; we cannot get 'behind' representation, 'before' culture. But the various modern and postmodern attempts to thematize this have been disastrous. The Kantian assertion of substantial subjects existing in pure self-relation beyond the level of appearance proves unsustainable. Theories of language as will, the imposing of meaning upon the blank surface of unstructured objects of sense, are no better. Symbolist fantasies of the magical powers of names revert to ancient speculation and simply take speech out of history. Postmodernist arguments about the inescapability of semiotic equivocation rightly accept that there is no 'realm' outside speech, but mistakenly conclude that this means an unbroken process of manipulation (violence) in which meaning can be related only to power since there is no ground for speech. The question, 'To what does speech answer?', is dismissed in diverse ways by all these styles of thinking about language. And if that question is nowhere to be located, we have no way of making sense of a range of actual practice in speech – difficulty, pleonasm (as Milbank puts it), that is, the development of non-identical repetition, praise, the verbal performance of self-scrutiny (repentance?), and more. In different ways, all these have to do with the frontiers of identity and otherness as a region of appropriate complexity.

Hence the interest of Bulgakov's scheme as outlined by Professor Arjakovsky. The triadic structure he sees in speech (subject/substance, verb, complement) embodies a sort of instability in the very idea of *the* subject – which is perhaps why he insists upon the priority of 'hypostasis' over nature. There is, so to speak, a unique 'locus' within the net of shifting relations which constitutes itself an identity precisely in the multiplicity of 'othernesses' which act in or through or across it. What there is not is a solid mysterious singleness on to which a variety of extras are bolted. The mysteriousness or inexpressibility of the subject is not a hinterland of self-relation, but the impossibility of finding one ultimate object at the heart of what is being spoken of. Hence the inseparability of naming from a whole practice of relation; and hence the insistence that the name is inseparable from the active presence of its subject – not as a quasi-magical presence, nor some sort of emanation, but simply as the location of the subject within the processes of sustaining meaning, within the *act* of communication which is set in train by the openness, the self-subverting instability of every subject.

The weaknesses of Ferry's account are correctly identified by Arjakovsky: if the process of communication finally folds into a rather Habermasian concern with sustainable validation in universal communicative practices, we are still left with questions about whether the entire communicative practice can be seen as relating to or answering to anything beyond itself. The answer that Bulgakov, like Milbank, points to is, in effect, the conceiving of the divine life, the Trinity, as the foundational and irreducible 'communicative practice'. Bulgakov hints at how this might be developed (though one would have to track the themes through the detail of his later theological work). The concept *of hypostasis* is for him, as for other Russian theologians of his and the next generation, one that goes deeper than any idea of the simple instantiation of a 'nature', a kind of life. His speculations about Sophia, the 'Wisdom of God', can be read in this light as an attempt to relocate talk about the divine nature by binding it to the concrete activity of the divine hypostases. God's nature is what 'happens' or what is done in the active, eternal interrelation of those moments or *loci* of agency that we misleadingly call 'persons'; and what is done is the creative, kenotic, 'loving of loving' which Bulgakov identifies as the 'wisdom' in and through which God makes and redeems the world. We begin neither with an abstract nature, a set of divine attributes which may be attached to three subjects, nor with a groundless divine selfhood asserting itself (this is more like Berdyaev's curious schema), but with just that simultaneous multiplicity of action through distinct nodes or centres which constitutes an active reality engaged in communication. It is a sameness in otherness – identity, otherness and simultaneous self-bestowal for knowledge and relation – which cannot be reduced either to a discourse about generic substances or to a discourse about atomic individuals. Bulgakov's model of language is manifestly bound in with his developing Trinitarian thought and with the way in which his complex speculations about Sophia increasingly come to be for him a way of speaking about divine essence, *ousia*, in a relational and active mode.

As I have said, his refusal of any idiom suggesting a priority of nature to person is something he has in common with many other Orthodox thinkers – notably Vladimir Lossky, in many ways one of his fiercest critics. Outside the Russian world, the same themes are found in John Zizioulas and Christos Yannaras; the latter's reflections, especially in his recent work on postmodern metaphysics, would bear looking at in this connection. But perhaps the main point for the question of the transfiguration of the world by the word is that there is a clear strand in Eastern Orthodox thinking, a strand with some patristic antecedents, even if not quite the clear roots that Lossky or Zizioulas claim, which offers a creative model for the theological grounding of the sort of linguistic theory argued for by Radical Orthodoxy.

However, it is not only in terms of strictly defined Trinitarian theology that the Eastern tradition finds itself entwined with a contemporary problematic. As Arjakovsky hints, Bulgakov is fully aware of the other great theme in twentieth-century Orthodox thought, the recovery of Gregory Palamas' distinction between divine *ousia* and divine *energeia*. Although Palamas' own presentation of the distinction presents a good many problems of conceptual clarity, modern retrievals of it (especially by Yannaras) have taken the matter further. The idea of the name as 'energy' in a Palamite sense is a fruitful one. It allows us to say that the name *is not* an essence or the emanation of an essence or the exhaustive presence of an essence; essences, in the sense of definitive encapsulations of identity, do not belong in language. Naming allows the subject (avoiding for a moment the freighted word 'essence') to be apprehended as mobile, plural, engaged, constituted as an active subject *in* its complex relations (though this is not the same as saying that it is constituted by the agency of others). It asserts a particular kind of indeterminacy – not an empty potentiality, but a range of possible identities-in-the-other. In relation to the Palamite doctrine of the relations between God and creation, it is a way of saying that God truly 'becomes' the God of Israel and of believers in Jesus, without thereby saying that God is incompletely God without creation. It is a conceptual tightrope, which Western as well as Eastern theology has had to negotiate.

But details aside for the moment, the Palamite structure, which insists upon a real participation of creatures in God by way of revealed words and contemplative experience, makes possible a view of language which accords to the name a genuine relation to what it names without committing us to some magical or otherwise manipulative doctrine of the name as embodied essence. I want to allude briefly here to another Russian thinker who develops this even more explicitly than Bulgakov – the elusive A.F. Losev, whose *Filosofiya Imeni* was published privately in Moscow in 1927. Losev had clearly digested the Imyaslavtsy controversy and almost certainly Bulgakov's contribution to it, though he does not refer to it directly (he does refer to Florensky, however, mentor of Bulgakov and many others). Losev attempts to engage with Husserlian phenomenology, responding positively to its interest in symbolic form but arguing that it is insufficiently 'dialectical'. 'The name is life', according to Losev, it is the life of a subject in the intelligent life of another, and thus the foundation of sociality as a system of actual participation (rather than a juxtaposition of monadic substances). The unity of any subject is in living fact a multiplicity; the fluidity and continuity together of acts of naming are what enable us to conceive of a unity in subjects that is real, not just ideal. The ideal unity of a thing is, for Losev, a fiction. He rejects any *Ding-an-sich* language, insisting that the phenomenon as *yavlenie*, revelation, is the ultimate object of knowledge; every intelligible life is 'embodied' life, that is, life in engagement with other lives. True 'essence' is not the inexpressibility or inaccessibility of some hinterland; it is precisely what the dialectical tracing of the linguistic presence and deferral and re-imagining of something embodies in the world.

Losev proposes thinking about substance as what he calls *energem* – the activating content of the name (or of other specific concretions of life in relation). The name is *energeia*, the substance is what is 'energized' in actual rather than abstract life. The knowability of substance is entirely to do with its activity in and upon what is other; the 'unknowable' in substance is not – as we have seen – some inner, hidden territory, but the sheer mobility, the capacity for different relations, characteristic of the subject involved in action and engagement in time. You can speak of an 'apophatic moment' in this sense; and it is this apophatic dimension that constitutes dialectic as a 'symbolic' discourse; it is a discourse that does not claim to deal with fixed essences but with histories of multiple representation unified by some sort of continuity in *energeia*. Only in this can we secure an adequate or precise intelligible form (*eidos*) of substance. The language of art is symbolic dialectic at its height, language or representation most adequately in harmony with the unifying *energeia*. Losev, like Bulgakov and Florensky, speaks here of 'sophianic' representation – a form of representation that is maximally open to the essentially personal act of communication that underlies all intelligibility. This is 'mythological' language, but the only idiom possible to express the all-pervasiveness of relation in the world of knowledge. This formulation, it should be added, is probably also a way of suggesting to censors or unsympathetic Soviet readers that the argument is not a religious apologetic; but an attentive unsympathetic reader will have already taken the point that an account of language without transcendental reference is manifestly thought by Losev to be impossible. Losev's final formulation of the character of substance certainly gives plenty of hostages to fortune here. Substance is asserted to be sevenfold: there is the fundamental apophatic indeterminacy, the fact of the capacity for multiple relation; there is *eidos*, intelligible form in the widest sense, followed by the 'eidetic *me on*', the capacity for multiple dimensions of intelligibility; then comes *logos*, the immediate specific animating force for particular action in time, then *sophia*, the moment of embodiment. The final two stages are the *energeia* flowing from embodiment, which is indistinguishable from the symbol, and the external fact of concrete related being (*inobytie*).

This is not exactly a lucid or wholly coherent structure, but its interest in our context is the way that it deploys a pretty overtly theological vocabulary to describe the connection of language and 'substance', attempting, as Losev says, to steer a path between agnosticism and rationalism. It is very clear, as with Bulgakov, that the Palamite model is being used in tandem with elements of Dionysian apophaticism to provide a tacit link between knowledge of God in the Eastern tradition and a theory of speech (of speech-acts, one might say) that will avoid the pitfalls of arbitrary labelling, magical emanation or Kantian redundancy. The apophatic is not a primitive mystery overcome in representation; it is more that which repeatedly reasserts itself in the very process of representation in time – the uncovering by speech itself of what is not yet represented, which will in turn reveal more of the un-represented.

So as we look at the many links between aspects of the Eastern theological tradition and the challenges of forming a theory of speech beyond violence and mere *jouissance* alike, Losev is perhaps a partner no less interesting than Bulgakov in the task. His likely association with the world of Bakhtin, which recent scholarship has begun to explore, gives a further turn to an intellectual agenda that should fully engage all those involved in today's theological and philosophical conversations.

Chapter 2
Sophiology and Theurgy: The New Theological Horizon

John Milbank

The Genius of Sophiology

At the dawn of the twenty-first century, it increasingly appears that perhaps the most significant theology of the two preceding centuries has been that of the Russian sophiological tradition. Latin theology within the same period has been characterized by a gradual recovery of a more authentic tradition, rooted in the Church Fathers, the earlier to High Middle Ages and the better contributions of the Renaissance legacy. This recovery eventually became focused on an attempt to retrieve the sense that there is no great gulf between creation and deification, since humanity, and even the cosmos through humanity, has always been orientated in its fundamental being towards receiving the gift of supernatural grace.[1] In this way it opened up the possibility, even if it has never completely been followed through, of restoring the integral links between theological and philosophical discourse. The Eastern tradition, on the other hand, had never posited such a gulf, because it had never given rise to the Western problematic concerning the relation between nature and grace, reason and revelation. Although it was indeed much corrupted by alien scholastic influences, and even by certain rationalizing trends of its own engendering, it was still possible for Vladimir Solovyov and other religious philosophers in the nineteenth century to resume a mode of thought in which the philosophical and the theological were seamlessly fused.

However, this greater rooting in ancient Christian tradition also allowed the Russians to respond to post-Kantian German thought in a manner not only significantly different from that of the West Europeans, but also, arguably, more attentive to the deep character of German idealism. Under the goad of Jacobi's contention that pure reason, without the support of faith, will have to confine itself to the supposedly graspable apparent truth of phenomena, thereby evoking the spectre of an underlying nihilism, Kant himself already sought to incorporate an understanding of faith, grace and even Christian doctrine within the scope of his philosophy. Still under the goad of Jacobi's incisive writings, which now called into question the very idea that reason could really round upon its own

---

[1]   See John Milbank, *The Suspended Middle: Henri de Lubac and the Debate Concerning the Supernatural* (Grand Rapids, MI, 2005).

presuppositions, or intuit what is required for thinking without thereby simply performing yet another move within ungrounded discursive reason itself, Fichte, Hegel and Schelling were forced to try to ground reason by incorporating in their philosophies an account of the entire history of human cultural and theoretical reflection. This endeavour inevitably appealed to the history of religion and the history of Christianity in particular, in order to try to elucidate how finite discursive reasoning is related to the infinite self-establishing *Logos*. The idioms of faith and belief were here respectfully seen as the vital clues to the comprehension of reason itself. In this manner, Jacobi's charge of nihilism was, it was hoped, held at bay, or else nihilism itself, as by Hegel, was given a more benign interpretation.[2]

Recent scholarship has emphasized the trajectory which I have summarized above, and what is striking is the way in which this accords with the older Russian reception of German philosophy. First of all, it remained far more emphatically aware, compared to the later Western reception (in the second half of the nineteenth and the twentieth century), of the way the nihilist problematic lurked always in the background of this tradition. Secondly, it realized that, in effect, German idealism had restored the integral unity of faith and reason, albeit in a mode which, even perhaps in the case of Schelling, was too biased towards the pole of reason. The Russian thinkers, from Solovyov through Pavel Florensky to Sergii Bulgakov in particular, then sought both to extend and to criticize this tradition, especially in the form it took in Schelling, in a manner that would free it of its rationalist and transcendentalist biases and render it more consonant with genuine Christian doctrine. In particular, they gradually purged away the notion, ultimately derived from Jacob Boehme, that is so pervasive in post-romantic German thought, according to which there is some sort of endemic conflict in the absolute which involves God himself in the Fall, the latter being regarded as an inevitable rather than a contingent event.[3] At the same time, the existential and conceptual issues that tended to support this notion were never skirted round by the Russians, who tended to provide more orthodox versions of the Behmenistic solutions.

---

[2]   See John Milbank, 'Knowledge: the theological critique of orthodoxy in Hamann and Jacobi', in John Milbank, Catherine Pickstock and Graham Ward (eds), *Radical Orthodoxy. A New Theology* (London, 1999), pp. 21–37; Paul W. Franks, *All or Nothing: Systematicity, Transcendental Arguments and Skepticism in German Idealism* (Cambridge, MA, 2005); Frederich C. Beiser, *The Fate of Reason* (Cambridge, MA, 1987); Andrew Bowie, *Schelling and Modern Philosophy* (London, 1993); on the German-Russian link, see Michael Allen Gillespie, *Nihilism before Nietzsche* (Durham, NC, 1995).

[3]   For Germanic Gnosticism, see Cyril O'Regan, *The Heterodox Hegel* (New York, 1994) and *Gnostic Return in Modernity* (New York, 2001). For the modern Russian sophiological tradition, see Paul Valliere, *Modern Russian Thought: Bukharev, Soloviev, Bulgakov – Orthodox Theology in a New Key* (Grand Rapids, MI, 2000); Antoine Arjakovsky, *La génération de penseurs religieux de l'émigration russe* (Kiev/Paris, 2002). For Bulgakov's adaptation of Schelling, see *Philosophy of Economy: the World as Household*, trans. Catherine Evtuhov (New Haven, CT, 2000).

Pavel Florensky's return to the Jacobian perspective was drastic: he argued that because reason lacks a 'reasonable' intuition to serve as foundation, and we cannot ground general truths upon isolated empirical intuitions, that therefore 'we revolve in the domain of postulates and presuppositions of certain knowledge'.[4] On the basis of this prodigiously 'postmodern' conclusion, he concludes that, according to pure reason itself, it is perfectly possible that there is no truth and that the 'true' horizon is rather a nihilistic one. Thus, in the long term wake of Jacobi and Hamann and beyond idealism, he concludes that reason of itself, in order to save itself, must 'postulate' by faith an infinite ground for the conclusions of reason which will confirm fleeting finite truths, snatched from the flux of time and the elasticity of space, only as participations in an infinite truth where the exclusivity of opposites on which finite logic must rely has necessarily (since in the infinite there are no boundaries to establish exclusive 'identities') ceased to apply. The Trinity, he suggests, is the revelation to faith and to a heightened reason of the logic of a coincidence of identity with non-identity in the infinite which is alone self-establishing.

For these reasons, it seems to me that the scope, ambition and modernity of Russian theology is greater than that of their Latin contemporaries. They tended to start at the point where de Lubac and Balthasar, to name but the most considerable names in the West, only finally arrived. This is because, by fusing the classical tradition with German idealism, heavily tempered, they did rather more than simply arrive at a *ressourcement*, plus certain thin post-Kantian glosses. Instead, in a more full-blooded way, an attempt was made, not simply to recover and defend orthodoxy, but even to extend it by attending both to untapped resources in the tradition, and to new problematics thrown up by the experience and reflection of modern humanity.

Here, I think, two brief remarks are in order. First of all, one respect in which orthodoxy might be 'radical' is in recognizing that orthodoxy is an always unfinished task. This is not only because new heresies may negatively pose to the Church new questions, but also because existing doctrinal formulations may enshrine unresolved problematics, as much as they successfully resolve old ones. It is also because, as Henri de Lubac says in his essay on the development of doctrine, the narratives and symbols of the Bible and the Liturgy contain a surplus of mysterious meaning that is infinitely in excess of our achieved speculative comprehension.[5] There always remains pre-discursive material, or even blocks

---

[4]   Pavel Florensky, *The Pillar and Ground of the Truth. An Essay in Orthodox Theodicy in Twelve Letters*, trans. Boris Jakim (Princeton/Oxford, 1997), p. 47 and see also pp. 47–9.

[5]   Henri de Lubac, 'The Problem of the development of Dogma', in *Theology in History*, trans. A.E. Nash (San Francisco, 1996), pp. 248–80. See also Lewis Ayres' insightful footnote to this essay in his *Nicaea and its Legacy: An Approach to Fourth-Century Trinitarian Theology* (New York, 2004), pp. 427–9. Ayres, is however, wide of the mark in construing Radical Orthodoxy as too 'systematic' in a modern sense and too neglectful of Scripture, Christology and the redemptive process (on p. 403 of the same

of such material, not yet done justice to. And any reflection on this material will involve a renewed engagement with philosophical resources that is able not just to borrow from these resources, but also to modify them in the light of the data of faith. Such a primary level of engagement has, I think, rarely been undertaken by theology since medieval or even since patristic times; but it is very clearly attempted by Florensky and Bulgakov. Clearly, the block of insufficiently explored primary material which they above all consider concerns the question of wisdom, of the heavenly Jerusalem and of the eternal humanity. Such a consideration rightly involves asking whether extra-canonical texts, some texts loosely considered to be 'Gnostic' and even certain pagan monotheistic texts, have not at certain points done more justice to these Biblical elements than that which hitherto has passed for mainline orthodoxy.

My second remark concerns the nature of the new questions posed by modernity, and treated in a certain fashion by the German idealist tradition. Above all, they concern the new awareness, since the Renaissance, that nature is a dynamic process, and that human nature is most of all dynamic and creative in character. In consequence, one becomes more aware of time, change and collective processes. The questions which then inevitably arise are, why, philosophically and theologically, is there life in time? Why are there successive human generations? Is human collective existence primary over individual existence? What exactly is it that binds together the human collectivity to compose human nature? If human creativity possesses a seemingly unlimited and potentially catastrophic power to transform non-human nature, then what exactly is our role within nature and what is the meaning of nature for us? In addition, the awareness of dynamic processes within nature is greatly increased by the discovery of biological evolution, which renders life a more unstable and violence-dominated process. Within a post-evolutionary climate, the traditional question of theodicy becomes much intensified: what can justify this endemic *agon* within life itself – this formed the thematic of Schelling's novella *Clara*.[6]

All these questions are taken up by the Russsian sophiologists and their genius here is to be able to distinguish that which is ineluctable and unavoidable within modernity – namely the thematics I have just named – from more questionable intellectual manoeuvrings in the face of these thematics: in particular the assumed normativity of the turn to the individual knowing subject and the primacy of epistemology and representation after Descartes and Kant. The Russians rather wager (in a manner similar to that of the French 'spiritual realists', especially Félix Ravaisson) on the possibility that a more traditional ontologically and

---

section of this important book). Indeed, it is precisely its lack of any 'overt' (i.e. presumably methodological) 'theology of scripture' and eschewal of pietistic rhetoric that renders Radical Orthodoxy 'non-systematic'.

    [6]   F.W.J. Schelling, *Clara or, On Nature's Connection to the Spirit World*, trans. Fiona Steinkamp (New York, 2002).

cosmologically focused mode of reflection can be renewed, so as to take account of the specifically modern issues.

And here their further genius is to link the under-explored matrix of material in the Bible concerning wisdom with the new issues posed by modernity concerning nature, humanity and evil. Often this linkage is brilliantly counter-intuitive: thus to take better account of the dynamism of nature, appeal is made to a non-temporal heart of nature which is created Sophia as the world-soul. In a similar fashion, in order to take better account of human historicity and collectivity, appeal is made to an ahistorical Adam-Kadmon figure. Finally, in order to come to terms with evolutionary struggle, the primacy of life and the unreality of death is invoked, along with a new insistence on the fallenness, and indeed, evil, of the natural world as we in time experience it. Later in this chapter, I will try to indicate the coherence of these counter-intuitive moves.

If sophiology contrives to connect new problematics with a renewed hermeneutic of neglected texts, it also tries to deal with the standing *aporias* of existing doctrinal formulations. In every case, I think, this has to do with the question of mediation. Thus between the persons of the Trinity defined as substantive relations (following a tradition successively elaborated across East and West by the Cappadocians, Augustine and Aquinas), there are no third terms: *media non dantur*. Likewise there is no third term between the essence of the Godhead and the persons of the Trinity themselves. Were there such *media*, then persons and relations and essence would become specific instances of something more general and fundamental. Likewise, if there were a third term between God and the Creation, if God were related to the Creation and not just the Creation constitutively related to God, there would be a greater than God and God would not be God.

Again, in the case of Christology, there is no third term between the two natures, nor between both the natures and the divine hypostasis. Nor is there any third term between the Holy Spirit and the collectively infallible Catholic Church. Finally, there is no third term between manhood in general and Godhead, nor between God who is able to become man and humanity which is destined to be deified. However, as the Irish Catholic philosopher William Desmond has abundantly pointed out, where there is no third, no between, no *metaxu*, to use the Platonic term also favoured by Bulgakov (as Desmond is well aware), then one tends to get a resolution of all relations into impossible free-standing univocal identities, resulting in an unexplained pluralism, or else alternatively into a monistic equivocal flux whose self-grounding remains equally inexplicable.[7] And as Desmond, a renown Hegel scholar, also contends, any merely dialectical version of mediation tends in reality to evacuate mediation by turning it into an agonistic shuttle between univocal pure self-standing identity on the one hand (perhaps with an accompanying hierarchy of an original identity over a secondary one), and an equivocal pure process of differentiation on the other. A little later on,

---

[7]   William Desmond, *Being and the Between* (New York, 1995); Sergii Bulgakov 'The Unfading Light', in *Sergii Bulgakov*, trans. and ed. Rowan Williams (Edinburgh, 1999), p. 134.

I shall consider how the traditional theological formulations, if left unmodified, can also fall prey to these sorts of dissolution.

For now the important thing to note is that one can take sophiology as the attempt to think through the place of mediation in instances like the theological ones mentioned where, it would seem, there cannot possibly *be* any mediation and yet, without it, everything threatens to fall apart. To anticipate, one could say that Sophia names a *metaxu* which does not lie between two poles but rather remains simultaneously at both poles at once. As such it does not subsist before the two poles, but it co-arises with them such that they can only exist according to a mediated communication which remains purely occult, a matter of utterly inscrutable affinity.

So we can now see that the notion of Sophia brings together three distinct things in modern Russian thought. First of all, it asks about divine wisdom in the Bible and the wisdom that is the first created of God's creatures (Prov 8:22–31). Secondly, it tries to confront the modern realities of dynamic collectivity and seemingly endemic evil in nature. Thirdly, it tries to tackle the problem of a necessary but seemingly impossible mediation that lurks within traditional speculative theology. By bringing these three problematics together, it arrives at a new sort of Trinitarian ontology which makes conjoined but distinguished relation and mediation the fundamental principles for all of reality, in such a manner that the dynamism of nature and humanity is both saved and accounted for. Here it is by no means exclusively Eastern, but tends to marry an orthodox understanding of the divine presence in the *economia* (for example, Maximus' ontology of the *Logos/logoi*) with the Augustinian Trinitarian legacy and what can be regarded as valid in the German idealist Trinitarian speculations.

The modern and postmodern relevance of Russian sophiology is seen more specifically in the way that it foregrounds the instability and uncertainty of understanding, the question of technology and the human relation to nature, together with the question of sexual difference and the preponderance of evil in finite reality. With respect to postmodern philosophy, Florensky's and Bulgakov's often somewhat surrealist thought appears much more at home in the world of difference, simulacra, life, the event and the question of mediation than any of the other early twentieth-century theologies.[8]

Impossible Mediation: (a) The Trinity

In what follows, I will try to give a schematic summary of how all this is done in my own idiom, which will not hesitate, where it seems necessary, to extend sophiological reflection beyond the conclusions arrived at by the great Russian masters.

---

[8]   See especially Florensky's *The Pillar and Ground of the Truth*, which was both conceived and presented in some sense as a symbolist-surrealist work, especially in its depiction and commentary upon a series of emblems at the head of every chapter.

In the case of the divine Trinity, Sergii Bulgakov insisted, as he thought, and most probably wrongly, against Aquinas, that the divine essence cannot in itself be considered something sheerly impersonal, even though it is not in itself a hypostasis, or in Latin language a *persona*.[9] Although it is not a hypostasis, it is still fundamentally 'hypostasizing', or formative of the personal as characterized, reflective and spontaneous. This, then, is the primary reality that can be named 'Sophia' – the divine essence, or the divine being itself. There is, indeed, apparently nothing that lies 'between' the persons of the Trinity, since they are substantive relations such as to ensure that the poles, so to speak, here encompass the entire globe. Insofar as the love that subsists between Father and Son can be considered to be a third reality, this is nothing that subsists between them, much less before them, but rather something that itself proceeds from them both (or from the Father through the Son, if you like – it makes little difference to reason, if it has made a lot to history) to constitute a third hypostasis. So exactly what space is left, for Sophia as a hypostasising power to carry out a mediation?

Rowan Williams explains:

> Sophia is certainly a concrete reality, but not as a *subject* in any sense at all. If love always loves love (and how very Augustinian Bulgakov is in this respect!), the loving persons of the Trinity cannot love what they are if that nature is simply an abstract set of divine qualities; what they love is the capacity for love which is the foundation (though not the cause or origin, as if the abstract came before the concrete) of the eternal life they actually lead.[10]

Bulgakov himself links this 'hypostasizing' love which is Sophia with the fully hypostasized 'love in person' of the Holy Spirit, in the following way. We can recognize a mutual kenotic 'sacrifice' between Father and Son which would be, in itself, a kind of tragedy, a strange kind of unlimited 'sadness', were it not that this ecstasy gives rise to a productive joy that is 'more' than them both. If one considers purely the dyad of Father and Son then, says Bulgakov, one has only a kind of 'ideal' formal relationship, such that for the Father the Son is merely his own perspective of generating, and for the Son the Father is merely the perspective of being generated. Bulgakov links this ideality with 'sadness', by remote analogy to the travails of human conception and birth. In the latter case, the actual birth of a child, which gives rise to joy, achieves a new separation of parent and child which causes humans to forget the preceding anguish. In the case of the Trinity, Bulgakov suggests, this anguish is so eternally surpassed that it never actually occurs. It is always already suppressed as the mutual joy of the

---

[9]   Sergii Bulgakov, 'The Unfading Light', pp. 133–61; *Sophia: the Wisdom of God; an Outline of Sophiology* (Hudson, NY, 1995), pp. 3–53; *Le Paraclet*, trans. Constantin Andronikof (Lausanne, 1996), pp. 171–82*; Du Verbe Incarné*, trans. Constantin Andronikof (Lausanne, 1982), pp. 13–39.

[10]   Williams, *Sergii Bulgakov*, pp. 166–7.

Spirit which yet hypostatically exceeds the first two persons, because this joy is something 'objective', communicable beyond themselves as the *ethos* or peculiar shared 'culture' of their mutual love (to elaborate Bulgakov's reflections) and for this reason one can say that the person of the Spirit as 'the spirit of truth' in some particular sense most of all *is* Wisdom, or Sophia, the person that most personifies the divine essence.[11]

But Bulgakov's most subtle point is that it is only this 'joy as mutual product' which permits Father and Son to be, as it were, 'separately' actual for each other, beyond the mere formality of relationship, just as parent and child gradually come to see each other as free-standing persons. In the case of the Trinity, of course, because of substantive relationality, this is not precisely the case, but nevertheless, the joyful upshot of mutual relation allows this relation to be constantly and dynamically renewed, precisely because it incites a tension between the two poles of the dyad that is a response of Father to Son as 'released' Son, and of Son to Father as 'persisting' Father. For insofar as the surprise of the joy of the Spirit exceeds them both, it rebounds as renewed mutual awareness of the alterity that could instigate this astonishment. In this way, double sacrifice is surpassed by that joy which is the ecstatic beholding of the integrity of the other.

The sacrificial, utterly self-abandoning moment of love is, according to Bulgakov, a crucial moment of love, and it is the ground for the possibility of love persisting in a world of evil as the experience of actual suffering. It is also the ground for the divine redemptive assumption of this suffering in the Incarnation, although one should stress that the anguished separation of the Son from the Father undergone in Gethsemane and on the Cross is only something which he experiences, through the *communicatio idiomatum, qua* possessing an individual human nature, and not *qua* divine *persona*. Bulgakov's appropriation of Schelling here is actually more cautious than that of Hans Urs von Balthasar: he speaks indeed, like the German romantic philosopher, of an internal divine 'Victory' over the shadow of something that has never really come to pass. But in Bulgakov's case this is the shadow of suffering, rather than, as for Schelling, the shadow of evil or else that the divine Father has arbitrarily not elected.[12] Nor, for Bulgakov, is there any reverse transfer of Christ's suffering rupture from the Godhead in time back into the life of the Trinity itself, linked with a lingering Hegelian sense that, from all eternity, it is the Spirit which ensures the union of Father and Son, who are otherwise in a certain anguished separation from each other. By contrast in the case of Balthasar, one has an element of *both* these still somewhat 'gnostic' notions (in a bad sense, because

---

[11]   In a similar fashion, Claude Bruaire argued that while the essence of the divine Trinity is personal spirit or 'gift' (a function which he saw as being very much like that of Sophia), the Holy Spirit nonetheless is most of all spirit and gift, most of all 'the personal essence'. See Claude Bruaire, *L'être et l'esprit* (Paris, 1983), pp. 159–204.

[12]   Bulgakov, *Le Paraclet*, p. 174.

they tend to ontologize the agonistic).[13] With far greater philosophical acuteness, Bulgakov associates the shadow of divine anguish not with the rupture of two mutually isolated subjects, but to the contrary with a relatedness to the other so absolute in its reverse solipsism that one loses the sense of the independent integrity of the other (and thereby of one's own integrity also?) altogether.

And also in contrast to Balthasar, he never allows that any shadow of separation is truly actual in the immanent Trinity, nor requires any 'theodramatic', dialectical healing. Whereas the Swiss theologian spoke of the Spirit as 'reminding' the Father, in the event of the Cross, of the shadow of redemptive suffering rupture that had always hovered between him and the Son, the Russian theologian again spoke much less dialectically, but actually far more catastrophically, of the extinction also – or rather especially – of the Spirit as Joy in the finite realm, on the night of Gethsemane and the following Good Friday. For here, in terms of the divine assumption of human sinful nature, the shadow of the mere dyad, of merely 'ideal' relations between Father and Son, of relations without *relata*, has, indeed, eventuated. Because of the reality of substantive relation, and because, also, of the 'ideal' moment of sacrificial love now activated, both the Father and the Spirit are also affected by the *communicatio idiomatum*: the Father is 'con-crucified' as freely giving his Son unto death, while the Spirit must not merely suffer but 'vanish', if she is but the joyful upshot of love between Father and Son and this is now obliterated through an extremity of suffering that reduces the Son to 'being generated' and the Father to 'generating'.[14] If neither can for the moment see the other's face, then this (as I think Balthasar failed sufficiently to see) is *not* because the dyadic substantive relation has been impossibly severed in the vertical dimension, but rather because it alone – on the human, horizontal level, by virtue of the communication of the human idiom of suffering – remains, without the 'comfort' of the Spirit's procession.

Yet Bulgakov strongly insists that nothing eternal has changed and that nothing eternal has been 'put-off' by the incarnate Christ: the only *kenosis* is the eternal one of the dyadic 'mutually sacrificial' relation: Father to Son and Son to Father. Because nothing eternal has changed, and because this is reversely communicated to the humanity, the absolutely desolate and joyless suffering of the Cross (the only absolute desolation that there is, since it appears to destroy the eternal possibility of joy itself) is instantly and spontaneously converted from the ecstasy of sorrow into the ecstasy of the resurrection of joy, which brings about the resurrected 'return' of the persons of Father and Son, as integral persons not 'exhausted' by their substantive relating (which of course paradoxically destroys also the relation, which requires a 'real two'). For if the Spirit was eternally the 'excess' product of mutual love, always already present beyond the merely 'ideal' mutually sacrificial

---

[13]   Hans Urs von Balthasar, *Theo-drama: theological dramatic theory*, trans. Graham Harrison (5 vols, San Francisco, 2002) vol. 3, pp. 183–92, 489–521; vol. 4, pp. 235–7, 336–85. See also my remarks in *The Suspended Middle*, pp. 74–5.

[14]   Bulgakov, *Du Verbe Incarné*, pp. 288–9.

love of a dyad, as their commonly emerging *ethos*, then when, in time, this sterile ideality is actualized on the Cross, then even so, or rather *all the more*, this excess product of joy will once again arise, to annul that death which is love only as sacrifice and not also as mutual positive ecstasy. This is precisely why Jesus was 'raised in the power of the Spirit', and we can see at once how, if 'communication of idiom' from the divinity to the humanity is a matter of personal putting on of a 'nature', that once again, it is the Spirit which most especially hypostasizes the divine nature or Sophia as such, and so makes this communication possible.

With such a nuanced Trinitarian *schema*, Bulgakov is able to achieve a remarkable synthesis which does justice both to the Augustinian sense that the Spirit expresses only the mutual love that flows between Father and Son, and to the Eastern sense that it is the Spirit which alone enables their fully personal relationship. The Spirit proceeds 'by way of' the Son, and yet is also received by the Son from the Father ('resting on the Son's head', as in Christ's baptism in the Jordan) and is in turn received back by the Father from the Son.[15] (In allowing this, Bulgakov shows a very Western-influenced perspective, and he speaks variously of the Spirit proceeding 'by' the Son, 'on' the Son and 'of' both the Father and the Son, thereby in effect conceding the *filioque*.)[16] So while the Spirit merely 'announces what the Son says of the Father', as the 'spirit of truth', but not 'the truth itself', it nonetheless 'establishes the reciprocity of Father and Son'.[17]

This joy that is the Spirit knows, in turn, no 'interval' or 'distance' between itself and the Son taken together with the Father: there is no shared medium between these two realities, any more than there is between Father and Son. Nevertheless, if there were in no sense a shared 'something' (*homoousios*, if one likes) involved in substantive relation, then the engendered would be sheerly 'other' to the engendering, and the proceeded to the proceeding, on analogy with a bifurcation between *natura naturans* and *natura naturata*: a dualism of process and upshot (which Bulgakov subtly avoids, in the manner above indicated) that would in fact entirely undo substantial relation. Instead, the Son 'is not' the Father as in pure relation to him, but at the same time he 'is' the Father (as Augustine indicates), insofar as the *persona* is not other to the essence and stands forth just as much in respect of being in itself the essence, as in respect of being in itself a substantive relation.[18] Hence *persona* for both Augustine and Aquinas *is not* just the name of a pure relation, but also the point of the intersection between the relational and the essential register.[19] It is this 'essential' aspect of the person which helps to ensure its 'actual content' and 'independence' (only so to speak) in the way which we have just seen was spoken of by Bulgakov. Here again we see a link between the role of essence as Sophia and the Holy Spirit as Sophia, insofar as both tend to

---

[15]   Bulgakov, *Le Paraclet*, pp. 174–77.

[16]   Ibid.

[17]   Bulgakov, *Du Verbe Incarné*, pp. 18–20.

[18]   Augustine, *De Trinitate*, VII, 3, 11.

[19]   Thomas Aquinas, *ST* I\u00aa Q. 9 a. 4 resp; Q. 39 a. 1.

actualize, to concretize, to insinuate 'beauty', 'sensation' and 'life' as Bulgakov puts it,[20] and so even to 'objectify' in such a fashion as to furnish a definite shape to Father and Son, or to 'supply character'. (For the latter notion see further below.)

Via this point of intersection between relation and essence in the person, the engendered is in some sense the unengendered and the proceeded is likewise in some sense the proceeding. It follows then, that there is in a certain fashion a dynamic substantive mediation between essence and relations which involves also a mediation between the persons themselves.

However, it is hard to understand how this can be so. If there is any third term between the essence and the persons (and in consequence between person and person), this threatens to become itself a fourth hypostasis, or else the persons to be reduced to mere modes of a super-fundamental process. Third terms regarded as fundamental are always liable to become genera which contain the linked items as specific instances of themselves. Hence the 'betweenness' involved here cannot really concern, even metaphorically, any intervening space. Instead, Bulgakov's point is rather that what is common to the three persons cannot itself be exactly impersonal, even if it is also not exactly in itself a person: therefore it is at once an essence and yet something already approaching the personal. His thought here is specifically and distinctly vitalist or organicist in character – thus he speaks of the deity as a super-organism. If one takes the analogy of a tree, then Bulgakov is refusing to say that what binds the forest together is an archetypal super-tree, but on the other hand he is also denying that the shared common form 'tree' is in itself a static intellectual abstraction.[21] Rather, if we want to account for why there is a certain dynamic stability of 'treeness' throughout the ages of the earth, we need to think of the universal form 'tree' as not apart from the entire arboreal process of growth and decay and formation, such that it is in a sense identical with the total life of all trees throughout all time as that which mysteriously enables a certain stability of shape and activity within a continuously non-identical repetition.

By analogy, in the case of God, the divine essence is not an impersonal being, substance, essence, set of realized truths or potential that is fully in force. Rather it has in itself, although infinite, a specific and definite 'character' which is the aesthetic shaping power of wisdom, or the manifesting power of the divine superabounding light which, according to the Bible, is 'glory'. This character is not as such in itself fully personal – somewhat as trees and houses or shared social practices can have characters as much as persons do, even though they are not themselves rational, willing or conscious.

Moreover, this 'character of things' is by no means merely a weak echo of that character which persons possess purely in their own right. To the contrary, one can argue that if the divine essence did not possess 'character' or rather, shall we say, a 'power to characterize', then the divine persons themselves would not

---

[20] Bulgakov, *Le Paraclet*, pp. 174–9.

[21] Bulgakov, *Du Verbe Incarné*, pp. 1–22; *Sophia: the Wisdom of God*, pp. 54–81; *Philosophy of Economy*, pp. 44–58.

be personal. This is because their relationality alone does not guarantee their possession of character. A stone, for example, can have 'a parent' in the sense of a physical origin, just as much as can a human being. Therefore why should not an eternal offspring that is a pure substantive being-engendered be a kind of infinite impersonal super-stone? The possessable and transferable character of all persons, human and divine, rather derives initially from the 'shape' that they derive from the objective world, consistently handled and transformed. A human aworldly self would be empty: 'character' only emerges through doing and making, through interaction with things and with other people through the mediation of things. Personal character arises from the subjective alteration of objectivity.

Nevertheless, 'character' is intensified by the greater reflexivity and spontaneity of the personal: by its power to sustain surprising continuities of form through willed changes of shape. It is just for this reason that the most *definite* human characters are precisely the most *enigmatic* ones – such that, indeed, character is enigma and enigma is character: it is *only* enigma that can generate characterizable variations, to allude to Elgar's unique musical composition.[22] Enigmatic persons impart the most singular shape to their actions, even though we cannot quite say what this is. Thus the people who convey the most unique flavour are also those who are sometimes the most unpredictable, or at least never *precisely* predictable, because no one else fully has the secret of that art which is these persons themselves. It is for this reason that, even though our contemporary sense of the word 'person' itself derives from the classical idea of the performance of a theatrical role,[23] *all* characters in plays and novels are caricatures (even Jane Austen's Emma, even Flaubert's) compared to the extraordinary people that we meet with in real life, who are destined to play roles of a far greater definiteness and complexity. And this is why the novelist should concentrate on creating 'another' world, not on placing invented characters in something like our world. Thereby she has more chance of creating, out of her own unique character, relatively life-like fictional characters whose uniqueness belongs to the unique *ethos* of the invented world. The consequent reality-effect then has more chance of illuminating our world, than any more direct attempt at *mimesis*. Even an apparently 'realist' novel like *Adam Bede* in fact succeeds, perhaps contrary to what George Eliot herself supposed, because

---

[22]   On this elusive topic, see Philippe Lacoue-Labarthe, 'The Echo of the Subject', in *Typography: Mimesis, Philosophy, Politics* (Cambridge, MA, 1989), pp. 139–208.

[23]   See Robert Spaemann, *Persons: the Difference Between 'Someone' and 'Something'*, trans. Oliver O'Donovan (Oxford, 2006), pp. 16–34. See, in particular, p. 23: 'the term "person" came to mean a subject relating to its nature like an actor to its role'. Spaemann goes onto to describe how this new sense of person as role or character (rather than as mere rational autonomous being, as for earlier Greek thought), was decisive in showing how the persons of the Trinity could be one yet distinct as 'playing different roles' in relation to each other, and how God incarnate could be 'personally' united by singularity of character, without confusion of created and uncreated, finite and infinite natures.

she has in effect created her 'own world' out of the characterized singularity of her intense perception of the real one that she knew about.[24]

However the necessary resources for the emergence of this intensified and enigmatic personal character lies initially in the idioms proper to things, and especially in the transfiguring power that is already proper to things. Hence even the infinite persons of the Trinity cannot be personal, which is to say 'enigmatically characterized', simply in themselves and as relational, unless they are always *mediating* and are equally *mediated by* an objective personifying power, or a 'power to characterize'. This power must combine a definite though infinite aesthetic shape with the pre-ground for conscious reflexive judgement and loving will in the mode of an impersonal 'bending-back upon itself' (without which there could never be any shape, only an impossibly abstract 'line') and unconscious spontaneity. What is thereby jointly unpredictable in objective formation is the ground for the enigmatic 'reserve' of the personal.

Why though, cannot the power to personify, Sophia, be herself a self-grounded hypostasis, akin to the Islamic Allah? The answer here has to do with fact that, as Bulgakov recognized, one cannot take Being alone to be the primary principle. What is, manifests itself, else it is unthinkable.[25] Therefore, as Gregory of Nyssa affirmed, Being is also *dynamis*, which is the power to affect. However, for Gregory *dynamis* is equally the power to be affected, because manifestation requires also a registering of this manifestation if it is to be there at all – whether or not this registering is taken to be 'conscious' in character.[26] In consequence, if we posit an initial Being which is 'one', and insist that it can only be if it shows itself, then we have immediately also to posit a 'second', which is the receiving capacity. The problem of mediation between the expressing first and the expressed – and so it would seem, reflexively expressed – second, then arises.

This can be resolved dialectically and dynamically after Hegel: the initial One is not just from our point of view, but really and truly ontologically lacking, such that it must express and define itself in order to move out of its own nullity. But in this conception, the *aporia* of a double beginning is in a sense evaded by recourse to a philosophical myth of a 'counterfeit double' as William Desmond so well expresses it, even if no knock-down reasons may be available to stop people believing it.[27] No real daemonic *metaxu* or sophianic principle is invoked here, since differing is the work of the original One itself, through a self-denial which it must of course later cancel in order to retain an integral identity. In eventually re-claiming for the One itself the *formal process* of othering, the finitude of multiple difference in its real substantively constituted content is abandoned to sheer

---

[24] See George Eliot, *Adam Bede* (Harmondsworth, 1985), Chapter 17, 'In Which the Story Pauses a Little' where she enunciates her realist aesthetic credo.

[25] Bulgakov, *Du Verbe Incarné*; *Sophia*, pp. 37–81.

[26] See John Milbank, 'The Force of Identity', in John Milbank, *The Word Made Strange: Theology, Language, Culture* (Oxford, 1997), chap. 8, pp. 194–216.

[27] See William Desmond, *Hegel's God: a Counterfeit Double?* (Aldershot, 2003).

equivocal contingency: this is the reverse face of Hegelian absolute identity, which so many commentators overlook. Moreover, since the One in-itself remains empty, even the content of the Absolute's 'for itself' can be nothing other than the sheer accidental randomness of unfated difference, outside providential governance – Hegelian shit, as Slavoj Žižek graphically regards it.[28]

This is why it remains possible to read Hegel as a kind of nihilist, as argued first by the remote if deviant disciple of Solovyov, Alexander Kojève, or indeed as a kind of atheist, as argued against Gillian Rose by Jay Bernstein.[29] And Schelling's more 'positive' version of this same dialectical mediation is really but a slight improvement. Here an original positive willing of determination which establishes the regime of love does, indeed, bring a finite contingent order within the sway of providence, and also announces a more final 'victory' (Schelling's preferred name for God) over the originally indeterminate and mechanically necessitated shadow reality, which God from the outset refuses as the ground for his 'pre-ontological' original willing of freedom. However, Schelling's essentially non-teleological concept of freedom – which fails to see freedom as only really free in its orientation to the good but rather tries to regard the good as without remainder the decision of freedom – assumes first of all 'the faculty to be one or the other of the contradictories' and secondly 'that incomprehensible primordial act in which the freedom of a person is decided for the first time'. This act reveals 'character' and Schelling (against the Aristotelian tradition of practical reason) takes it to be obvious that the 'choice' of character is entirely prior to 'reasoning or reflection'.[30] In this way Schelling extended the post-Scotist negative understanding of free choice as rooted in a fundamental 'indetermination' into a validation of the purely positive 'existential' character of an actual choice when it occurs. He also, as we have just seen, ontologized and theologized this scheme by conceiving God as fundamentally a decisive choice for actual particular things over against a refused realm of indeterminacy and indifference. But this means that the positive peaceful affirmation of difference is for him always grounded upon a refusal of both the unrelated self as same and of the other as external and alien.

In Trinitarian terms, as Schelling later expressed it in his *Philosophie der Offenbarung*, this means that the pre-ontological 'Father', in his ungrounded decision to be as a character or 'person', at once generates the Son *as* the location of this now 'existing' decision, and *also* as the thereby conjured-up hinterland of unrealized possibility. It is in terms of this latent tension that the Son possesses an independent personality, and he is therefore potentially the site of a constant

---

[28]   See his essay 'Not only as Substance, but also as Subject', in Slavoj Žižek, *The Sublime Object of Ideology* (London, 1989), pp. 201–31 and Slavoj Žižek and John Milbank, *The Monstrosity of Christ: Paradox versus Dialectic* (Boston Mass: MIT Press, 2008).

[29]   Alexander Kojève, *Introduction to the Reading of Hegel: Lectures on the Phenomenology of Spirit*, trans. James H. Nicholas Jr (Ithaca, NY, 1969).

[30]   F.W.J. Schelling, *The Ages of the World* (Third Version, 1815) trans. Jason M. Wirth (New York, 2000), p. 78.

impulse to return to the Father, but equally of a constant impulse to re-establish his independence. (One should contrast here Bulgakov's 'shadow of suffering', because this does not proceed from any implicit tension between Father and Son, but only 'anticipates' – from our *modus cognoscendi* – a trouble to both that might arise from outside them both.) This *mélange* of simultaneous affirmation of, and yet exception to the Paternal character gives rise immediately to the third person of the Holy Spirit who establishes the divine reclaiming of itself as the union of both the *actus purus* of eternal positive decision and the affirmation also of the other, necessarily at first excluded possibilities, so permitting a full 'acceptance' of the Son's inevitably independent moment.[31]

So within God, for Schelling, there is no *actual* eternal tension, struggle, alienation or refusal, not even in sublated form. In this respect he is far closer to patristic orthodoxy than Hegel, just as he also approaches Aquinas' distinction between being and essence to affirm the priority of the former and the 'secondariness' of human thought with respect to existence. In addition he recovers the reasonableness of revelation by linking it with the (essentially Aristotelian) notion that it is always actualities, including historical actualities, which alone disclose truth and he also re-affirms at last Hamann's (and Jacobi's) view that, this being the case, every act of reason continues to rest upon an unsurpassed act of faith.[32] Unfortunately Schelling also invented 'existentialism' by extending the primacy of being over intellect to God himself and then by grounding the divine being upon the divine will – for Aquinas by contrast, infinite being, thought and will all coincide, without any priority, in the divine simplicity. By doing so he betrayed, at the most fundamental metaphysical level, his own insight into the primacy of action and the embedding of truth within an actual state of affairs, to which true desire is responsive. By admitting possibilism and indeterminate freedom to ultimate status within God, he replaced a true positive mediation within God with a latent tension between the realized and the unrealized and ensured that within the creation itself this tension will become really and truly fundamental.

For the notion of an original necessary shadow of indetermination ensures that creation, unlike the creator, must be seen as necessarily grounded in ontological violence. By rooting evil as a 'positive' possibility within this pre-original (but never infinitely actualized) divine estrangement, Schelling renders inevitable and paradigmatic for nature a process of initial reactive suffering and agonizedly resistant overcoming and so fails really to grasp the primacy of the good as self-giving plenitude. This follows, because the 'revelation' of God in actuality or in being, which is also the constitution of the *cosmos*, demands the simultaneous

---

[31]   F.W.J. Schelling, *Philosophie der Offenbarung, 1841–2* (Darmstadt: Leske, 1843) II, p. 15, 16. For a modern abridged version, see that of Manfred Frank (Frankfurt am Main, 1977). But for the most conveniently available complete edition see the French translation: *Philosophie de la Révélation, livres I-III*, translated under the direction of J.-M. Marquet and J.-F. Courtine (Paris, 1989–94).

[32]   Schelling, *Philosophie der Offenbarung*, I, 8.

instantiation of the 'No' as well as the 'Yes', since they are mutually conditioning, even though they are also ineradicably opposed, and the 'No' is the only ground of an other to God which he yet negatively contains. In consequence, the finite world of nature emerges initially as the actualization of the divine 'No' and therefore involves also the temporary actualization of the indeterminate and mechanical which this very 'No' refuses, now that the *agon* which is merely latent in God becomes the heart of living reality. For this reason, the diversity of nature *cannot* be explained 'by the peaceful eisemplasy [*Ineinsbildung*] of various forces'; rather, 'everything that becomes can become only in discontent'.[33] The products of love for this vision are – since they are rooted in a primordial gesture of the will that establishes once and for all (outside any real historical accumulation of habit in the case of human beings, or any rational adoption of a desirable pattern in the case of God) personal 'character' – unmediably diverse.[34] They therefore reduce to so many various subjective affirmative gestures whose different content, in the case of finite spirits, is inextricably linked to the different paths of negation which they have traversed. If a single affirming will is to achieve this affirmation in affirming the will of another, then it must always first negate the other's exteriority such that (effectively against the teaching of Saint Paul about the uniquely non-reactive character of charity) 'a root of bitterness lies even in sweetness' and 'a root of hatred lies in love' which 'although concealed ... is necessary for its support'.[35]

So as with Hegel, so for Schelling, mediation remains linked to an instable and agonistic process, not, as for the greater radicalism of Orthodox Trinitarian thought, with the perpetual and peaceful dynamic *stasis* of a genuinely doubled and so tripled eternal beginning and end. Hence for even the final Schelling, the generation of the Son inevitably involved the realization of the latent possibilities conjured up by the Paternal decision as the created world whose otherness is inseparable from its tensional alienation. An immediate and yet contingent human fall (here again, Schelling improves upon Hegel) proceeds from a will infinitely to actualize the pre-given positive tendency in nature to establish itself as a power separate from God and not, as for Augustinian tradition, form a pure negation of the fullness of created reality which, without remainder, is tending back to its Creator.[36]

Neither Hegel nor Schelling therefore, entertained the truly radical thought of a real original difference exceeding any tensional process of development. But if one does entertain this, then one can project the epistemological necessity of original two-ness onto the ontological plane (as seems already to have been obscurely affirmed by Plato).[37] Then one is confronted with the mystery of Sophia, of original mediation, or of original supplementation without Derridean deception

---

[33]   Schelling, *The Ages of the World*, p. 91.

[34]   Ibid., pp. 77–8.

[35]   Ibid., p. 39.

[36]   Schelling, *Philosophie der Offenbarung*, II, 16.

[37]   See Hans Joachim Krämer, *Plato and the Foundations of Metaphysics*, ed. and trans. John R. Catan (New York, 1990).

and anguish.[38] That which *is*, is dynamic self-expressive life, but as such it is also the otherness of active reception of this dynamism. It is, indeed, super-eminently sperm and womb, forever conjoined and forever apart. But this eminent life is also eminent intellect, or precisely 'wisdom', because, in our experience, the reception of *oneself* as a gift, or the receiving of a gift such that one *is not* outside this reception, is, as the French Catholic philosopher (in the tradition of spiritual realism) Claude Bruaire argued with explicit reference to both Bulgakov and de Lubac, most of all characteristic of conscious life, capable of gratitude.[39] Merely in gratitude one can already *be* according to a new mode, and one cannot think at all without receiving something and without understanding oneself *to be* this reception, such that one reflexively gives what one has received from another again to oneself. But in the Trinity of course, these two moments of reception and reflexivity absolutely coincide, such that there is, strictly speaking (and in contrast to Hegel) no reflexivity of the second, expressed and cognitive principle. Here indeed, process (paternal generation) and upshot (sonship) are entirely coterminous.

All the same, the process is not a mere univocal essence that 'distributes' the three persons. Were it so, then modalism would threaten, as it would likewise if we took the essence itself, or Sophia, to be a fourth hypostasis. And such modalism would either tend towards an original monism, raising power or will above love (which is always relational), or else to a primacy of triadic pure difference beyond oppositional duality, grounding a general priority for difference as such throughout all being. Or else again one could have a dialectical version of the latter position, which would aporetically oscillate between the supremacy of an empty one and the supremacy of an accidental difference, in the fashion we have already seen. Hegel or Deleuze: it makes fewer odds than most suppose.

Where difference enjoys priority then, in the absence of mediation, one has a situation of implicit incompatibility and so of latent conflict: mediation will here be required for the sake of a liberal peace, but it will only be able to assume an extrinsic formalist mode which will therefore have to suppress to some degree the expressiveness of difference and thereby will only operate through the exercise of a re-doubled violence. Without original mediation, external conventional mediation can only itself be in reality one more instance of arbitrary difference.

To avoid this ontological and socio-political upshot, one must indeed conceive of the divine essence as Sophia, a characterizing power. As we have seen, process and relation do not guarantee an instance of personal character, but, on the other hand, character can be communicated from one person to another, and there can arise a kind of collective character. Indeed for character to be character at all as an expressive showing-forth, it must be in principle communicable and must even be actually communicated in some measure. Thus all of the godhead is characterized, and all the persons of the Trinity share in and hypostasize the power to give which is also the power to receive that marks life as such and supremely intellectual life.

[38] See Milbank, *The Word Made Strange*, pp. 55–123.
[39] Bruaire, *L'être et l'esprit*, pp. 51–87.

It follows that Bulgakov's Trinitarian ontology is not just an existentialism but rightly and equally a vitalism and an intellectualism.

Impossible Mediation: (b) God and Creation

In the above fashion one sees the sophianic principle of 'impossible' mediation operating most supremely in the case of the divine Trinity. The same principle is then participated in, in various modes, by the Creation, by Humanity, by the Incarnate *Logos*, by the Mother of God, by the Church, and by what one might call the liturgical-economical process.

In the case of the whole of the Creation, how can it possibly exist at all? There is nothing but God, in his ubiquity. If there is also the Creation as well as God, then the Creation must lie within God. The internally emanated Son and Spirit are already the Creation as gift and response, expression and interpretation – as Aquinas in his earlier work affirmed, at least in relation to the Son.[40] More specifically, Sophia as the feminine power of active reception is super-eminently the Creation, while Son and Spirit are super-eminently the Creation as hypostasized by the angels and by humanity, while the latter more differentially images Son and Spirit as masculine and feminine – to such a degree that the divine love, as Bulgakov argues, is most especially manifest in male/female relationships of every conceivable type (Mother-Son, Brother-Sister, etc. as well as Man-Wife).[41] He says in this respect that Eve proceeds from Adam in a dream because she is a 'spiritual' donation of a second flesh; hence the union of man and woman and their resultant reproduction is also always symbolically the union of flesh with spirit. The Son is for this reason already prototypically the divine humanity, in a clear echo of Swedenborg, while the 'feminine' Spirit alone 'actualizes' and 'manifests' this *theanthropos*.[42] The Spirit, as it were, brings the eternal divine humanity to birth, while equally she simply reflects it, in such a way that, according to Bulgakov, she is the prototype of deified humanity, rather than humanized deity, the incarnate God. Likewise, she is the prototype of Mary and of the Church, which is why, together with the bride, she says 'come' in the *Apocalypse* (Rev 21:21). Meanwhile, although the Father is *only* manifest in this double 'theandrism' of Son and Spirit, he himself stands in a certain monarchic

---

[40]   See Philipp Rosemann, *Omne ens est aliquid: Introduction à la lecture du 'système' philosophique de saint Thomas d'Aquin* (Louvain/Paris, 1996), pp. 191–210.

[41]   Bulgakov, *Du Verbe Incarné*, pp. 35–6.

[42]   Bulgakov, *Sophia*, p. 79: 'We can say of the *Logos* that he is the everlasting human being, the human prototype, as well as the Lamb slain "before the foundation of the world".' See also p. 80, but there are translation and typographical errors here, so see also the French version, *La Sagesse de Dieu: résumé de sophiologie*, trans. Constantin Andronikov (Lausanne, 1983); *Le Paraclet*, pp. 311–13 for the passage about the creation of Eve and *Du Verbe Incarné*, pp. 34–7.

and mysterious reserve above it – although it is, of course, just this height and reserve and mystery which is alone shown in the eternal human image.

But if the Creation lies within God, God must inversely lie within the Creation. God must be also that in himself which goes outside God, as Dionysius the Areopagite indicated.[43] Since God is all in all, at the bottom of that nullity which is alone proper to the Creation must lie God – who, for Augustine, is 'closer to us than we are to ourselves'. Or, in Maximian terms, just as the one *Logos* in God is also the many *logoi* that are the inner principles of created things (things as most fundamentally divine thoughts, which Augustine described in similar terms as created divine 'numbers'),[44] so these many *logoi* in creatures are in themselves the unity of the one *Logos* in the created order.

Since the Creation is not God, and yet God is everything, this constitutive divine intimacy of word or number must, in some sense, be 'created God', as John Scotus Eriugena put it.[45] This is why there is an earthly as well as a heavenly Sophia. But like the heavenly, uncreated Sophia, the earthly, created Sophia is not, in herself, an hypostasis. Rather, for Bulgakov, as the world-soul, she is that power of self-engendering life which logically must be prior to death and which undergirds the non-organic as well as the organic – he stood very close to Bergson at this point.[46] She is that which forms and patterns and orders and empowers creatively – not by arbitrary power, nor yet according to a fixed formula. She is an artist, albeit an unconscious one, and she is supremely shown through her prime attribute of beauty, which Bulgakov, following Dostoyevsky's dictum, believed would 'save the world'.[47]

But why, in the face of a modern temporalization of nature, invoke the pre-modern notion that, at the heart of nature, lies something supra-temporal? The answer is surely that Bulgakov, in the wake of Solovyov and Florensky, realized that if all arises through a process of action and reception, ever non-identically

---

[43]   Dionysius the Areopagite, *The Divine Names*, Book 4, chap. 1. See also Thomas Aquinas, *ST* I^a Q. 20 a. 1 ad 1.

[44]   Augustine, *De Musica*, Book VI; *De Libero Arbitrio*, Book II, chap. 45, xvii, 45–7; *De Quantitate Animae* – where the fundamental element is 'the point' rather than the number. See also Emilie zum Brunn, *St Augustine: Being and Nothingness* (New York, 1988); Catherine Pickstock, 'Music: Soul, City and Cosmos after Augustine', in *Radical Orthodoxy*, pp. 243–8.

[45]   John Scotus Eriugena, *Periphyseon*, Book I, ed. I.P. Sheldon-Williams (Dublin, 1999), 453c30–454a10, pp. 62–5. See in particular, p. 65: '[the Divine Nature] is (also) created because nothing except itself exists as an essence since it itself is the essence of all things' and, earlier, pp. 63–5: 'in all things the Divine Nature is being made, which is nothing else than the Divine Will. For in that nature being is not different from willing, but willing and being are one and the same in the establishment of all things that are to be made'.

[46]   Bulgakov, 'On the Transcendental Subject of Economy', in *Philosophy of Economy*, pp. 123–56; *Sophia*, pp. 54–82; *Du Verbe Incarné*, pp. 39–52.

[47]   Rowan Williams, *Sergii Bulgakov*, p. 128.

repeating itself, then things are bound together in a more organic, more unified and even a more quasi-personal way than within an Aristotelian cosmos. It is not that there are abstract *genera* external to their specific instances which would involve an oscillation between the concretely particular and the abstractly universal. It is rather that universality consists more Platonically in the process of engendering and being engendered itself, in the totality of this process. For if one wants (to echo Florensky's and Bulgakov's way of posing the problem), to think of the ontological 'transcendental condition' for the possibility of consistent yet varied processes in time,[48] then no appeal can plausibly be made, after Darwin, to a set of fixed kinds, nor yet to an ontic first cause – since, within the material universe, this cannot originally precede what is caused, and in any case the notion of 'cause' is a pragmatic fiction which disguises the fact that 'what causes' is only something changing into something else – such that all ultimate causes are more primarily effects, or, as Neoplatonism and Aquinas had it, 'emanations'.[49]

Instead, given that time-space is a relative framework (a point already invoked very early on by Florensky), it becomes possible to pose the question of how all instances of a process might exist, simultaneously, from a perspective above and outside time. From this vantage point, one can think of all natural processes and the one process of nature herself as Sophia, as created wisdom, the first of God's works according to the Biblical Wisdom literature, and so not as anything abstracted, but rather as a concentrated universality of aesthetic character.[50] Clearly a belief in a transcendent, creator God validates this notion that there is an eternal inner dimension to the finite and the temporal. And this dimension, since it does not abstract from time and complexity, actually guarantees the irreplaceable significance of process and becoming with all their manifold concrete instances. It does not replace it but sums it up and presents it to the Godhead, while at the same time supplying it with its regular but inexpressible bounds, without which it would lapse into indistinction.

Between God and Creation then, there is no between. To suppose so would be idolatry. On the other hand, if the created order univocally enjoys its own existence which sufficiently possesses existence as finite being, then there is after all, by the working of an inexorable dialectic, a third term, namely 'being', invoked as lying

---

[48]   Bulgakov, 'On the transcendental Subject of Economy'; Pavel Florensky, 'Letter Ten: Sophia', in *The Pillar and Ground of the Truth*, pp. 231–84.

[49]   See John Milbank and Catherine Pickstock, *Truth in Aquinas* (London, 2001), p. 31, citing Jean-Luc Marion's correct recognition that Aquinas thinks of divine causality more fundamentally in terms of the Dionysian aitia or 'requisite' than of strictly Aristotelian 'cause' and this is why he describes an effect more frequently as *causatum* than as *effectus*. This view (to elaborate Marion) renders 'causing' much more as 'giving', such that the cause is a going out of itself as an effect, while the effect is wholly 'from' the cause, in which it 'eminently' abides. For Marion, see 'Saint Thomas d'Aquin et L'Onto-Théo-Logie', in *Revue Thomiste*, TXCV/1 (1995): 31–66.

[50]   Bulgakov, *Philosophy of Economy*, pp. 13–156; Florensky, 'Letter Ten: Sophia'.

between God and the Creation and thereby threatening idolatrously to include them both. To avoid this outcome one must rather say that all created being borrows its being from God who alone fully 'is' or is 'to be'. Finite being shares in and is remotely like the *esse* of God.

Yet at the limit of such an analogical conception one must admit, with Eckhart, who is merely extending Augustine's *dictum* to its logical conclusion, that by an unforeclosed and mysteriously harmonious dialectic (unlike that of Hegel), what shares in God through its very unlikeness to God can only do so because it is also precisely like, indeed identical with, the Godhead in its hidden heart.[51] If nullity shares in being, then at bottom created things are God in some sense and God is in some sense created. To avoid at this point either acosmism or pantheism (and thereby lose the ultimacy of gift and relation), the best we can do is to affirm both these further strange impossibilities at once. Sophia is the Creation in God; Sophia is also God in the Creation. There is not one Sophia, hovering onto-theologically between God and the Creation; there are two Sophias on two sides of the chasm, yet somehow their deep-beyond-deep affinity renders them after all but one. But not 'one' in the sense of an hypostasis; one rather in the sense of a shared essence or character or power-to-personify.

For Bulgakov, the created order is in the image of the Trinity because it has to be constituted by the sophianic capacity to hypostasize, plus actual hypostases which alone render this power actual and operative.[52] Hence the idea of a reality without spirits is unthinkable and impossible. Here one can re-invoke my argument about giving that was intended to prove that primary created reality must be intellectual. Again following Bruaire, the inner reality of the Creation is a gift that establishes a receiver, a pure recipient whose entire being is reflexive gratitude, and this, for reasons already seen, must be intellectual being. It then follows that the inner reality of created Sophia is created angelhood and humanity. Humanity has itself an eternal and atemporal aspect because it is another, and indeed the supreme example, of a natural community of generation. Here again, the notion that there is an eternal 'collective personhood' of all humanity does not detract from, but rather confirms, the significance of life in time, following the same logic that I have already unfolded with respect to life in general. This might not seem to be the case if one supposes that the eternal humanity is, unlike Sophia, an hypostasis, but it is not. Although it is a more intense degree of the power-to-hypostasize, the only actual human hypostases for Bulgakov are real human beings existing in the course of time.

Nevertheless, a significant difference ensues from traditional Christian emphases. It is also the eternal Adam as created (not as uncreated, not as the *Logos* itself) who has fallen, and the original unfallen eternity or else benign time enjoyed by actual human beings has likewise been lost to fallen view. It is also this Adam

---

[51] See John Milbank, 'Preface to the Second Edition: Between Liberalism and Positivism', in *Theology and Social Theory* (Oxford, 2006), pp. XI–XXXII.

[52] Sergii Bulgakov, *The Bride of the Lamb*, trans. Boris Jakim (Grand Rapids, MI/ Edinburgh, 2002), pp. 79–124.

– the dynamic human essence – which must be restored if we are all to be restored. Hence Bulgakov – much more directly than hitherto within the Christian tradition (but there are analogies here with Jewish Cabbalistic and Hasidic thought) – saw salvation in collective and historical terms. It is a gradual work, culminating in and enabled by, the work of Christ. Deification itself now incorporates and criticizes the bastard Promethean insights of the West concerning godlike human power emancipated from a transcendent horizon, and recovers the earlier non-Promethean perspectives of Neoplatonic theurgy and the Hermetic *Asclepius* – that astonishing Egyptian work which at once prophesied the technological era, *and* warned against its potential excesses leading to ecological catastrophe, once a sense of reverence for the earth and the need to cherish it have been lost.[53] To become divine now means for Bulgakov also constantly to shape better images of deity (as the Hermetic corpus suggests),[54] and to mediate the divine creative economy such that all human working is a coming to know and, inversely, coming to know is a constant process of collective just distribution: 'economy is knowledge in action; knowledge is economy in theory'.[55]

Also, in coming to know by working, we arrive at a new vision through the images we have made, the songs we have sung, the words we have uttered, and this 'seeing through' is the theurgic invocation of the divine by which alone God can descend to us – the infusion of our own works with his inspiration. Strictly speaking, for Bulgakov, human theurgy (as opposed to 'theurgy' proper, which is simply the divine work) is 'sophiurgy', since 'Sophia' names the synergic fusion of human and divine work which is brought about through the Incarnation and Pentecost and sustained by liturgical activity, focused upon the transformation of bread and wine into God's body in the Eucharist.[56]

In this way, resuming after a long time the work of Dionysius the Areopagite, who first mediated the best pagan monotheism to Christian thought, and of Maximus, Eriugena and Cusanus, Bulgakov explicitly and by name adds theurgy to *theosis*, thereby enabling, with this ancient resource, more justice to be done to the modern sense of the importance of human fabrication. Outside an ultimate liturgical reference, economic activity sinks into sensual and greedy debasement, while, as Rowan Williams has underlined, aesthetic activity falsely pursues an immanent spirituality which seeks to abandon the body, in default of any recognition of sacramental mediation of the real transcendence of the Creator God by all modes of embodiment.[57] On the other hand, modern Christianity, Bulgakov suggests, must now more fully grasp that the theological is always also theurgic: that God only reaches us through the liturgical invocations latent in all human

---

[53]   'Asclepius' in *Hermetica*, trans. Brian P. Copenhaver (Cambridge, 1992), pp. 67–92, esp. paras 8–9, pp. 71–2 and para 25, p. 82.

[54]   'Asclepius', paras 22–4, pp. 79–81.

[55]   Bulgakov, *Philosophy of Economy*, p. 131.

[56]   Bulgakov, 'The Unfading Light', pp. 149–59.

[57]   Rowan Williams, *Sergii Bulgakov*, pp. 113–31.

creative bringing forth of the unanticipated.[58] These invocations reach their highest pitch in language, which synaesthetically blends the imaginative work of all the senses: thus Bulgakov defended the contemporary Russian revived Palamite notion (much refracted by Russian aesthetics' reception of French symbolism), that by uttering the name of Jesus the energetic presence of the divine person is thereby brought about, because in some ineffable way the sonorous patterns and other sensorial resonances of human language have become attuned over the ages to a certain receptivity of transcendence.[59] Or, as the symbolist forerunner Charles Baudelaire realized this thought in words: '*Comme de longs échos qui de loin se confondent/ Dans une ténébreuse et profane unité, / Vaste comme la nuit et comme la clarté/ Les parfums, les couleurs et les sons se répondent*'.[60]

Indeed, only this sort of theurgical perspective helps us to understand, in theological terms, just why there exist many human generations. It is because the work of praise takes time and is collective, like a cathedral taking many centuries to build. For this reason, I would say that generation, including sexuality, can be seen as belonging to our original humanity. This should be asserted against the austere and dubious Eastern-derived views of Louis Bouyer, cautiously supported by Hans Urs von Balthasar, who cites more or less approvingly the German idealist view that where there can be no death, neither can there be any birth, and who erroneously regards a restoration of paradisal virginity alongside the salvific need for the incarnation as the ground for the requirement of the virginal conception. My own, opposite view is, however, in keeping with that of Augustine, who acknowledged marriage and therefore possible descendants of Adam and Eve before the fall, and still more Aquinas, who – in keeping with an Hebraic outlook – regarded successive generations of children as an intrinsic 'blessing', rather than as a contingent post-lapsarian remedy. He also considered that sexual sensible pleasure before the Fall would have been more intense, despite the fact that (in agreement with Augustine by the time of the *Summa*, revising his position in his *Sentences* commentary), Eve's hymen would not have been broken and there would have been no concupiscence, since both mind and the entirety of the body would have integrally consented to the maximum to the performance of the sexual act. Rather, precisely *on account* of harmony with reason, ecstatic bodily pleasure (perhaps because true ecstasy is other-directed?) before the Fall would have been far greater, just as, in the absence of irrational lust (that is wrongly directed and inappropriate desire) there would have been no merit whatsoever in sexual abstinence. So for Aquinas, it is an unlimitedly erotic and procreative being that humanity has denied and lost through sin.[61]

---

[58] Bulgakov, 'The Unfading Light'.

[59] See Rowan Williams, 'General Introduction', in *Sergii Bulgakov*, pp. 1–19.

[60] Charles Baudelaire, *The Flowers of Evil [Les Fleurs du Mal]*, parallel text, trans. James McGowan (Oxford, 1993), *Spleen et Idéal* 4; 'Correspondences', pp. 18–19.

[61] Thomas Aquinas, *ST* Iᵃ Q. 98 a. 1 resp; a. 2, esp. ad 3. In the latter article he explicitly refutes Gregory of Nyssa on this point. See also Louis Bouyer, *Le Trône de la sagesse. Essai sur la signification du culte marial* (Paris, 1957), p. 257; Balthasar,

Nevertheless, it is true that, after the Fall, generation becomes a prime means of mercy: constantly putting an end through death to our inadequacies, but also holding out the hope through birth that our unfinished work of self–redemption may be renewed and taken forward by our descendants, just because this work must also be part of the work of collective redemption.

For nothing that we do can be a good action, save in a certain receptive situation where others are able to pick up and continue the peculiarly 'characterized' action which we have initiated. Indeed, it is often the case that we can only judge a past life as 'happily fulfilled' (or otherwise) when we see posthumously what it was really leading to: this has nothing to do with 'consequentialism', but rather concerns the limited and fragmentary nature of our insight into teleological ends and the *intrinsic* trajectory of our activities – a limitation which demands an inescapable element of 'moral risk' whose misadventures may often require retrospective pardon. Here one has to say that while, indeed, moral failing is not as such attributable to finitude (which is only a necessary but not sufficient condition

---

Theo-drama, vol. 2, pp. 365–82; vol. 3, pp. 331–44. One can qualify Balthasar's account of Mary's virginity to say that it is in one respect necessary in order to restore female integrity and sexual painlessness, but not in order to restore an asexuality. This ground for necessity is not, however, the main one – in theory one could imagine *ex potentia absoluta Dei*, the creation of two new, uncorrupted parents for Jesus. Rather, the Virgin Birth, which of course all Christian Orthodoxy must uphold as literal truth (there is something sadly comic about the many Anglican theologians who deny this, yet still insist on the literal truth of the Resurrection) is 'aesthetically appropriate', first of all, as returning for the sake of redemption to the original creative power of God which can override the normal physical laws. As Aquinas argued, with the virginal conception, God completes the quadrilateral repertoire of possible ways of creating the human being: from the earth with Adam, from Adam with Eve, normally from man and woman and now purely from woman: *ST* III[a] Q. 31 a. 4 resp. One can add to this that the fact that the last mode is the final one and generates not just a human being but the God-Man, suggests that woman is especially the partner of God, and that woman rather than man is the highest as regards the 'purely human'. The male relative physical-spiritual lack of self-enclosure, inability to enfold things and then to creatively bring forth a new physical being, ensures a more nomadic character which is only completed in the hybridity of the God-Man and the 'entire enclosure' of the male human subject within the divine Sophia. It is interesting in this respect that the Sufi theologian Ibn 'Arabi, argues that Mary was the new Adam, since Jesus preceded from her alone (as Eve from Adam's side), while symmetrically Jesus was the new Eve: see Henry Corbin, *Alone with the Alone: Creative Imagination in the Sufism of Ibn 'Arabi* (Princeton NJ, 1997), 'The Creative Feminine', pp. 157–75. Secondly, the *convenientia* of the virginal conception derives the birth of the *Logos* entirely from an act of human assent – thereby revealing to the most extreme degree the mystery of female 'active receptivity' and power of integral self-enclosure which can also bear fruit. It is in these respects that Mary is already in person the Church, and that in her we see that the seemingly secondary human 'reception' of Christ is also, paradoxically, a pre-condition for his very coming into being. This understanding of the necessity of the Virgin Birth therefore, is in line with the idea that the historic saving event involved a 'double descent' of Sophia. And see further below.

of its possibility), that nevertheless in a fallen world it is frequently impossible to disentangle culpable from innocent ignorance, so that much of the time 'we know not what we do' in a double sense (both as already blinded and as self-blinding). It is just because of this double ignorance that we can be forgiven, since the unforgivable sin against the Spirit would be an evil performed despite the full light of the good – and because evil just is, following Socrates, blindness as to the vision of the good, we can confidently say that this 'maximum' sin is also not a possible sin, even in the case of Lucifer.[62]

For Bulgakov, such a collective and historical aspect of Fall and salvation extended also to the natural world. Uncompromisingly and rightly, citing Wisdom 1:13, 'God made not death', he insisted that for the Wisdom literature and then clearly for the New Testament, death is no part of the original divine order.[63] In league with death and in opposition to life are 'blind necessity, unintelligible raging elements' besides 'deadened mechanism, iron fate'. Both the divine and the human economy (the latter in only a slight extension of the usual sense) seek constantly to oppose the 'disintegrating forces and deeds of death' with the 'organizing forces of life'. For given that the Creation only subsists through hypostatic beings, angels and humans, it becomes possible to understand that, when they refuse the supreme gift of intellectual life, all life falters and is impaired in the wake of this catastrophe. But this means that also the heart of Creation, Sophia, is somehow dragged downwards: '*Viens-tu du ciel profond ou sors-tu de l'abîme,/ O Beauté?*' as Baudelaire asked.[64] Thus Bulgakov declared that 'Sophia – primordial humanity – as the soul of the world' may realize the dark side of its being in exercising a blind and chaotic will. So there is, as the Christian Gnostics intimated, albeit in a heterodox mode, also a fallen Sophia to be constantly sought out and recovered through art, through good science, through the contemplation of nature – for there is something here not merely to be redeemed, but also a lost spark of beauty presently trapped under the spell of evil, that is yet for the moment missing from the plenitude of beauty as such: '*Grain de musc qui gis, invisible,/ au fond de mon éternité!*'[65] Surely a too-limited orthodoxy is quite wrong to ignore this obviously 'Gnostic' aspect to Christ's parables of the lost sheep and the lost coin?

So nature, as Schelling expressed it in *Clara*, lies as it were under the hand of a malign enchanter, but looks to Humanity to free it from its imprisoning spell. Here I think, very important and complex questions arise as to the relationship between the modern medical attempt to 'defeat death' and the Christian Eucharistic working for resurrection. How do we distinguish between an impious attempt to lead us into a pseudo-eternal life and a possibly genuine medical collaboration with the

---

[62]   For all this, see Robert Spaemann, *Happiness and Benevolence*, trans. Jeremiah Alberg SJ (Notre Dame, IN, 2000).

[63]   Bulgakov, *Philosophy of Economy*, pp. 68–76.

[64]   Charles Baudelaire, *Les Fleurs du Mal, Spleen et Idéal*, p. 21, 'Hymne à la Beauté', pp. 44–5.

[65]   Baudelaire, *Les Fleurs du Mal, Les Épaves*, X; 'Hymn', pp. 302–3.

process of ushering-in the *eschaton*? This, I suspect, is a very Russian question – invoking the 'God-building' philosophy of Nikolai Fyodorov, in particular.[66]

Because the Creation only subsists through hypostasization, the presence of Creation in God and God in Creation is also of itself the process of deification. Here again though, mediation does not lie between, but at once on one side and the other through an obscure but crucial echo or attunement. Above all, we cannot distinguish, in Gregory Palamas' fashion (and I think that Bulgakov in the end implies a rejection of this),[67] between the divine essence and the divine uncreated energies which enable the economy of human redemption. It is clearly not the case that Palamas distinguished them in any simple fashion that would entirely forego the divine simplicity. Nonetheless, the distinction which he did make appears to have something in common with the almost contemporary Western Scotist 'formal distinction' – less than a real one, more than merely one made by our minds: rather a kind of latent division within a real unity permitting a real if partial separation on some arising occasion.[68]

---

[66]   See Rowan Williams, *Sergii Bulgakov*, pp. 45–6.

[67]   Bulgakov, *Le Paraclet*, p. 236. Here Bulgakov seems to say that he agrees with Palamas that 'energy' is God but not identical to the divine *ousia*, only because the essence comprehends 'many energies'. One could elaborate as follows: a single divine energy, like truth or inspiration or beauty, is not the divine essence because it is only an aspect of God. But by the same token it is therefore a created energy, even though it acts with the power of the uncreated. When, by contrast, one is speaking of 'all' the divine energies, and therefore truly of energy as such, then in their uncreated simple unity they are identical with the divine essence.

[68]   Denials that this is the case generally deploy language which only confirms that it is, indeed, the case. Gregory Palamas' own language seems directly to confirm it. See, for example, referring to Gregory Nazianzus and to – a misreading of – Dionysius: *Triad III*, 2.13, in Grégoire Palamas, *Défense des saints hésychasts*, ed. and trans. Jean Meyendorff (Louvain, 1959), pp. 666–7: 'How cannot the shinings-forth [ellampsesi – of the good and the beautiful], without beginning and without end be other than the imparticipable essence of God, and different, even though inseparable from the essence?'. And again see *Triad III*, 2.22, pp. 680–3, where Palamas says that the energies pre-exist in God outside his creative activity like the faculties of seeing and hearing in the soul when these faculties are not actually being exercised, and so 'just as the soul is not simply these faculties, likewise with God; and just as the soul remains unique, simple and without composition, without any multiplicity or composition entering into it on account of the faculties which rest in it and proceed from it, likewise God is not deprived of his unicity and simplicity on account of the powers which are in him, he who does not merely possess many powers, but who is all-powerful.' Hence it would seem that there must be some 'ground' for the separation of the powers (energies) from the essence in the 'all-powerfulness' of God, apart from the divisions which follow upon createdness and the perspectives of the creation. So while Palamas rightly opposed the crude onto-theology of Barlaam which imagined that God could act not as God but by created mediators as his real powers, he still falls himself into a more subtle onto-theology which is like that of Scotus in wanting to see the distinction of powers which reach us as distinct as in some 'formal' way distinct in the divine essence as opposed to become distinct only when this essence is refracted as creation and created

In this respect the Palamite theology does appear slightly to ontologize the epistemological truth that God 'in himself' remains beyond the grasp of even the beatific vision, as though this reserved aspect were a real ultimate 'area'. By contrast, and following Dionysius, this God in himself is in no sense whatsoever 'other' to the God who goes kenotically forth from himself in his *dynamis* which is also the plural *dynameis* towards the creation, and likewise his eternal essential *energeia* (*actus*) which is equally the diverse economic 'energies'. The divine intrinsic outgoing kenosis (freely willed as a reach into contingency, and yet God eternally *is* this willing), or the divine *Logos/logoi*, or the divine uncreated/created Sophia, or the Platonic 'daemonic' *metaxu*, simply *is* the divine essence and not something even formally apart from it, lying in an impossible no man's land between God and the world.

By and large, as I have just indicated, Bulgakov refuses this over-literal 'between'; when he does lapse into affirming it, he also and inevitably tends to erect Sophia as too literally a fourth hypostasis, possessing a kind of uniquely independent substantiality.[69] Clearly, for Bulgakov, the Palamite energies played the same role as Sophia, and infused human actions with theurgic power. Nevertheless, sophiology is superior to the Palamite theology precisely *because* it moves away from a literal between and allows the energies simultaneously to be identical with the divine essence itself and yet also to be created as well as uncreated. This actually brings Eastern theology more in line with the best Thomism for which grace has to be created as well as uncreated if it is ever to reach us – but occupies no phantom and limboesque border territory.

The Theurgic Dimension

To suppose that there is even a formal division between essence and energies risks two things: first of all, it risks supposing that deification is merely an irradiation by the light of the divine energies, lying in this sort of idolatrous 'between', or false mediation, with the final divine darkness reserved. Secondly, it risks a contrasting of the divine darkness with the divine dazzling and overwhelming light, such that one is supposed, rather in the manner of Vladimir Lossky, once and for all to exceed the cataphatic, and as it were finally to access God in a sheerly negative mode by abandoning all images and their anticipations and plunging super-theoretically into the absolute night.[70] Of course such a stance means that one has, dialectically,

---

powers – which are not directly divine powers as Barlaam supposed. To give a pertinent created example: the colours of the rainbow all indeed display pure light in its many aspects when refracted – yet pure light as the 'eminent' reality of these colours is not in itself even latently red, green, blue, yellow, orange, violet and indigo.

[69]   On this, see Rowan Williams' remarks in *Sergii Bulgakov*, pp. 113–20, 165–7.

[70]   See Vladimir Lossky, *The Mystical Theology of the Eastern Church* (Cambridge, 1973), pp. 23–44.

in fact positivized the negative and tried to make it do a concrete work. To some small degree this perspective may be encouraged by Gregory of Nyssa's almost proto-Scotist view that God is most of all an uncircumscribed positive infinity, to which there corresponds, on the part of finite spirits, an endless 'epectasic progress'. Likewise by Gregory's presentation, in his version of a *Vita Moysis*, of Moses as in some hyper-sense 'seeing' the divine darkness, possessing a *theoria* of an infinite 'luminous' darkness that of itself dazzles counter-wise to the shining of light: 'this is the seeing that consists in not-seeing, because that which is sought transcends all knowledge, being separated on all sides by incomprehensibility as by a kind of darkness'.[71]

But in both cases, as Ysabel de Andia argues against Jean Daniélou and Balthasar, Dionysius the Areopagite, ironically (perhaps) under pagan monotheistic influence, supplied important correctives which were crucial for the later history of Western mysticism. In the first instance, he more construed God as the coincidence of bounded and unbounded, with a corresponding stress that mystical access to God has supereminently to exceed *both* the cataphatic and the apophatic. Here I see no warrant whatsoever for Denys Turner's contorted and anachronistic attempt to 'grammaticalize' this and so to regard this exceeding as a kind of meta-*apophasis*, whose corollary would be to turn the negatively and yet eminently known God of Dionysius into the *Deus Absconditus* of the post-Ockhamite Luther.[72] This is to treat the Areopagite as if he were a post-Kantian delineating the transcendental bounds of our finite cognitive speculative powers, rather than as a pre-modern mystic who is describing the ontologically real psychic motions of negative and positive ascent from the finite to the infinite. This latter perspective is also quite clearly the way in which Dionysius is read by Aquinas when he develops his own account of 'eminent' or 'super-eminent' attribution.[73]

In the second instance, Dionysius speaks of Moses' communion with the divine darkness *not at all* as a seeing, even as a seeing that blinds, since *theoria* is for him confined to the sight of the 'heavenly place' wherein God is sought within the heavenly cloud, but is rather purely and entirely a liturgical 'plunging into' the inner sanctuary of the divine darkness. In contrast to Gregory of Nyssa, this liturgical entering-in is not exceeded by an epectasic 'desire to see' which at once holds God at a slightly greater distance and also considers him ontologically

---

[71]   Gregory of Nyssa, *The Life of Moses*, trans. A.J. Malherbe and E. Ferguson (New York, 1978), pp. 163, 95 and see further pp. 162–5, 94–6; Ysabel de Andia, Henosis: *L'Union à Dieu chez Denys l'Areopagite* (Leiden, 1996), pp. 304–75. On p. 338, she cites Gregory at *In Cant.*, home XI: 'the divine night ... gives to the soul a certain sense of its presence, while escaping from the grasp of evidence, hidden by the invisibility of its nature' [my translation from the French].

[72]   Pseudo-Dionysius, 'The Mystical Theology', Chapters One to Three, 1032D–1048B in *The Complete Works*, trans. Colm Luibheid (New York, 1987), pp. 138–41. Denys Turner, *The Darkness of God: Negativity in Christian Mysticism* (Cambridge, 1995), pp. 19–50.

[73]   Thomas Aquinas *ST* I^a Q. 13 a. 6.

in more absolutely negative terms. Instead Moses, by plunging into the night, is absolutely and finally united with the One in which finite and infinite coincide.[74]

This makes it sound as if Dionysius is more the mystic of the night than is Gregory. But in fact, just the opposite is the case, as Abbot Suger in the twelfth-century West perhaps realized, in probably deploying Dionysius thought to promote the fractal aspirations of gothic architecture (even if it is untrue that this is the unique source of this architecture, and that the Islamic *arabesque* was also an important influence, the latter still does not have much stone-dissolving, glass-deploying quality – and may in any case in turn have Christian Syrian roots).[75] Dionysius is supremely a mystic of light, and still more so than Gregory. For when Moses enters blindly into the darkness, he is at once overwhelmed by a divine excess of illumination. Thus whereas, for Gregory of Nyssa, the infinite darkness is said of itself to coincide with light, for Dionysius the infinite-finite darkness of the One is said to be also a 'super-luminous darkness' – *hyperphotos gnophos*, a linguistic hyperbole added to an oxymoron, whereas Gregory deploys *only* the oxymoron of 'brilliant darkness' (*lampros gnothos*). Dionysius' hyperbolically and asymmetrically augmented oxymoron represents rhetorically an inconceivable eminence of light that is the supereminence of all forms and not just, as with Gregory's mere paradox, a sort of positive counter-shining of indefinite obscurity. Thus Dionysius declares: 'if it is invisible because of a superabundant clarity, if the excess [*hyperbolē* – now ontological] of its luminous and superessential effusions remove it from every regard, yet it is here that is found everyone worthy to know God and to look upon him'.[76] God is in this passage only an absolute darkness, because he is the Platonic sun of the Good, the donating source of light by which all see and can be seen (and so *are* at all in their characterised forms) which cannot itself be seen because it blind. While we cannot in any way regard this absolute light-darkness, we can, at the height of mystical ascent, liturgically 'be' at this source itself.

So curiously, while Gregory retains the 'seeing' of Paul's 'then we shall see as we are seen', and Dionysius appears to abandon it, Dionysius retains the sense of identity with the divine that Gregory appears to refuse. Moreover, the blinded identity with absolute light suggests indeed that we may after all 'see as we are seen': for while we remain blind in the end, since we can never grasp the divine essence, as this blinding is by the very excess of light, we do come to coincide, in the highest possible measure with that divine radiation which *causes* things to be seen by causing them to be, and so cannot be any 'looking at' in an ordinary sense. For Aquinas God only 'sees us' in terms of a sense of the capacity of his

[74]   Pseudo-Dionysius, 'The Mystical Theology', Chapter One, 3, 1000D–1025A.

[75]   For a qualified defence of Erwin Panofsky's Dionysius-Suger thesis, and dismissal of Bernard McGinn's critique, see L. Michael Harrington, *Sacred Place in Early Medieval Neoplatonism* (London, 2004), pp. 158–64. See also Erwin Panofsky, *Abbot Suger: on the Abbey Church of St. Denis and its Art Treasures* (Princeton, NJ, 1946).

[76]   Pseudo-Dionysius, 'The Letters', V, p. 265 [the very loose translation has here been modified].

own power[77] – it is *this* kind of looking, which defines the 'as we are seen,' with which, for Dionysius, we can eventually be united.

Gregory, by contrast, still in a partially Plotinian fashion, suggests that the mystic encounters, hyper-theoretically, the removed, infinite, 'in-itself' and ontologically dark divine presence, by ascending the inward mountain heights of the psychic, beyond passion and intellect, even if he regards this ascent more collectively than Plotinus, and insists far more than the latter that the psychic is the inner reality also of the corporeal.[78] But the unknown Syrian writer is rather the legatee through Proclus of neo-pagan theurgical perspectives (as well as very probably, their Christian equivalents before Dionysius himself), for which the human soul is 'fully descended' into the body, and even in its knowing aspect can never escape from the mediating contemplation of surrounding *locus*.[79] The soul must always *be in a place*, whereas for Plotinus – and perhaps to a degree Gregory – it could escape place. For Iamblichus, again opposing Plotinus, even the gods had to be approached through place, since sacrifices are not simply 'sent heavenwards' but also draw the divinities downwards, by invoking those resonances and sympathies which hold the cosmos together. Likewise in Dionysius, the mystic comes liturgically to the place where God dwells – so even the One God has in himself a temple, a dwelling place, which is something like the cosmos in its eternal aspect and this point must clearly be linked both to God's outgoing in Creation and his full descent in Incarnation. So for Dionysius the Mosaic journey towards God leads upwards only by going first outwards through cosmic and socio-historical (ecclesial) mediations and the passage upwards is not an inner seeing, but rather a raising up by being externally overwhelmed by the divine through liturgical processes in which God himself has eternally come to meet us in the eternal spaces of his cosmic temple.[80]

It might be objected here that theurgy intrudes something non-Christian: a sense that one can influence the divine, which affronts any genuine sense of apophatic mystery. But quite the opposite in fact pertains, and we should remember here that *just because* they were involved, unlike Plotinus, in anti-Christian polemics, Iamblichus and Proclus tended, sometimes unconsciously, to search for pagan equivalents for what people found attractive in Christianity.[81] Thus the pagan Neoplatonist Iamblichus

---

[77]   Thomas Aquinas, *ST* I^a Q. 14 a. 5 resp: 'He [God] sees other things not in themselves but in Himself; in as much as his essence contains the similitude of things other than Himself.'

[78]   See Milbank, 'The Force of Identity'.

[79]   See Gregory Shaw, *Theurgy and the Soul: the Neoplatonism of Iamblichus* (University Park, PA, 1995).

[80]   On both Iamblichus and Dionysius, see L. Michael Harrington, *Sacred Place in Early Medieval Neoplatonism*, pp. 51–125.

[81]   Augustine, in *The City of God*, Book X, chap. 9–10, criticized theurgic practices all too simplistically as pagan polytheistic delusion and devil worship. Yet on the other hand, as others have pointed out, it is possible to see strong parallels to theurgy in *Confessions*, Book IX and XII. For in the first case the aporias of time are only pragmatically resolved in terms of the idea that in uttering the psalm to God Augustine is able to synthesize without 'dispersal' past,

already rejected the metaphor of 'seeing' God, precisely because God is not an idolatrous onto-theological object. To the contrary, he is that which utterly surrounds and perfuses us, and therefore he cannot be subject even to a non-intellectual gaze, since even this suggests that something (looking) can be done to him.[82]

Iamblichus argues that the theurgic rites do not change the minds of the gods, or even bring us into the relation of seeing the gods, but rather bring us close to the divine presence through procedures that allow us to resonate with it: 'by the practice of supplication we are gradually raised to the level of the object of our supplication and we gain likeness to it by virtue of our constant consorting with it'.[83] The immediate reaction to this of some Christians, however, may be that any sense of 'grace' is here lacking. Such, however, is not the case, because our transformation is *not* (as it is slightly more for Plotinus) a self-alteration based upon a better 'regard' of the divine. To the contrary, the liturgical-magical procedure of theurgy, by achieving an attunement with the divine, allows us more to receive 'the excellent gift of the gods' and 'the divine care which has been denied us' and which is founded upon the fact that the gods 'embrace in unity within themselves all beings together' because 'the light of the gods illuminates its subject transcendently, and is fixed steadfastly in itself even as it proceeds throughout the totality of its existence'.[84] Thus while prayer and invocation does not, indeed, change the minds of the gods, it is not simple a disguised mode of self-therapy because it permits us, through achieving the right topological, bodily and spiritual dispositions, to receive more fully the divine flow of grace. For this reason one can speak of a 'persuasion' of the gods: 'the persuasion (*peithō*) which expiatory rites exercise upon the higher class of being, recalling them once again to care and goodwill towards us …'.[85] One can indeed speak of grace (*charis*) here because the gods have no need, says Iamblichus, of sacrificial 'service' from us:[86] this is not the point of the theurgic rites at all; rather it is the case that 'earthly things, possessing their being in virtue of the *pleroma* of the gods, whenever

---

present and future as an echo of eternity. Here liturgy 'shows' an answer which theoria cannot really comprehend. And this liturgical act is only possible because God himself has descended into time in order to counteract his dispersive tendencies which have been activated by sin. In the case of Book XII, Augustine's quest for his own identity passes beyond the 'confession' of all that is only himself and therefore not his true self towards the true 'confession' of divine praise in which he truly finds himself. But this finding is ecstatically impersonal because it consists in a praise of the cosmos and of God through the cosmos. Hence it is quite untrue that Augustine follows the spiritual road of 'interiorization' that was later taken by Bonaventure. To the contrary, somewhat like Dionysius and later Aquinas, he strives towards God only with the entirely of his fellow creatures – by exteriorizing himself.

[82]   Iamblichus, *On the Mysteries*, trans. E.C. Clarke, J.M. Dillon and J.P. Hershbell, (Atlanta, 2003), I.11–15, pp. 47–61.

[83]   Ibid., I.15 pp. 58–61.

[84]   Ibid., I.9 pp. 38–9; I.15 pp. 58–9.

[85]   Ibid., I.13, pp. 54–5.

[86]   Ibid., I.11 pp. 48–9.

they come to be ready for participation in the divine, straightway find the gods pre-existing in it prior to their own proper essence'.[87] (This is the first known occurrence of the New Testament/Christian Gnostic term 'pleroma', linked initially to cosmic Christology, in a Neoplatonic text.) So in Iamblichus, as in many Christian writers, grace and participation lie close together, and in his case this is supported by his view that the entire 'divine world', comprising the One beyond the good, the good beyond being, and the gods, daemons and heroes, is in 'in itself' and as such imparticipable, while at the same time this entire divine world descends into the earthly one and is mysteriously participated in by the realities of the temporally and spatially extended cosmos: 'the gods ... and all the multitude which is generated around them constitute a totality in unity, and the totality is the unity and their beginning and middle and end consist in the very mode of unity'.[88]

Hence despite Iamblichus distinctions between the unparticipated One or monad and a 'participated' going forth in the divine which is constituted by the 'dyad' of goodness which mixes the limited with the unlimited, 'going forth' in general lies either, as the 'dyad' or 'the Good', on the 'ontological' or para-ontological (divine) side or else, as 'the participating', on the ontic (cosmic) side of the ontological difference, and *does not* hover in any limboesque 'between'. Indeed it is partly a denial of this literal 'between' which encourages the theurgic sense that the divine must kenotically descend into the cosmic. However, we know from Damascius, and from certain indications in surviving texts of Iamblichus himself, that he posited an ultimate One beyond even the One that gives rise to the dyad, and so beyond the contrast of 'unparticipated' and 'participated'. Damascius explicitly affirms that his own 'unique principle' is 'before the two', and continues to say that 'it is therefore that absolute which Iamblichus affirmed as an intermediary between the two principles, and as that which is absolutely ineffable, whereas the two are, for example, the limiting and the unlimited or again, if one prefers, the one and the many, understanding here the one opposed to the many, not the one [ie the absolute just referred to] anterior to the many and without opposition'.[89] So, as Gregory Shaw correctly argues, this ultimate One is not 'still more unified' and entirely cut off from everything that follows from it, but rather is a secret ground *beyond* the later division between the one and the many, entirely in keeping with the general theurgic thrust towards elevating matter and multiplicity. Iamblichus himself seems to refer to the generative one as 'the monad' which the Pythagoreans 'call ... "matter" and the "receptacle of all", since it is the cause of the dyad and of all receiving ratios',[90] suggesting a certain identity of this one and the dyad which is then grounded in the

[87]   Ibid., I.8. pp. 36–7.

[88]   Ibid., I 5–7, pp. 20–31; I.19, pp. 72–3.

[89]   Damascius, *De Principiis* R.I. 103 6–10; in the French bilingual edition, *Traité des Premiers Principes, Tome II: De La Triade et de L'Unité*, trans. Joseph Combès (Paris, 2002), pp. 27–8.

[90]   Iamblichus (?), *Theologoumena Arithmetica* 5, 12–15. This text may however be by a follower of Iamblichus and not Iamblichus himself.

one beyond both; a further passage in *On the Mysteries* also makes a Pythagorean distinction between the ultimate one and the unity that 'governs the many'.[91] This would mean that Iamblichus is not, as Rowan Williams once suggested in his now classic *Arius*, taking further the Plotinian tendency to posit an ultimate one that is radically alone and cannot, as such, be in any sense participated-in, but rather moving in the very opposite direction: a direction which from the Christian point of view is more tending towards 'orthodoxy' than any encouragement of Trinitarian heresies, Arian or otherwise, for it turns out that he, and in his wake Damascius, was shifting to a perspective, perhaps in line with the original view of Plato, that would render 'mediation' still more ultimate than the One. (Nor, I think, is Iamblichus at all guilty as Williams suggests, following E.F. Osborn, of a 'bureaucratic fallacy' of multiplying entities for the sake of it. Rather, Thomas Taylor in the eighteenth century understood better that his 'luxuriance' is to do with a sense that the divine *is* proliferation; that it lies in otherness as well as identity, in the many as well as the one, the material as well as the spiritual, the mediating as well as the singular, the outgoing and returning as well as the remaining.)

It follows, then, that the Palamite notion of 'energies' is not at all a recursion to Iamblichus, but a Christian deviation which, if anything, is more in a Plotinian line. While, indeed, Iamblichus' dyad does not quite attain an equality with the generating One – in a way that would approximate to the Christian Son-Father relation, there is still a tendency in his writings to see this dyad as an 'inner emanation' proper to the divine sphere as such, while the 'absolute' ultimate one can to some degree be approximated to the 'one essence' (or 'sophia') of the Christian Trinity. Of course it is also true that Christianity realizes a much fuller sense of grace; however, since this is by virtue of the Incarnation, one could also say that this is because it realizes a far fuller sense of the *theurgic* in that it thinks of worship as only possible at all because God himself has descended in person to offer worship to God and so to re-attune all of humanity to its divine origin and goal.[92]

From the above analysis it can be seen that Iamblichus fully grasps the link between oracular revelation on the one hand, and apophatic mystical ascent on the other. Because God is unknowable he must reveal himself to us, he must descend, though still as unknowable. But we encourage our awareness of this descent not when we merely look, but when we act in accordance with the processes of nature, which means being alert to the subtle affinities between matter and spirit and between one material thing and another. Mysticism is therefore for Iamblichus entirely liturgical and located, and surprisingly it appears to be this pagan current which bequeathed to Christian mysticism a more rigorously ritual, cosmic, topographical and collective focus.

Thus for Dionysius, as for Iamblichus and Proclus, God is 'there' for us not when we 'look' at him, but rather when we call upon him and perform actions

---

[91]   *On the Mysteries* VIII. 3 pp. 312–13.

[92]   See Gregory Shaw, *Theurgy and the Soul*, pp. 33–4; Rowan Williams, *Arius* (London, 2001), pp. 194–5.

attuned to him. This 'higher magic' is not merely automatic, but then no magic ever is, according to the profound researches of Marcel Mauss,[93] and it is not possible to influence God, but rather it is possible to attune ourselves and the cosmos to a greater receptivity of the divine. How else are we to understand prayer without reducing it either to a mythical attempt to change God's mind, or else to mere self-therapy? Clearly liturgical prayer is indeed a kind of higher magic.

Dionysius also took over the pagan Neoplatonic insistence that to receive an emanation from above, or a *doron*, a descending gift, is at once to contemplate this gift and actively to pass it on.[94] In this way he was able, with pagan assistance, to make better sense than hitherto of the Christian centrality of love: to love is at once to know and to receive and at the same time practically to communicate goodness. As I earlier indicated, the final Pauline *telos* is still in place, but here we only 'see' God, not through a Nyssan un-exhausted desire to see God, but rather, indeed, 'as we are seen', namely through God's super-surrounding and sun-like sight of us, a communicative light which remains something that we distribute downwards in the very act of regarding it.

Now these Dionysian perspectives appear to me only to be resumed in their full implications within the sophianic tradition – and we have already noted the theurgic elements in Bulgakov's thought, which even extended to a cautious embrace of notions of occult sympathy. Deification is active and liturgically creative as well as contemplatively passive. It does not mean to 'see' God across a mythical intervening distance, nor to be grasped by God's energetic outskirts on the brink of an always inaccessible pool of darkness. Neither of these false mediations pertain. But on the other hand, the ascent of deification is impossible unless God constantly descends to us – meeting liturgically with our acts in time, which are our modes of being in time. Were it possible for us to ascend under our own efforts (in that Pelagian or semi-Pelagian sense which Augustine in the West resisted), then grace would be denied and this ascent would itself constitute an impossible mediating ladder between humanity and God. No, we can become God, because God is constantly becoming us. Here again there cannot be mediation, yet there must be mediation in the sense of something that abides simultaneously on both sides of an absolute rift, held together by an ineffable attunement.

Sophiology and Christology

But does this 'God constantly becoming us' displace the unique incarnation of the *Logos*? Not at all. Recall that the eternal Adam is only the universal human hypostasizing power. The Fall of man impairs this essence, but by rights this should lead to absolute extinction for both human essence and human hypostases. It only

---

[93]   Marcel Mauss, *A General Theory of Magic*, trans. Robert Brain (London, 2001).
[94]   Pseudo-Dionysius, *The Celestial Hierarchy*, Chapter Three, 2, 165A–165C, p. 154; *The Divine Names*, Chapter Eight, 5–6, 889D–893A, pp. 111–13.

does not do so because, in some sense, when Sophia falls to become the sinister 'Achamoth' according to Bulgakov, the heavenly Sophia is 'impossibly' affected, and God cannot suffer, even for a hypothetical 'instance', a loss to his glory.[95] It is as if he only maintains his aseity, which of course he cannot not do, through the retrieval of languished glory, the lost wailing woman who forever in time wanders through the streets of Babylon, and according to *Proverbs* accosts young men at the crossroads in a way which so oddly echoes the conduct of the virtuous beauty, Sophia herself, who cries to them from the housetops: '*cette nature étrange et symbolique/ Où l'ange inviolé se mêle au sphinx antique …*'.[96]

Hence, if the essence of humanity is not after all extinguished, and hypostasized humanity along with it, this is because through all eternity the essence is immediately restored. So much is this the case that, when God as the divine Son descends in the Incarnation, so also does the eternal humanity or the Son of Man, as some problematic passages in the New Testament attest – this quasi-figure emerges from the Hebrew priestly and wisdom traditions given a middle Platonic gloss by Philo. Thus, for example, one can read First Colossians, Chapter 1 verse 15, which refers to Christ as the image of the invisible God as being nevertheless, like Sophia, the *first-born of Creation*, more honestly and critically, and yet not in an Arian mode, if one takes it to refer to the Philonian primal man rather than to the pre-existent *Logos*, whose reality is not thereby, of course, denied.

So for Bulgakov, in the Incarnation, not only is it the case that a human being is hypostasized by the *Logos*, it is also the case that here, uniquely, the human essence coincides with an individual human being. Though not, of course, with a human hypostasis; rather with the divine hypostasis which is the second person of the Trinity. But the eternal divine humanity, or human essence, or *Adam-Kadmon* – at once the first and the second Adam spoken of by Paul – is itself eternally saved and united with God *entirely because* of the unique descent of the *Logos* at one specific point in human history. Here alone occurs the event of the final finding and retrieving of the lost and fallen Sophia.

Nevertheless, the ground of the possibility of incarnation is the eternal descent of God into the Creation as Sophia, and the eternal raising of humanity through deification. In Christ, the 'obscure echo' becomes coinciding resonance that itself echoes throughout the cosmos and along all the corridors of human history. In Christ the divine Sophia, like the divine *esse*, works to hypostasize a natural creature without any finite hypostatic supplement. Here a pure mediation is carried out from the divine pole alone. Because of the general echo, the general indwelling of God in the world as Sophia, this full descent is possible, but once it is accomplished, the *aporia* of mediation is, so to speak, practically resolved – if scarcely in theory. God is now more than God simply by remaining God. The world through humanity is now also God by remaining the world, since something other than God has come

---

[95]   Bulgakov, *Du Verbe Incarné*, pp. 77–80, 127. And see John Milbank, 'The Name of Jesus', in *The Word Made Strange*, pp. 145–71.

[96]   Baudelaire, *Les Fleurs du Mal, Spleen et Idéal* 27, 'Avec ses vêtements …', pp. 54–7.

to be enhypostasized by the divine *Logos*. Otherwise, it would seem, God lacks the lack of God which is the positive good of dependence and seeking desire; God, as Pierre Bérulle said, lacks the worship of God, but now even this lack is made good, such that human beings can now adore God adequately, through God alone.[97] So from all eternity God has always been the God-Man and the Russians are right: the theanthropic exceeds even the theological. 'God appears and God is light/To those poor Souls who dwell in Night./But does a Human Form Display/To those who Dwell in Realms of day', as William Blake put it, in his gloss upon Swedenborg.[98]

Christology, so regarded, reverses the business of mediation. For now it is not hypostasizing that mediates, but rather the hypostasis of the *Logos*. He indeed sustains through his concretely realized character the separation of human and divine nature. At the same time, they are mediated by an extremity of mutual echo: the divine nature impassibly suffers; the human nature is conjoined to the divine attributes – such is the *communicatio idiomatum*. Moreover, the character of the divine hypostasis is fully and only displayed through the two natures and their characterological fusion. For, in keeping with Bulgakov's trajectory, we are no longer to see these essences as abstract and static; instead, they are both, of course, hypostasizing powers, the uncreated and created Sophia.[99] Hence because they display one and the same character of the hypostasis of the *Logos* in the respective idioms of finite time and infinity, they tend also radically to fuse these idioms together in a very Cyrilline fashion. Christ as personal, one might say, has fully assumed human traits; Christ as in two natures has finally blended the divine and the created Sophia.

What this adds to Chalcedon is subtle but crucial, and also tends to integrate atonement doctrine with Christological ontology. It is not satisfactory merely to say, with Chalcedon, that Christ is divided by nature and united by person or character. For this suggests that he is in one aspect (the personal) the God-Man or incarnate, but in another aspect (the natural), he is not. An entirely personal union on its own, involving no unity of nature whatsoever, would, in Nestorian fashion, render the communication of idioms impossible and suggest that Christ was only identical with the *Logos* in terms of a kind of distilled 'ideality', emanating from his concrete, embodied life like a perfume, but not truly including that life. Hence to allow for this, and yet to avoid monophystism which would abolish the Creator/created divide and in effect suggest, in an over-Oriental fashion, that Christ was

---

[97]   Pierre Bérulle, *Opuscules de la Piété*, ed. Miklos Veto (Grenoble, 1997) III. 72. viii p. 364. See also Veto's long essay in the same volume, 'La Christo-logique de Bérulle', pp. 7–136. Bérulle's defence of the view that God would have been incarnate even without the Fall is in line with Maximus' and Eckhart's arguments for this more than those of Scotus. For this difference, see my contribution in Žižek and Milbank, *The Monstrosity of Christ*.

[98]   William Blake, 'Auguries of Innocence', in William Blake, selected by J. Bronowski, p. 71.

[99]   Bulgakov, *Du Verbe Incarné*, pp. 121–7.

entirely an uncreated divine *avatar*, one requires a category that mediates between personhood and nature.

This, of course, is for Bulgakov provided by 'Sophia'. Because the two natures are 'characterizing powers', the exchange of idioms is not extrinsic, since both natures are fluid and dynamic, rather than fixed and substantive. Furthermore, the two characterizing powers are at bottom one, since the uncreated and created Sophia are more fundamentally one in 'foundation and content' according to Bulgakov – given that God is the all and the creation itself is 'nothing but' the outgoing of God, even though God is in himself mysteriously the 'self-exceeding'.[100] They differ only as to their 'conditions' of respectively eternal glory and finite becoming, and for this reason the two conditions can come together in the Incarnation not just actually on the basis of the one divine hypostasis, but also transcendentally on the conditional basis of the more fundamental unity and tendency to unity of the two essences taken as the two Sophias or objective characterizing powers. Just as, for Aquinas, the orientation of humanity to deification is an ontologically transcendental condition for the 'appropriate' possibility of the Incarnation, so, for Bulgakov, the fundamental divine-human unity of Sophia performs a similar role.

And it is this same fundamental unity which for him permits God to assume even fallen human nature. This would be impossible, given the nature of sin as *absolute* estrangement from God, an 'impossible' removal from the 'all' that is and can ever be, were it not for the fact that the human hypostasing power, Sophia, even as fallen, remains, in her fallen heart, insofar as she remains actual at all, like a *fleur du mal*, 'ontologically unbreakable', still entirely united with her heavenly counterpart.[101]

Sophia, Israel and the Church

What remains briefly to be considered with respect to the problematic of mediation is Mariology, ecclesiology and liturgical theology. However, they can all be considered with respect to a problematic that Bulgakov, uniquely to my knowledge, raises and yet partially shies away from. This is the following: if the personhood of the Son is substantively relational, then how is it possible for the Son alone to be incarnated and not the whole Trinity?[102] That is to say, if the personality of the Son can be expressed in time, this must itself be a relational expression, even if not, of course, at the human level, a fully substantially relational one, and therefore the Father and the Spirit must in some fashion be also incarnated, since the Son simply *is* his relation to the other two hypostases.

This problem can then be combined with a modern sense that Jesus' expressed personality must have been more social and historical than the tradition allowed.

---

[100] Ibid., p. 124.

[101] Ibid., p. 127.

[102] Ibid., p. 119.

But Augustine indeed was near to combining these two insights: for him in *De Trinitate*, the Son as relational has to be incarnate in the relations of time which he repairs and restores, so allowing a recuperation of all true psychic life in time. Moreover, for Augustine the incarnate Son through his humanity only relates to the Father and the Son through temporal images or voicings of these realities – not to an impossible mythical hovering of these divine persons in their economic function between the Creator and the Creation.[103]

Can one possibly go further than Augustine and say that the Father must in some fashion be 'incarnated' as the voice of human memory, especially as the memory of Israel? After all, if Christ is sinless, then this memory now becomes retrospectively perfected. By retroaction, the temporal source that is Israel becomes one with the eternal Paternal source – and such a perspective would also act as a salve against the grosser forms of supercessionism. And can one also say, with Bulgakov this time, that the Church in its eschatological totality is collectively personified by the Holy Spirit?[104]

Here, once more, one sees the playing through of the sophiological schema in its fully incarnational mode: for salvation to arise, there must be a retrospective remaking of the past through forgiveness: this is possible since the past is only ever 'there' through the traces it leaves in the present and its promise of the future.[105] In this manner, all human paternity or cultural legacy is restored, because it is imbued with the character of the true, infinite origin. Here also, then, the divine Sophia now fully plays the role of the earthly one.

Similarly, salvation is only possible because it is fully anticipatory. Hence if there is the presence of redemption, then, given the present is only the promise of the future and has always already given way to the future, the perfect future must be entirely imbued with the Holy Spirit as the united mutual expression of memory and awareness. The Holy Spirit has descended as displaying the actively receptive, feminine and so perhaps most fundamental aspect of Sophia while, equally, as in the case of *Adam Kadmon*, the eternal power collectively to deify humanity which is the celestial city, heavenly Jerusalem, has descended here on earth.[106] Memory as collective is relatively impersonal; yet as personal it is also collective and capable of being transmitted. Future hope, likewise, is sustained collectively and is a sacramental anticipation of eternal consummation, without which it would be mere optimism; at the same time it is only fully expressed and given concrete character in individual members of the Church. Hence in a full economic, or rather

---

[103] Augustine, *De Trinitate*, Books I–IV.

[104] Bulgakov, *The Bride of the Lamb*, pp. 97–102.

[105] See John Milbank, *Being Reconciled: Ontology and Pardon* (London, 2003), pp. 44–61.

[106] Bulgakov, *The Bride of the Lamb*, pp. 79–103. Here he stresses that all human males are hypostasized through Christ and all human females through Mary who is identical with the Church which is in turn hypostasized by the Holy Spirit who is eminently female.

actually incarnate Trinitarian display, there is a triple mediating without mediation between collective process and individual fully personal embodiment.

Bulgakov acknowledged that Christ is only incarnate through the Church by means of the person of Mary, and only personally expressive in human time through the always already begun receptivity of the Church.[107] In this way he faintly pointed to the radicalism of the surely logical view that the Bride is collectively and eschatologically the equal of the Bridegroom. Given his sexual ontology of the eminent 'maleness' of the Son-*Logos* and the eminent femaleness of the Spirit-*Donum* that is a crucial part of his vitalism and which I broadly endorse, this suggests also gender equality. Bulgakov only evades this by insisting, quite wrongly, that in some sense the eternal Son in his activity has a kind of hierarchical superiority over the essentially passive Spirit. We should surely reject this and link gender equality to the equality of Bride with Bridegroom, thereby not abandoning the essential significance of Biblical engendered typology, nor the Biblical and theological significance of sexual difference.

These radical proposals seem to me to complete sophiology by suggesting, indeed, that Sophia as such becomes incarnate, since the three substantive relations become incarnate in the retrospectively, repletely and prospectively perfected human temporality of past, present and future. These moments are specifically represented by parenthood as past performance and redeemable memory, woman in her fertility as proleptic and eschatological, and man as elusively present and immediate – exhausted by his current deeds of love for the sake of the future, which nonetheless enshrine their own intrinsic worth.

 Such a radical perspective avoids the perennial dilemma of Mariology, which appears to require that her *fiat* is an instigation of the Church as the community of the redeemed before its foundation by Christ. It is this dilemma which gives rise to the solution of the immaculate conception in Anselmian and Scotist terms, whereby Mary is required to give the highest possible honour to Christ, just as Christ is ontologically required to give the highest possible honour to God, in default of any proper understanding of human deification in general. But instead one can say, thereby evading the need for this doctrine, or rather perhaps finding a way to recast it, that since the *fiat* is not merely the opening occasion for the Incarnation, but also relationally constitutive of the Incarnation, that Mary must already be the presence of the Church, yet as such must be from the outset of her life so composed that her orientation to the supernatural is also the beginning of the actual birth of the *Logos* within her. Here again, on the ground of Sophia's double presence in God and creation, we have the possibility of heavenly wisdom's full descent to earth at a certain point in time.

The Church, however, is not just Marian and spiritual. It is also the body of Christ. Here the physical aspects and evocations in icon and in the Eucharist of Christ's humanity continue to unfold the hypostasing power of his human nature which is fully stamped with the character of the hypostasis of the *Logos*.

---

[107] Ibid.

Thus the Church in its physicality most acutely poses to us the question, why is there a physical life in time?[108] As regards its temporality, as Rowan Williams has often indicated, this has something to do with the positive value of lack, of dependence and of slow coming to be, not just in a lifetime, but also across the generations. As regards its corporeality, here again it seems that Christian theology needs to have some recourse to the resources of pagan monotheism. For it is Proclus, and not one of the Church Fathers untouched by his influence, who seems to supply the radical answer which then gets remotely echoed right down to Aquinas. Human and daemonic (Christians would say angelic) intelligence, says Proclus, is removed by its constitutive doubling of being in the conceptual image from the absolute simplicity of the One and from the non-reflexive understanding of the henads or gods (Christians would say from the non-reflexive and intuitive intelligence of the Triune God). But material things, as non-reflexive, although lower than intellect, are also in a certain way simpler than intellect: automatically, in a kind of slumbering innocence, physical things have to praise the gods and God simply by existing and showing themselves forth in their integrity.[109]

This means that there is a limit to the corruption of nature spoken of by Bulgakov: it is always imposed upon nature, and always silently opposed by her. It follows that while, indeed, sinful humans descend from spiritual things to rational ones and then to sensual ones, the cure for that is homeopathic. First of all, that is because the perverse descent loses by definition the power to re-ascend; it corrupts the freedom of the will. Hence fallen humanity can only be rescued by the descent of the divine – in this sense quite clearly, the Incarnation, or the restoration of true worship, is the supreme theurgic action. But secondly, because material things of themselves lead back in their simplicity, despite every degree of fall. Hopkins was right: 'there lives the dearest freshness deep down things'. So it is just for this reason that divine incarnation must reach beneath even humanity into the material, the Eucharistic. Or rather for a double reason: because humans have degenerated just this far, and because simple material things are the only true allies of deity in a fallen world.

So this supplies the only plausible reason for the instance of material creation: it captures something of the highest which reflective intelligence – the gift to itself of a gift – does not. At the same time, one can inversely point out that, without the 'suspension' of matter by spirit and form, matter itself evaporates into all the various shapes through which it can alone ever be or appear. There is no coherent 'materialism', because every materialism always dissolves matter into atoms, laws, processes and rhythms which are strictly speaking always formal or spiritual in character. Pure matter by contrast is, as Aristotle and still more Aquinas realized, a

---

[108] This is the question insistently and poignantly asked (if not perhaps adequately answered in non-sentimental terms) in Marilynne Robinson's novel *Gilead* (London: Virago, 2004).

[109] Proclus, *Elements of Theology*, pp. 57–8 and see Jean Trouillard, *La Mystagogie de Proclos* (Paris, 1982), pp. 119–42.

pure mystery, the subject of an *apophasis* for knowledge, since its potential is only ever 'there' when in some degree it is already actualized by form. In consequence, hylomorphism is the *nearest* one can get to materialism; hylomorphism saves matter by regarding it as the vast shadow cast by form which ensures that there is a distinction for human being between the ideas they intend and the real external things they intend by those ideas. In the case of angels, there is no such distinction, which means that angels encounter their internal ideas also as the presence of other discrete beings. In the case of the Trinity however, the reduction of hypostasis to pure relation means that 'the idea' of the other is also a purely *external* (as it were) relation to the other. In this way the divine coincidence of idea and otherness recovers something of the quality of that spatial and temporal exteriority which humans enjoy and which is unknown to angels. The play of the divine essence through the Trinitarian relations is therefore in a sense eminently matter, and this coincides with the sense that Sophia is eminently a female womb. So just as matter 'recovers' in the mysterious depths a lost simplicity and a lost negative mystery, so also it recovers in a 'weak', strangely absent and yet by that very token creative form, the power and integrity of Sophia.[110]

It is for this reason that the cosmos requires there to be humans as well as angels – they alone reflexively synthesize, as microcosms, all of the cosmos, because they are at once both spiritual and material and combine material externality with an intimation of angelic intimacy in a manner that ensures that they, most of all creatures, exhibit an image of the Trinity. But given the fact of the Incarnation, sophianic, theandric, metaxological ultimate reality is also both spiritual and material, or radically kenotic, and its characteristic double echo across no gulf applies also to the ineffable union of body with soul, matter with mind.

So from a final sophianic-theurgic perspective, matter is not a mere contingent residue, like Hegelian detritus according to Žižek, but nor is it simply a sacramental mirror to be ultimately left behind. Rather, as for Maximus the Confessor in his thoroughly theurgic *Mystagogy*,[111] it is always to be returned to, because the ultimate points all the way back, always to the rain falling silently on the remote beautiful pond in the earthly countryside. Sophia rests in the Godhead and in the pond: there lies nothing between the two, but – as 'the true intermediary *metaxu*'[112] – she brings them most intimately together.

---

[110] Bulgakov, 'The Unfading Light', in Rowan Williams, *Sergii Bulgakov*, p. 145.

[111] Maximus Confessor, 'The Church's Mystagogy', in *Selected Writings*, trans. George C. Berthold (New York, 1985), Chapter Two, pp. 188–9.

[112] Bulgakov, *The Bride of the Lamb*, p. 123.

COMMENTARY

Antoine Arjakovsky (translated by Adrian Pabst)

'On ouvre de nouveaux les grands livres:
Ceux qui parlent de châteaux à enlever, de fleuves
à franchir, d'oiseaux qui serviraient de guides ...'[113]

Theses are the glory days of Sergii Bulgakov! Professor Milbank's paper makes this case convincingly. I do not say that in any triumphalist way. We know full well that the rehabilitation of Bulgakov in the conservative circles of Eastern Orthodoxy has still not happened. And if one were to speak about the Wisdom of God, the orthodox world is far from acknowledging its importance.

If you ask in a Moscow Church about an icon of Wisdom, all you will see is an expression of horror which is typical of any 'pure' person in the face of heresy. This of course is not new. I was recently told that the Cathedral of the Holy Wisdom of God in Grodno in Belarus was destroyed in 1961 in a situation of total public indifference. But it is not only the Russian or Belarus people who have just escaped the yoke of Soviet atheism. Even in an Orthodox seminary in the Anglo-Saxon world where I spoke about the place of Sophia in the Orthodox patristic, iconographical and liturgical tradition, a teacher asked me what all the fuss was about given that we all know Sophia is no other than Christ himself. ...

Let me speak directly to such and similar reactions.[114] Of course it is true that Christ is, as Saint Paul said, 'power of God and wisdom of God' (1 Cor 1:24). But we should remember that these words concern Christ, God-Man in the sophianic union of the two natures, not the *Logos*, the eternal God-Man, the hypostasis of the second person of the Holy Trinity. Bulgakov himself had noted that in the text of Saint Paul, power and wisdom were not preceded by any article. He interpreted this identification of wisdom with Christ in a Trinitarian fashion: 'Christ, on whom the Holy Spirit rests, has revealed the Father and disclosed the Wisdom of God'. Thus Bulgakov positioned himself in continuity with Saint Augustine who wrote that 'Wisdom is the Father, Wisdom is the Son, Wisdom is the Spirit. Not three Wisdoms but one Wisdom'.[115]

Does however the rediscovery of sophiology warrant the claim to a new theological horizon as set out by John Milbank? I am profoundly convinced of

---

[113] Philippe Jacottet, 'Le Mot Joie', quoted in epigraph by John Milbank, in *The Word Made Strange*.

[114] Cf. Antoine Arjakovsky, *Essai sur le père Serge Boulgakov, philosophe et théologien chrétien* (Paris, 2006).

[115] Sergii Bulgakov, *Bratstvo Sviatoi Sofii: Materialy I Dokumenty 1923–1939*, ed. N.A. Struve (Moscow, 2000), p. 134.

this and I am delighted that his account of the sophianic horizon points to theurgy. Vladimir Iljine, a good friend of Bulgakov, remarked that Christianity cannot be appreciated with moderation, as if it were a matter of tasting a good cognac. Alexander Men, who transmitted the works of Bulgakov behind the Iron Curtain and died a martyr, used to say that '*Le christianisme ne fait que commencer*'. Milbank is right to argue that the highest theurgic action is the Incarnation of the *Logos*, the restoration of genuine rite and worship. For theurgy is the infinite authority that Christ has conferred upon his friends Christ, that of walking on water, healing the disabled and resuscitate the dead!

Interestingly, this is not only true for Anglo-Saxon thought but also extends to continental philosophy, at least those who are questioning the very foundations of contemporary positivism. For instance, Jean-Luc Marion, in his recent book *The erotic phenomenon*, writes that 'to love without being defines love without being … To say that love resuscitates should be construed as an analytic proposition'.[116] What does this mean? Nothing more and nothing less than a new epistemology. For Marion, mathematics and the natural sciences seek by way of epistemic reduction to measure in objects that which is repeatable and permanent. By contrast, the humanities – philosophy, history or sociology – seek by way of ontological reduction to retain of things their status of being (*étant*) in order to reduce it to being (*l'être*) and thereby to discover in man 'a being (*étant*) that has a stake in being (*l'être*)'. In both cases it is the relation of being to time that was determining for Einstein as well as for Heidegger.

In developing Marion's argument, it is possible to say that the 'ecumenical sciences' that are promoted by Radical Orthodoxy, belong to both natural sciences and the humanities, insofar as they search within the Church for what is temporal and what is eternal. But these 'ecumenical sciences' require a further effort of intelligence and will on our part. In their proposed method of reduction – which one could describe with Marion as 'loving reduction' – time is no longer that of repetition or anxiety but become the times of those who love; as Paul Ricœur put it at the end of his book *La Mémoire, l'histoire, l'oubli*, the time of *le temps des lys des champs et des oiseaux du ciel*! By way of loving reduction, space loses the homogeneity it had acquired in the ontological relation. The 'here' and the 'there' are no longer exchanged within a neutral space, when the beloved is not in the arms of the lover anymore. By discovering the Church as a loving reality and as a gift of God, as a body whose limbs all suffer when a single limb hurts, we come to understand that love is the source of all knowledge and of the whole of Creation.

The Orthodox philosopher Christos Yannaras says exactly that in his book *Postmodern Metaphysics*, because for him contemporary science in general and quantum physics in particular, show that reality is constituted by the participation of human beings in it. There is no intermediary realm between reality and us. As John Milbank argues, there is a *metaxu* which is simultaneously on each side of

---

[116] Jean-Luc Marion, *Le phénomène érotique* (Paris, 2003), p. 125 [my translation].

these two poles.[117] Yannaras draws the same conclusion as Marion and Milbank from the idea of the theurgic power of love:

> In our experiential model of a semantics of human language, only a will-to-existence unfettered by any natural-essential presupposition or intentionality can be absolutely non-self-interested love. Only love as an ontological (rather than an ethical) category, can express self-transcendence and self-offering – a communion with being – as a volitional mode of existence: only love can refer to an existence which exists not through necessarily acquiescing to the fact of its existence, but through freely hypostasizing its being (by coming forth as distinct hypostases of its being) – producing hypostases by 'generation' and 'procession' with which it structures being as a communion of love.[118]

Moreover, it is not only philosophy or quantum physics that discover at the end of modernity the new horizon of sophianic love. I will now turn to economics and the new economy of ever more rapid globalization, as well as the new politics that is emerging out of the ruins of the modern natural law tradition.

At the outset, Bulgakov was of course an economist. In his lectures at Kiev University, he had demonstrated the lacunae of the thinking of Marx, Kant and Schelling. Already in his book *The Philosophy of Economy* of 1912, he had presented Sophia as the real transcendental subject of economics. Like Milbank he spoke about the theurgic mission given to man by his Creator. In a chapter on the sophianity of the world, he wondered 'in what does the nature of man's creative activity consist?'. His answer was that 'in knowledge, in economics, in culture and in art, it [this nature] is sophianic. Its metaphysical foundation is the real participation of man in divine Sophia which communicates to the world the divine energies of the *Logos*'.[119]

Nowadays a great number of economists, such as those who meet in France as part of the *Assises chrétiennes de la mondialisation*, question the classical economic theory of *laissez-faire* grounded in a natural order willed by God. Instead they are interested, without necessarily knowing how to name it, in the sophianic dimension of economics. They retrieve 'an approach – too often forgotten – of Creation, out of respect for the Creator and Creation given to man', thus reflecting on the realization of a genuine sustainable development.[120]

This approach highlights the numerous problems of the global economy, in particular the failings of global governance, the growing gap between rich and poor countries, a properly endemic gap (as Milbank would put it) – especially when one remembers that Sub-Saharan Africa has today a total Gross National

---

[117] See, *supra*, chapter one, section 1.

[118] Christos Yannaras, *Postmodern Metaphysics*, trans. Norman Russell (Brooklyn, 2005), p. 176.

[119] Sergii Bulgakov, *La philosophie de l'économie* (Paris, 1987), pp. 100–101.

[120] *Assises chrétiennes de la mondialisation, Livre blanc, Dialogues pour une terre habitable* (Paris, 2006).

Product (GNP) lower than that of the Netherlands and that between 1983 and 1994, Africa paid to the International Monetary Fund (IMF) US $5 billion more than what it received from it – and also environmental degradation. Faced with this crisis, these economists have called upon Pascal Lamy, the Director of the World Trade Organization (WTO) to create a new 'alternational democracy' founded upon values (justice, freedom, peace, trust, etc).

According to this approach, economics should no longer be based on profit but on gift exchange.[121] For the new index of growth is not GDP or GNP but instead the Index of Human Development, as defined by the economists of the UN's Programme for Development, an index that takes into account health and education standards, as well as democratic structures and other similar factors.

This marks a reversal which radically distinguishes the liberal school as represented by Michael Novak from the thinkers of the new world economy such as Robert van Drimmelen, the Secretary General of the Association of World Council of Churches related Development Organizations in Europe (APRODEV).[122] Like van Drimmelen, Michael Novak, who according to John Milbank, Stephen Long and Daniel Bell is the leading voice of the liberal school, speaks of love as the foundation of economic life.[123] But for him this love is such that it privileges a policy of welfare and a moralist outlook on the environment in order to correct the laws of the free market.[124]

On the contrary, for Robert van Drimmelen – author of the book *Faith in a Global Economy* published by the Ecumenical Council of Churches – to acknowledge the love between God and his creation obliges mankind to create new laws, in order to render visible the invisible play of the two hands of God's Wisdom. The Swiss economist Christoph Stückelberger set out in 2002 the principles of such a new ethical economy in his book *Global Trade Ethics*. In France, Jean-Baptiste de Foucauld has argued for a new reflection based on the Gospel about money and divine gifts.

The advent of a new era of global governance means that we have to question the nature and operation of international relations since 1648, based upon the acceptance of unlimited sovereignty of the nation state, but also the need to question the principle of parliamentary decision-making based on the law of the stronger.[125] The European Union has shown how it is possible to move from a logic of sovereignty to a logic of

---

[121] Pascal Lamy, *La démocratie monde. Pour une autre gouvernance globale* (Paris, 2004), p. 85.

[122] APRODEV is a consortium of 17 ecumenical organizations in the field of development aid based in Brussels (www.aprodev.net).

[123] Michael Novak, 'The Love that moves the Sun', in Michael Novak (ed.), *A Free Society Reader. Principles for the new millennium* (Boston/New York, 2000), p. 98.

[124] Michael Novak, *On cultivating Liberty. Reflections on Moral Ecology*, ed. Brian C. Anderson (Boston, 1999).

[125] It is also possible to cite other examples of this questioning of nation state sovereignty. I am thinking in particular of the notion of the right to intervene which was

community in a mutually beneficial fashion. This passage, made possible by engaged Christians such as Robert Schuman and Aldo di Gasperi, relied on the following principles (as pointed out by Michel Camdessus, Denis Badré and Pascal Lamy): the mutualization of the war industries, the primacy of European law over national law, the defence of the principle of subsidiarity, and the monopoly of initiative granted to the European Commission.[126]

The method of consensus that is now being deployed by the great ecumenical forces is also profoundly innovative. This method of decision-making which takes everyone's advice into consideration is not a method of the lowest common denominator but on the contrary a method of a maximum of truth in the Spirit. The objective of this method is to rediscover after five centuries of parliamentarianism the spirit of the first council of the Apostles. Jill Tabart has argued in her book *Coming to Consensus*[127] that the decision-making procedure according to a parliamentarian and argumentative mode based on the law of majorities was only formalized in 1583 in the *Lex Republica Anglorum* of Thomas Smyth. At that time, this procedure has the important advantage of enabling European countries to overcome the feudalist configuration of power.

But after the tragedies of the twentieth century, the Churches have gradually understood that majority voting does not mean any guarantee in making just decisions and on the contrary can produce growing frustrations within the new personal conscience of the citizenry. Mainly for reasons of long-term efficiency, certain Churches such as the United Churches of Australia have decided to go by the Holy Spirit in the most serious possible fashion. The aim is no longer to prevail over others by way of arguments but to engage in a process of discernment in which the will of God is sought in an attentive mutual listening to the position of each and everyone involved. According to this perspective, the diversity of opinion is a guarantee of success to the extent that all share a common credo.

So yes, when one closely observes the new theological horizon that John Milbank has outlined so forcefully, there is reason to think that Orthodoxy is a task that remains to be accomplished.

---

introduced, unfortunately without limits, within the United Nations by the current French Foreign Minister Bernard Kouchner.

[126] For Pascal Lamy, 'The monopoly of initiative concerns the widely recognized necessity to grant the exclusive initiative of policy and policy instrument to a third instance, independent of member states, an instance that is trusted by them (trusting in a way which they would be prepared to do bilaterally) in order to propose policies required by the common interest of the Union … This means that a Commission proposition can only be amended without its agreement by unanimity among the member states … The Commission takes initiatives that deepen integration and amends them in such a way that these produce a majority'. Lamy, *La démocratie monde*, p. 39.

[127] Jill Tabart, *Coming to Consensus. A Case Study for the Churches* (Geneva, 2003).

PART II
Sophia, Politics and Ecclesiology

Chapter 3

The Metaphysics of Hope and the Transfiguration of Making in the Market Empire

Michael Northcott

Multitude and Market Empire

One of the more provocative accounts of the material conditions and metaphysical underpinnings of the global market economy in recent years is the book *Empire* by Michael Hardt and Antonio Negri.[1] The book presents the global market as the new form of empire and as the logical end of modernity, and in particular of European political economy. The roots of this development are traced to medieval philosophy, and especially the work of John Duns Scotus whose affirmation of the powers of *this* world subverts the traditional Christian conception of the analogical duality of being in which all beings in themselves and in their relations participate in the being of God as well as in the material world. The Scotist move focuses attention on the powers of singular, univocal being in material existence, which, as Dante recognized at the time, was the origin of the drive to 'realize all the powers of the possible intellect', whose first fruit was the Renaissance.[2] The influence of transcendence in human affairs is thereby undermined, and humans become 'masters of their own lives, producers of cities and history, and inventors of heavens'.[3]

This new focus on immanence paves the way for the assertion of monarchic power as the only true transcendent, with the gradual monopolization of armed force and fiscal authority by sovereign kings. The multivocal loci of economic and political power in independent cities, trade guilds, monastic foundations, and baronial estates are forced through a long history of violent struggle and vicious wars to cede power and authority to univocal monarchic forms which ultimately achieve their legitimacy in the birth of nation states, and subsequently of national parliaments. The result, as Hardt and Negri put it, is that by the time of Spinoza 'the horizon of immanence coincides with the horizon of the democratic political

---

[1] Michael Hardt and Antonio Negri, *Empire* (Cambridge, MA, 2000).
[2] Ibid., p. 71.
[3] Ibid., p. 70.

order' and in the absence of any external mediation we find that 'the singular is presented as the multitude'.[4]

This drive towards singular sovereignty in political economy is given added force by Europe's outside, its colonies. The colonies provided a terrain in which resistance to singular sovereignty was first coercively conquered, and on the model of which domestic resistance could also be pacified. In the civil wars over modernity which began in the Renaissance and were concluded in the misnamed 'wars of religion', Europeans began to realize that they could both subjugate native peoples in extra-European territories and the peasantry at home by removing all mediating and local forms of authority. And so the modern artifice of sovereignty, the imperious nation state, with its illusory appearance of naturalness and representativeness, emerged from this combination of coercive subjugation at home and violent conquest abroad. The idea of the nation state was sustained by the mystification of its true origin under the claim of the naturalness of the enclosure of common land and property as narrated in John Locke's account of property rights and Thomas Hobbes' account of the state as the social artifice which defends the claims of property owners.

According to Hardt and Negri the nation state comes to be identified in the modern age with 'the people', a deceptively unitary concept that is the product of the nationalist ideologies and projects of emergent nation states which bend both national and popular claims to sovereignty toward the spiritual construction of national identities.[5] And in time these ideologies and claims are transformed by the emergence of capitalist sovereignty, which is 'a form of command that over-determines the relationship between individuality and universality as a function of the development of capital'.[6]

The market empire challenges this over-determination with its creation of fluid and irregular global flows of commodities, ideas and peoples which displace and deconstruct the monopolistic powers of nation states and subvert the spiritualized ideas of the people and sovereignty which legitimate these powers. In other words, late capitalism's generation of a new global market empire generates a range of supranational structures which contain within them the seeds of new forms of counter-empire. Whatever the sacrifices of human and ecological goods that the emergent form of the neoliberal market empire requires, Hardt and Negri suggest that it nonetheless contains within it a liberatory dimension in the potential sovereignty of the global multitude. The dominion of the market empire and the inequalities it creates and exacerbates are inevitable and will be decisive in all those regions of the world that were formerly colonized. Though global production chains, and the information networks on which they depend, operate through diversity and diversification, the end paradoxically is unification, the drawing of all peoples and regions of the planet into one disciplinary regime. And with the

---

4   Ibid., p. 73.
5   Ibid., p. 104.
6   Ibid., p. 87.

new mobility of capital there follows a new mobility of labour so that the Third World and the First World get intermingled in the new market empire:

> The Third World does not really disappear in the process of unification of the world market but enters the First, establishes itself at the heart as ghetto, shantytown, favela, always again produced and reproduced. In turn the First World is transferred to the Third in the form of stock exchanges and banks, transnational corporations and icy skyscrapers of money and command. Economic geography and political geography both are destabilized in such a way that the boundaries among the various zones are themselves fluid and mobile. As a result the entire world market tends to be the only coherent domain for the effective application of capitalist management and command.[7]

The borderless nature of the market empire requires 'a new mechanism of the general control of the global process and thus a mechanism that can coordinate politically the new dynamics of the global domain of capital and the subjective dimensions of the actors'. On this account, it is an illusion to imagine, as anti-globalization critics do, that it is possible for individual countries to de-link themselves from the global market through new forms of protectionism. Any such attempt at economic isolation 'will mean only a more brutal kind of domination by the global system, a reduction to powerlessness and poverty'.[8] Instead, the market empire gives rise to a new global political entity – the 'multitude' – who are connected across borders and nation states via jet travel and the internet, and as the multitude coalesce in new groups and movements it will acquire the power to challenge and resist the rule of the market empire and its constituent agencies including economic corporations and nation states.

This conceptualization of the productive power of the multitude is analogous to Spinoza's account of divine power as immanent world-making.[9] The potential power of the multitude is manifest in new kinds of collaboration, organization and resistance among individuals, ethnicities and classes who are drawn together across continents and nation states by the ineluctable flows of the global empire. Counter-empire takes form in transnational political organization made possible by the internet and international travel, and exemplified in such developments as the World Social Forum, or international protests such as the global demonstration against the invasion of Iraq by the United States and Britain in 2003.

While beguiling in its simplicity, and in its resurrection of a Marxian view of the unfolding of new possibilities within the capitalist revolution, this approach is however not without major problems. Foremost among these is that, because of the Spinozist theological underpinnings of their project, Hardt and Negri give no

---

[7]   Ibid., p. 254.

[8]   Ibid.

[9]   Malcolm Bull, 'You can't build a new society with a Stanley knife', *London Review of Books*, 23/19 (4 October 2001).

account of the kinds of proper exercises of power which might be presented as an alternative to the malign forms of over-determination that they so imaginatively describe other than reactive protest. And this inability to specify the positive uses of political power arises from the libertarian foundations of their account of the new liberties and forms of self-government to which the borderless multitude lay claim. As Malcolm Bull suggests, at this point Hardt and Negri show themselves to be inheritors of the Jeffersonian Republican tradition, rather than radical Deleuzian Marxists.[10] Like the neoliberals they decry, they too only have a negative definition of liberty on offer. Self-government for them is Hobbesian – the self, even as part of the multitude, can do no more than protest and survive.

The Distorted Theology of Free-Market Global Capitalism and its Critics

This is why in their account of the condition of the market empire Hardt and Negri share a surprising degree of common ground with contemporary theological advocates of free-market global capitalism, such as the Roman Catholic Michael Novak. Novak's central claim is that deregulated market capitalism offers the best hope of any social structure for the liberty of citizens and their realization of material comfort, meaningful work and purposeful leisure because, unlike so many social (and socialist) revolutions which 'promise a reign of saints', capitalism is designed for sinners.[11] While certain civic virtues are required for capitalism to flourish, nonetheless the market system is in essence a system which enables the self-interested actions of sinners to work towards the common good of others through what Novak calls the 'doctrine of unintended consequences', or what Adam Smith called the invisible hand of the market.[12] Markets are superior to other forms of organization because they involve voluntary action on the part of individual service providers and consumers; people get what they want when they want it 'without waiting in line'. The watchword throughout his apologia is freedom: 'theologically speaking, the free market and the liberal polity follow from liberty of conscience'.[13] Where economic and industrial production and consumption are not ordered according to market principles of supply and demand, or where the fruits of capitalism are not properly appropriated, they generate dependency and therefore the opposite of freedom. The spread of the market promotes 'exchange relations' and these are 'more fully human than relations of dependency'.[14]

Novak rejects the critique that capitalism's constant transformation of social life, and the invasiveness of international trade, produce more suffering than they ameliorate and create new kinds of enslaving dependency. On the contrary, he

---

[10] Ibid.

[11] Michael Novak, *The Spirit of Democratic Capitalism* (New York, 1982), p. 85.

[12] Ibid., pp. 88–92.

[13] Ibid., p. 114.

[14] Ibid., p. 205.

argues that in the Americas international trade has consistently resulted in a shift of investment from the richer US economy to poorer economies in the South, and that if these economies remain poor, it is not because this investment creates poverty or dependence on the North but because of the ignorance of economics in traditional Latin and Catholic cultures.[15]

For Novak the critics of capitalism rely on accounts of the social which require people to be virtuous and which hence enforce virtue: their God is a God of command, and their goal is a utopia here on earth which, in a sinful and fallen world, is not realizable this side of heaven. 'Democratic capitalists' on the other hand believe in a God who works providentially through 'the practical providential intelligence embodied in singular agents in singular concrete situations'.[16] This does not mean that capitalism does not rely upon, and help to reproduce, community. On the contrary, Novak contends that nowhere is it possible to find the range of interaction of individuals in shared interest groups and networks than in North America.

But even Novak is prepared to concede that there are dangers in the system he so praises. For the very virtues on which capitalism relies – thrift, honesty, hard work, self-reliance, trust – are capable of being dissolved by the experience of growing up in the midst of wealth and plenty:

> The commercial virtues are not, then, sufficient to their own defense. A commercial system needs taming and correction by a moral-cultural system independent of commerce. At critical points, it also requires taming and correction by the political system and the state. The founding fathers (of America and America's economy) did not imagine that the institutions of religion, humanism, and the arts would ever lose their indispensable role. They did not imagine that the state would wither away. Each of the three systems needs the other.[17]

And at this point we encounter a crucial flaw in Novak's theology of capitalism, for under the conditions of the emergence of the market empire the state is losing some of its powers. And further the institutions of religion, humanism and the arts have no global mechanisms to match those of the institutional structures of governance and subjectivity creation represented by international capitalism, and in particular transnational corporations and supranational agencies such as the World Trade Organization. In effect, capitalist institutions and practices are free-riding on moral and social capital which capitalism itself is not able to reproduce. Instead, the constant process of upheaval, and the built-in requirement of resource and labour mobility, constantly undermines the moral foundations on which the market society relies for its effective functioning.

---

[15]   Ibid., pp. 275–6.
[16]   Ibid., p. 112.
[17]   Ibid., p. 121.

This analysis exposes a deeper metaphysical problem with Novak's defence of global capitalism. He argues that the market is a unique device for the release and mobilization of human creative powers and potentialities, and that it is therefore the key social dynamic which enables humans to mirror, share and release the creative powers hidden by the creator in the creature. However, viewed in an ecological perspective, far from being the fulfilment of creation, capitalism appears to be on a collision course with the planet.[18] This collision course springs from the ontological assumption, which Novak shares with Hardt and Negri and which they trace from Scotus through Spinoza, that it is human willing which is the source of fertility, productiveness and value in the natural order and in human being. For the modern economist, and here there is no difference between Hardt and Negri and Novak, wealth and value are human products, and not divine gifts, and material existence, or what Christians call creation, is in effect redeemed *through* human effort and human making. As Novak puts it 'nature is not regarded as achieved, completed, finished. Creation is unfinished. There are things human beings have yet to do'.[19] Humans also in Novak's view are achieved, completed and redeemed *through* their choices, and in particular through the productive activities of invention and exchange fostered by democratic capitalism.

This account of the centrality of human willing and making to the redemption of being, both human and non-human, is deeply connected to Novak's view that the material world is unfinished, incomplete, and to be transformed and completed through global capitalism. It is also connected with the doctrine of unintended consequences, which Novak, like Adam Smith and Reinhold Niebuhr, identifies with an account of divine providence. Its origin may be traced to Vico's *New Science* and Bacon's *Novum Organum* and it is mediated by Adam Smith to the European Enlightenment. For Smith, divine providence works through the invisible hand of the market to produce the common good from individual acts of willing. But what kind of god is this who works in this way? It is clearly not the God who is revealed in Jesus Christ to redeem all creation and human being from sin and death. For the god of the market is a god who redeems through human acts of willing, and through a long chain of destruction, and not through divine action to reinstate the peace of the reign of God. As Stephen Long points out, Novak's is a vestigial Christian theology designed to make theology *relevant* to the global market while not challenging the autonomy of the market from divine sovereignty.[20] Like Hardt and Negri, Novak believes that human beings, and the collectively constructed global market, are the transcendent agents operative within history from which value, and liberation, originate. The principal difference between Novak and Hardt and Negri is that whereas for the latter it is the 'multitude' of displaced workers, migrants and unemployed who will rise up to redeem the global condition of

---

[18]   See Michael S. Northcott, *A Moral Climate. The Ethics of Global Warming* (London, 2007).

[19]   Novak, *Democratic Capitalism*, p. 73.

[20]   D. Stephen Long, *Divine Economy: Theology and the Market* (London, 2000), p. 78.

humankind, for Novak it is the regnant lords of the market – industrial corporations – who will provide for all human needs and aspirations.[21]

For Novak the immanent conditions of the market empire, and in particular the competitive scarcities of food, land, water and other resources that it introduces to traditional societies, are the source of political transition to law-based, democratic and therefore 'free' nation states.[22] This is why American neoconservatives embrace the language of empire, and vaunt America's newly discovered imperial role in shaping a 'new Middle East' and even a 'new American century'. Liberty, productive power, the invisible hand of the market are the means through which human societies are redeemed. The inventor, the maker, the manager and the warrior are the transformative agents in the neoconservative social vision, but only when they can exercise this agency in a context of conflict and competition for markets and resources, and for such values as 'freedom', 'liberty' and 'democracy'.

The anthropological assumptions shared by Novak and Hardt and Negri are more profound than their differences. The core assumption is that the human condition is one of inherent conflict and struggle for limited and scarce natural resources, an assumption which assumes foundational violence and original scarcity. They also share the view that the conditions for the liberation of humanity lie within the unfolding of certain amoral and impersonal processes and tensions which lie beneath the surface of history. And finally they share the view that sovereignty over human society emanates from the ability of individuals and collectivities to engage these unfoldings creatively, or in other words to derive agency from immanence. Where Hardt and Negri differ from Novak and other advocates of neoconservative and neo-imperial dogma is in their recognition that this location of sovereignty in the immanent domains of history and social process, and in particular in the sovereignty of the market empire, necessarily supplants other sources of sovereignty, and especially the transcendent sovereignty of God. As they suggest, the global market draws individuals and whole societies into its net and in so doing imposes its own particular form of subjectivity on all who participate in it. This subjectivity necessarily opposes the spiritual submission of Christians to the suprahistorical divinity, and substitutes the idolatrous god of the market – and its pantheon of lesser idols – for divine sovereignty. And as with all forms of idolatry this substitution involves a range of sacrifices, both human and ecological.

These sacrifices include the enslavement of communities of persons and ecosystems in the South in corporation-friendly, tax- and regulation-free 'free trade zones'; the selling of the common goods of topsoil and water in the capitalistic incorporation of Third World agriculture, often driven by the local state; and the destruction of the common lands of indigenous peoples from the Amazon and

---

[21]   Novak, *Democratic Capitalism*, pp. 176–80.

[22]   See further Robert Kagan, *Of Paradise and Power: America and Europe in the New World Order* (New York, 2004).

Borneo to the Kalahari and the Congo.[23] These sacrifices go hand in hand with the larger ecological extinctions of species, over-fished oceans, and melting glaciers and ice sheets, as the earth and its multitudes are drawn into a collective sacrifice of history-defying proportions. In place of the small-scale sacrificial offerings of traditional religions the new imperial religion produces a multivalent victimage system on a planetary scale but the libertarian projects of Negri's sovereign multitude and Novak's sovereign corporation provide no grounds for hoping that this immanent destruction can be ended. In place of the political claim of the Church in Christendom to enact the reign of God through participation in the divine Spirit and through such economic practices as the just wage and the just price, we have a theological description of an economy which operates mechanistically and independently of any moral frame. But in the context of the immanent collapse of ecological systems under the assault of a neoliberal economy which is rapidly racheting up its emissions of greenhouse gases and its assault on natural systems including forests and oceans,[24] and which is at the same time actually increasing human immizeration and poverty in both First and Third Worlds, the claim that the market empire will ultimately redeem looks increasingly quixotic.

The negative neoliberal account of liberty as freedom from the restraints of geography or virtue is in reality an ideological mystification of the imperial nature of the global economy and the sacrifices it requires of people and planet. All that the advocates of this ideology can offer in the way of hope that things will come out right is the realized eschatology of the 'end of history'. This inability to imagine alternatives to the present system despite the myriad sacrifices of human and ecological goods the present system requires indicates, as Frederic Jameson suggests, the need to recover an earlier tradition of utopian visioning of alternative futures,[25] the roots of which may be traced in Western literature to the anti-imperial invectives of the Hebrew Prophets and the Revelation of St John of Patmos.

The Idolatry of Empire and the Hope of the Apocalypse

The Apocalypse of St John the Divine has been a significant source of hope through Christian history to which the victims of successive empires have turned for its consoling message that the sovereignty of the lamb has already overthrown imperial Babylon in heaven and that soon within human history it will restore the Church which is the bride of the lamb to its rightful place alongside the returning King. As Christopher Rowland suggests, the Apocalypse is an unveiling

---

[23]   As Timothy Brennan points out, the colonized victims of contemporary Empire are hardly mentioned in Hardt and Negri's *Empire*. See Timothy Brennan, 'The Empire's New Clothes', *Critical Inquiry* 29 (Winter 2003): 337–67.

[24]   Northcott, *A Moral Climate*.

[25]   Frederic Jameson, *Archaeologies of the Future: The Desire Called Utopia and Other Science Fictions* (London, 2005), pp. 4–9.

of empire and its imaginative appeal arises from its 'challenge to the *status quo* and its evocation of a better world, all linked to a passionate concern for present responsibility'. The Apocalypse also indicates that

> the world is no longer to be accepted as it is, that what passes for reality is to be unmasked and the frequent collusion of the world of 'common sense' with evil forces revealed. Its whole drama represents a struggle for wholeness, in which the separation between heaven and earth, God and humanity are at last overcome when God tabernacles with men and women.[26]

The real meaning of the Book of Revelation is that the Roman Empire, variously the 'beast', the 'dragon' the 'whore of Babylon', and the Roman emperor or antichrist, are already defeated.[27] The Roman Empire may appear still to reign supreme, but the time is not long before all nations, and even the 'whore of Babylon', will come to acknowledge the Lordship of Christ. Revelation is, in other words, a powerfully anti-imperial tract. Its coded and symbolic language pointed the first Christians to the real truth of history which is that all empires, including Rome, will ultimately fail and be supplanted by the direct rule of God through the communion of the saints. In relation to the Roman Empire we might even say that the prophecy was quite literally fulfilled.

But what of the present market empire? In the United States, whose corporations and cultural products assume such a vital hold on the market empire, there is a growing tendency among evangelical and fundamentalist Christians to reinterpret John of Patmos as indicating not so much a this-worldly triumph of the sovereignty of the lamb over the sovereignty of emperor as a great conflagration at the end of history in which the faithful are 'raptured' from an earth over which the antichrist acquires unrestrained and malign sovereignty. Like the secular historicists Novak and Hardt and Negri, the heresy of dispensationalist millennialism puts Americans in charge of the events which will bring on this end. Instead of the divine Spirit sustaining the faithful in their anti-imperial fealty to the Messiah – the lamb that was slain – the empire becomes the Messianic agent of Israel's recapture of the biblical lands and of the rebuilding the Solomonic temple on the temple mount which is said to usher in the end time. This dispensational millennialism involves a veiling rather than an unveiling of empire. And curiously the grounds for distinguishing between those who will be raptured or left behind are not their resistance to the idolatrous sacrifices of empire but instead their sexual mores. The mark of the beast is on the homosexual and the abortion clinic but those who worship at the temples of capitalism will escape Armageddon unscathed provided they also acknowledge Christ as 'their personal saviour and Lord'.

---

[26]   Christopher Rowland, *Revelation* (London, 1993), p. 3.

[27]   Michael S. Northcott, *An Angel Directs the Storm: Apocalyptic Religion and American Empire* (London, 2004).

And yet it is precisely in the sphere of economic management and the monopolization of civil society by economic actors that we see the gravest threat to the sovereignty of Jesus Christ over the lives of Christians, their families and communities, in America. One clear example of this is the extent to which the long hours and small number of holidays which characterize the pattern of working life for most Americans have subverted traditional Christian restraints on work, and taken away time from parenting and worship.[28]

In the light of the dispensationalist turning of the originary utopian text of the Book of Revelation into another ideological support to the sovereignty of the market, Jameson's suggestion of the need to recover the utopian impulse as a way to imagine the positive conditions for an alternative future seems all the more pertinent. The utopian impulse finds contemporary form in science fiction of both a novelistic and filmic kind and it is these science fiction visions in late modernity which can help to overcome the anamnesis of left and right in holding on to the 'memory of happiness' as a 'standing reserve' of 'personal and political energy' at the end of history. Jameson suggests that utopian science fiction offers a more hopeful vision of the outcome of recent history than the imperial ideology of neoliberalism since, like the Revelation of St John of Patmos, it aims at the alleviation and elimination of the sources of exploitation and suffering rather than at the composition of blueprints for bourgeois comfort.[29]

The question Jameson does not fully address however is the 'great trench' between the imagined utopian spatial enclave and the empirical reality of the late modern condition.[30] To bridge the trench utopian thought seems to require the Marxist elision of the hoped for future with the work of creating it of the kind which is evident in Hardt and Negri's *Empire*. And as Nicholas Lash suggests, this elision is not one from which the Christian hope is immune either. The difference with the Christian hope is that the coming of the hoped for liberation does not rest upon the agency of the victimized multitude but rests instead on the resurrection of Christ whose triumph over sin and death puts an end to the need for victimage as means to liberation.

Christianity is 'irreducibly eschatological in character' but this character always looks backwards as well as forwards. In Christian eschatology, as opposed to utopianism, there is, as Lash suggests, a narrative connection between past, present and future hope which sets Christian hope apart from the historicism of other forms of utopianism. And it is this narrativity which breaks the intrinsic Marxist and neoliberal identification of victim and agent which Hardt and Negri, and Novak, sustain. It also makes all Christian liberative projects both more provisional and less programmatic than those of Marxism or neoliberalism.[31]

---

[28]   Richard Sennett, *The Corrosion of Character: The Personal Consequences of Work in the New Capitalism* (New York, 1998).

[29]   Jameson, *Archaeologies of the Future*, p. 12.

[30]   Ibid., p. 39.

[31]   Nicholas Lash, *A Matter of Hope* (London, 1981), pp. 234–7.

Against the modern capitulation to the 'condition of pure agency', the Christian knowledge of the resurrection of the crucified one affirms that even in the midst of the exigencies of history the future liberation of humankind in Christ is already begun.[32] Against the utopian claim of the market empire to unite all peoples in a potentially liberatory coalescence, the Incarnation of God in Christ is the originary source of *koinonia* between all creatures and all peoples. Unlike the coerced unity of the market empire, this Incarnational metaphysics is truly global because it affirms that in Christ God reconciled all things to God himself (Col 1:20). On this account the Church, and not the global market, is the place where Christians discover and sustain this unity in the sacred mysteries which are the 'vital core of the Kingdom of God'.[33]

The Church as an Alternative Christian Economy

The metaphysical foundation of the alternative unity of the global ecclesia is the orthodox belief that the creative and redeeming acts of God are revealed as intricately related in the Trinitarian unfolding of the drama of the incarnation and in the early Christian confession and worship of Jesus Christ as the divine *Logos*. As Douglas Meeks suggests, the doctrine of the Trinity is crucial to unmasking and resisting the condition of scarcity of resources that the global empire imposes upon humans and the earth, with corporate schemes to privatize everything from the water coming off the mountains and out of the sky to the healing arts of medicine and the nurturing skills of child care and teaching. The God revealed to the Israelite prophets, and in Jesus and the Spirit, is a generous God whose intention is to restore the plenitude, the fullness of created being in God's redeeming purposes. Scarcity, and the exclusion of so many from the artificial cornucopia of consumer goods, are opposite conditions to the form of life God reaffirms in the Incarnation, Crucifixion and Resurrection.[34]

The early Christians witnessed to this alternative form of generous life against the Empire of Rome in their communities when they adopted an ethic where everyone who had more than enough property shared out of their abundance with those who did not have enough.[35] The first Christians were faced by an emergent market empire just as we are. We know from recent archaeological findings that rural areas in Palestine in Jesus' day were being turned into places of extraction

---

[32] Ibid., p. 249.

[33] Archbishop Anastasios, *Facing the World: Orthodox Christian Essays on Global Concerns* (Crestwood, NY, 2003), 27–8.

[34] M. Douglas Meeks, *God the Economist: The Doctrine of God and Political Economy* (Minneapolis, 1989), p. 65. See also Michael S. Northcott, *Life after Debt: Christianity and Global Justice* (London, 1999).

[35] Justo L. Gonzalez, *Faith and Wealth: A History of Early Christian Ideas on the Origin, Significance, and Use of Money* (San Francisco, 1990).

for the Empire of Rome. Archaeologists have uncovered evidence of large-scale farming premises in Galilee and neighbouring regions, including substantial grape and olive presses, fish bottling factories and other such facilities, and hostel style housing for landless labourers.[36] The economy of Jesus' day was turning from a self-sufficient regional economy into a satellite of the metropolitan economy of Rome whose cities and armies required new sources of food and wealth in distant parts of the empire. The famous roads, and impressive sea ports, which the Empire established from Egypt through to Northern France are testimony to the sheer scale of this trading economy, a truly global economy for peoples living in a world whose known borders were the Atlantic ocean and the mountains of West Asia. And it is against this background that the early Christians developed an ethic of economic sharing which did not recognize the absolute demands of property as these were being imposed on the peoples of the Mediterranean under the Roman Empire.[37]

There is an ongoing recognition in the Christian ethical tradition of such theological and communitarian limits to property rights. For Thomas Aquinas, all persons have natural rights to sustenance and domicile given to them by God in the created order and these natural rights represented a permanent check on the property rights and claims of the rich. Consequently, where the poor were denied their natural needs, it was legitimate for them to steal from the rich:

> in case of necessity everything is common property and thus it is not a sin for someone to take the property of another that has become common property through necessity ... Human law cannot violate natural or divine law. The natural order established by Divine Providence is such that lower ranking things are meant to supply the necessities of men.[38]

Thomas' position is connected to his account of idolatry and his elaboration of the first commandment of Moses. Only when humans are rightly ordered as persons, and as creatures, towards worship of the creator, and set human making in the context of gratitude towards a generous creator, can they recover the analogical relationship between human making and exchange and the moral and spiritual economy of the divine Trinity which is enacted in the mystical and participative space of Christian liturgy.

How though might this liturgical metaphysic offer any genuine mediation between the market empire and the utopian enclaves sustained by Christian worship? The danger of the liturgical metaphysic is that it does not escape the criticism of utopian thought – that it provides no viable pathways from the utopian enclave to the larger world, or from the present to the imagined future. Thus while

---

[36] Sean Freyne, 'Herodian Economics?' in Philip F. Esler (ed.), *Modelling Early Christianity: Social-Scientific Studies of the New Testament in Its Context* (London, 1995), pp. 23–46.

[37] See further in this vein Northcott, *Life after Debt*.

[38] Thomas Aquinas, *ST* II-II, Q. 66, a. 7.

Stanley Hauerwas, a passionate advocate of a liturgical metaphysic, suggests that the only hope that the world has to be redeemed from the evils of liberalism is for Christians to live and worship virtuously, and so resist liberalism, he rarely names ways in which this transformation might be discerned beyond the practices of the liturgical community.[39]

John Milbank argues that the form of exchange that provides a real alternative to the market empire is gift exchange and so suggests a contiguity between the French anthropological and philosophical recovery of the category of gift – and its theological recovery in the work of Jean-Luc Marion – and the attempts of Christians to resist the colonizing effects of neoliberalism on civil society and in economic exchange. But what form does the category of gift take? Milbank's concrete example is good design.[40] Good design, beauty in art and even in consumer objects, is a form of generosity which can be expressed within market relations but this is only the case when there is a clear and traceable link between design and making. Apple Computers proudly boast on their software and hardware boxes that they are 'designed in California'. But so long as they are constructed in the deregulated, low wage and highly toxic environments of the free trade zones of Southern China even the beauty of an Apple I-Pod or MacBook cannot be construed as analogous to divine generosity. This is why in the Middle Ages the church was locally engaged in setting just wages and prices – because aside from shared deliberation over the worth of the maker and his skills the possibilities of exploitation always exist in monetized relations.

Russian Orthodox theologian Sergii Bulgakov also suggests that aesthetics in the sphere of industry and technology is crucial to the redemption of the modern project. If technology is the 'spiritualizing of matter', then aesthetic considerations can indeed contribute to the humanizing of the technological society.[41] However, Bulgakov identifies the danger of the technological aesthetic which is that a society that excels in stimulating new needs and devising new forms of luxury and wealth is in danger of submitting men and women to the rule of mammon. A technological aesthetic without moral constraints is therefore likely to result in the creation of new scarcities and to exacerbate poverty, and to increase inequality between rich and poor. In other words, a surfeit of luxury, however beautiful some luxury objects may be, produces a moral decline into sensual hedonism. Modernity attempts to

---

[39]   See further Stanley Hauerwas, *A Community of Character: Toward a Constructive Christian Social Ethic* (Indiana, 1981), pp. 1–35. In more recent work he has begun to do this; for example in his *A Better Hope. Resources for a Church Confronting Capitalism, Democracy, and Postmodernity* (Grand Rapids, MI, 2001), he suggests that marriage is a central practice for resisting modern capitalism.

[40]   John Milbank, 'Liberality Versus Liberalism' at http://www.theologyphilosophy centre.co.uk/papers.php: see also Michael Northcott, 'The Parable of the Talents and the Economy of the Gift', *Theology*, 107 (2004): 241–9.

[41]   Sergii Bulgakov, 'The Economic Ideal', in Rowan Williams (ed.), *Sergii Bulgakov: Towards a Political Theology* (Edinburgh, 1999), pp. 23–54.

create procedures and systems which are designed to keep people virtuous – or at least the outcomes of their market decisions virtuous – even when they themselves have been corrupted by hedonism. But virtue may only be had through moral struggle, and this struggle must be taken up in the effort to redeem industry and technology from luxury, sensual overload and injustice. There is consequently a need to add *ascesis* to aesthetics: not the kind of *ascesis* which rejects all modern technological achievements, but the kind which recognizes that an excess of luxury and wealth can displace God and the good as centring goals in the inner desires of men and women, and that devotion to these idols can create societies which are both deeply unequal and deeply corrupt. Bulgakov's combination of aesthetics and *ascesis* suggests that through moral struggle it is possible for Christians to engage in the transfiguration of economic activity and of human making. But they can only do this when the material world which human action works on is understood as grounded in the divine *Sophia*. If it is characteristic of human beings to work on and transform the biophysical environment, then for this transformation to be *transfiguring* it needs to be characterized by 'theurgy' of the kind which takes place above all in the sacramental life of the Church.[42] Theurgy represents the mystic incorporation of being *and* action into the priesthood of creation by the Church, and through life enfolded by liturgy the aesthetic dimension of making is married to ascesis *and* ethics. Such a marriage may indeed be responsible for the transfiguration of economics and of human making in late modernity. But for it to be sustained it requires that the communities where this marriage is enacted actively seek to engage the material economy in genuinely transformative ways.

I began this chapter in considering the injustices and imperial exploitations advanced by the market empire under present conditions of globalization. We are all caught up in these trades as people who travel from place to place, buy food or computers, books or clothes. If Hardt and Negri are wrong to suggest that the liberative possibilities of the market empire are contained in the internal tensions, and in the flows of information and of people that it involves, how might the utopian enclaves sustained by participation in Christian liturgy act as a resource for the transformation of a market empire? I suggest that Fair Trade is the clearest exemplar of a mediating practice between late capitalism and the Christian hope for the transfiguration of the market empire. The practice of fair trade involves a recovery of the kinds of moral order and restraint over economic activity such as those suggested by the property relations of the first Christians, and by the medieval practice of just wage and just price. Fair Trade organizations establish long-term relationships with their suppliers and they ensure that a just wage is paid to producers and that this wage is reflected in the just price of fair trade goods.[43] The anonymity of the global market is resisted by the Fair Trade model

---

[42] Rowan Williams, 'The Unfading Light: Introduction', in Williams, *Sergii Bulgakov*, pp. 128–9.

[43] Geoff Moore, 'The Fair Trade Movement: Parameters, Issues and Future Research', *Journal of Business Ethics*, 53 (2004): 73–86.

which reconnects consumers and producers in a moral economy where economic exchanges acquire again the character of gift exchange.[44] It is therefore particularly significant that fair trade began in Britain in the worshipping community of a theological college, namely St John's College in the University of Durham. It was members of this college who first established a cooperative trading venture in a vicarage in Newbottle in County Durham which led to the establishment of Traidcraft, the first Fair Trade organization in Britain.[45] Traidcraft remains Britain's largest Fair Trade organization and in its mission statement it continues to affirm the moral and spiritual basis of its trading relationships. The Christian origins of Fair Trade indicate that the utopian space opened up by the theurgic actions of Christian communities is not a sectarian option but a genuine source of transformation which already shows the possibility of the moral transfiguration of the market empire.

---

[44]   Gavin Fridell, 'Fair Trade and the International Moral Economy: Within and Against the Market', Centre for Research on Latin America and the Caribbean, York University, CERLAC Working Paper Series (January 2003).

[45]   Chris Sugden, *Fair Trade as Christian Mission* (Bramcote, 1999).

Chapter 4
Wisdom and the Art of Politics

Adrian Pabst*

> God is called wise not only insofar as he produces wisdom, but also because insofar as we are wise, we imitate to some extent the power which makes us wise.
>
> St Thomas Aquinas[1]

The Division of Christendom and the Loss of Universality

The catastrophic state of contemporary politics is unprecedented in modern history and betrays a wider intellectual and cultural crisis. Never before since the French Revolution have the West and its allies seen a centrist convergence of left and right and the ensuing absence of any robust ideological contest. The imposition of the neo-liberal 'Washington consensus' across the globe is usually cited as the main cause for this state of affairs, but this is merely a symptom of a much more fundamental change in politics and culture – the ruling classes have abandoned the notion of a public good that can blend personal well-being and the global commonweal in favour of naked individual self-interest and a new plutocracy that centralizes power and concentrates wealth. This is true not just of the authoritarian capitalists in Russia and China or the socialist autocrats in Central and Latin America but similarly of the governing elites in the West and their worldwide client states.

Indeed, the growing polarization of societies between an underclass that is trapped in poverty and an offshore aristocracy that is virtually exempt from taxation bears the potential for economic crises and for social conflict and unrest perhaps unseen since the industrial revolution and the troubles in the 1920s and 1930s. Global capitalism is once more haunted by Marx's spectre that the free market uproots long-established social relations and undermines the fabric of organic cultures, thus creating the conditions for a class war beyond the narrow confines of the nation state. Coupled with renewed ethnic and religious strife and the resurgence of nationalism and messianism, the predicted 'clash of civilizations' and new 'wars of religion' seem to have become reality – less than two decades after the West's self-proclaimed victory in the Cold War and eight years after the rise to power of neo-conservatism. Furthermore, the downfall in Iraq and Afghanistan and the gradual shift of the world's geo-political centre of gravity from the Euro-Atlantic Community to Central Asia, India and China appears to suggest that the

* I am grateful to the Leverhulme Trust for awarding me an Early Career Research Fellowship which supported this research.

[1] St Thomas Aquinas, *Summa Contra Gentiles*, Book I, chapter 31, paragraph 2.

West has suffered an overwhelming military defeat and is losing the battle of ideas. The twin utopia of liberal democracy and free-market capitalism – whose advent after the Cold War was hailed as Hegel's promised 'end of history' and the fulfilment of Kant's avowed 'perpetual peace' – now lies in utter ruins.

The decline of the West and the demise of its dominant ideologies is of course not in itself a new phenomenon. It was in fact one of the dominant themes of nineteenth- and twentieth-century philosophy of history, from Jacob Burckhardt and Friedrich Nietzsche via Oswald Spengler and Arnold Toynbee to Pitirim Sorokin, Fernand Braudel and Alexandre Kojève. These and other thinkers share an emphasis on the primacy of civilization over culture and religion and a reading of world history in terms of the rise and fall of Western universalism. One key assumption is that Christianity was only one among many determinants of the West's universalist tradition and that this tradition owes more to Antiquity and modernity than it does to Jerusalem and the Middle Ages.

However, the writings of Catholic and Orthodox intellectuals and historians like Hilaire Belloc, Christopher Dawson, Nicolas Zernov and Georges Florovsky suggest that such and similar accounts understate the centrality of Christendom in the formation of Pan-Europe and the extension of a Christian order to other continents and cultures.[2] Their revisionist reading corrects the erroneous claims in much of contemporary theology and philosophy of history that a universal Christian political and social order is a departure from the teaching of Jesus and the life of early Christian communities and that the modern Enlightenment State was a necessary corrective to pre-modern feudalism and medieval crusades. Here we can go further. Theologically, neither the idea nor the historical reality of Christendom from Constantine's Empire in the West to medieval Byzantium in the East can be dismissed as a perversion of Christianity. God's Incarnation in Jesus of Nazareth has revealed the filial relation between the infinite absolute and the concrete particular; Christ's Resurrection has reconfigured the dualism between the one and many in the direction of each person's universal singularity which shares in the Trinitarian relationality of the Godhead.[3] The historicity of these events marks the irruption of the *eschaton* in world history and as such manifests the participation of time in eternity. Christ's living embodiment in the Church has prepared the advent of God's Kingdom on earth and thereby transformed the Christian community into the only universal dominion – precisely the meaning of Christendom. As John Milbank has argued, Christendom is cultural and territorial

---

[2]   See, *inter alia*, Hilaire Belloc, *Europe and the Faith* (London, 1924); Christopher Dawson, *Religion and the Rise of Western Culture: Gifford lectures delivered in the University of Edinburgh 1948–1949* (London, 1950); Christopher Dawson, *The Formation of Christendom* (London, 1967); Nicolas Zernov, *Eastern Christendom: A Study of the Origin and Development of the Eastern Orthodox Church* (New York, 1961); Georges Florovsky, *Christianity and Culture* (Belmont, 1974).

[3]   See Adrian Pabst, 'The Primacy of Relation over Substance and the Recovery of a Theological Metaphysics', *American Catholic Philosophical Quarterly*, 81/4 (2007): 553–78.

as well as spiritual and political; it is the body of Christians, the Church. Without Christendom as *ecclesia* that orders the natural *oikos*, *polis* and *cosmos* to their supernatural end in God, the Christian promise of universal salvation remains unintelligible. Without Christendom as the anticipation of God's Kingdom, the Christian promise of peace and justice remains equally unintelligible. Without Christendom, the Christian claim to universality remains largely abstract and strangely disincarnate.

Likewise, the historical reality of Christendom, though imperfect and never fully realized, was an integral part of Christianity. The 'Constantinian turn' was in line with the public political dimension of the Christian faith; more importantly, it marked the recognition that Christianity is universal and thus more than simply another creed that deserves protection from persecution. The problem was not the action of Constantine but instead later developments that reduced Christianity to a state cult and, in so doing, subordinated the logic of Christ to that of Caesar.[4] Rather than legitimating a Christian pacifist or a secular liberal response, this shift requires a theological critique and alternative which was already provided by St John Chrysostom and St Augustine's critique of the sacralization of power and Pope Gelasius' distinction of the two swords. For Chrysostom and Augustine who followed and developed St Paul's teaching, secular rule is confined to the temporal *saeculum* (destined to pass into God's Kingdom) and falls inside the Church insofar as it concerns justice and the orientation of human existence to the Good. The distinctness of State and Church was preserved and enhanced by Pope Gelasius I who emphasized the difference between ecclesial *auctoritas* and secular *dominium*, with the former having absolute priority over the latter[5] – since eternity enfolds time and the finite realm only *is* to the extent that it mirrors and reflects God's infinite being and goodness. So configured, politics and the law are secular (in the sense of belonging to the *saeculum*) without being divorced from religion – a unique legacy of Christendom to Europe and the world at large.

The defenders of Christian universality from St Paul via the Church Fathers and medieval scholastics to modern and late modern Christian philosophers like Ralph Cudworth and Vladimir Solovyov all shared a commitment to the idea of government as a divine gift and the subordination of all institutions to natural law in line with divine wisdom as mediated through the Church. In his exposition of the Epistle to the Romans, Chrysostom exhorts Christians not to reject the public political realm as profane but instead to judge secular rule in terms of its divine

---

[4] Emperor Theodosius' decree in 391, which established Christianity as the official religion of the Empire, was in some respect an antecedent of the later secular *dérive*, but Theodosius' legacy also includes the abolition of state support for paganism, the ecumenical Council of Constantinople in 381 and the last reunification of the eastern and western part of the Empire before the fall of Rome.

[5] Gelasius I, 'Letter to Emperor Anastasius' in Oliver O'Donovan and Joan Lockwood O'Donovan (eds), *From Irenaeus to Grotius: A Sourcebook in Christian Political Thought, 100–1625* (Grand Rapids, MI, 1999), pp. 177–9.

foundation and finality: 'Don't raise objections about one or another abuse of government, but look at the appropriateness of the institution as such, and you will discern the great wisdom of him who ordained it from the beginning.'[6] Within a Christian order, wisdom and politics are inseparable because, as I shall argue below, politics is the just and harmonious ordering of relations within the city according to the supreme Good – an account that can be traced to the theological transformation of Neo-Platonism by both the eastern and the western Christian tradition. Drawing on St Augustine and Solovyov, I will argue that knowledge of the Good is only given to us through divine wisdom that has made all things and ordered them to their end in God. To restore politics therefore requires the recovery of divine wisdom and the re-conceptualization of human knowledge – an integral vision that we owe in large part to Christendom and that was lost after its demise.[7]

Returning briefly to the earlier point about its historical reality, it is hard to overstate the importance of Christendom in European and world history. First, Christendom was not simply a Roman invention that was confined to the Latin West. Following Dimitri Obolensky's ground-breaking work, there is amply evidence to suggest that from late Antiquity to early modernity large parts of Eastern Europe from the Balkans and Romania via the territories on both sides of the Danube to the Ukraine, Russia and beyond lay within the orbit of Byzantium's religious, political and cultural influence. Taken together, these lands constituted a commonwealth of kingdoms and nations which over time built a shared civic tradition.[8] Only the 'Byzantine Commonwealth' and its lasting legacy can explain how the East was christianized and why it has since then formed an integral part of Pan-Europe.[9] Without Eastern Christendom (and the defence of Western Christianity by Charlemagne and King Alfred the Great in the ninth century),[10] Christian Europe might have succumbed to the invasion by Muslims in the South and the East and by pagan Vikings in the North-West. Moreover, from the eleventh to the fourteenth century, the periodic religious and monastic revival in Byzantium provided a bulwark against the Mongols and gradually shifted the focus of the

---

[6]   John Chrysostom, 'Twenty-Fourth Homily on Romans', in *From Irenaeus to Grotius*, p. 95.

[7]   The emphasis on Aristotle at the expense of Plato and the misreading of Augustine's Neo-Platonism as the source of the western proto-secular turn towards the independence of the natural realm are to my mind the main problems with the otherwise important book by David Bradshaw, *Aristotle East and West: Metaphysics and the Division of Christendom* (Cambridge, 2004).

[8]   See his seminal book, *The Byzantine Commonwealth: Eastern Europe, 500–1453* (London, 1984).

[9]   Dimitri Obolensky, *Byzantium and the Slavs: collected studies* (London, 1971); *The Byzantine Inheritance of Eastern Europe* (London, 1982).

[10]   I owe the point about the historical significance of King Alfred to conversations with John Milbank.

Russian Orthodox Church away from national power towards trans-national reconciliation of the Northern periphery with its centre in Constantinople. Coupled with a spiritual and artistic renaissance, this realignment favoured political unity among hitherto rival principalities, even though the unification of Russian lands around Moscow introduced a growing split with the Roman Catholic Kingdom of Poland and Lithuania and did not prevent the later dissolution of the supra-national commonwealth into its constituent parts – empires, monarchies and national churches.[11]

Second, the shared reality of Christendom in the Latin West and the Greek East also helped sustain a common theological and philosophical framework, as evinced by a range of works from Boethius and Maximus the Confessor via John Scotus Eriugena and Anselm of Canterbury to Thomas Aquinas, Gregory of Palamas, Meister Eckhart and Nicholas of Cusa. The growing network of monastic communities and religious orders facilitated both textual exchanges and personal contacts. Despite important doctrinal and political differences, the shared body of works framed debates and ensured a degree of theological coherence. Even at the time of apparent isolation, figures such as St Anselm met Orthodox monks and bishops at the Council of Bari in 1098 to address the eastern and western divergence on the *filioque*.[12] Nothing in these (or earlier and later) discussions suggested that the Church was already in schism; on the contrary, there was agreement on the issues at stake and on the need to solve the semantic and creedal differences theologically. As Giles Gasper has documented, Anselm's mention of the universal Church (*ecclesia universalis*) in his *De processione* illustrates how Greeks and Latins were bound together by the same faith and a common – though disputed – theological tradition.

Third, it was the dissolution of Christendom which led to the division into East and West – a break-up that foreshadowed the Reformation and the Enlightenment, both of which fatally weakened the Christian foundation of European politics and culture. The Great Schism was a complex process that cannot be reduced to the events of 1054 but began earlier and culminated later. The affirmation of Petrine primacy by Pope Leo I after the Ecumenical Council of Chalcedon in 451 was part of a wider ecclesial vision to restore unity after the controversies following Nicea and Constantinople; as such, this event cannot be viewed as the origin of the later disintegration. What did cause a lasting theological-political split within Christendom was a territorial dispute between Pope Nicholas I and Photius of Constantinople in the 860s, after which the Pontiff characterized for the first

---

[11]   John Meyendorff, *Byzantium and the Rise of Russia. A Study of Byzantino-Russian Relations in the Fourteenth Century* (New York, 1989).

[12]   For evidence that St Anselm was influenced by the Greek Fathers and that he had access to Latin translations of Greek patristic works in the monastic and cathedral libraries of England and Normandy, see Giles E.M. Gasper, *Anselm of Canterbury and His Theological Inheritance* (Aldershot, 2004), esp. pp. 107–73 and 201–6. On the discussions at Bari, see pp. 174–97.

time the papacy as the Patriarchate of the West.[13] Though partly in response to Photius' anti-papist tirades, this Western shift reinforced Rome's monopolization of the universal Church at the expense of communion with other patriarchates and Episcopal sees and it thereby fuelled a growing estrangement between East and West. What followed was a series of attempts to reunite the Church and the divided polity by holding ecumenical councils such as in Lyons in 1274. Paradoxically, the Council of Ferrara-Florence (1438–39), which reached agreement on a range of contentious issues, marked the end of eastern and western efforts to reunify the churches. Nicholas Loudovikos has argued that in its wake, Augustine and Aquinas were described as heretics by important Orthodox figures such as Scholarios (later patriarch of Constantinople). Moreover, Pope Eugene IV's emphasis on papal supremacy seemed to eliminate the hitherto common ground for ecclesial union. After Florence, the division became entrenched and the abandonment of a shared theological vision rendered reconciliation increasingly difficult.

The schism was finally consummated in 1453 when the Byzantine Commonwealth centred on Constantinople was destroyed by the invasion of Turkish troops. Subsequently, pan-European Christendom gave way to national kingdoms and churches in the East and the growing tension between the papacy and the princes in the West. This event and its aftermath shattered the Œcumene and polity that bound together East and West around a shared – though contested – Christian legacy. The absence of a mediating ecclesial tradition undermined the remnants of Christendom from within and reinforced some of the worst tendencies of Eastern monocracy and West dualism. Thus, the Great Schism helped destroy the theological and political underpinning of Europe's Christian culture and its common intellectual basis. In this sense, it remains historically much more significant for Europe and the rest of the world than the discovery of the New World or the American, French and Russian Revolutions. Without the disintegration of Christendom, neither modernity nor secularization would have emerged triumphant in the way they did.[14]

Indeed, the demise of an overarching ecclesial and political order helped create the conditions for the passage from patristic and medieval catholic orthodoxy to secular modernity. Theologically, the loss of a shared vision was decisive in the shift from intellectualism and realism to voluntarism and nominalism. When on 7 March 1277 the Archbishop of Paris Stephen Tempier prohibited the teaching of 219 theses, he rightly rejected rationalist tendencies in the Faculty of Arts (some strands of radical Aristotelianism and Averroism) but wrongly condemned the autonomy of philosophy and legitimated the incipient separation of *potentia*

---

[13]   Interestingly, upon his election Pope Benedict XVI refused the title of 'Patriarch of the West'. Far from claiming universal jurisdiction, Benedict seems to think that the primacy of Roman See is only defensible by distinguishing apostolic function from patriarchal power and by working towards the reunification of all episcopally-based churches, beginning with Rome, Moscow and Constantinople.

[14]   Christopher Dawson, *The Dividing of Christendom* (London, 1967).

Dei ordinata and *potentia Dei absoluta*. In so doing, he censored those western and eastern patristic and medieval traditions that had argued for a hierarchical yet mutually reinforcing relation between reason and faith and philosophy and theology. Equally, when John Duns Scotus eschewed the analogy of being in favour of univocity, the natural theology he championed failed to preserve the ontological difference between Creator and creation that had been defended by both eastern and western Church Fathers and scholastics. And when William of Ockham denied the reality of universals in things, his conception of theology eliminated divine revelation from nature, relegating it to the supernatural realm knowable by faith alone – a nominalization that aborted the tradition of metaphysical realism which had spanned much of the Greek East and the Latin West.

Politically, the gradual decline of Roman and Byzantine Christendom opened up a space for rival powers and hegemons. The distinction of State and Church within a common polity always carried with it the potential for competition and imbalance. Over time emperors, kings and popes vied for primacy. With the weakening of the Empire in the West and the Commonwealth in the East, national states and national churches asserted themselves against the hitherto shared trans-national political and ecclesial identity, a process that goes back to the eleventh and the twelfth century.[15] (But important antecedents can been traced to earlier periods in both East and West: examples include the monopolization of political power in Byzantium in the eighth and the ninth century and the control of the papacy by Emperor Otto I in the tenth century. The difference between the early medieval and the later medieval events is that other factors, including a joint theological tradition, mitigated monopolization and thus limited division.)

Once the edifice of Western Christendom and the Byzantine Commonwealth was swept aside in the fourteenth and the fifteenth century, Christian Europe began to fracture along theological, ecclesial and political lines. The loss of a shared political framework was a key factor in the rise of the Protestant Reformation, which in large part was a dispute over papal authority, national sovereignty and the power balance between the peasantry, the nobility and the monarchy. In conjunction with the theological shift to nominalism and voluntarism and the concomitant ecclesial-political division (for example when Ockham sided with King Louis IV of Bavaria against Pope John), the political upheaval sealed the exit from a Christian order. The end of Christendom inaugurated the emergence of secular modernity and the rise to power of liberalism in its religious, political and economic guises – a direct intellectual lineage that has been clearly established by historians.[16]

---

[15]   Brian Tierney, *The Crisis of State and Church, 1050–1300* (Englewood Cliff, NJ, 1964); Alain Boureau, *La religion de l'Etat: La construction de la République étatique dans le discours théologiques de l'Occident médiéval, 1250–1350* (Paris, 2006).

[16]   Among many others, Louis Dupré, *Passage to Modernity. An essay in the hermeneutics of nature and culture* (New Haven, 1993); Alain de Muralt, *L'unité de la philosophie politique. De Scot, Occam et Suárez au libéralisme contemporain* (Paris, 2002).

Since the triumph of secular reason, Western civilization and its purported universal validity has become almost exclusively associated with certain strands of Renaissance humanism and the Enlightenment; most recently perhaps, this is reflected in the influential contemporary attempts by Francis Fukuyama and Samuel Huntington to defend the West against its apparent enemies and to chart a path for Western supremacy.[17] As a result of confining Christendom and traditional religion to the dustbin of history, modern republicanism has denigrated Christian universality in favour of two rival variants of abstract universalism that compete for pre-eminence: first, American Calvinist exceptionalism based on divine election and America's messianic destiny as 'a city upon the hill' and a 'beacon of democracy' for all the nations; second, European secularism based on the primacy of reason over faith and Europe's mission to extend the Enlightenment to the rest of the world. Both these types of universalism are abstract insofar as they replace catholic orthodox realism (grounded in the historic encounter of biblical revelation and ancient philosophy and the mediation of divine sovereignty via the distinctness of state and church and the autonomy of intermediary institutions) with the formalism of the central state and the free market and the subordination of religion to the secular logic of God's absolute unmediated power knowable by blind faith (Calvinist America) or man as the measure of all things based on the autonomy of reason (Enlightenment Europe).

Without Christian universality, modern American and European ideals of freedom, prosperity, solidarity and human rights are vacuous and can be manipulated at will. Indeed, the formalization of being, which (as I argue in the following section) is the mark of modernity, has privileged abstract values *vis-à-vis* embodied virtues and elevated procedural values over and above substantive values, thus hollowing out the principles and the finalities of the universal Christian religion and its manifold mediations in and through particular organic virtue cultures.[18] The breakdown of Christendom thus spelled the end of a distinctly Christian political order which – albeit imperfect – to some extent reflected and mediated divine wisdom. Before I can chart its recovery and extension, I need to show how the loss of universality destroyed a politics that sought to order relations within the city according to the highest Good.

Modernity and the Formalization of Being

Since the fall of Christendom and the rise of modernity, ethics and politics are no longer framed by the pursuit of the common good in which all can participate through particular practices that mediate universal ideals. Instead, ethics is

---

[17]   I refer of course to Francis Fukuyama, *The End of History and the Last Man* (London, 1992) and Samuel Huntington, *The Clash of Civilizations and the Remaking of World Order* (New York, 1996).

[18]   The best account of the impact of modernity on ethics and politics remains Alasdair MacIntyre's seminal book, *After Virtue. A study in moral theory* (2nd ed., London, 1985).

reduced to the formulation of abstract and disembodied laws (Kant's categorical imperative or Mill's principle of liberty) at the service of an impoverished variant of utilitarianism. Likewise, politics is little more than the arbitration of rival interest and conflicts between individuals, groups and states. Arguably, much if not virtually all of modern and contemporary political philosophy is trapped in the logic of Hobbes' perpetual war of all against all (*bellum omnium contra omnes*) in the state of nature that legitimates the invisible hand of the free market (Adam Smith) and the central state's monopoly on the use of force (from Kant to Weber) in order to regulate the violence which is apparently endemic to humanity.[19] The modern dualism of pure nature and the supernatural ensures that the promise of peace is relegated to the heavenly city and that the earthly city cannot escape the reign of violent conflict, except by waging a perpetual total war. In patristic and medieval theology peace is already (though only partially) actualized in the Church as the living body of Christ and thus foregrounds the social and the political. By contrast, modern philosophy radicalizes the (predominantly Protestant) focus on evil and sin in the direction of the primacy of violence over peace. The regulation of conflict is therefore the condition of possibility for human relations, and violence – not peace – is foundational of society and politics. Contrary to Augustine's account of evil as *privatio boni*, modernity grants violence its own independent station and thereby eliminates the ontological priority of the Good.

As Alasdair MacIntyre has shown, the passage from a pre-modern virtue ethics to a modern morality of values had lasting consequences for philosophy, politics and culture. Deprived of any notion of transcendent goodness, hierarchies were progressively flattened and organic cultures dissolved. The idea of a lived covenant between Creator and creation gave way to theories of an abstract social contract among individuals, and the practices of universal brotherhood in Christ were replaced by formal and contractual ties that neither mediate universals nor particularize individuals. The formalization of being, which is the mark of modernity, consisted of a mapping of reality that privileges spatiality over temporality and abstracts all individual beings from the mysterious profundity of universal being, devaluing real actuality in favour of virtual possibility. The whole of reality was reduced to a set of spatialized relations that are determined exclusively by the mind and manipulated at will. The transcendence of the sacred *cosmos* which exceeds intellectual cognition was supplanted by the immanence of nature which can be controlled and dominated by individual reason, itself liberated from the limits of communal authority and collective discernment.

Conceptually, this shift can be traced to a strand in theology stretching from Gilbert Porreta via John Duns Scotus to Francisco Suárez. As already indicated, this tradition abandoned the shared patristic and medieval emphasis on intellectualism

---

[19]   On the lineage from Thomas Hobbes via Adam Smith and Immanuel Kant to Max Weber and the contemporary apologists of the market state, see Adrian Pabst, 'On the Theological Origins of the Secular Market State', in Roberto Scazzieri and Raffaella Simili (eds), *The Migration of Ideas* (Sagamore Beach, MA, 2008), pp. 99–122.

and realism in favour of voluntarism and formalism and thereby paved the transition to modern philosophy and contemporary liberalism.[20] Porreta's embrace of a purely 'grammatical Platonism' (Jean Jolivet) introduced an irreducible dualism into ontology by dividing that which is (*id quod est*) from the transcendence of being itself: divine creative and 'concretive' activity produces copies which bear but a weak resemblance to their exemplar (*secundum extrinsica*) – a resemblance which can only be ascertained by abstraction in the mind and which is absent from the phenomenal manifestation of material forms[21] (as for Boethius, whose ideas were well known and extensively commented upon by Gilbert).

The consequences of this questionable variant of Platonist metaphysics are far-reaching. If particular actual things only reflect a general similarity with their universal cause and do not in some sense disclose God's singularity, then actuality lacks particularity. If this is so, then that which exists merely represents one possibility in an infinite set of equally probable possibilities. As Simo Knuuttila has documented, Porreta, 'inspired by Peter Damian's more pious than philosophical ideas',[22] asserts that the actual world and its history are no more compelling than any other possible set of alternative providential projects: 'All things are similarly subject to His power, so that as those, which have not been existent can have been existent, and those which do not exist or will not exist, can exist, in the same way those which have been existent can have been non-existent, and those which are

---

[20]   On the centrality of Duns Scotus in the rise of modern epistemology and politics, see Catherine Pickstock, *After Writing. On the Liturgical Consummation of Philosophy* (Oxford, 1998), pp. 121–61. On the link between late medieval nominalism and the entire liberal tradition, see A. de Muralt, *L'unité de la philosophie politique*. My argument is that the origins of this tradition go back to Gilbert Porreta (c. 1085–1154), whose work (transmitted by the powerful Porretan school) contributed to the rise of twelfth-century radical Aristotelianism. Thomas Aquinas' Christian Neo-Platonism can be seen as the last great defence of realism against formalism before the 1277 condemnations and the unravelling of the Neo-Platonist synthesis in the wake of Scotus and Ockham. See Adrian Pabst, 'De la chrétienté à la modernité? Une lecture critique des thèses de *Radical Orthodoxy* sur la rupture scotiste et ockhamienne et sur le renouveau de la théologie de Saint Thomas', *Revue des Sciences Philosophiques et Théologiques*, 86/4 (2002): 561–99. For a longer exposition of the arguments in this section, see my forthcoming book *Metaphysics: The Creation of Hierarchy* (Grand Rapids, *in press*).

[21]   Lauge Olaf Nielsen, *Philosophy and Theology in the Twelfth Century. A Study of Gilbert Porreta's Thinking and the Theological Expositions of the Doctrine of the Incarnation during the Period 1130–1180* (Leiden, 1982), p. 73 *et sq.*

[22]   Simo Knuuttila, 'Possibility and Necessity in Gilbert of Poitiers', in Jean Jolivet and Alain de Libera (eds), *Gilbert de Poitiers et ses contemporains. Aux origines de la logica modernorum* (Naples, 1987), pp. 199–218. On Damian's conception of *potentia Dei absoluta*, see William Courtenay, *Capacity and Volition: A History of the Distinction of Absolute and Ordained Power* (Bergamo, 1990), pp. 25–8, 65–79.

or will be, can be non-existent.'[23] According to Gilbert, the actuality of particular beings does not reveal anything about God's creative and concretive activity other than his absolute will. Strictly speaking, actualization does not matter because the actuality of particular things can retrospectively be undone. In turn, this implies that the Creator has no stake at all in his creation, except as a demonstration of his utter omnipotence. All that creatures can know of God through created nature is his inscrutable will and arbitrary power.[24] As such, the real relation between Creator and creation is reduced to a purely formal resemblance between the divine exemplar and its human copies.

Duns Scotus reinforced and extended the formalization of being. By equating the cause of individuality with the formal principle of *haecceitas* that is internal to particular beings, he separated the question of individuation from God's creative action. Coupled with the univocity of being and the formal distinction of existence and essence, he elevated the formality of essence over above the actuality of existence and severed the existential relation between creation and the Creator's act of being. Once the relation between God and the world is purely formal and independent of actual materiality (which, for Christian Neo-Platonism bears the metaphysical trace of divine creativity), it is but a step from Scotus' formalism to Ockham's nominalism that denies the reality of universals and thus rules out human cognition of God's phenomenally intelligible presence in created nature.

If divine revelation is no longer naturally knowable and divine will inscrutable, then God is relegated to the supernatural realm knowable by faith alone. It was Francisco Suárez who radicalized the division of revealed theology and metaphysics and the dualism of reason and faith and nature and grace. By privileging abstraction and reason over sense perception and judgement, he claimed that the human mind could know the *cosmos* by reason alone – rational knowledge of pure nature, purged of all supernatural infusion. As the science of being in general, metaphysics threatens the independence of theology by predefining the space within which *sacra doctrina* can operate. Moreover, if knowledge of first principles and final ends that govern the universe does not require theological import, then the question of how things are individual and why they desire to be individuated no longer falls within the remit of theology. If in turn the cause and principle of individuation is no longer transcendent but immanent, then God is also eliminated from relations between individuals and the operation of the *polis*.

---

[23] '*Eque etenim uniuersa eius subiecta sunt potestati ut silicet sicut, quecumque non fuerunt, possunt fuisse et, quecumque non sunt uel non erunt, possunt esse ita etiam, quecumque fuerunt, possunt non fuisse et, quecumque sunt uel erunt, possunt non esse*', in Gilbert Porreta, *In De Trinitate*, I, iv, 72; translation in Simo Knuuttila, *Modalities in Medieval Philosophy* (London/New York, 1993), p. 78.

[24] Grzegorz Stolarski, *La possibilité et l'être. Un essai sur la détermination du fondement ontologique de la possibilité dans la pensée de Thomas d'Aquin* (Fribourg, 2001), pp. 204–5.

Suárez' metaphysics views relations as the product of the will and the intellect which is disconnected from divine creativity and which in no way reflects divine relationality. The ensuing conception of politics replaces divine agency with human agency and his critique of the divine right of kings produces a defence of popular power which lapses into alienation because the transfer of sovereignty from the people to the king is irreversible. Suárez' attempt to establish a natural democracy therefore foreshadows the rise of the modern secular absolutist state. This is reinforced by his account of the mystical body as a political body which is prior to that of the *ecclesia* and grants the State primacy over the Church. Individuation is thus rendered immanent and made subordinate to the secular logic of state power and sovereignty. This move is mirrored by the emphasis on the transcendental nature of unity and the relegation of God to a separate realm which is disconnected from the natural drive towards the supernatural.

The conception and institution of a universal *mathēsis* and the subordination of theology to metaphysics as transcendental ontology marks the reversal of the shared patristic and medieval primacy of relation over substance because this replaces God's individuating act of being and substantive relations within creation with self-individuated beings that are autonomous. Thus emptied of relationality, substances are individual before they enter into contact with other individual substances – the ontological foundation of liberalism. The rise and expansion of liberal philosophy and politics has had a profound and lasting impact, denigrating and abolishing both universal concepts and particular practices in favour of general and disembodied categories and structures, as evinced by a gradual shift away from a virtue culture of public ethos to an ideology of abstract, individual and private values. What caused this was the denial of a transcendent good that individuates everything relationally and infuses all things with goodness, enabling them to desire and to know the first principle and final end of being, the one true living God of love and goodness who revealed himself in Jesus of Nazareth – a relational God, the *Logos* that was always already with God and was God (Jn 1:1).[25]

Ultimately, this process undermines practical wisdom and the art of political judgement privileges modern knowledge and the formalization of politics (and economics). The hallmark of modern epistemology is to reduce knowledge to data and emplotment that is rationally grounded and empirically verifiable. Once the whole of reality has been drained of its depth and profound mysteriousness and is reduced to a universal *mathēsis* of abstract and spatialized relations, the known object is already predefined in order to correspond to the knowing subject. Indeed, the formalization of being is not confined to nature but extends to the mind. Just as objects now no longer bear the imprint of their divine source which they reveal to the intellect via the senses, so the subject now no longer knows being itself by abstracting form from sensation. Instead, the modern mind operates on the basis of *more geometrico* (demonstration from axioms) and in so doing it constructs concepts and representations of the objects that belong to the external world,

---

[25]   See A. Pabst, 'The Primacy of Relation over Substance...', pp. 566–78.

outside and independently of us. The mental invention of a universal mapping of reality turns on itself and is projected back onto the intellect. In other words, the mind does not mirror nature but determines the structures of reality.

As a result, the modern mind is emptied of the pre-modern idea of the plenitude of God's wisdom that is embodied in the active love for knowledge and that directs desire and will to the Good; thus devalued, the intellect is reduced to a purely formal entity that can produce knowledge exclusively through representation[26] – whether it is Descartes' innate ideas making sense of confused sensory impressions, Locke's passive and contentless mind turning sensations into reflections or Kant's *a priori* forms of apprehension and the categories of reason reducing the diversity of sensuous data to the unity of self-consciousness secured by transcendental apperception. Since actually existing phenomena do not disclose the noumena that ground and found them, all that the mind can know is its own representations. Consequently, it is mental construction which provides the ultimate foundation of, and verification for, both existence and essence. In addition to the separation of reason and faith, the subject is now divorced from the object and the mind determines the structures of reality. Vladimir Solovyov puts this well:

> A dualism lies at the beginning of modern philosophy as well, this time not between reason and faith, but between reason and nature, the external world, the object of reason … in modern philosophy, reason as an independent principle had to engulf its object – i.e., the external world, nature – to liken this object to itself.[27]

By elevating the mind to the measure of all things and the 'master of nature' (Kant), modern philosophy privileges possibility over actuality, in this sense that knowledge of essence precedes and exceeds that of existence and the actuality of beings does not disclose either their form or being itself. Particular things are little more than the actualization of logically possible entities – a sharp contrast with the metaphysical conception in Christian Neo-Platonism of potency as a disposition of real powers to be, i.e. a tending towards ever greater actuality as a perfection of participated being. So unlike Boethius' and Aquinas' account of beings in terms of participation in the act of being that brings them into actuality, modern philosophy inverts the shared patristic and medieval metaphysical priority of act over potency and posits the absolute primacy of possibility over actuality, grounding the ontologically desirable on the logically feasible. For ethics as for politics, this means that the Good is either relegated to the transcendental realm which is absolutely separate from nature and sensory perception (and thus only knowable by faith alone) or else the Good is a matter of positivistic individual choice that ultimately leads to conflict and requires arbitration by the central

---

[26]   Cf. Olivier Boulnois, *Être et représentation. Une généalogie de la métaphysique moderne à l'époque de Duns Scot* (XIIIe–XIVe siècle) (Paris, 1999).

[27]   Vladimir Solovyov, *The Crisis of Western Philosophy. Against the Positivists*, trans. and ed. Boris Jakim (Hudson, NY, 1996 [1873]), p. 17.

market state. Once religion and culture abandons metaphysics and embraces positivism, the formalization of being opens up the whole of society to mapping, measurement and management and thereby consecrates the triumph of utilitarian modernity (based on competition, proceduralism and violence) over pre-modern charity (centred on fraternity, civility and a shared practice of peace).

Since this shift from the patristic era and the Middle Ages to the modern age, epistemology has held supreme sway over metaphysics and the knowing subject now determines the known object rather than being illuminated by the highest cause and principle of knowledge – God's wisdom. As I shall argue, without God's wisdom that orders all things according to divine intentionality, knowledge and politics lack the *telos* of a transcendent Good that elicits the natural orientation towards goodness and perfection in union with God. So configured, divine wisdom does not replace human knowledge but enables, sustains and directs the natural desire for knowledge and justice to a supernatural end and thereby accomplishes and fulfils nature in a way which nature by itself does not and cannot.

From Positivism to Metaphysics

To say that human knowing and political judgement require divine wisdom is to say that epistemology and politics require theology. But such and similar claims seem to meet easy refutation. Did not the modern philosophy of Descartes, Hume and Kant falsify the assumptions and conclusions of classical theism? Did not Nietzsche expose the irreducible dualism of Platonist metaphysics at the heart of Christian theology? Have not Husserl, Heidegger and Marion demonstrated that the universal science of ontology and phenomenology must take precedence over the regional science of metaphysics and theology? Well, no. The trouble with these and other similar claims is that they oppose the immanence of nature which is accessible via the senses and reason to the transcendence of the supernatural that is knowable by faith alone. As a number of historians and philosophers have documented, the idea of pure nature was a modern theological invention linked to Duns Scotus' substitution of univocal being for analogical being and Suárez' theory of general and specific metaphysics.[28] Taken together, these two strands laid the ground for the shift from the patristic and medieval symphonic relation of reason and faith and philosophy and theology to the modern primacy of reason over faith and the separation of revealed theology from the onto-theological science of transcendental ontology. Following Scotist univocity and Suárezian general metaphysics, the German thinker Johannes Clauberg (1622–1665) replaced the term 'metaphysics' with '*ontosophia*' or 'ontology' to describe the science of

---

[28]   For an overview and important extension of this argument, see Jacob Schmutz, 'La doctrine médiévale des causes et la théologie de la nature pure (XIIIe-XVIIe siècles)', *Revue thomiste* 101 (2001): 217–64.

being *qua* being[29] – a common nature or degree of being that is both in God and creatures. In turn, this invention gave rise to two traditions that have dominated philosophy ever since: the transcendental philosophy of Descartes, Wolff and Kant and immanentist ontology from Spinoza to Deleuze.

Partly as a result of their shared theological origins, these two traditions run into similar conceptual problems. Philosophically, neither can give an adequate account of infinity and finitude and the link that may pertain between them. For instance, Spinoza and his (contemporary) disciples, by positing the separation of the infinite and finite (e.g. *Ethica* I, P28), struggle to explain why the *infinite* substance would express itself not just in infinite immediate and infinite mediate modes but in *finite* modes too. Here concepts such as self-expression or production are descriptive, not explanatory. If the link between substance and finite modes is unclear, then the reverse is also true: in the absence of final causation, finite modes rely on their own *conatus* and do not need the substance for their sustenance in being (e.g. *Ethica* III, P6). Likewise, according to Kant (in the section on Transcendental Aesthetics in the *Critique*) the idea of infinity is regulative, not constitutive; it cannot condition actual knowledge because to say that 'the universe is infinite' would be to transgress the limits of the sensible within which human knowledge operates. If infinity cannot be an object of knowledge for Kant, then only the 'architectonic nature of reason' and ideas of reason such as God, freedom and immortality can accomplish reason's natural striving for unity. But it is not clear why there are such ideas or why there is a natural desire for a higher unity. Ironically, immanentist ontology fails to explain the finitude of being, whereas transcendental philosophy cannot account for what lies beyond the realm of the natural world.

Politically, a similar conceptual problem arises. The transcendental defence of freedom and the immanentist case for equality fail on their own terms because in different ways they are unable to demonstrate the validity of their assumptions. Transcendental philosophy posits the idea of freedom but its denial of a transcendent Good that endows all beings with a natural desire for justice means that the foundation of an ethical quest and a substantive (rather than merely procedural) moral vision remains unexplained. Immanentist ontology asserts natural equality but its rejection of a transcendent Good which brings all things into actuality means that in reality groups of individuals (i.e. Spinoza's finite modes) are locked into competition with rival groups of individuals. This conflict mirrors the nature of finite modality which is at once a necessary reality and a contingent illusion. Only the sages transcend this aporetic condition and can grasp the commonality of the substance below and beyond the individuality of finite modes. The Spinozist vision of politics oscillates between a *de facto* autocracy of the wise and a *de iure* democracy of the ignorant.

---

[29]   Johannes Clauberg, *Elementa philosophiae sive ontosophiae* (1647). See Etienne Gilson, *L'Être et l'Essence* (2nd ed., Paris, 1972), pp. 144–86; Jean-François Courtine, *Suarez et le système de la métaphysique* (Paris, 1990), pp. 246–92, 436–57.

Moreover, post-modern pluralism – like modern liberalism – is caught between a transcendentalism that is blind and a positivism that is empty: just as liberalism appeals to unintelligible transcendental foundations in order to ground universal ideas that legitimate procedural values like representation, so pluralism can only secure positivistic notions of diversity by appealing to difference or alterity, both of which are residually transcendental. As such, both pluralism and liberalism represent a false universalism that is, first of all, predicated on abstract and disembodied principles and categories and, secondly, denies the existence of a substantive transcendent Good which can order conflicting freedoms and direct the diversity of difference to the unity of common being in which all beings participate. So the more radical move is to view liberalism and pluralism as mirror images of each other and to re-establish theology as the only metaphysics and politics that can defend the universal ideals that liberals and pluralists purport to offer but fail to deliver.

Contemporary attempts to re-instate a theological metaphysics and politics can no longer ignore the work of Vladimir Solovyov.[30] Perhaps more so than any other nineteenth-century figure, he shows that the speculative philosophy of rationalism and the practical philosophy of empiricism share the same conceptual basis – a metaphysics that seals the exit from metaphysics and consecrates the triumph of positivism in all areas of theory and practice. Ten key 'moments' are identified by Solovyov in the long transition from late medieval scholasticism to nineteenth-century nihilism:[31] first, separating the rationality of individual thought and the authority of communal faith from their single source, divine wisdom (wrongly attributed to Eriugena); second, elevating reason over faith and mind over nature (late medieval nominalism); third, dissociating individual beings and their knowledge from the wholeness of reality and the divine wisdom that infuses the entire created universe (Descartes and Spinoza); fourth, bridging the gap between the internal unity of the knowing subject and the external unity of known reality through representation (Leibniz, Bacon, Hobbes, Locke, Berkeley and Hume); sixth, dividing phenomena from noumena and replacing realism, rationalism and empiricism with transcendental idealism (Kant); seventh, rethinking the Kantian knowing subject in terms of self-consciousness and the absolute subject and, concomitantly, developing critical philosophy in the direction of pure subjective idealism (Fichte and Schelling); eighth, redefining the absolute principle of all being as the very form of concept and overcoming the split between idealism and rationalism by way of absolute panlogism (Hegel); ninth, positing a concept-independent reality and reconfiguring empirical philosophy in the direction of materialism (Marx); tenth, reducing matter to its atomic constituents and the human intellect to the physical brain, thereby equating consciousness with the

---

[30]   The absence of Solovyov and other leading Russian religious philosophers of the nineteenth and the twentieth century is one of the main shortcomings of Frédéric Nef's book *Qu'est-ce que la métaphysique?* (Paris, 2004).

[31]   Solovyov, *The Crisis of Western Philosophy*, introduction and chapter 1, pp. 11–69.

sensory perception of external, material phenomena (Comte, Mill and Spencer). In short, positivism constitutes the end-point of late medieval scholasticism and represents the triumph of 'positive science' (Comte) over theology and metaphysical philosophy[32] – a victory with profound consequences for religion, culture and politics.[33]

Leaving aside the detail of his reading of history, Solovyov's argument that only theology can guard against the separation of mind from world and the primacy of subject over object in modern philosophy outwits in advance Nietzsche's attack on Platonism as inherently dualist and Christianity as otherworldly. It also refutes Heidegger's charge that metaphysics is constitutively onto-theological, Derrida's accusation that the whole of Western thought is coterminous with Plato's 'phallogocentrism' and Levinas' assertion that philosophy is totalizing and must be overcome in the direction of an ethics of alterity. The significance of Solovyov's argument becomes fully clear when seen in conjunction with his conclusion that positivism is valid exclusively in natural sciences because only 'external relative phenomena as such must be studied in an external relative manner'.[34] The implication is that positivistic physical sciences, on account of their premises and their method, bracket the reality of transcendence and God and are thus incapable of refuting metaphysics or theology. The problem, as Solovyov already foresaw, is that positivism in the natural or the social sciences claims universal validity and arrogates for itself the monopoly on truth: the whole of reality can be reduced to external empirical phenomena that are scientifically knowable, and it is the physical brain that alone can determine what is real and how it is structured. (This impoverished view has led philosophers and natural scientists from Russell and Popper to Dennett and Dawkins to propound a militant form of atheism that is scientifically questionable and philosophically illiterate.) Thus, the mark of positivism is to enthrone the mind as the sole source of knowledge – at the expense of nature and the link that might pertain between them. But rather than annulling the possibility of religion and philosophy, this opens a space for the recovery of a theological metaphysics. For only theology can give an account of the relation between subjectivity and objectivity and the higher unity that binds them together.

This is what Solovyov explores in his book *The Critique of Abstract Principles* of 1880, where he develops a 'critique of critiques' of the entire tradition of post-scholastic philosophy by arguing that modern abstraction either separates the mind from the world or reduces reality to particular aspects and as such cannot encapsulate the 'unity-of-all' (*vseedinstvo*, literally the 'whole of things').[35]

---

[32]   Ibid., pp. 150–68.

[33]   Andrew Wernick, *Auguste Comte and the Religion of Humanity: the post-theistic program of French social theory* (Cambridge, 2001), pp. 1–21, 81–115, 186–220.

[34]   Solovyov, *The Crisis of Western Philosophy*, p. 167.

[35]   Vladimir Solovyov, *Critique of Abstract Principles*, pp. v–vi, quoted in Paul Valliere, *Modern Russian Theology. Bukharev, Soloviev, Bulgakov – Orthodox Theology in a New Key* (Edinburgh, 2000), p. 121.

Whereas the rationalist philosophy of Descartes or Hegel is 'a system of concepts without any reality', the empiricist philosophy of positivism is 'a system of facts without any inner connection'. In consequence, neither is equal to the unity of being. Solovyov's critique is not limited to theoretical philosophy but extends to aesthetics and to practical philosophy, including ethics, politics, economics and the social sciences. Modern theories of aesthetics deny that beauty is objective and universal; instead, it is claimed that 'beauty in things exists merely in the mind which contemplates them' (as David Hume wrote in his *Essays, Moral and Political* of 1742). Similarly, modern accounts of ethics absolutize one element of the social and political reality (like the law or utility) to the detriment of the rest. The same problem applies to politics: the liberal defence of individual freedom and the socialist emphasis on collectivity represent two extremes that mirror each other and cannot meet 'the ideal of a free communality' (*svobodnaia obshchinnost*).[36] By adopting the same positivistic approach as the natural sciences, the humanities and social sciences reject any import from metaphysics and are therefore unable to describe or conceptualize the integral nature of being.

Taken to its logical conclusion, Soloyov's critique of positivism transforms itself into an argument for theology. In a more radically metaphysical fashion than Schelling and Blondel, he demonstrates that consciousness and the physical world are not purely immanent but refer to a transcendent unity that binds together the human and the cosmic. For Solovyov, it is the freedom of consciousness that intimates something in excess of the brain's physical functions. The human spirit cannot be reduced to nature because it is able to reflect upon the universe as a whole. Likewise, nature is not simply a mass of inert materiality but instead constitutes a living reality that makes itself known to the mind via the senses. What the human and the cosmic share is an energy or power of existence that brings them into actuality and sustains them in being. Just as consciousness cannot be its own ground or object, so the world cannot be its own foundation or finality. Both human consciousness and the physical world stand in some reciprocal relation that cannot be reduced to either. The interaction between the human and the natural discloses the transcendence of immanence and the existence of an all-encompassing unity, both of which escapes the positivist prism. That is how Solovyov refutes positivism and restores metaphysics. The natural desire of all human and cosmic reality to surpass itself in the direction of the absolute is a sign that the absolute is always already related to the universe. Such an asymmetric relation calls forth a theological metaphysics because the freedom that is expressed in the act of self-transcendence can only be the gift of a supremely free God who did not need to create the world but chose to do so out of love and goodness. And we know the Creator God because he made himself known to us, as the living God of Israel and the incarnate God in Jesus of Nazareth. All of which points to the truth of Christian universalism.

---

[36]   Solovyov, *Critique of Abstract Principles*, p. 166, quoted in Valliere, *Modern Russian Theology*, p. 127.

Here Solovyov's reasoning is neither logically circular nor theologically self-validating. Instead, he begins his reflections on revelation with a conceptual history of religious evolution and then argues that Christian theology offers a re-description of reality which reveals the Christic orientation of the human-cosmic realm and the triune structure of the whole of reality, divine and natural. First of all, Platonist metaphysics is indispensable to theology because it demonstrates how the divine infinite is intelligible to the finite human intellect. Instances of beauty and harmony in the world are not illusions of the mind but imperfect reflections of the perfect beauty and harmony that characterizes the divine Good which endows all things with the natural desire for knowledge and justice. The crucial contribution of biblical revelation is to show that the divine is a living personal God who established a covenant with the people of Israel. Christianity is the fulfilment of all religions: Jesus Christ does not merely subsume and accomplish all pre-existing notions of divinity; uniquely, he reveals himself as the Son of God, the divine humanity, the living incarnate truth, the *Logos* that sustains everything which has been created out of nothing.

Second, the form of the human-cosmic order is indeed Christic. To make this point, Solovyov does not invoke either supernatural faith in scriptural revelation or pure reason and logic; instead, he argues that the history of humanity and the whole of reality are in some sense ordered towards the Christian God:

> Strictly speaking, the incarnation of Divinity is not something miraculous, that is, it is not alien to the general order of being. On the contrary, it is essentially connected with the whole history of the world and humankind ... This appearance of God in the human flesh is only a more complete, more perfect theophany in a series of other, imperfect, preparatory, and transformative theophanies ... Both these new and unprecedented appearances [the birth of the first and the second Adam] were prepared for in advance by all that had happened before; they constituted what the former life desired, what it strove and moved towards. All nature strove and gravitated towards humanity, while the whole history of humanity was moving toward Divine humanity.[37]

Unlike the logic of necessity that governs Hegel's rational idealism, Solovyov inaugurates something like an existential realism that links free divine kenotic self-renunciation with cosmic and human self-transcendence of natural limits in the actually existing person of Christ. The real event of the Incarnation thus marks the ontological and historical coincidence of divine kenosis that upholds the natural order and of human-cosmic anagogy that reveals divine humanity and deifies creation. As such, the Incarnation confirms and fulfils rather than annuls nature, and nature discloses and describes rather than conceals God's manifestation in the world. Only Christian theology can give a rationally intelligible account of

---

[37]   Vladimir Solovyov, *Lectures on Divine Humanity*, trans. and ed. Boris Jakim (Hudson, NY, 1995 [1880]), p. 157.

divine revelation because only in and through Jesus Christ is God visible and can be known as a personal Creator God.

The higher unity that pertains between subject and object – the 'whole of things' – is, according to Solovyov, best understood as the union of the divine with the cosmic and the human in the unique person of Christ. Perhaps more so than any other nineteenth-century figure, Solovyov shows that Christian theology is metaphysical in this sense that it describes the Christic form of humanity and the cosmos and conceptualizes how and why this might be so.

Here we must ask what is it that we know when we know that the world describes Christ and that Christ is God made man. For Solovyov, we know that there is a distinction – though no separation – between the principle that produces the unity underlying 'the whole of things' and the unity itself that is produced. He calls the principle the *Logos* of God and the unity the Sophia of God: Christ is Word and Wisdom of God. This rules out any notion of a fourth divine person and ensures that God comprises both the oneness of substance and the multiplicity of divine ideas that form the divine world, eternally begotten, not made – Christ or Sophia, *not* creation.[38] In the words of Solovyov, 'Sophia is ideal or perfect humanity, eternally contained in the integral divine being, or Christ'. As *Logos*, Christ is the self-manifestation of God, but '[this] manifestation presupposes that other for which, or in relation to which God manifests himself, i.e. it presupposes humanity'.[39] As Sophia, Christ is the divine humanity which God knows and loves

---

[38] '... to God, as an integral being, together with unity belongs multiplicity, the multiplicity of substantial ideas, of potencies or forces with a determinate, particular content' (ibid., p. 109).

[39] It is worth quoting the entire passage from Lecture Eight because together with Lecture Seven, it inaugurated the modern Russian tradition of sophiology: 'Thus, Sophia is ideal or perfect being humanity, eternally contained in the integral being, or Christ. Since it is beyond doubt that God, to exist in actuality and reality, must manifest himself, manifest his existence, i.e. must act in the other, the existence of this other is thereby established as necessary. And, since in speaking of God, we cannot have in mind the form of time ... the existence of this other in relation to which God manifests himself must be acknowledged as necessarily eternal. This other is not *absolutely* other for God (that would be inconceivable), but is God's own expression, or manifestation, in relation to which God is called the Word. But this disclosure, or inner revelation, of the Godhead and, consequently, the distinction of God as *Logos* from God as primordial substance, or Father, necessarily presuppose that in which the Godhead is revealed or in which it acts, and which in the Father exists substantially, or in a latent form, while being manifested through the *Logos*. Consequently, for God to exist eternally as *Logos*, or as active divinity, it is necessary to assume the eternal existence of real elements that receive the divine action. It is necessary to assume the existence of a world that is patient of divine action, that makes room in itself for the divine unity. The specific, produced unity of that world – the centre of the world and the periphery of Divinity – is humanity. Every actuality presupposes an act, and every act presupposes a real object of that act – a subject that receives it. Consequently, God's actuality, based upon God's activity, presupposes a subject that receives this activity, namely humanity, and

from all eternity. Solovyov's contribution to modern and contemporary theology is a new account of the relation between God and humanity in Christ who is both *Logos* and Sophia (later modified and extended by Pavel Florensky and Sergii Bulgakov). As God incarnate who was crucified and resurrected, Christ reveals God's love for his creation, such that it may be once more reconciled to its Creator. Sophia describes the power of deification that is Christ – the force that divinizes the whole of human nature and culture. Divine wisdom is required in all forms of human activity, in particular politics as the pursuit of justice according to the highest Good in God.

As I will argue in the remainder of this chapter, Solovyov's conception of the Good as relational and his use of Neo-Platonist triadic schemes links his theological metaphysics to his account of a specifically Christian politics and strongly resonates with St Augustine's Trinitarian theology. Taken together, Augustine and Solovyov highlight the convergence between the Eastern emphasis on the symphonic relation between philosophy and theology and the Western emphasis on the link between knowledge (*scientia*) and wisdom (*sapientia*). As such, the legacy of Augustine and the work of Solovyov help pave the way for a catholic and orthodox theology that transcends the false theological and political divide between the Greek East and the Latin West.

Divine Relationality and the Sapiential Structure of the Cosmos

As indicated earlier, Solovyov argues that the whole of actually existing reality, both divine and natural, is triune. The concept of God's triunity is not specific to Christianity but, according to Solovyov, can be traced to Hellenic Judaism and Greek Neo-Platonism: within the oneness of divinity there is a distinction between the personal and the essential, between God as an existing being or subject and his absolute essence or 'objective content'. Independently of Christian revelation, Philo of Alexandria developed the doctrine of the *Logos* as the 'expresser' of divine essence and the mediator between the one God and all that exists. Likewise, Plotinus and other Neo-Platonists spoke of the three divine hypostases which express the relation between the oneness of God and the multiplicity of beings. The innovation of Christianity, explains Solovyov, is to say that the *Logos* became incarnate in the living singularity of a historical person and that the Spirit descended into the material and is now the dynamic principle at the heart of the cosmos. Contrary to the gods of natural religion and the first cause of ancient metaphysics which privilege the one over the many,

---

presupposes it eternally, since God's activity is eternal. The objection that an eternal object for God's activity is already presented in the *Logos* is not valid, for the *Logos* is God made manifest. This manifestation presupposes that other for which, or in relation to which, God manifest himself, i.e. it presupposes humanity (ibid., pp. 113–4, translation modified; cf. Lecture Seven, pp. 96–111).

early Christians drew on Hellenic Judaism and Greek Neo-Platonism to make the point that the triunity of God and creation charts a radical middle way that overcomes the sterile opposition between the one and the many and brings divine oneness and human-cosmic diversity into harmonious relation. For the absolute infinity of God upholds the finite multiplicity that testifies to his goodness, beauty and truth which it participates in and reflects and mediates. The implication is that Christology and Trinitarian theology are inseparable and that any attempts to divide the Jesus of history from the Christ of faith go against the catholic orthodoxy common to East and West.

Prior to Barthian neo-orthodoxy and *nouvelle théologie*, Solovyov's work did not just help rehabilitate the early Christian blending of Greek metaphysics with biblical revelation and the insistence on cosmic mediation, human deification and the transformation of the *polis* in preparation of God's Kingdom on earth. His metaphysical theology also extended the patristic legacy in at least two ways. First of all, Solovyov insists that the doctrine of the Holy Trinity is intelligible to reason. Logically, to say that God is or exists is to say that he is an actual existent being or subject with a certain objective content or essence. Since nothing in potency is outside God and everything in actuality is inside God, the distinction between existence and essence amounts to the simultaneous relation and difference of God and the 'unity-of-all'. So the first mode concerns God's pure actuality, whereas the second mode denotes the actualization of all that is (i.e. the real expression of what is already in the first, albeit latently so). The unity that preserves the oneness of pure actuality and the multiplicity of its expression is the third mode. The triadicity of relations is not just true of the modes of existence 'but our own spirit necessarily exhibits a similar triadicity, once we recognize that it has an independent existence, that it is a genuine entity'.[40]

Second, as Solovyov goes on to explain, our inner life is also structured triadically: the psychic actuality of immediate consciousness; the inner actuality of our integral subjectivity; the overarching actuality of our self-consciousness. Of course, the triadic relations of the human subject are periodic phases that succeed one another and are mutually exclusive, whereas God's three modes of existence are eternal and simultaneous acts that belong to three distinct but unified divine subjects or hypostases. But how, if at all, can the human mind make a distinction between the triadicity of the human spirit and the triadicity of God? Solovyov operates this second extension of the patristic tradition by fusing orthodox theology with Leibniz and German idealism. Following Leibniz and Schelling, he says that reason – when it returns upon itself in self-consciousness – constitutes an inner triunity that consists of that which is conscious (the subject), that which it is conscious of (the object) and the very act of consciousness that unites them. As the first and the second only exist in the presence of and within the third, so the third only exists in the presence of and within the first and the second. Solovyov then draws on St Augustine's account of the mind's triadic structure (being, knowing

---

and willing) to overcome the binary logic of German Idealism: instead of a third 'moment' that binds together the first two, the human spirit is now viewed as fully triune, in each and every act. Unlike Descartes' *cogito ergo sum*, Augustine's *ego* is always already the one who knows and wills (*sum sciens et volens*), just as knowing necessarily involves being conscious that I am and that I will (*scio me esse et velle*) and willing necessarily involves that I will myself as one who is and knows (*volo me esse et scire*). As Solovyov explains,

> these three acts are identical not only according to their content, insofar as the one who is knows and wills itself. Their unity goes far deeper. Each of them contains the other two in their distinctive character, and consequently, each inwardly already contains the whole fullness of the triune spirit … Each of these three fundamental acts of the spirit is completed in itself by the other two and thus becomes individualized, as it were, into full triune being.[41]

Insofar as each act is only fully actualized by being triune, mental triadicity mirrors God's triunity, albeit approximately and imperfectly. Solovyov's appeal to Augustine seeks to extend and radicalize the German Idealist use of triadic schemes in a more Trinitarian direction. But what remains unclear is how the human mind reflects divine nature without transgressing the ontological difference between God and creation.

Here we can go even further than Solovyov in recovering and developing a patristic and medieval vision that balances the resemblance and difference between the triadic mind and the triune God. Augustine's emphasis on divine wisdom (*sapientia*) is central to his Trinitarian theology and his conception of a Christian politics. He relates the triadic structure of the human mind to the presence of divine wisdom in creation, and he links God's *sapientia* to sensory and cosmic mediation and to the relationality of the *ego*, the *oikos* and the *polis*. I will begin with the latter argument. Whereas Solovyov restricts analogies with the divine trinity to the logical and the psychic, Augustine extends such analogies to the material and the formal, arguing that individual corporeal forms are relational and that they disclose the triune God. How can this be so? In the *Confessions*, Augustine recalls how his love for material things sparked reflections on the nature of beauty and harmony and led him to compose his first treatise, *On the Beautiful and the Harmonious*, in 380–81.[42] Beauty manifests the unity of a composite and

---

[41]   Ibid., p. 95.

[42]   'To my friends I would say "Do we love anything but the beautiful? What then is the beautiful? And what is beauty? What is it that entices and unites us to the things we love; for unless there were a grace and beauty in them, they could not possibly attract us to them". And I reflected on this and saw that in material objects themselves there is a kind of beauty which comes from their forming a whole and another kind of beauty that comes from mutual fitness – as the harmony of one part of the body with its whole, or a shoe with a foot, and so on. This realization welled up in my mind from my innermost heart, and I

harmony describes the agreement with other composites. Material things are both beautiful in themselves and stand in harmonious relations with other things – they are individual *and* relational.

In the *De Musica*, Augustine shows that the beauty and harmony of things is a function of their 'numberliness' (*numerositas*). Each and every thing and the universe as a whole are governed by numbers and ratios which constitute the individual forms and the relations that pertain between them. Numbers and ratios are defined as measurements or modulations (*modulationes*) over time and across space. Modulations describe motion, rest, and the transition between them.[43] As such, they are neither part of a perpetual succession of anterior and posterior moments nor determined by fixed proportions but instead particular discrete 'moments' within the universal passage of time in space. Each 'moment' comes into existence and passes into nothingness, intimating a higher act of being, a higher number with a greater equality and likeness with the One – individual beings are relational substances in time that emanate from the substantive relation of the triune God in eternity.

In other writings, Augustine expands his re-description of the world to say that all things, corporeal and incorporeal, share three common features – 'measure', 'number' and 'weight': 'every being, substance, essence or nature, or whatever better word there may be, possesses at once these three: it is a particular thing; it is distinguished from other things by its own proper form; and it does not transgress the order of nature'.[44] Measure places a limit on everything, number gives everything form and weight draws everything to its station in the hierarchy of being. Taken together, 'measure' (or limit), 'number' (or form) and 'weight' (or order) are universal principles that govern all particular beings; they characterize the metaphysical structure of reality. This depiction echoes the wisdom tradition of the Old Testament, in particular the Book of Wisdom 11:21 where it is said of God that he has 'ordered all things in measure, and number, and weight'. Augustine's appeal to this tradition throughout his trilogy of commentaries on the Book of Genesis highlights his cosmological understanding of wisdom. He quotes repeatedly the Book of Wisdom 8:1, where it is written that wisdom 'reaches from end to end mightily and governs all graciously'.[45] Here natural and scriptural revelation reinforce each other, so to speak, as nature interprets the signs of scripture and scripture reflects the reality of nature and alerts us to the presence of the divine in the world.

But how can we see sapiential or sophianic nature of the cosmos? This question is related to Augustine's second argument which I indicated earlier – that we can know the triune God because divine wisdom is somehow in us and directs our

---

wrote some books entitled *The Beautiful and the Harmonious*, two or three books I think –you know, O God, but it escapes me, for I no longer have them; they have somehow been lost' (*Confessiones* IV, xiii, 20; cf. *Confessiones* IV, xiv, 23; xv, 24).

[43]   *De Musica* VI, ii, 3; VI, vii, 18.

[44]   *De Vera Religione*, VII, 13.

[45]   See, *inter alia*, *De Genesi ad litteram*, III, xii, 18; III, xiv, 22; IV, xii, 23; IV, xxxiii, 51.

natural desire for knowledge to its supernatural fulfilment in God. Unlike Solovyov, Augustine does not restrict the presence of triadic schemes to self-consciousness but extends it to the senses and judgement. Indeed, the reason why we can delight in the beauty and harmony of material things is because forms in things appeal to our senses that are themselves structured by forms: 'the very sense of delight could not have been favourable to equal intervals and rejected perturbed ones, unless it itself were imbued with numbers; then too, the reason laid upon this delight cannot at all judge of the numbers it has under it, without more powerful numbers'.[46] Augustine's reasoning is not circular: his argument is that contact with the material world via sensory experience elicits our desire to know that which we apprehend imperfectly and do not as yet fully grasp. Far from supplementing human knowledge with divine illumination to bridge the gap between the natural and the supernatural, Augustine's epistemology fuses Plato's theory of *anamnesis* (ἀνάμνησις) and Aristotle's scheme of act and potency and develops both in a fully theological direction.

Following Plato, he argues that knowledge of forms exceeds recollection because sensory experience awakens the soul to the presence of intelligible forms in sensible things.[47] Beyond Plato, he denies that the soul effects bodily sensation and the memory. Both sensation and the memory are activated by the numbers and ratios in objects which kindle our desire for beauty and harmony.[48] He agrees with Aristotle that the coming into being of finite material things is the result of an act of being which actualizes a potency to be and that sense perception is at the origin of knowledge of forms that inhere in matter because the senses mediate species to the mind. Against Aristotle, he contends that matter is not purely passive but instead contains a capacity to receive form, not unlike a seed whose form unfolds in the presence of active forces.[49] Thus judgement of beauty and harmony is a capacity which, like sensation and memory, is activated by the numbers and ratios in objects. Augustine's innovation is the idea that the presence of numbers and ratios in objects, sensation, the senses, the memory and judgement intimates a hierarchy of forms (numbers) which is governed by ordering relations (ratios) of equality:

> These beautiful things, then, please by number, where we have shown equality is sought. For this is found not only in that beauty belonging to the ears or in the motion of bodies, but also in the very visible forms where beauty is more usually said to be … For there's not one of these sensibles [which] does not please us from equality or likeness. But where equality and likeness, there numberliness. In fact, nothing is so equal or like as one and one.[50]

---

[46]   *De Musica* VI, ix, 24.

[47]   Jean-Louis Chrétien, *L'inoubliable et l'inespéré* (Paris, 1991), pp. 15–64.

[48]   *De Musica* VI, iii, 4 – iv, 5.

[49]   *De Vera Religione* XVIII, 36; *De Musica* VI, xvii, 57; *De Natura Boni*, xviii.

[50]   *De Musica* VI, xiii, 38.

For Augustine, 'numberliness' is the ordering principle of all which is. The mind is enticed by beautiful and harmonious things because they embody varying degrees of likeness with the One; individual things are beautiful and harmonious insofar as they reflect the unity of oneness. The hierarchy of numbers and ratios is coextensive with the equality of all things in relation to the perfection of the One. The conjunction of hierarchy and equality suggests an irreducible link between metaphysics and politics in Augustine's cosmology. So knowledge of beauty and harmony is knowledge of the triune Creator God whose wisdom governs the whole of reality.

Moreover, there is an analogy between knowledge of the world and knowledge of the self because both are grounded in God's wisdom. Just as knowledge of the world reveals a relational ordering of all things which intimates God, so knowledge of the self discloses a self in relation – being, willing and knowing (as Solovyov recognizes), as well as memory, love and understanding – i.e. mental triads that reflect the image of the Holy Trinity in us. However, Augustine insists that mental triads only resemble the triune God insofar as we are not exclusively focused on the internal self or the external other but instead seek to know that which sustains them both. Love is indispensable to knowledge because love always already involves the lover, the loved and love itself, none of which cannot be reduced to each other.[51] Love is relational and ecstatic because love for the self and love for the other (or the neighbour) is *love for love* – the incarnate God, Christ as *Logos* and Sophia. That is why Augustine concludes that 'this trinity of the mind is not really the image of God because the mind remembers and understands and loves itself, but because it is also able to remember and understand and love him by whom it was made'.[52] The love that is involved in knowing the real structure of the world and the real constitution of the self is God's loving wisdom, for this is how God communicates himself to creatures. To discover divine *sapientia* at the heart of the *cosmos* and the self is to discover the integral and ecstatic openness and direction of all that is to God – our creatureliness and the createdness of the whole universe. Rowan Williams puts this well:

> Its [the mind's] knowing and loving of God in this context is also a knowing of its proper place in creation's hierarchy, its freedom from temporal and material conditioning in its deepest orientation. It is possible for human minds to be set free for God, because there is nothing in the order of creation that intrudes between the mind and God's self-communication.[53]

---

[51]   Rowan Williams, 'The Paradoxes of Self-Knowledge in the *De Trinitate*', in Joseph T. Lienhard, Earl C. Muller and Roland J. Teske (eds), *Collectanea Augustiniana. Augustine: presbyter factus sum* (New York, 1993), pp. 121–34.

[52]   *De Trinitate* XIV, iv, 15.

[53]   Rowan Williams, '*Sapientia* and the Trinity. Reflections on the *De Trinitate*', in Bernard Brunning, Mathijs Lamberigts and Jozef van Houtem (eds), *Collectanea Augustiniana: Mélanges T.J. von Bavel* (Leuven, 1990), pp. 317–32, quote at 320.

To know that we are created is to know that we are good in virtue of proceeding from the supreme Good itself. Our emanation from the One God constitutes an ontological relation that was broken by the Fall and restored by the Resurrection of Jesus Christ, the incarnate Son of God – Word and Wisdom. The divine free gift of creation grants us both freedom from and freedom for the Creator, but what we discover at the heart of being is that 'God is more interior to me than I to myself' (*Deus interior intimo meo*).[54] That is why we need to keep God firmly as the object of our being, willing and knowing. To do so is to share in his loving wisdom and to transform ourselves and the world according to the highest Good, so that we may preserve the goodness that we have by participation and perfect the justice that we attain by acting in line with God's will. In the concluding section of this chapter, I shall argue that a Christian politics must therefore be grounded in the wisdom of the living God.

Wisdom's Power and the Art of Politics

Both Augustine and Solovyov link theology and metaphysics to politics. The focus on relationality leads each to reject atomism and to develop an organic vision that avoids the false binary between the one and the many. Reality is a vast ensemble of interlocking bodies whose members are equally participant yet hierarchically ordered. Indeed, each distinct entity is, according to Solovyov, best described as an organism composed of parts that are inseparably related to each other and form a whole. Likewise, the entire order of being is an organism in which each part is 'a necessary organ of the all'.[55] If nothing comes from itself and everything mirrors the source of all existence, then God is the universal organism in which all have their origin and end. That is why in *De Civitate Dei*, Augustine likens peace to the well-ordered concord of the diverse members to a body as a whole and order to 'the distribution which allots things equal and unequal, each to its own place'.[56] The distinction but non-separation of the two cities enables Christianity to resist the earthly city where it violates divinely-given natural law, whilst also transforming all existing arrangements in the light of God's wisdom and to change the very nature of power – away from violent coercion towards peaceful persuasion and faithful conversion. The image and reality of the body illustrates the coincidence of hierarchy and equality within Augustine's 'musical metaphysics' where different numbers and ratios reflect in diverse ways the unity and perfection of the one triune God.

Based on such a hierarchical ordering that is incompatible with the false egalitarian utopia of socialism and the empty freedom of secular liberalism, Solovyov defends a theocratic model that is grounded in the ultimate metaphysical,

---

[54] *Confessiones* III, vi, 11.

[55] Solovyov, *Lectures on Divine Humanity*, p. 106.

[56] *De Civitate Dei*, XIX, 13.

ethical and political principle – the solidarity of all things within 'the living divine unity-in-all'.[57] Theocracy does not designate the unilateral control and power of the Church over all other institutions and communities. Rather, for Solovyov, theocracy represents the expression of this solidarity in the political, social, economic and cultural sphere, i.e. the connecting of all the institutions and practices of society to the loving wisdom of God, as mediated in and through the Church. Here the Church neither aborts all existing constitutional arrangements nor monopolizes politics and economics but instead ensures that each realm occupies its own proper station in the overall configuration. In order to avoid false theocracy and abstract clericalism, Solovyov's account of a theocratic model fuses the primacy of God's living reality with the freedom of the other spheres that constitute the entire societal order. Translated into more concrete terms, this means that the Church is only the highest institution insofar as it mediates God's love and wisdom by embodying the gift of peace and extending it to the whole of creation. In turn, this requires institutions and practices of justice that govern the entire political, social and economic system that must stand in reciprocal yet hierarchical relations. There can thus be no authoritarian central state, no unbridled free market, no independent civil society and no neutral civic culture. Such a hierarchy is not a mask for a totalitarian theocracy but instead the dynamic expression of relationality based on the principle of relative autonomy and relative dependence – an imperfect mirroring of the absolute independence of the three divine persons. In the words of Solovyov,

> in a society embodying the norms of free theocracy, all the various elements of society, all the aspects and spheres of social relations are preserved, and they exist not as isolated, introverted, mutually irrelevant fields, or as fields that compete for exclusive dominance, but as necessary parts of one and the same complex entity … Here we cannot have contradiction and exclusivity between the elements, for if all are necessary to each other, then all are autonomous and also dependent on one another at the same time.[58]

Taken together, Augustine's distinction of the two cities and Solovyov's conception of a 'free theocracy' avoid the dualism and secularization of power that tend to be associated with the West and the monism and sacralization of power that tend to be associated with the East. Augustine's emphasis on the *ecclesia* as the only universal polity is preserved and extended by Solovyov's conception of a 'free theocracy' where all spheres of activity are framed and ordered by Christian principles of charity, solidarity, equality and the pursuit of the common good.

Let me recapitulate. The catastrophic state of contemporary political culture reflects the demise of a theological metaphysics and the rise of positivism in

---

[57]   Solovyov, *Critique of Abstract Principles*, p. 168–9.

[58]   Solovyov, *Critique of Abstract Principles*, p. 185, quoted in Valliere, *Modern Russian Theology*, p. 133.

philosophy and politics, leading to the secular liberal dictatorship of political absolutism and moral relativism. If it is true that the origins of this trajectory can be traced to the division of Christendom and the loss of Christian universality, then it follows that any attempt to overcome the current predicament and to offer an alternative will rest on a revivified Christian theology that recovers and extends a theological metaphysics and politics centred on the Good in which all participate. Paradoxically, the West can learn from the East how to retrieve a theological metaphysics, whereas the East can learn from the West how to connect Sophia to self-knowledge and knowledge of the world's triune structure that mirrors symmetrical relation within the Trinitarian Godhead and provides the foundation for peaceful practicing relations across creation. Relationality so configured is not only metaphysical but also political. It translates into practising relations which establish human association at all levels – from the family and the household via communities to a common polity. Even though these may have distinct ends, they are all hierarchically ordered and governed by the unity of the common good. Conjointly, Solovyov's theological metaphysics and Augustine's account of wisdom can help reconfigure politics – not as a science of mapping, measurement, management but instead an art of discerning the harmonious ordering of the cosmos and making this idea real by re-ordering relations within and among the *ego*, the *oikos*, the *polis* and the *cosmos* according to the supreme Good that individuates all beings relationally. Thus to conceptualize the self and the world to surpass the narrow confines of inwardness and to 'spend' oneself ecstatically in the world – to embrace the world, to discern at the heart of its materiality the infinite divine actuality that deifies human power and uplifts creation to an ever-closer union with God, so that 'we evermore dwell in him and he in us' (1 John 4:12–13), 'for of him, and by him, and in him, are all things' (Rom 11:36).

PART III
Ontology, East and West

Chapter 5

Ontology Celebrated: Remarks of an Orthodox on Radical Orthodoxy

Nicholas Loudovikos

I

When I first arrived in England in October 1999, as a Visiting Lecturer of the Institute for Orthodox Christian Studies, which was trying to make its first academic steps, some of the first words I heard here were 'Radical Orthodoxy'.[1] 'Another Protestant radicalism' I thought scornfully, with the usual self-sufficiency of the Greek Orthodox. After some weeks, things went worse and I started to investigate this matter with my school English. I thought, 'What is going on here?' The first thing I managed to discover was that the whole project was about 'participation'; a thought model in a way familiar for an Orthodox person, but at the same time also very suspicious. 'Another Protestant effort of a narcissistic outlet out of suffocating individualism' said the former clinical psychologist in me and I decided not to give a penny for this movement. Note that in Greece (as well as in France, where I did my postgraduate studies in a most traditional Catholic Institute), to be Protestant means to be either totally indifferent or to be 'radical' and full of 'participational desires', and that means interiorism, psychologism and sentimentalism.

Six months later, when I was about to leave, I came across Catherine Pickstock's first book and was particularly struck by its subtitle: *On the Liturgical Consummation of Philosophy*.[2] That was a scandal! That would have been the perfect subtitle for my own book, published in 1992 in Athens under the title *A Eucharistic Ontology*; a publication much talked about in Greece, which cost me my academic post in the Theological Faculty of Thessaloniki. Soon I bought all the books published by RO and soon terror filled my mind since I realized that I seemed to be myself a Radical Orthodox! Fortunately this book, which was the first book of mine, is already translated into English and will be published in the United States. Thus I will soon be able to share my 'fears' with my English-speaking friends.[3]

---

[1]   Henceforth RO.

[2]   Catherine Pickstock, *After Writing. On the Liturgical Consummation of Philosophy* (Oxford, 1998).

[3]   I have published, in Greece, various books on *Philosophical Theology* and *Systematic Theology*, as it is called in the UK, but very few readers will be aware of their content. This obliges me to make references to my own work in order to explain how I understand RO and everything else.

Needless to say that I am deeply touched by RO. A sense of deep, poetic proto-Christian nostalgia is communicated to my soul each time I see a book of a RO author. Not only as a 'ceaseless re-narrating and 'explaining' of human history under the sign of the cross',[4] as John Milbank says, but, first of all, as a deep anticipation for grace. This desire is what touches me most in RO. Although it is not mentioned very often, it is, I think, the hidden cornerstone of the RO building. I will come back to this later on.

Nostalgia, desire, participation: we already have three passwords to the Radical Orthodoxy universe and we will get some more by reading the introduction to the RO volume, published in 1999.[5] This *new theology*, as the subtitle reads, is a passionate manifesto for a new enterprise, which has to become as soon as possible an interconfessional project, that is a nostalgia for the theology and experience of the primitive Church, if it really wants to be something new – and not only a Protestant revival. My aim here is to help towards this direction.

RO thus attempts to 'reclaim the world by situating its concerns and activities within a theological framework'.[6] This is neither a sterile gazing at the past nor a vague apophaticism but 'an indeterminacy that is not an impersonal chaos but infinite interpersonal harmonious order in which time participates'.[7] Indeterminacy, harmony and time are thus three other keywords of RO thought. This order is expressed as 'a fully Christianized ontology and practical philosophy',[8] as divinely illuminated knowledge of an Augustinian type, where faith and reason, grace and nature supposedly coincide. Christian ontology, ethics and epistemology are thus three other pillars of the RO tower of truth. This ontology is expressed, so to speak, as an immanent transcendentalism, where 'all there is *only* is because it is more than it is'[9] – against any 'rational metaphysics, claiming to comprehend being without primary reference to God',[10] inaugurated by John Duns Scotus. Fighting against secular nihilism, RO seeks to establish a non-metaphysical ontology which consummates Neoplatonic inspiration in the Eucharistic experience. That means that all the great biblical issues concerning man and cosmos are reworked within a Platonic framework and in dialogue with post-modern thought. Thus the group of RO passwords is completed: will, language, vision, of course, but also touch, imitation, along with *ecstasis* and, the top of the tops, intersubjectivity, with its necessary Augustinian allusions to state or *polis*. Let me discuss these terms in turn.

---

[4]   John Milbank, *The Word Made Strange. Theology, Language, Culture* (Oxford, 1997), p. 32.

[5]   John Milbank, Catherine Pickstock and Graham Ward (eds), *Radical Orthodoxy. A new theology* (London/New York, 1999).

[6]   John Milbank, Catherine Pickstock and Graham Ward, 'Introduction. Suspending the material: the turn of radical orthodoxy' in ibid., p. 1.

[7]   Ibid., pp. 1–2.

[8]   Ibid., p. 2.

[9]   Ibid., p. 4.

[10]   Ibid., p. 5.

II

Encounter, friendship, marriage, coition understood as that which is described by the Greek word *sunousia* (συνουσία),[11] is the very core of RO. In a word: *eros*, which is impossible to translate into English, as the readers of Plato or Plotinus can understand in the West. If I were asked to sum up RO's quest in a phrase I could say that it is a deep erotic exploration and, at the same time, foretaste of harmony through participation. That means that if I were asked to use only one word for my description I would say: desire, the proper existential synonym for *eros*; given that *eros* is not only human in the Greek patristic tradition. And here we are at the core of our discussion: Platonic, and even more, Plotinian *eros* is exclusively human. As Plotinus says the One 'ἡμῶν οὐκ ἐφίεται' [the One 'does not desire us', *Enneads* VI, 9, 8]. Let me quote the whole passage in the excellent translation of A.H. Armstrong:

> The One, therefore, since it *has no otherness* is always present, and we are present to it *when we have no otherness*; and the One does not desire us, *so as to be around us*, but we desire it, so that we are around it. And we are always around it but do not always look to it; it is like a choral dance: in the order of its singing the choir keeps round its conductor but may sometimes turn away, so that he is out of their sight, but when it turns back to him it sings beautifully and is truly with him; so we too are always around him – and if we were not, we should be totally dissolved and no longer exist – but not always turned to him; but *when we do look to him, then we are at our goal and at rest and do not sing out of tune* as we truly dance our god-inspired dance around him.[12]

'Looking' here means participation and harmony. But let me continue with Plotinus:

> And the soul's innate love makes clear that the Good is there, and this is why eros is coupled with the Psyches in pictures and stories. For since the soul is other than God but comes from him *it is necessarily in love* with him, and when it is there it has the heavenly love, but here love becomes vulgar … And every soul is Aphrodite; and this is symbolized in the story of the birthday of Aphrodite and Eros who is born with her … But there is our true love, with whom also we can be united, *having a part in* him and truly possessing him, not embracing him in the flesh from outside. But 'whoever has seen, knows what I am saying', that the soul then has another life and draws near, and has already come near and *has a part in him*, and so is in a state to know that the giver of true life is present and we need nothing more ….[13]

---

[11] Synousia, *syn* + *ousia*, '*syn*-' means 'co-' and *ousia* means 'essence', 'substance'.

[12] Plotinus, *Plotinus in seven volumes*, trans. A.H. Armstrong (7 vols, Cambridge, Mass./ London, 1966–88), vol. 7 (Enneads VI, 6–9), Enneads VI, 9, 8, pp. 334–5. All italics are mine.

[13] Ibid., VI, 9, 9, pp. 337–9. All italics are mine.

What we have here is a specific kind of participation which has marked Western mysticism as a whole. Let me expound some of its characteristics. First of all, the One or God does not need to love anyone, but he is 'necessarily' loved by inferior beings. Second, the souls have a sort of a natural kinship with him and thus they can be *part* of him. Third, the One has no otherness and thus participating in him means losing my own otherness. Fourth, harmony and order mean exactly participation in the One's non-otherness. Fifth, as there is no providence at all, our love is not an existential fulfilment but rather a 'necessary', volitive 'spiritualization', that is an outlet, an *ecstasis* of our nature in order to find its source, brought about by our will. Sixth, because of the natural kinship mentioned above, I am by definition, in my very essence, mind, destined to dominate what is not mind; that is matter – or the passive part of my soul.

Some of these aspects of Neoplatonic participational mysticism have passed through Augustine to the so-called 'Christian mysticicm' – and were then secularized in Western philosophy. Augustine had read Porphyry in Marius Victorinus' translation and he had also probably read works by Ambrosius such as *De Isaac el anima* and *De boino mortis* which contain important passages from the *Enneads*.[14] I thus completely agree with RO that the Platonic tradition is deeply melted into the original 'mystical' Christian experience, especially in the West. But even if that is helpful for the expression of the Christian experience, it also raises some major anthropological and ontological problems. Let me substantiate this.

1.   First, the image of a needless and self-sufficient God, who does not need to love anyone, caused the constant temptation of his apprehension as a 'great unmarried' (according to Olivier du Roy's ironical expression): a tendency which dominates Augustinian Trinitarian theology until 391. At the same time man discovers his own private castle of self-sufficiency, i.e. his interiority.

This makes easy an ontological anagogy from the human to the divine. In fact, during especially the first period of Augustine's spiritual development (until 391), the soul is the real revealer of the Trinity, while Christ simply offers an example of a modest and moral way of life. The psychological characteristics of the human soul can be referred to the persons of the Trinity and thus we have, anagogically, an ontology of the Triune God based on our physical experience of our selves. The first of these psychological triads (*De Trin.* VIII, IX–X) is that of the lover, the loved one and love. But this triad is not satisfactory as it is possible for it to be interrupted by hatred; the triad of the spirit, its knowledge and love for itself is more suitable. Thus the human *cogito* becomes a Trinitarian *cogito*. Finally, the bishop of Hippo speaks of the triad of *memoria*, *intelligentia* and *voluntas*, and finds the perfect triad in the absolutely narcissistic one of self-memory, self-thought and self-love. Combining Plotinus and Porphyrius, Augustine finally reaches a Platonic analogy, which recognizes God by means of his creation and particularly by man's soul.

---

[14]   Kurt Ruh, *Geschichte der abendländischen Mystik* (3 vols, München, 1990–99), vol. 1, p. 87.

As already mentioned, I believe that this anagogical method represents only one of the steps (that is the first one) in Augustine's Trinitarian ontology. I do not think that he ever abandoned it at all. But in his mature work we also find a step beyond that, a further development and improvement of his previous thought. I cannot present here the arguments in detail, but I think that some of the main aspects of Augustinian Trinitarian theology are very close to those of the Cappadocian fathers, although almost all contemporary Eastern theologians (for example John Zizioulas, Christos Yannaras, John Romanides) tend to reject this fact strongly. I would like to mention as an example his fight against anthropomorphism in the *De Trinitate* (XI, 15; 23; 24), or his clear distinction between *Divinitas* and *Deitas* and his consideration of the Father not as the source of essence but as a *principium deitatis* (*De Trin.*, IV, 20, 29), or the identification, in God, of the mind with being and life (*De Trin.*, VI, 10, 11). I also think of his understanding of the divine essence as a relational reality, which is of paramount importance both in St Athanasius' and the Cappadocians' theology (*De Trin.* VII, 1, 1), and of his frequent use of the example of the three human persons (friends, relatives or neighbours, as he says) instead of that of the one closed spiritual subject. He uses this idea in order to underline the independence and reality of the three divine persons. This is what the Cappadocians usually do, even though they do not insist on anagogy, as Augustine occasionally does.

I therefore do not think that we can speak of an essentialism of Western Trinitarian theology against the personalism of the Eastern one – as G.L. Prestige would have us believe. If we consider at least the case of the Augustinian triadology, we may rather speak, I think, of two types of personalisms in East and West, depending on how each of them understands the notion of consubstantiality (ὁμοούσιον). I believe that in Augustinian theology we have a *sui generis* ontology of personal communion, based on a Plotinus-inspired understanding of consubstantiality. This constitutes the end and consequence of his anagogical method and at the same time a correction and a new penetration. This 'voluntaristic' Trinitarian ontology considers the mystery of God's essential Tri-union as a transcendental subjectification of himself by the force of his will. That means that the three persons are one God because they are determined and unified under the only one goal, the only one supreme meaning, which the will can provide. Here we have a direct influence from the Plotinian identification of the hypostasis of the One with his will (*Enneads* VI, 8, 13), in a new Christian transformation. This will in Augustine is transformed into the essence of God's love, which is, in its turn, the essence of his absolute spirituality (see *De Trin.* XV, 17, 27, cf. XV, 20, 38 – XV, 21, 41). As his spiritual essence, God's will/ love unifies his substance and endows the three persons with their subjectivities, by giving the only ultimate meaning to their communion. Thus we see that this communion does not have a meaning *per se*, but obtains its ontological identity from that transcendental meaning, will/love can provide. We can say that this doctrine represents a philosophical explanation of the mystery of God's union, which is the model of many Western personalisms until today. We also could say that the difference between this personalism and the Greek patristic one seems to lie in the fact that in the latter will is absolutely distinguished from essence. Thus the meaning of Trinitarian communion lies within itself and there is no need of an external meaning or goal, for it to be justified. Here communion is more 'existential' and less 'institutional' (I cannot spell this out further here).

What I mean is that desire emerges here indeed but it seems marked from the beginning with self-fulfilment. The long Western history of the difficult balance between existence as divine gift and existence as human offering begins here. If God's primary desire is his self-fulfilment, man's primary desire is his self-fulfilment, too, that is man's desire is not clearly God's desire and God's desire is not clearly man's desire. Of course, I agree with Michael Hanby that Augustine deserves a more favourable reading than mine. I am very eager to agree that there is a 'doxological subject', which '*is* only as it participates in the ever-arriving gift of its doxological – which is to say, teleological – existence'.[15] Hanby concludes that for Augustine '*all that is not doxology is nihilism*',[16] but when knowledge precedes love, as happens in the eighth book of the *De Trinitate* (VIII, 4, 6) there are still traces of this 'nihilism', because all this exchange does not remove that perspective of self-fulfilment. I may be wrong, but in the following chapters of *De Trinitate* the problem remains: a self-fulfilled God and a man who needs to love him in order to fulfil himself too. I will get back to this later on.

2.   Second, there is the problem of kinship between the 'spiritual' part of creation and God himself and the kind of participation it generates. In order to have 'a doctrine of mystical return to God as unknown source …'[17] as John Milbank in a characteristically Neoplatonic manner calls it, we need first a description of divine ecstatic outgoing and then an affirmation of its human reception. Concerning the former, Milbank and Pickstock write:

> Thus if what creation discloses of *esse* is that it somehow can exist outside of itself, what the ontological revision that is the hypostatic union discloses is that *esse* is in itself this ecstatic going outside itself. For divine *esse* is now shown to be such that *a new thing can inhere in it* [italics mine], to be such that it can become entirely the *suppositum* of a creature outside itself, yet without real addition to itself. This last negative safeguarding of divine aseity might seem to deny that divine *esse* is also divine event, but in fact it achieves the opposite. It denies that divine *esse* can *become* event, but affirms that it *is* event, since an event can entirely come to belong to it without adding anything new. The point must be that God already was, eminently, the new event.[18]

[15]   Michael Hanby, 'Desire. Augustine beyond Western subjectivism' in J. Milbank et al. (eds), *Radical Orthodoxy*, p. 116.

[16]   Ibid.

[17]   Milbank, *The Word Made Strange*, p. 42.

[18]   John Milbank and Catherine Pickstock, *Truth in Aquinas* (London/New York, 2001), p. 85.

We need here – if we are to avoid pantheism – a solid theological ground, which cannot be offered by Aquinas. Milbank and Pickstock speak of a 'created exterior to God, because God's interior is self-exteriorization'.[19] Besides the obvious confusion – so usual in the West – between theology and divine economy, we enter, theologically speaking, a deep darkness. God is the subject of a new event, which is creation and that is 'neither essential not accidental' for him: 'That is to say how the proper accident of the new organic instrument can come entirely to belong to God's being, and yet not add anything to this, nor be related to it.'[20] But although this inconceivable belonging without relating is so strongly affirmed, a few lines further we read that 'from the internal perspective God is *eternally* the God in whom a man inheres, just as he is eternally the God *who has shared his being with the Creation*'.[21] This sharing is so decisive that creation enters finally God's being since 'God, as *esse*, exceeds the contrast of being with becoming, and is eminently becoming'.[22] From an Orthodox perspective, in spite of the good intentions, this seems to be sheer pantheism.

Of course RO are not pantheists. They simply lack the kind of theology which, by overcoming Neoplatonism, can help them express their deeply Christian notion of participation. And this is why I shall insist again and again that RO has to become interconfessional if they want to stay radical. Here, the only way of expressing this 'sharing of being' is the notorious distinction between divine essence and divine or uncreated *logoi* of energies, made by the Greek fathers and elaborated upon for many centuries, from the Cappadocians and Maximus the Confessor, to Gregory Palamas and some modern Orthodox theologians today.

There is no room here to present this very old doctrine, which belongs to our common Christian tradition. I have written a whole book to explain this in terms of an 'Eucharistic Ontology' – my own 'RO book' as it were. The term '*logoi* of beings' is not translatable in English. *Logos* means 'constitutive principle', 'inner principle', 'essential principle', 'rationale', 'reason' or simply 'word'. Identified with God's living will, the uncreated *logoi* are acts (ἐνέργειαι) of his loving divine will in constant dialogue with creation: *logos* means always *dia-logos* (dialogue) in the Greek patristic tradition and particularly in St Maximus the Confessor's thought. *Logos* is uncreated but distinct from uncreated divine being. It is personal (*enhypostatos*) not in the sense that it is a being itself, but in the sense that it is the volitive expression of a personal being who moves his essence to act *ad extra*. *Actus* does not mean here, as in the Aquinatian tradition, the real and active existence of God himself, but his work and 'world' outside of himself. This is a very crucial and substantial difference between the Christian East and West. But it may not be a direct disagreement but rather a misunderstanding. While the West understands by the term *actus* God's real and active existence, the East means by the same

---

[19]   Ibid., p. 86.

[20]   Ibid.

[21]   Ibid. (second italics are mine).

[22]   Ibid., p. 87.

term God's activity outside of him (which proceeds from his personal essence – existence).[23] By the *logoi*, to return to our discussion, God creates, that is *proposes* to beings their own essences and an ontological dialogue follows. If essence is thus given, its 'mode of existence' is only the result of this dialogue between the *logos*-word of God and the *logos*-word of man. That means that the final *esse* of created beings is unknown, indeterminate, because it is the eschatological result of a long dialogue between God and man, a dialogue which culminates in the cross and the resurrection of Christ. Christ, the divine *Logos*-Son of the Father, is himself in his incarnate composite *hypostasis* the ontological presupposition of this ontological dialogue. Christ, the only begotten *Logos* of the Father, the bearer of his will, takes with him in his Incarnation all the *logoi* of beings which rest in him and holds them together in an ontological, hypostatic mode of existence. By this hypostatic union the *logoi* or divine wills are made fully apparent in the flesh of Christ (and can be offered to us by the sacraments). So our participation in the divine energies is simply the way of our participation in the crucified and resurrected Christ. We thus easily understand that the question of the *logoi* or energies is *not* the fundamental theological crux regarding our salvation. The hypostasis of the incarnated Son and his relationship to the Father, which we enter not by nature but by grace (that is by adoption through baptism and the Eucharist), is our primary theological concern here. Consequently, that which is given to us is a personal *tropos hyparxeos* (mode of existence) by grace and not a participatory 'essentialist' connection between different substances. This new mode of existence, our *adoption by the Father in Christ through the Spirit*, is only *realized* in this *syn-energetic* participation in Christ's deified human nature. Although it is accompanied by the contemplation of the *logoi* or the famous vision of the 'uncreated light', these spiritual experiences are *not* sources or causes, or even proofs of this new mode of existence. What happens is just the opposite! What is true, however, is the fact that created being is thus in becoming and this becoming is becoming-in-communion, explained finally by the Eucharistic experience (that is the Eucharistic incarnation of Christ in which we can participate) as a *non-metaphysical ontology that can only be celebrated*.

Thus the uncreated *logoi* or acts/energies of God explain how creation is fully divine – 'always more than it is' according to the RO expression – without being confused with or added to divine being. Consequently, divine being is not divided into a participated and a non-participated part. Creation does not need to lose its otherness while God does not lose his own otherness either. Participation in God is essential, without fully entering God's essence, while by becoming 'well-being', creation does not introduce becoming into God's very being. Theology and economy remain deeply connected but ontologically distinct – Neoplatonism is honoured but at the same time overcome. Western theologians have to understand that the distinction between essence and energies/*logoi* in God, made by the Greek fathers, is not a formal one, but, as Palamas many times stresses, made only by

---

[23]   See David Bradshaw's extremely important book, *Aristotle East and West. Metaphysics and the Division of Christendom* (Cambridge, 2004).

the mind (κατ᾽ ἐπίνοιαν). That means that this distinction here is not a *separation* but an expression of the fundamental *distinction* between will and essence in God which is not of course a separation either. This distinction derives exactly from the fact that God is personal and that means in relational and loving communication *ad intra* as well as *ad extra*. Consubstantiality expresses this loving relationality *ad intra* while the energies, or *logoi*, or grace (which is another name for the same thing) express this loving relationality *ad extra*. Thus the only purpose of this distinction is to explain the very presence of God himself in creation without losing his transcendence. It is true that some modern Orthodox theologians give the impression that divine energy or *logos* is something *between* God and creation. Thus we have a kind of 'ontologization' of energies, as if we had two separate 'beings' in God: essence and energy. In that case Rowan Williams would be right, at least partially, when he compares these ontologized energies with the Neoplatonic henades, reifying what are merely distinctions made 'by mind'.[24] But energies or *logoi* are not quasi-personal agents, mediating the divine perfections to lower beings but personal acts of an '*ek-sisting*' God. Divine energy is *God himself ad extra*, as a manifold expression of his grace, while divine essence is *God himself* not *ad intra* but as *he is in himself*. As David Bradshaw points out: 'This distinction enables Palamas to say what Aquinas so much wanted to say, but could not: that God can *do* otherwise without *being* otherwise'.[25]

Created being is divided, also 'by mind', in created essence and created energies. There is not enough room in this chapter to explain everything, but the uncreated energetic action is absolutely inconceivable without its created energetic reception.

3.   Now how does a human being receive divine ecstatic love/energy/grace? 'By his mind', is the RO response; 'by his respective enhypostatic *logos*-act-energy' is the Greek patristic answer. This difference is essential. Following the Neoplatonic tradition, Augustine[26] and the whole of Western mysticism considers the human mind capable of seeing, in a way, the divine essence. The respective RO position is that because 'we are mind, humans specifically are destined to be deified'[27] – by grace, of course. Elsewhere Milbank writes that 'the capacity of intellect to "be" all things also shows for Eckhart (as for Aquinas) that it is itself unlimited Being and precisely the site of coincidence of *esse* with *essentia*'.[28] How far is this position from what Charles Taylor called a 'disengaged subject' or 'punctual

---

[24]   See Rowan Williams, 'The Philosophical Structures of Palamism', *Eastern Churches Review*, 9 (1977): 27–44.

[25]   Bradshaw, *Aristotle East and West*, p. 272. This distinction can also be found in Maximus the Confessor.

[26]   Nicholas Loudovikos, *Closed Spirituality and the Meaning of the Self. The Mysticism of Power and the Truth of Nature and Personhood* (2nd edn, Athens, 1999), p. 42 (in Greek).

[27]   Milbank and Pickstock, *Truth in Aquinas*, p. 38.

[28]   Milbank, *The Word Made Strange*, p. 45.

self',[29] referring to Descartes and Locke respectively, as a kind of 'worldless I', as Fergus Kerr calls it,[30] which is pure mind and dominates traditions, communities and history? Of course, RO tries to 'existentialize' this mind by connecting it with the whole of human experience. However, human essence is not 'mind' but a human being's 'whole', as Maximus the Confessor puts it.[31] And this 'whole' is not an adding of body and soul but an active process of 'catholicization'. A human being acts as a whole in order to give – by the reception of God's act – a 'hypostasis' to the whole created being, to become *cat-holicos*, pan-human and pan-cosmic.

This is also why in Symeon the New Theologian, for example, the ascetical life implies a full ontology of the real self. The Mind (νοῦς) is absolutely and forever embodied. The appearance of God is a fact concerning not only the logical soul but also the senses, vision, hearing, touch, taste, smell, transformed in the Spirit.[32] Real life is a catholic sense in God, the gathering of the mental and the sensual, the essential and the existential in Christ and not a volitive spiritual outlet. Four centuries later St Gregory Palamas, the defender of the Hesychasts, makes a very significant contribution to the ontology and anthropology of the 'life in Christ' (the latter expression is used by the Byzantine authors; the term 'mysticism'is completely misleading, as we will see, if we are to understand Orthodox spiritual life). Palamas reacts against the ontological distinction between essence (or nature) and existence, which Plotinus needs in order to explain the contemplation of the One. We can indeed find in Plotinus' work this distinction (and a deep anxiety that follows it) between the existent being, which represents a loss of real existence, and the contemplating being, who possesses, by contemplation, the real heavenly life. Real existence, the real human self, means by definition an elimination of being, which constitutes a false existence. And we have to absolutely accept this ontological bisection, to put in brackets our physical existence in order to find our supposed transcendental essence by contemplation, when the soul becomes, like the One, ἐπέκεινα οὐσίας ['beyond (the) essence', *Enneads* VI, 9, 11]. 'Spirituality' here means the sacrifice of the human in order to succeed in taking root in eternity. So we have plenty of 'mystical' life, but no real creatures to participate in it. In this sense I don't think, as already mentioned, that the so-called 'Byzantine mysticism' is really a mysticism or, even, a 'spirituality', although sometimes it is understood in this way by some Orthodox theologians. Palamas, fighting against Neoplatonism, considers the distinction between nature and existence as opening up the possibility of a free completion of the full human nature in Christ, as existence in the Spirit, where all the elements of the self and creation are completely accepted, in order to constitute the Body of Christ. Here existence means, as in Maximus, an

29   Charles Taylor, *Sources of the Self* (Cambridge, 1989), p. 159, cf. pp. 143–76.
30   Fergus Kerr, *Theology after Wittgenstein* (London, 1997), p. 46.
31   Loudovikos, *Closed Spirituality and the Meaning of the Self*, chapters II & III.
32   Symeon the New Theologian, trans. A. Golitzin, *On the Mystical Life: The Ethical Discourses* (3 vols, Crestwood, NY, 1995–7), vol. 1, discourse III.

ek-stasis not out of nature – as some existentialist philosophers and some modern Orthodox theologians, such as John Zizioulas consider personhood – but an *ek-stasis* of the nature itself in the Holy Spirit. Thus, Neoplatonic contemplation of the One does not mean union, says Palamas against Varlaam. This contemplation is imaginary, he says, because it is only intellectual, that is without the body. By contrast, the elevation of the Hesychast to God is real, because it happens by the grace of the Holy Spirit and carries together 'every kind of creature' (μετά παντός εἴδους κτίσεως) 'in order for the *eikon* (image) of God to be completed' (ἵνα τό τῆς εἰκόνος ἀπηκριβωμένον ᾖ).[33] Thus not only the mind, but all the forces of the soul and even the body participate in God. The saints are not only contemplators but participate in God with their whole nature according to grace.[34] This absolutely real, empirical and non-metaphysical union with the divine is precisely the meaning of the theology of the natural, enhypostasized and uncreated energies of the Triune God. The uncreated energies give God (Father, Son and Spirit, because the uncreated energies proceed from the Father through the Son by the Holy Spirit) the possibility to be not only transcendent but also immanent, to be really present in creation. Thus, the 'mysticism' or 'spirituality' becomes non-metaphysical and is part of an empirical eschatological ontology of the whole human nature. What is important is not to cling to a certain terminology but to express in some way this valuable spiritual inheritance. Terms can be altered or even replaced.

4.   What remains to be added briefly is that every volitive *ecstasis* out of nature is in danger to become practically a will to power if it is not rooted in *homoousion*, the only theological term we have if we are to find a solid *ontological and at the same time ecclesiological* ground for intersubjectivity.[35] Maximus the Confessor claims that it is exactly this ontological *tropos* of 'consubstantiality' which is transferred, as Church, to creation, by God's uncreated energies. I think that I agree with Milbank's correction of Western intersubjectivity based on 'the event of reciprocal but asymmetrical and non-identically repeated exchange'.[36] This safeguards at once communion and the fullness of the self. There are important Greek theologians today, such as Yannaras and Zizioulas, who are very eager to sacrifice the real self in order to achieve communion. If personhood is identified with communion, while at the same time the so-called *gnomic* or personal will does not play an important role in our anthropology, then we simply reverse the

---

[33] Gregory Palamas, 'Contra Acindynum', in *Writings of Gregory Palamas*, ed. Panagiotes K. Chrestou et alii. (5 vols, Thessaloniki, 1962–92), vol. 3, Ant. 6, 36, 11 (in Greek).

[34] '... οὐ θεωροὶ μόνον ἀλλὰ καὶ κοινωνοὶ τῆς θεότητος κατὰ χάριν γεγονότες ...', ibid., Ant. 6, 38, 12–13.

[35] See Nicholas Loudovikos, *The Apophatic Ecclesiology of Consubstantiality. The Primitive Church Today* (Athens, 2002), pp. 19–188 (in Greek).

[36] John Milbank, 'The Midwinter Sacrifice', in Graham Ward (ed.), *The Blackwell Companion to Postmodern Theology* (Oxford, 2001), p. 124.

notorious Western individualism. Personal truth now lies not in autonomy but in heteronomy, and the self is simply flooded by the other, instead of communicating with him by his own personal natural will or energy.[37]

This subtle existential balance between the self and other, beyond Levinas and Marion, can only be theologically achieved and understood today. And this is the only way to avoid the transformation of desire into will to power. Desire is fundamentally (and unconsciously) intersubjective and not individual – and the West owes much to Lacan for rediscovering this truth.[38] Lack or assimilation of the other means that my desire becomes gradually a will to power, while lack or assimilation of myself means that the other's desire dominates and annihilates me. Post-enlightenment secularized Christianity gave birth to both distortions – but this is another big issue. Nihilism is something which started not outside but within the Christian Church. Christian spirituality of a 'worldless I' is practically a fundamental nihilism (and the most dangerous one) which annihilates worldly existence in the name of God. Secular nihilism merely inverses the poles of the Christian one. Nietzsche is simply a secularized 'Christian', for he – unlike Kierkegaard, who lives in deep anticipation of the other – violates communion by his will to power. This is exactly the core of Christian individualism.

5.   In this respect I would like to say something about the RO claim to consider mind as naturally and constantly illuminated by God, in an Augustinian fashion. This is a significant but also dangerous claim, a really 'risky poetics'. According to the Greek patristic tradition, mind as well as the 'passions' (which are positive powers of the self) need not be left behind but must be transformed by repentance, which gradually 'harmonizes' our *gnomic* or personal will, with the grace of the sacraments. Any other idea of 'natural' illumination, which is based on the view that *as minds*, we are supposedly close to God, who is the supreme mind, risks the danger of a deep intellectual narcissism and its consequences. That means again the great retirement of the self into its solipsistic castle. Of course the RO intentions are different. Indeed, the greatest philosophical impasse nowadays is, I think, exactly this post-Kantian overbearing anthropocentric immanentism, with its analytical, linguistic and deconstructive consummation, which 'cuts reality down to size' as Thomas Nagel said.[39] We have thus not an overcoming but a transformation of idealism.

---

[37] See Nicholas Loudovikos, *Orthodoxy and Modernization, Byzantine Individualization, State and History in the Perspective of the European Future* (Athens, 2006), pp. 15–42 (in Greek).

[38] Of course Lacanian 'otherness' is not exactly the same as Christian 'otherness', but the convergences and divergences cannot be discussed here. See on this Nicholas Loudovikos, *Psychoanalysis and Orthodox Theology. On Desire, Catholicity and Eschatology* (Athens, 2003), pp. 15–42 (in Greek).

[39] See Thomas Nagel, *The View from Nowhere* (New York, 1986).

Or, as Michele Marsonet puts it:

> The idealist claims:
> (A) We cannot step out of thought: if we admit that there is an external reality which transcends thought, then, by the same act of thinking it, this alleged external reality is no longer transcendental. It follows that we can never overcome the cognitive identity between being on the one side, and thought on the other.
> But most analytic philosophers would paraphrase it in the following manner:
> (B) We cannot step out of language: if we admit that there is an external reality which transcends thought, then, by the same act of thinking it, this alleged external reality is no longer transcendental. It follows that we can never overcome the cognitive identity between being on the one side, and language on the other. We might say, thus, that for classical idealism whatever is foreign to thought is unknowable, while for the analytic tradition whatever is foreign to language is unknowable as well.[40]

This modern non-representational 'nominalism' culminates in the controversial Wittgensteinian radical mysticism where the world is left untouched by God in a fundamentally post-Kantian fashion, while the 'language games' are supposed to 'console' some theologians repenting from Cartesianism.[41] Wittgenstein's mysticism cannot understand Incarnation, although he undermines the epistemological ambitions of the 'worldless I'.

But the problem still remains: can we liberate ontology from immanentism without making it vaguely and falsely transcendental? Can we liberate knowledge from idealist or realist epistemology without making it either darkly mystical or arrogantly positive? Between an Apollinarian, monophysitisizing abolition of mind and an optimistic Platonizing theological exaltation of it, the Greek patristic tradition has to offer a subtle and delicate theology of illumination, based on the distinction between mind (νοῦς) and reason (λογική). In his Sermon 53 (*On the Entrance of the Theotokos in the Temple*) St Gregory Palamas recapitulates the whole issue. Sensation, imagination, *doxa*, reason and mind are considered to be the parts of the embodied human soul. What the young Mary discovers in the temple during her intensive and deep prayer for all suffering humankind is really amazing: through deep prayer, the 'prayer of the heart', and only through that, the mind becomes, by grace, the created mirror of the uncreated God, elevating and separating the mind from reason. But the mind is not illuminated because it is a mind, but it is a mind because it is illuminated. That means that

---

[40]   Michele Marsonet, 'Linguistic Idealism in Analytical Philosophy of the Twentieth Century', in Paul Coates and Daniel D. Hutto (eds), *Current Issues in Idealism* (Bristol, 1996), pp. 114–15.

[41]   See Kerr, *Theology after Wittgenstein*. I extensively agree with Connor Cunningham's 'Language. Wittgenstein after Theology' in John Milbank et al. (eds), *Radical Orthodoxy*, pp. 64–90.

illumination, in its real meaning, is something we need to receive by grace; by a prayerful harmonization of our personal or *gnomic* will with the grace of the sacraments, and not something we already possess *ex officio*. The mind's natural light must thus become an uncreated one, not of course by essence but by grace. This is extremely essential, because in this way we not only avoid the dangers of any latent identification of God and mind but we also avoid the possibility of a separation between mind and the whole creation. The illuminated mind is illuminated because of the presence of grace and not because it is ontologically superior. Being deified while remaining absolutely ontologically equal to creation and bound to it, the mind joins then again reason, imagination and sensation and, through the last one, the human body; and through the body the whole creation, conveying divine illumination everywhere and transforming the world into the Body of Christ. We do not need then the perennial Derridean postponement of meaning or its Wittgensteinian dilution into language games: that is the meaning of theological apophaticism, as the affirmation of Incarnation, as the possibility of the material world to be illuminated and deified by grace. This happens by changing creation's mode of existence without losing its substance.

This is why I call this illumination a 'eucharistic illumination'. This illumination teaches us the very mode of existence of the Trinity, helping us to transform God's world into God's Church. There is another point here where I find myself in a happy agreement with John Milbank. Reconciliation, if it has to do with ontology, is no less than a deep gift-exchange. Indeed, it 'is only meaningful in the perpetual synergy of human offering and divine gift, eternally transferred and renewed through infinite and multiple reciprocities'.[42] In reconciliation, 'the bond of love is an exchange of infinite love',[43] which makes forgiveness an 'unlimited positive circulation', rather than 'a mere negative gesture'.[44] If reconciliation concerns ontology it concerns it as, I think, a 'Eucharistic-ontology-of-becoming-in-communion',[45] where being is a circulating divine gift. In other words, this is the celebrated ontology of being as gift.

6.   Last but not least, let me say something on the RO consideration of the *polis*. I have read Milbank's *Theology and Social Theory*, a book of invaluable importance for someone who wants to understand the political problems in the West. I would need to write another chapter to comment on this issue. What I would like to say very briefly is that the so-called Byzantine state had a very different character. In any case, the Augustinian separation of the two cities was never of any importance in the Roman East. The state, which gradually assumed the form of a perverted

---

[42]   John Milbank, *Being Reconciled. Ontology and Pardon* (London/New York, 2003).

[43]   Ibid., p. 47.

[44]   Ibid., p. 48.

[45]   Nicholas Loudovikos, *Eucharistic Ontology. Maximus the Confessor's eschatological ontology of being as gift* (Athens, 1992), pp. 251–72 (in Greek).

Church, of an anti-Church, is the seminally totalitarian state of Machiavelli and Joachim de Fiore, which culminated in the various fascisms of our epoch. The analysis of this state by Milbank is again excellent, as is his theological suggestion for a new understanding of the 'political' problem. Anyway, in the Byzantine 'existential' state – as I call it in my latest book – the problems are different. I would say that here the problem is not the historicization of Christian eschatology, as in Hegel, but the eschatologization of history, so that the latter, along with the state, may sometimes lack solidity and 'reality'. A kind of reconciliation may be needed here.

III

Let me conclude provisionally. I really appreciate the RO 'erotic' project. I could say that it is one of the most insightful theological projects I know today in the West. But I would like to see RO less Platonic (although Plato is the greatest theologian of Antiquity)[46] and more patristic, more Christian than Western, more interconfessional than High-Anglican. As I am one of the very few Orthodox theologians who insist on the necessity of a reconciliation between the Eastern and Western patristic traditions today (and especially that of the first millennium), I think that you will give me the right to suggest to the RO brothers and sisters to do the same thing: to reconcile Aquinas with Maximus the Confessor, for example, exactly because Christian experience is much richer than the textbooks allow us to imagine. Reconciliation here does not mean any disgusting ecumenistic melting, but, again, a 'circulation of gifts'. Finally, theology is not a matter of intellectual arrangements – the theologian's radical need is to deepen his life in Christ, which is a sort of life 'that comprises body and soul', as Rimbaud wanted life to be; and that means to draw grace whereby that is possible …

---

[46] Nicholas Loudovikos, *Theological History of Ancient Greek Philosophy* (Thessaloniki, 2003), pp. 153–202 (in Greek).

Ecumenical Orthodoxy –
A Response to Nicholas Loudovikos

John Milbank

I was absolutely delighted to hear and then to read Nicholas Loudovikos' positive responses to the various attempts of the RO group, whose efforts are still in their early stages. He identifies what is most essential about the movement, namely its *ethos*, extremely well and correctly recognizes that at the heart of this ethos lies a stress upon an 'erotic' mode of Christianity in precisely the ancient and patristic Greek sense of *eros*. It is this erotic emphasis of 'Catholic' cultures in general which the historian Christopher Dawson once defined as constituting their 'warm' character, as opposed to the 'cold' character of Protestant cultures, which tends to instrumentalize nature and society, in accordance with precisely that isolation of a self-sufficient, punctual and yet solipsistically 'redeemed' self, which Loudovikos takes to be the tendency of the West in general to promote.

As to his recommendations for the future evolution of RO, I am also wholeheartedly in agreement in the most important respect, namely that it needs to become still more interconfessional in character. Already it is a deliberately interconfessional theology – both 'Catholic' and 'Orthodox', but it needs to increase its blendings of West with East: indeed with both the Orthodox and the 'oriental' Christian East. Moreover, this theoretical project should be matched with a practical one: to assist the reunification of the episcopally-based churches under the primacy of Rome, but in terms of a new consensus as to the nature of papal power and its relation to conciliar power, once we have rid ourselves of late medieval and early modern distortions of the theology of the papacy. I believe that such a project is logically consistent with the dominant lines of the Roman Catholic *nouvelle théologie*, as well as with the fact that vast swathes of modern 'Orthodox' territory in fact acknowledged both Rome and Constantinople in the Middle Ages: 'uniate' Catholicism is if anything the older Eastern norm and not at all a post-reformation aberration as the Moscow patriarchate has too often suggested.

As to the second respect, a need to become 'less Platonic and more patristic', I can only agree up to a point. RO has deliberately tried to undertake again the 'original' encounter of Christianity with Platonism, which is in part constitutive of its very nature, in the light of more recent readings of Plato and Neoplatonism, which stress their religious as well as philosophical character. It has also tried to engage with more accurate accounts of the history of the development of the original encounter, insisting upon its diversity and complexity. There is, in fact, a strange tendency for both Eastern and Western Christendom to identify the differences of the other as 'too Platonic'. Thus Loudovikos, like many others in the East, traces the over-intellectualism, individualism and pantheistic tendencies of the West to a Platonic root. Yet just as frequent is a Western suspicion of Eastern concentration upon participation, the sharing in the uncreated light, deification and the Jesus prayer as all too Platonic or even quasi-pagan, and as underplaying New Testament notions of free grace, justification and atonement.

My personal view is that this symmetrical mud-slinging misfires on either side. The characteristic differences of East and West are not in any way to do with a greater or lesser influence of Platonism from the outset (though after the high Middle Ages the latter is much more dominant in the East than in the West), but rather with different specific and often quite contingent historical developments, that involved somewhat different construals of both Biblical texts and the Platonic legacy.

I strongly welcome the fact that Loudovikos distances himself from certain too-frequent Orthodox caricatures: thus he fully allows, for example, that interpersonalism has been important in the West as well as in the East. Nevertheless, I still do not think he as yet gets the comparative place of Platonism in either tradition quite right. To my mind, as he at one point allows, Augustine is in essential continuity with the Cappadocian modification of Origen and if, in his late thought there are the beginnings of something very different, then this is more to do with a slight commencement of a more 'positivist' and 'voluntarist' approach to the word of the Bible and if anything a certain removal from Platonic influence, not its over-confirmation. Certainly the more drastic tendencies towards a 'worldless ego' at the end of the Middle Ages were clearly to do with an abandonment of the Platonic legacy, which often went along with a downplaying of the role of subtle symbolic exegesis (and therefore of an appropriate exegesis) of the Bible.

Moreover, as many commentators have now suggested, one cannot read Augustine's Christian modifications of Plotinus as simply a 'retreat from Platonism'.[47] To the contrary, Augustine's greater interest in sensory and cosmic mediation and in inter-personal relations may in some ways also take him closer to the original Plato. This is most strikingly true of his recovery of the doctrine of recollection in the mode of a doctrine of illumination – whereas recollection plays a marginal role in the *Enneads*. Thus it has been remarked that, in some ways, Augustine's shifts are parallel to those of the pagan 'theurgic Neoplatonists' Iamblichus and Proclus, even though ironically these shifts were intended in part to help shape a rival pagan monotheism to that of Christianity.

One could see also a third parallel in the response of the Cappadocians to both Plotinus and Origen. However, it was the Eastern tradition, not the West, which first of all integrated certain insights of pagan theurgic Neoplatonism through the later writings of Dionysius the Areopagite.[48] The subtle change this wrought in some ways appears contradictory, if one does not fully understand the nature of the

---

[47]   For a summary and development, see Michael Hanby, *Augustine and Modernity* (London, 2003); see also Lewis Ayres, *Nicaea and its Legacy. An Approach to Fourth-Century Trinitarian Theology* (New York, 2004), pp. 364–84.

[48]   See Ysabel de Andia, *Henosis: l'union à Dieu chez Denys l'Areopagite* (Leiden, 1996).

theurgic current. For under this influence Dionysius, and then Maximus, on the one hand actually speak rather more than before of *theosis* in terms of *henosis*, while on the other hand they also stress, yet more than the Cappadocians, the continual dwelling of the soul in the body, together with the liturgical context for spirituality, the eschatological transformation of the cosmos, the eminent containment of the many and diverse in the one and infinite and the 'pointing back' of the spiritual to the material, and the contemplative to the practical. This makes *total nonsense of all the textbook assumptions*, because the still greater 'material' emphasis is arguably at once truer to the Bible *and* in keeping with a certain genuinely Platonic current of understanding.

These remarks may help the reader to see that, if RO stresses 'the Platonic', this does not at all betoken the sort of thing that might immediately come to mind when that phrase is heard. Ultimately, we need to approach this whole matter in a fresh spirit, just as we need to realize that the Hebrew Bible is just as concerned with cosmic order as with historical change and that by the time of Jesus Hebraic, Hellenic and Roman cultures had become thoroughly blended.

Nicholas Loudovikos then raises a series of six specific issues which he wishes to put RO. I should now like to respond briefly to each of these in turn.

1.   First of all, there is the issue of the Western understanding of subjectivity. Loudovikos severely qualifies the usual Orthodox accusation against Augustine regarding the Trinity and the self and this is to be greatly appreciated. However, I do not think that there is any evidence that Augustine moves from an earlier more solipsistic view to a later more relational one, even if his thought gets constantly refined. To the contrary, I think that from beginning to end of his thought he embraces a kind of 'musical ontology' which puts relation before substance and relation in time before relation in space. This 'relationality' is for him at once internal and external to any related thing, to avoid reduction either to 'self' or to 'other' – a balance whose desirability Loudovikos in his essay explicitly recognizes.

But the balance is for Augustine only perfectly achieved in the Trinitarian relations, which involve real differences and yet which, precisely as *pure* relations, are compatible with the divine simplicity. For us to image this Trinity must involve an oscillation between relations 'within us' and relations with those outside us that nonetheless constitute us (somewhat like Lacan's scheme, as Loudovikos suggests). This ecstasis towards the other that is repeated 'as ourselves' is ultimately founded upon our integral ecstasies towards God, as Rowan Williams has suggested: the image of the Trinity is in us only because we actively relate to the Trinity. Perhaps Augustine can too much make it sound as if he favours the internal over the external relations: however, a careful reading of *De Trinitate* shows that the self which we know and love is the self which knows and loves with true intention and true *dilectio* both God and neighbour.

Nor do I see any evidence for a favouring of the will in Augustine: the precedence according to *taxis* (not dignity) of knowledge over love, to which Loudovikos ironically objects, precisely prevents this. For the true knowledge of the filial *ars* is what expresses the Father, not something which the Father arbitrarily wills. Nor is the 'will' of the Spirit the ultimate essential upshot of the Paternal-Filial relation; rather it is the excess of ordered desire which enables that relations and which that relation in turn engenders, so returning the Spirit's attention to the original source and the co-original expression. Nothing here suggests that Trinitarian communion is not in itself an ultimate, nor that it exists in order to unfold some sort of trans-relational unified upshot. Such a 'Hegelian' development is *not* latent in Augustine. One can agree with Loudovikos that Christianity surpasses the Greek desire for 'self-fulfilment' in the direction of an 'ecstasy' that rejoices both in self and in other and in their specific relating. But this surpassing is sustained in the West as well as in the East. If it is eventually in the West lost sight of, then this is much more to do with a later Avicennian (and in the long-term Plotinian) contamination of Trinitarian theology in the course of the Middle Ages. It was only this contamination which raised the essence in ontological dignity above the Trinitarian persons and grounded their distinction not in relationality but in formal distinctions between origin, intellect and will and between all three and the essence. But here Loudovikos should be alert to the fact that he himself seems to espouse a 'formal distinction' of essence from will that is dangerously close to just these tendencies. To really identify will with essence is not to promote a voluntarism, nor inversely is it to render will impersonal; rather it is apophatically to affirm that in God there is not a distinction between what he is and what he decides – nor between both and what he knows. This is because he is absolutely one and simple, as Dionysius and Maximus (partly in the wake of Neoplatonism) rightly insisted. This emphasis was bequeathed by them to Thomas Aquinas.

2.   Secondly, there is the issue of participation. This concept, I think for both of us, alone does justice to the idea of creation *ex nihilo*, because it stresses that finite being can only be 'from God' – can only image him as sharing in him, but equally can only share in him as imaging him, not as a literal part, since creation is also 'other' than God. This medium, described by Aquinas with the phrase 'quasi-part', is what RO always seeks to maintain. However, that does not mean that such a middle path resolves the *aporia* of just how God can be 'all' and yet give rise to something else. One can hint at resolutions and yet the *aporia* remains as a mystery, even though one believes that it is resolved in God – thereby avoiding a postmodern hypostasization of *aporia* à la Derrida, as though dilemma should itself be the object of a religious cult. But I think that for Loudovikos even this position remains unsatisfactory and that is why he advocates, in the common Eastern Orthodox manner, the essence/energies distinction as a 'solution' to the aporetic mystery. Here I believe there are several confusions.

First of all, I do not consider that the Cappadocians ever regarded this distinction as a real rather than a human mental one – but so far Loudovikos is in apparent agreement. Secondly, though, I think that the revolutionary Pauline use of *energeia* for the divine presence to us and the divine synergic co-working with us (later paralleled in pagan theurgy, as David Bradshaw has argued)[49] is upheld and not betrayed by Aquinas' understanding of God's essence itself as *energeia* or *actus*. This is because the whole point of the Pauline usage is that it implies that God acts on us as God, without intermediaries, precisely because, as our creator, he is utterly near us with a nearness beyond nearness. But God being absolutely One, simple and omnipresent, cannot do anything that he is not, cannot be present to us with a mere 'aspect' of himself. To desire, like Bradshaw as cited by Loudovikos, that God should be able to do something other than what he eternally 'is', is to fail to conceive of God's absolute ontological difference from mere beings. It is, in reality, to fail to be apophatic enough by negating our distinction between 'is' and 'does'.

But the third point is that here Aquinas is as close to Maximus as could be desired: his view that in the eternal actuality of the second person of the Trinity are contained all the real realities and truths of every single created thing to a degree more eminent than their finite containment of themselves (such that things are more themselves 'away from themselves' in God) is a precise continuation of the Maximian *Logos/logoi* doctrine.[50] For Maximus *never* spoke of a distinction between the *Logos* and the *logoi* in God, nor of the two as representing a distinction between the divine essence and the divine action: to the contrary he says that the *Logos* is also the *logoi* because the divine one is also many: 'the many *logoi* are the one *logos* to whom all things are related and who exists in himself without confusion...'.[51] Conversely, the many created *logoi* that constitute creatures are also 'one' because they are led back by nature to the one *Logos*. Hence, for Maximus, the many *logoi* and even the one *Logos* itself are on both sides of the Creator/created divide at once, but never in any way at all hover 'between' the two.

Now Loudovikos of course wishes to deny any such 'betweenness' – which incidentally would *not* even be Neoplatonic, as the 'henads' in Proclus are somewhat like angels and there is an absolute ontological chasm between them and the One. However, when he declares that the Palamite distinction of essence from energy (and so of *Logos* from *logoi*) is not a Scotist–type 'formal distinction', he disproves himself in the very next sentence by declaring that 'this distinction here is not a *separation* but an expression of the fundamental *distinction* between will and essence in God which is not of course a separation either'. This suggests that while the distinction is made purely *kat epinoian* according to Palamas, it must have some sort of *fundamentum in re*, as for the Scotist formal distinction – for otherwise what could it mean, given that the West of course recognizes a purely mental distinction between God's providence and his essence? Any denial

---

[49]   David Bradshaw, *Aristotle East and West: Metaphysics and the Division of Christendom* (Cambridge, 2004), pp. 119–53.

[50]   See Philipp W. Rosemann, *Omne ens est aliquid; Introduction à la lecture du 'système' philosophique de saint Thomas d'Aquin* (Louvain/Paris, 1996), pp. 48–72.

[51]   St Maximus the Confessor, Ambiguum 7 (PG 91:1077C), in *On the Cosmic Mystery of Jesus Christ* trans. P.M. Blowers and R.L. Wilken (New York, 2003), p. 54.

that *actus ad extra* and *actus ad intra* are in reality identical and *in no way* really distinct (Aquinas' position), must involve either a real or a formal distinction between the two. I think that it is clear that Palamas intended indeed nothing as crude as the former, but nonetheless something like the latter.

This implies, in the fourth place, that we should replace the story of an eternal division between East and West over this issue with a more accurate and far more interesting story which involves a certain parallel between the Scotist and the Palamite moment – even if the latter was nothing like such a serious *caesura* as the former. Finally, in the fifth place, as I try to explain in my chapter in this volume, I think that modern Russian sophiology, especially as articulated by Bulgakov, sustains better than Palamas the Maximian imperative, and is far more compatible with Aquinas than it supposes. For as with the *logoi*, Sophia lies on both sides of the creator/created divide and does not hover in any imagined middle limbo. Her role surpasses Maximus' conception by conveying the third term (which is again no mere 'between'), according to our *modus cognoscendi*, common at once to essence and to persons, in order to avoid the notion of an impersonal essence. This 'personifying power' mediates within the Trinity, while it is also this power that is externalized as creation and is immanent within it. If one denies that there is any real or formal distinction between the *theologia* and the *economia*, then one can say that participation is also aporetic and mysterious. For there is not a 'part' of God which he shares and a reserved part which he does not share. Rather, all participation is in the imparticipable, just as it is the unsharable itself which shares itself, and that which is all-sufficient which incomprehensibly goes out from itself and therefore, somehow (in order to 'resolve' the *aporia*) must also return to itself. However, I thoroughly agree with Loudovikos that we should interpret this alternating rhythm as an 'ontological dialogue'. As he says, if all creatures are most profoundly *logoi*, then this is, indeed, a kind of 'proposal' of their existence to them by God, to which they must perforce freely respond. And certainly the Eucharist is at once the renewal and the consummation of this dialogue. To say that it exceeds metaphysics as 'performed ontology' is precisely in accord with the liturgical metaphysics of Catherine Pickstock's *After Writing*, and with our shared argument in *Truth in Aquinas* that for Thomas theology self-exceeds itself as transubstantiation.[52]

3.   The third issue concerns the supposed RO over-rating of the importance of the mind. Here I simply want to register a collective plea of 'not guilty', because I think we all clearly resist the kind of 'onto-theological' or 'zero-sum competition' account of *ascesis* which would suggest that we are to trade body for mind, senses and imagination for intellect and finally intellect along with other people for God. We have all often stressed that human intellect is explicitly bound up with a

[52]   Catherine Pickstock, *After Writing. On the Liturgical Consummation of Philosophy* (Oxford, 1998), pp. 253–67; John Milbank and Catherine Pickstock, *Truth in Aquinas* (London, 2001), pp. 88–111.

certain kind of embodiment – with handedness, erect posture, touching, common-sensing and materially-based language.[53] We are also in accord with Loudovikos in affirming that the supernatural destiny of mind as such elevates the human body and the whole cosmos along with it.[54] If, indeed, as Maximus taught, we are to ascend from the senses through contemplation of the cosmos to mystical union, then nevertheless this ascent transfigures our bodies, senses, imaginations and minds. Moreover, what is proper to the lower stages is always fulfilled in a higher mode in the upper stages, not simplistically left behind by a sacrifice involving an absolute loss. Here Aquinas would be at one with Palamas in denying that existence is to be surpassed in favour of essence.

4.   The fourth point concerns the question of intersubjectivity. Here I much welcome Loudovikos' agreement with me that slavery to the other is but inverted and disguised egoism (which must also contradictorily exalt the egoism of the other) and that what we rather require is the achievement of reciprocal exchange where the integrity and legitimate self-care of either party is respected. Earlier I suggested, following Robert Spaemann, that the common term between *eudaemonism* on the one hand and other-regarding on the other is 'the ecstatic'.[55] If RO is indeed lacking the sense that this is grounded in the *homoousion* then this should be remedied! Interpersonality certainly implies a communion in and an exchange of 'the same' (essence, substance, being, power–to–personify) whose 'sameness' is nevertheless only constituted and sustained within this exchange.

5.   The fifth point concerns 'Illumination' which is also a crucial trope for RO. We tend to argue that Augustine's illuminationist doctrine is not in any sense ontologistic (as in Malebranche) since he fully insists that we only know 'in God', not by alien transfer to the divine side, but rather in the same sense that we 'live, move, have our being' and sense things in God, by participation. Therefore the illumination of the mind by God by no-means involves some sort of side-stepping of sensory mediation. Inversely, we also consider that Aquinas did not abandon the Augustinian doctrine of knowledge by illumination, even if he places renewed stress on sensory reference and discursive process. But for Thomas discursive *ratio* is still situated within the partial intuitions of the transcendentals by the human *intellectus*.[56] To know anything is to see to some degree within the divine light. There is therefore nothing wrong, as Loudovikos avers, in seeing even our natural

---

[53]   See for example, Milbank and Pickstock, *Truth in Aquinas*, pp. 60–88.

[54]   See John Milbank, *The Suspended Middle: Henri de Lubac and the Debate concerning the Supernatural* (Grand Rapids, MI, 2005), pp. 88–104.

[55]   Robert Spaemann, *Happiness and Benevolence*, trans. J. Alberg SJ (Notre Dame, IN, 2000).

[56]   See Milbank and Pickstock, *Truth in Aquinas*, pp. 21–4.

understanding as divinely illumined: it merely applies to the mind a general sense of participation.

On the other hand I have also argued that, if everything that participates in God seeks to return to him, then the specific mode of intellectual return is the aspiration to see God, to partake in the beatific vision. At one point Loudovikos speaks as if this trope were too Platonic, when of course it is derived directly from St Paul! But if, in this way, even the natural participation in mind by God implies an orientation to the supernatural, even though this is the free gift of grace, then *in concreto* one can agree with Loudovikos that illumination is by grace and most certainly agree (as RO writers have often indicated) that mind is *only* mind as illuminated by God. And I would also thoroughly concur that without this view, the correlation between the knower and the thing known implies no genuine realist reference: this only follows if one affirms that our minds and all real things have the same creative source and that things are ordained to be known by minds. In this respect Loudovikos is quite right to say that Wittgenstein's later position is ultimately another transcendentalism which cannot resist the kind of scepticism I have just indicated and that by comparison Derrida's 'deconstructed linguistic transcendentalism' is far more rigorous, since it foregrounds the sceptical implications.

6.   In the sixth and final place, it is certainly true that we need to explore much more the relative strengths of the Eastern and Western models of Church/State relations. Although the duality of the two cities in the West as Rowan Williams has argued, tended to prevent sacralization of the state and to foster constitutionalism through the emergence of 'free associations' and their interrelations, it is also right to say with Loudovikos that the secularization of the church ideal itself has led to totalitarian excesses. On the other hand, as he hints, the Byzantine model has sometimes sacralized and frozen in time and absolutized the imperfect structures of state ruling.

Nevertheless, in positive terms, this more monistic, integral model has also served to remind us that even political government must be permeated by charitable purposes, as in the Byzantine setting-up of state welfare institutions, and that the full Christian order involves the body as well as the soul: this is the political counterpart to the ascetic raising-up of the body discussed earlier. It was because of *the resurrection of the body and the deification of humanity* that the 'West Byzantine' 'Anonymous of York' or 'Norman Anonymous' placed regal authority within the single Church-society (Christendom) above the papal, as representing Christ in his divine and kingly, rather than his human and priestly aspect.[57] While this viewpoint may involve a certain semi-Nestorianism and also misses the Augustinian point that the regal arm is relatively secular because of its lesser goals of mere restraint and

---

[57]   Norman Anonymous, extracts from *The Consecration of Bishops and Kings*, in *From Irenaeus to Grotius: a Sourcebook in Christian Political Thought*, eds Oliver and Joan Lockwood O'Donovan (Grand Rapids, MI, 1999), pp. 251–9.

not entire transformation of the moral subject, it still indicates a certain danger in the clericalization and spiritualization of the post-Hildebrandine Western Church.

And in fact the actual Eastern Byzantine outlook at times started to realize something of a synthesis: the emperor was indeed a priest, and yet not a priest of the highest kind since he has to shed human blood. In like manner, the image of the emperor had to be subordinated to the icons of Christ and the saints for Nicephorus and John Damascene. In this way a proper Byzantine sense that there is something *ersatz* about denying that the effective and coercive power is not to be seen as in any way the spiritual real thing, did not entirely preclude Augustinian and Gelasian perspectives about the temporal compromise of secular rule. Anglicans are perhaps in a good position to see this, since their legacy is, at its deepest roots (as the poet and theologian Charles Williams saw) at once Roman and Byzantine.

Without question therefore, the development of a more ecumenical and balanced political theology is an important and even an urgent task for today. I believe that RO and Fr Nicholas Loudovikos would stand together in affirming that the scandal of Church division is in large measure responsible for the emergence of secular reason, and that only when this division is overcome will we really start to discover how there can be a modern Christian alternative.

Chapter 6

Kenosis, *Poiesis* and *Genesis*:
Or the Theological Aesthetics of Suffering

Graham Ward

In this chapter I wish to explore, a little further, certain Greek terms that have been important to my theological thinking and offer some reflections on why I believe they help to furnish that vision, which not only responds to the social atomism and the nihilism and so on, but also challenges, even unmasks it. The terms are not chosen at random: they play an important part in patristic theology even though I am going to examine them primarily as they appear in the Pauline epistles and the epistle of St James.

Let me frame the analysis with a well known quotation from Athanasius on the work of Christ: 'He made men gods by himself becoming man.' The quotation is taken from the first book of *Orationes Contra Arianos* and it is followed by a number of mini exegeses on New Testament texts, most particularly Philippians 2:9 which is the turning point of Paul's kenotic hymn on the descent, death and exaltation of Christ: 'Wherefore God has highly exalted him, and given him a name above all names.' The doctrine of kenosis provides a significant context then for Athanasius' account of deification; deification being understood here as the human participation in the ontology of Christ's resurrection. The verb Athanasius uses for 'made men gods' is *theopoieo*. It is a word found again and again in the Greek fathers, taken from what appears to be a specific locale: Alexandria.

The earliest use is in Clement of Alexandria, who, following Origen and Eusebius is accredited with using the Letter of St James polemically in his debates with the Gnostics.[1] The Letter of St James is highly significant, as we will see. For the moment, we can note that Clement exalts James (ironically in the same way as the Gospel of St Thomas) above the other Twelve disciples. We will see more of the possible importance of this when we come to treat the position of Christ in the epistle. From Clement we find the term occurring in the work of Origen (another supporter of James' exalted position) and Athanasius (as we have seen), Cyril and Didymus of Alexandria, and (presumably via Origen) it turns up in the writings of Basil, Gregory of Nyssa and Maximus the Confessor. With this verb we are treating the soteriological import of the incarnation that situates God as

---

[1] There are a number of verbal echoes on the letter in the first-century writings of Clement of Rome, but it is Clement of Alexandria, it seems, who first accepts the letter as Scripture.

both efficient and final cause, in the language of Aristotle. God is both the creator and, in some sense yet to be unfolded, that which is created.

In this theological framework, then, I wish to examine in the relation between *kenosis, poiesis* and *genesis*: the inner theo-logic of their connectedness. Because from out of the treasures of these words will emerge a Christology, a soteriology, an anthropology, a doctrine of creation, and a doctrine of God. Not surprisingly, perhaps, one of the best places to examine the theological connectedness of these words is the New Testament.

There is only one mention of *poiesis* in the New Testament and that happens to be in the Letter of St James and it is part of his exhortation to Jewish-Christians of the diaspora:

> [R]eceive with meekness the implanted word (*ton empsuton logon*) which is able to save your souls. But be doers of the word (*poietai logou*), and not hearers only, deceiving (*paralogizomenoi*) yourselves. For if anyone is a hearer of the word and not a doer (*poietes*), he is like a man who observes his natural face (*to prosopon tes geneseos*) in a mirror; for he observes himself and goes away and at once forgets what he was like. But he who looks (*parakypto*) in the perfect law (*eis nomon telion*) of liberty and perseveres, being no hearer that forgets but a doer that acts (*poietes ergou*), he shall be blessed in his doing (*in te poiesei*) (Jas 1:21–5).

James is also the only NT writer employing the word poietes ('doers') other than Paul who uses it once in his Letter to the Romans in a way which echoes James: 'it is not the hearers of the law who are righteous before God, but the doers of the law (*oi poietai nomou*) who will be justified' (2:13). We will return to Paul later (and leave aside questions concerning whether the Letter of St James was written before most if not all the Pauline epistles and the exegetical wars that have been waged between James and the Pauline teaching of justification by faith).[2]

Allow me to make a number of observations on this text. A few of them have the support of critical commentators but most of them do not because: (1) the epistle is generally taken as pastoral and so all too quickly this passage is read as a

---

[2]   There are many scholars who would concur the Letter showed evidence of 'a chronological distance from Paul's missionary activity', S.R. Llewelyn, 'The Prescipt of James', *Novum Testamentum*, 39/4 (1997): 385–93, especially p. 386. These would include: Alfred Wikenhauser and Josef Schmid, *Einleitung in das Neue Testament* (Freiburg/Basel, 1973), pp. 573–7 and Werner G. Kümmel, *Einleitung in das Neue Testament* (Heidelberg, 1970), pp. 297–301. Martin Hengel even views the Letter of James as an antipauline polemic: 'Der Jakobusbrief als antipaulinische Polemik' in *Tradition and Interpretation in the New Testament*, eds Gerald Hawthorne and Otto Betz (Grand Rapids, 1987), pp. 248–78. But, more recently, this chronological distance that places James after Paul has been challenged. See Luke Timothy Johnson, *The Letter of James: A New Translation and Commentary* (New York, 1995).

moral injunction against the hypocrisy of hearing and saying but not doing; and (2) they read *poieo* as a synonym for *prasso*. Of course it can be a synonym. We know this from the employment of these verbs in the LXX. But there is also an important Hellenistic philosophical distinction made by both Plato and Aristotle between the terms in which *poiesis* names a unique and creative act, a new bringing forth or *genesis*. And not only does Plato use this word to describe divine creativity (in *Timaeus* 41d–42e) as distinct from the activity of the demiurge (who does not create out of nothing), but the LXX has around 3,200 references to *poieo* as God's action with respect to the created world. Furthermore, since at least the time of W.L. Knox's influential paper on the Letter of James,[3] attention has been drawn to the Hellenistic elements (echoes of Plato, Philo and the *Corpus Hermeticum*) in the writing. So there are grounds for believing there is something more subtle and more theological going on here that attention to the Greek might reward.[4]

First, we have to note the tension in v.21. The *Logos* has to be received before it can be enacted (v.22), and it is because of that reception that there is potential for salvation. Christian praxis does not follow merely from the Christian's own decision; it follows and is in accord with a reception that is prior to the decision. Nevertheless what we are told is that what is received (the *Logos*) is also what is already implanted within the soul. Knox interpreted this as a contradiction, while also making an interesting observation on *empsutos* (inborn, innate): 'The writer is trying to express the thought of the divine *Logos* as a gift of 'mind' which comes from God', and he draws a parallel between this text and a similar idea in the *Corpus Hermeticum*.[5] We will return to this idea in a moment. For now I only wish to point to the paradox or what I would call the chiasmic structure of Christian agency: any action involves a movement that issues from both that which is received or revealed and that which is innate – that which is given and that which enables a response to what is given. Using a Johannine formula we can talk of the 'I in you and you in me'. I am empowered by the Word to perform that Word and the basis of that empowerment is both the grace of God and what Augustine describes as '*interior intimo meo et superior summo meo*'.[6] The work of de Lubac in both *Surnaturel* and *Le mystère du surnaturel* offers a great unfolding of this theme in terms of *desiderium naturale* and le '*donum perfectum*'[7] – though

---

[3]   Wilfred L. Knox, 'The Epistle of St. James', *The Journal of Theological Studies*, OS–XLVI, 181–2 (1945): 10–17. Knox's observations are affirmed in Hubert Frankemölle comments on the relationship between James and Philo. See Hubert Frankemölle, *Der Brief des Jakobus* (2 vols, Gütersloh, 1994), vol. 1, pp. 305–20.

[4]   For a thorough examination of the language of James see J.B. Mayor, *The Epistle of Saint James* (3rd edn, New York, 1913) and Peter Davids, *The Epistle of James* (Exeter, 1982), pp. 57–9.

[5]   Knox, 'The Epistle of St. James', pp. 14–16.

[6]   Augustine, *Sancti Augustini Confessionum libri* XIII / quos post Martinum Skutella iterum edidit Lucas Verheijen (Turnholti, 1981), 3.6.11.

[7]   Henri de Lubac, *Le mystère du surnaturel* (Paris, 2000), pp. 105–34.

something remains unthought in de Lubac which I associate with the physical condition of being embodied.

Secondly, observe what happens when the reception of this dynamic *Logos* fails to be performed: *Logos* is perverted into the condition of *paralogizomai*; a deponent action, caught between active and passive. The active element seems, literally to be 'acting against' or resisting (*para*) the *Logos*; the passive element is the resultant state of mind: becoming deceived, not thinking correctly, and even cheating oneself. Not only will such an event work contrary to the soteriological effect of the *Logos*, but it will result, ethically, in disobedience. Throughout the epistle, James insists the primary state of being before God is obedience. In the opening verse he describes himself as '*Jakobos ... doulos*' – the Jacob who is slave of both God and the Lord Jesus Christ. The mention of *doulos* connects with Paul's kenotic hymn in Philippians (2:7) – where Christ, in his pouring of himself out, takes the 'form of a slave' (*morphe doulou*). I am not suggesting James is quoting Paul, in fact Paul may be quoting a baptismal hymn known in various Christian communities. What I am pointing to is the fundamental disposition with respect to the Word is as a slave – such that one receives the Word with meekness. What the kenotic hymn points to is that this disposition is a Christic one first and a Christian one by participation in Christ. Now this disposition is fundamental for understanding all Christian praxis, because the disposition of the Word as that which gives, that which serves, is the condition for the same disposition in those who are *poietes* of the Word. Later in the letter (3:15, 17), James, appealing to the Wisdom tradition (a tradition that cannot be disassociated from the early understanding of kenosis) writes about: the wisdom from above (*anothen*) that is true, set over against the false wisdom which does not come down from above (*ouk ... anothen katerchomene*).[8] He moves easily from a *Logos* theology to a *Sophia* theology, and while not making any distinction between an earthly and created Wisdom and a heavenly uncreated Wisdom, he does relate both *Logos* and *Sophia* to a creative work such that *Logos* is correlated to *legein* (to talk, to discourse) and *poiein* (to act, perform).

In fact, we can take this further and suggest it is the performance of the Word by the Word in human acting that constitutes the *poietes*, the *poiesis* and the *poiema*. I put it this way because although it has been insisted upon that '*poiema* and *poiesis* [and therefore presumably *poietes*] ... have in the NT ... nothing whatever to do with poetry'[9] and this extends a conclusion drawn about the LXX that *poietes* is not used of God. I would contend this claim. In the Letter of St

---

8   The Wisdom tradition is filtered through Hellenism, but nevertheless as Verseput notes with respect to James 1:17: 'the reference to God as the creator of the heavenly luminaries ... admits of no convincing explanation on the hypothesis that Greek theological reflection motivates the author's remark', Donald Verseput, 'James 1:17 and the Jewish Morning Prayer', *Novum Testamentum*, 39/2 (1997): 177–91, here 178.

9   Herbert Braun, entry for '*Poieo*', in Gerhard Friedrich (ed.), Geoffrey W. Bromiley (trans.) *Theological Dictionary of the New Testament*, Vol. VI (Grand Rapids, 1971), p. 475.

James all commentators have observed the literary nature of the Greek. In fact, most commentators view the Greek as pretentious because of its 'mirroring [of] the higher *koine* language … Its fluent and elegant style [that] would appeal to readers living in the Greek world'.[10] The literary Greek is complimented, as we note throughout, with a Hebraic use of parallelism, such as is found in the Psalms. In addition, associations, as we have seen, with Philo and the *Corpus Hermeticum* are frequently made. And Philo does employ *poiesis* and *poietes* as poetic terms.

Furthermore, Philo like his secular Greek context, also saw a strong connection between *poiein* and *legein* in a way James does. For in the epistle, at the forefront of James's concern for Christian praxis is the restraining of the tongue, as Chapter 3 demonstrates. 'How great a forest is set ablaze by a small fire. And the tongue is a fire!' It is later in Chapter 3 that the Wisdom tradition is introduced. Participation in the *Logos* will affect how one speaks, not only how one acts. In fact, *poiesis* brings together creation, action and discourse. For James, there is 'speaking evil' (4:11); there is cursing (3:9) and arrogant boasting (4:16); there is the grumbling against one another (5:9); and there is the irreverent swearing of oaths (5:12). But the *legein* rooted in the *Logos* creates knowledge and understanding. The Wisdom tradition articulates a theology of creation.[11] 'The Lord by wisdom founded the earth' (Prov 3:19). Wisdom is understood as Yahweh's artificer, craftsman, the agent ensuring creation is not only ordered and meaningful but also a work of art, a work of beauty.

Read in terms of a theological aesthetics, what this language in James suggests, I would argue, is that the doer of the Word performs a poem in which the divine is both the subject and the object; the praxis is ontologically poetical, for it inscribes a divinity into the world through a divinity from above. The *poietai logou* (the doer of the Word), parallel to a later reference to the *poietai ergou* (the doer of the work), performs in his/her submission a doxological response; and this performance constitutes the salvation of both the one who is faithful and the world in which s/he is being faithful. I will return to this theological aesthetics later with respect to another aspect of kenosis and serving that is key to James: suffering. Though we might emphasize here that I am suggesting James' use of *poietai ergou* in the context of a *Logos* and a *Sophia* tradition relates theology to *theurgia*.

The dialectical nature of the epistle's argument, contrasts, as we have seen, good talk and bad talk; a control of the tongue and the tongue's licentiousness. But this dialectic is crossed by another: one concerned with money. In an analysis of the Letter's rhetorical structure, Lauri Thurén describes how the use of *exordium*, or appeal to a shared ethos in order to 'shape the original rhetorical situation to

---

[10]   On the sophistication of the rhetoric see Wilhelm Wuellner, 'Der Jakobusbrief im Licht der Rhetorik und Textpragmatik', *LB* 43 (1978): 62–3.

[11]   For a discussion of the Wisdom tradition and the Letter of James see, Donald L. Verseput, 'Wisdom, 4Q185, and the Epistle of James', *Journal of Biblical Literature*, 117/4 (1998): 691–707.

suit the author's message'[12] reflects the audience's internal questions that 'can be classified into two groups: the abuse of speech and the abuse of money'.[13] This is an intriguing connection, especially when related to a question asked emphatically throughout the last part of Chapter 2: 'What profit (*ophelos*)' is there in having faith without works (2:14, 2:16)? The thread of thinking that connects *poietai ergou* with speaking and acting well, also connects those that resist or refuse participation with speaking and acting badly. Under acting badly is the misuse of money, fraudulent and decadent behaviour, and rank injustice (5:4–6). Riches, like words that are spoken, are not in themselves wrong, but they have been 'corrupted', 'cankered', 'rusted' (5:1–2) through misuse. What connects language and money theologically here is 'economics', understood as the operations of good or bad management. As a participator in the creativity or economy of the Logos, just as one will learn speak well, so one will learn the best stewardship of riches. Outside of the economy of *Logos*, just as understanding is darkened so ways of behaving err. Such doing are a negative *poiesis*. Wealth is employed here metonymically as a corrupted good, and the indices of a fall from 'every good and every perfect gift' (1:17) into sin.

This brings us to a third observation on *poiesis*, concerning its content. There is a creative doing, there is a creative agent who does this doing – but what is done? I have indicated that it is a response to and therefore a witness of that which has been received from the Word. We might speak then of the thing done as an intensification of the incarnation of the Word. The action then, to use a much later word, is sacramental. But there is more than this. For in such an account, one who performs the Word while respected in the integrity of their selfhood is crossed by another, the divine. So that ultimately, as James points out, the ergonomics of the action lead to blessedness. In other words, the agent is not simply a vehicle for the expression of that which has been received. We return to that which is innate; that which is fundamental to being human. James embarks upon a complex analogy of the man who looks into a mirror and turns away. The one who performs the Word remembers *to prosopon tes geneseos*, and the one who hears the Word only forgets *to prosopon tes geneseos*.

The curiosity here lies in the use of *genesis* (which concerns birth, origin, engendering). Whatever is performed concerns not only the Word received but the remembrance of *to prosopson tes geneseos*. Furthermore, in terms of a content or form for the *poiesis* the only object that is specifically represented is *to prosopon tes geneseos*. This is not the language of Plato. It is a Hebraism. I suggest that what the doer of the Word comes to see in and through that doing, is his or her true likeness, true character (*prosopon*). He or she is recalled to an *imago* that is both fundamental to be who they are, who they were called out to be, but obscured. Obscured, that is, by all that which resists the service and the reception of the Word, that we might call sin if by sin what is understood as everything that refuses

---

[12]   Lauri Thurén, 'Risky Rhetoric in James?', *Novum Testamentum*, 37/3 (1995): 262–84, here 276.

[13]   Ibid.

to obey 'the royal law' (Jas 2:8) of love. The praxis of sin is twice mentioned in James as a negative *poiesis* (4:17 and 5:15) – a usurpation of divine creativity to bring about an inversion of creation, a decreation. One can observe here verse 3:16 about the tongue as a fire 'staining the whole body and setting on fire [*phlogizouos* – inflaming, but also a punning play[14] on and consumption of *Logos*] the cycle of nature [*ton troxon tes geneseos*]'. Evil speaking distorts the economy or course of what was established at the beginning. As such, the one who hears the Word only is in a dangerous position, on the threshold of unpicking the fabric of the created order (in which they themselves are the clearest image of God's work). But the doing that brings forth the *poiema* – what is performed, painted, composed, written, danced, drawn – is both the Word received and a *genesis*, an expression of what was created originally. The expression is not a copy as distinct from the original; it performs something of the fulfilment, the realization or perfection of the original.

We are on the frontiers here of a profound theological anthropology that is inseparable from a Christology and a doctrine of the Trinitarian God. I am aware there are heated debates among commentators as to the extent Christ is at the forefront of James' epistle. There is no reference to the cross and the resurrection and the word 'Christ' only occurs once in the text, in the opening apostrophe that has been declared by eminent scholars as indicative that '*Seine Briefform ist blosse Einkleidung und Fiktion*'[15] (the form of letter is merely a disguise and fiction). But other cognate Christian terms for Christ are employed: the Word, the perfect law, and Wisdom.[16] There are conflicting opinions about how embryonic is James' conception of a Triune God; how close to the Jewish monotheistic tradition he remains. But there is also a recognition that no other epistle so closely parallels Jesus' words, especially as recorded in the *Gospel of Matthew*.

I will not enter into these textual frays directly, but offer a theological reading that affirms a Christology that underwrites the whole epistle and gives attention not so much to Christ as a person but to a messianic operation with respect to the recreation of the world. And that recreation is not a second creation bearing no relation to the first, it is the recreation of what was always so *en Christo*. For I suggest that what the *poietes* gives form to is the truth of the doer, of himself or

---

[14]   The Letter delights in forms of *homoeopropheron*. See Duane F. Watson, 'The Rhetoric of James 3:1–12 and a Classical Pattern of Argumentation' *Novum Testamentum* 35/1 (1993): 48–64.

[15]   Wolfgang Schrage, 'Der Jakobusbrief,' in Horst Balz and Wolfgang Schrage, *Die Katholischen Briefe* (Göttingen, 1973), p. 6. His sentiment is in line with the groundbreaking study of the letter by M. Dibelius, *Der Brief des Jakobus*, revised by H. Greeven (Göttingen, 1964), p. 67.

[16]   By the time of Eusebius of Caesarea, to describe Christ as 'the first-begotten and first-created Wisdom of the God, the pre-existent Word Himself' was commonplace. Eusebius of Caesarea, *The History of the Church*, trans. C.A.Williamson (Harmondsworth, 1965), p. 39.

herself, in Christ, in some analogical sense *as* Christ. For in the Wisdom tradition creation is born from the speaking of the Word; creation is God's *poema*, and our *genesis*. James writes: 'He gave us birth by the word of truth, so that we would become a kind of first fruits of his creatures' (1:18). In seeing something of what we truly are, through the Word, we see something of what the Word itself is. The Christian act then, the *ergon*, realizes an unfathomable paradox in which that which is created in the image of God is crossed by that which is God himself. The activity of God crosses through the activity of being human. The *imago dei*, whose self-understanding is inseparable from Christ as the prototype *imago dei* – between which there is all the difference of the created and the uncreated creator – finds a unique singular expression as a praxis. Vocation here is a practice spoken already by God.

One thinks immediately of the patristic exegesis of the difference between image and likeness and Paul, who uses *eikon* both to speak of the new human being after Christ (Rom 8:29) and Christ himself as the *eikon tou theou* (2 Cor 4:4). The precise content of the Christian praxis, the poetic expression, is formed in a response to and in a recognition of an asymmetrical relation of utter dependence: the knowledge that I am because Christ is. It is also an expression of a surrender – the perfection or *telos* of one's act as service (*leitourgia* undertaken as *doulos*). In this realm of paradox, freedom is realized only in the most profound obedience to the perfect or final law. The perfect law parallels the Word, and later both are drawn into the description of Wisdom that comes from above and whose descent brings forth a new creation (3:17, 18) for those who make peace (*tois poiousin eirenen*).[17] The verb *parakypto* (in 1:25) means not only 'to look intently' but 'to bend or stoop in one's examination of' – as Mary stoops to gaze into the empty tomb.

If this *poiesis* brings forth blessing, the making of peace (3:18), and the production of what is good (*kalon poiein*) (4:17) which is also the production of what is beautiful, it is also, for James, inseparable from endurance, patience and suffering. *Poiesis* is a labouring; being obedient is not passive but a work undertaken in the transit of grace. In the kenotic *carmen Christi* of Paul's letter to the Philippians the action undertaken by Christ in 2:6–8 is inscribed in three verbs: he emptied himself (*ekenosen*), he humbled himself (*etapeinosen*) and he became obedient (*genomenos upekoos*). *Upeko* is not just to become subject to, to submit, it is also to suffer. In the kenotic hymn, Christ suffers to the point of dying. But, significantly, the suffering is indissociable from the practice of submission. Let us follow this more closely. The Letter of St James begins and ends with the call to endurance. The suffering is associated with 'trials of any kind' (1:2) and temptation (1:14).

---

[17]   This relation in the Letter between Law, Wisdom and creation provides a strong endorsement of the sentiment that there is 'every reason to suppose that James' Christian community still considered itself to be part of the religious culture of Israel,' Verseput, 'James 1.17 and the Jewish Morning Prayer', p. 188. Verseput is arguing for the relation between both the Wisdom genre and the Letter and verse 1:17 and the 'creation motifs of Jewish morning prayers' (ibid., p. 178).

The trials can have an external cause. He speaks of the oppression of the rich and being dragged into court (2:6). But the temptations come from within oneself and are related to desire: 'one is tempted by one's own desire [*epithumia* – which is a general word covering all sorts of desiring], being lured and enticed by it' (1:14). The endurance required issues from remaining in obedience such that the external trials and the inner wrestling with an errant desiring do not give birth to doings that are faithless acts of unrighteousness: like the misuse of wealth. James is insistent that the temptations are not from God. They are rooted in our human condition.

However, the one who is a doer of the Word, as we saw above, is more than human. S/he participates in a divine economy in which riches are employed fruitfully. What is important in this account of human acting is that the suffering is endemic to the kenotic disposition that is Christic first and ours by participation. The suffering is inseparable from being open and responding to the world in Christ. *Kenosis, poiesis,* and *genesis* which constitute the fundamental axioms of Christian praxis and the operations of God with respect to salvation can never be divorced from such responsive suffering. The theological condition for this suffering lies in the Godhead itself. In a gnomic phrase, James writes: 'God yearns [*epipothei* – an intensification of the verb *potheo,* to miss] jealously for the spirit he has made to dwell in us' (4:5). A more theologically rigorous account of the inner Trinitarian economy lies in the future, but the verb *epipotheo* points to a suffering that arises out of love, a love that acknowledges Trinitarian difference whilst also in its responsive kenotic acts towards that which is different, and suffers the distance that difference installs. That is, suffers the distension necessary to meet and respect that difference. That which is created good and true and beautiful and exalted (for what is emptied, humbled and obedient is exalted also according to a Christic logic there is James as it is explicitly there in the *Gospel of St John*) is suffered, passionately. To return to a Pauline vocabulary: *kenoo* is intimately associated to *plero. Kenosis* is not then endless emptying, endless exile; it is simultaneously fulfilment, perfection, and doxology. While a theological aesthetics can be orientated around the manifestation of the glory of God, the glorification is not without its passion, its cross. We might go further here, answering Moltmann, and suggesting that this intratrinitarian pathos is the basis upon which God can both identify with our sufferings, in fact also be in solidarity with us in them, while remaining impassable.

We need to deepen this analysis of suffering, for clarification; for there is a suffering that is the consequence of sin. James lists several: the double-mindedness of the doubter, the greed of the rich oppressor, the arrogance of the boaster, to name a few. The suffering here is both with respect to the person committing the sin (in terms of delusions and instabilities) and those others affected by the praxis of sin (in terms of the perpetration of violences and injustices). And so the question arises: are there two forms of suffering – an evil form and a good one? Put this way, the implicit Gnosticism of such a view becomes apparent. So what then, might be the relationship between the suffering born of unrighteousness and the suffering born of a profound kenotic yearning for the other? There must be a relationship such that grace may be effective and salvation operative. I suggest we have to return to that condition prior to the practice of obedience in Christ or the practice of sin – desire (*epithumia*). Suffering is always related to desire. Either the desire of those with riches who wish, at all costs to others to increase their wealth. This is a self-protective desire that gives in to temptation for it cannot bear the suffering born of being constrained by the love of Christ. Evil is not a substantial thing; it is an act in which love is rejected. This rejection of the pathos of love that will lead to a recognition pointed to right at the beginning of our observations on the *Letter of St James*: we do not live just to ourselves. There is that implanted *Logos*, that image as an imprint forgotten, that renders all our self-sufficiency fissured and opens us to the possibility of knowing Christ as the one within whom we dwell (and who dwells in us). We suffer if we reject love and we suffer if we embrace it. But, and this is the most significant difference between these sufferings, the suffering born of love's rejection is devoid of meaning or rationale: *paralogizomenoi*. It is ultimately self-destructive because it acts against the order of creation. Whereas the suffering born of embracing love is creative in the way we have seen the relationship between a *theopoiesis*, *kenosis* and *genesis* is creative. In our own sufferings we need patience, James tells us, because it is only in patience that we can learn how to discern the true nature of such sufferings.

The doctrine of God and the theological anthropology I have begun to sketch here resonates with Gregory of Nyssa's description of Christian praxis and the Godhead in his homilies on the *Song of Songs*: 'the finding of whom is always to seek him; for it is one thing to seek and another to find; but the proceeds of seeking is the seeking itself'.[18] Nyssa is, of course, in the tradition of what we might call 'theopoetic thinking' going back to the school of Alexandria. He understands that this longing or desire has a spiritual pathos: 'Here too, man is circumcised, and yet he remains whole and entire and suffers no mutilation to his material nature.'[19] I am aware that theological battles have been waged over the endless incompleteness of Gregory of Nyssa's account of spiritual desire – that actually has analogues with similar accounts in St John of the Cross and Nicholas of Cusa (as de Lubac has shown).[20] I leave those debates to one side as they have been answered elsewhere – namely by those who acknowledge there is a beatification, a seeing of God face to face, whilst nevertheless a continuing spiritual yearning. In de Lubac's language, there is '*une finalité sans fin*'.[21]

I obviously share much with this tradition among the Greek fathers: their doctrines of participation and *theosis*, rooted in Christology; the centrality of

---

[18]   Quoted by de Lubac in *Le mystère du surnaturel*, p. 249.

[19]   Gregory of Nyssa's *Commentary on the Canticle of Canticles* in Herbert Musurillo, S.J. (ed.) *From Glory to Glory: Texts from Gregory of Nyssa's Mystical Writings* (Crestwood, 1995), p. 193.

[20]   De Lubac, *Le mystère du surnaturel*, pp. 249–50.

[21]   Ibid., pp. 231–55.

desire and its discipline; the emphases in soteriology on *dunamis* and *energeia*; and their positive doctrine of creation that must take sin and evil seriously (even if, ultimately, they are ontologically void). I also share with these Church fathers (and I would include Augustine here also) a concern to allow Scriptural exegesis to guide and inspire theological reasoning. And if my work represents something of that theological sensibility associated with Radical Orthodoxy then there are certainly correspondences between the two that need to be explored more thoroughly, more systemically. That is because a profound relationality lies at the heart of a Trinitarian ontology shared by both the Catholic, High Anglican and Orthodox traditions that we both share. No doubt New Testament scholars would accuse me of a circular hermeneutic: I am reading the *Letter of St James* through Greek fathers like Clement, Origen and Athanasius, and then attempting to demonstrate how the theology in James' epistle anticipates those same Greek fathers. There is some truth in this. But while the circle I would maintain is inevitable, it is not vicious whilst I can reflect upon it and point to the fact that the exegesis is not an end in itself. The exegesis, like appeals to correspondences with the Greek fathers, facilitates a further theological end: the recitation or performance of the tradition in today's cultural context. For the hope and logic of what I have been saying is that there might be here too, in this *ergon*, in this doing, a *theo-poiesis*. It would be a scandal to claim it, but the operation of desire within these words and the flows of these ideas between us cannot but hope it, and pray it.

I return, finally, to my opening position. I am not a patristics scholar, nor a New Testament scholar, nor a scholar of Eastern Orthodoxy. As a contemporary theologian I am pursuing a theological vision that has driven the Christian tradition from its inception in the resurrection. For it seems to me only such a vision: of a world *en Christo*; of praxes within such a world that are liturgical (acts of serving); of a doing that is redemptive because it creates what is good and what is beautiful; and of a profound theo-poetic operation in which sin is exposed and love suffers its yearning for the other – only such a radical vision, a vision beyond utopian dreaming (for it is rooted in a mystery that belies the instrumental reasoning of all utopianism) – only such a vision can transform the ways in which contemporary culture imagines what is possible.

Silence, Intellect and Discourse in the Quest for the True Teaching – Reflections on Hermes Trismegistos' 'Definitions'[22]

Igor Dorfmann-Lazarev

In his article, Graham Ward offers us a reflection on verses 1:21–25 of the Epistle of James, in which, as he observes, the *Logos* (the 'Word' or a 'discourse') ought first to be received – to the point of becoming 'im-planted' (*emphytos*) – and then 'enacted'. Here the Epistle's author observes fundamental Biblical logic, according to which the word uttered by a prophet is always preceded by the word received by him from God. In the most striking way, perhaps, the link between the letting in of the word and its public expression is found in the vision of Ezekiel 2:8–3:3 in which the 'son of man' is told first 'to eat a roll of a book' – to the point of 'filling with it his bowels' – and then 'to speak unto the house of Israel'. This episode also inspired the author of the book that closes the Christian Canon (cf. Rev 10:9–11).

In the Epistle of James, however, it is not the prophecy, or more generally the speech, that is in question but 'working the righteousness of God' (1:20). Ward suggests reading James' binomial 'hearers (*akroatai*) of the Word/doers (*poiêtai*) of the Word' in the perspective of the Alexandrian exegetical theory of divinization. This provides him with a new key for the interpretation of this book which, ever since Luther, who had found it contradictory in every respect to Paul, has presented a particular challenge to Protestant Biblical commentators. Man, situated between the Word Creator and the created word, occupies according to Ward an intermediate position in the process of *theopoiesis* in which the 'word' appears contemporaneously as both the subject and the object of creative action. Ward thence comes to a consideration of human activity in the world, thus contributing to the discussion of the ontological value of man's acts, the underlying exegetical problem regarding both James and Paul.[23] His emphasis on the aesthetical aspects of human activity and human experiences drives him away, however, from the central concerns of the Epistle's author.

---

[22] The author expresses his gratitude to Christoph Schneider for his invitation to take part in this exchange and to the Rev. Peter F. Johnson, Charles Lock and John Lindsay Opie for helping the author improve his English style.

[23] Cf. Hubert Frankemölle, *Der Brief des Jakobus* (2 vols, Gütersloh 1994), vol. 1, pp. 339–40, in which the author discusses the *Rezeptionsgeschichte* of the Epistle of James in twentieth-century Germany, stressing the role of this text in the activity of the Resistance under the Nazi regime.

Reflecting on James' language, Ward mentions a brief observation made more than half a century ago by W.L. Knox on the similarity between the 'types of speculation' proper to the Epistle of James and to the writings attributed to Hermes Trismegistos (Hermes 'the Thrice-Greatest').[24] A closer glance at Hermes will allow us to place James and his vision of man's activity in the wider perspective of coeval religious thought. The Hermetic corpus reaches back to the ancient Egyptian wisdom texts, but in its extant form reflects the cosmopolitan intellectual ambience of Roman Egypt[25] and in some parts notably carries traces of the Bible and Apocrypha, as well as of Alexandrian Jewish exegetical thought. The texts attributed to Trismegistos were therefore shaped in the same area in which, towards the end of the second century, the Alexandrian Christian theology was born.

As in Christianity, the relationship between God and man is at the core of the Hermetic tradition. The various texts of Hermetic literature reveal different perspectives on this matter however, and although they could have been studied and meditated upon in the same circles of adherents, each of them ought to be treated in its own right. We suggest here bringing James' anthropology, which Ward's article discusses, into juxtaposition with one of the older of the Hermetic philosophical works, which has only recently become accessible to western readers and has not yet received sufficient attention from New Testament scholars. We refer to the 'Definitions' attributed to Hermes, which are preserved in their fullest form in Armenian.[26] Jean-Pierre Mahé, the author of the critical edition of the Armenian text, dates the original Greek to the period from the first century BC to the first century AD, suggesting that its sources may go back much further.[27] The 'Definitions' or their direct sources, therefore, might have been known to the author of the Epistle of James.

The 'Definitions', addressed by Hermes 'the Thrice-Great' (*Eŕamec*, in Armenian ← *Trismegas*) to his disciple Asclepius, were translated into Armenian in the second half of the sixth century. They belonged to the numerous Greek

---

[24] Wilfred L. Knox, 'The Epistle of St. James', *The Journal of Theological Studies*, OS–XLVI, 181–2 (1945): 14–16.

[25] The latest Hermetic texts were put into writing before the end of the third century AD; see A.D. Nock, in *Corpus Hermeticum. Asclepius*, ed. A.D. Nock, trans. A.-J. Festugière (4 vols, Paris, 1945) vol. 2, pp. 259, 275.

[26] The *editio princeps* of the 'Definitions' was published in 1956 by H. Manandian. 26 years later, J.-P. Mahé prepared a new critical edition, translation and detailed commentary; cf. Jean-Pierre Mahé, *Hermès en Haute Egypte: les textes hermétiques de Nag Hammadi et leurs parallèles grecs et latins. Le fragment du Discours parfait et les Définitions hermétiques arméniennes* (2 vols, Québec 1978–82), vol. 2, pp. 358–405. Later, an edition of the surviving Greek fragments of the 'Definitions' datable by the eleventh century was prepared jointly by J. Paramelle and J.-P. Mahé, 'Nouveaux parallèles grecs aux Définitions hermétiques arméniennes', *REArm*, XXII (1990–91): 115–34.

[27] Mahé, *Hermès en Haute Egypte*, vol. 2, p. 278.

texts from which the Armenian divines, followers of the Alexandrian exegetical and doctrinal traditions, sought to obtain the dialectical instruments for defining Christological orthodoxy independently of the imperial Church.[28] The interest in Hermes could have been provoked in particular by the positive appreciation given him by Gregory of Nazianzos, one of the most quoted Greek fathers in Armenia, and by Cyril of Alexandria, the major authority for the Christology of the Armenian Church.[29] To evoke this text in connection with the present encounter between the orthodoxy shaped by the first half of the ninth century in the west of Asia Minor and a new, 'Radical', orthodoxy elaborated today at Cambridge has a particular significance: it offers us the opportunity to recall still another orthodoxy, that which had been sought by Armenians, Syrians, Egyptians and Ethiopians during several centuries following the rejection of the 'Definition' of the council of Chalcedon (451) across the area extending from Transcaucasia in the north to the Horn of Africa in the south.

The Hermetic 'Definitions' therefore link the Nile valley with the mountains of the Caucasus, that ancient frontier between Asia and Europe, thus bequeathing to Christendom the wisdom of ancient Egypt. The survival of this text in numerous Armenian manuscripts,[30] in spite of the adversities of Armenian history, as well as the wide use of the 'Definitions' made by mediaeval Armenian authors,[31] demonstrates its importance for the articulation of Armenian orthodoxy in the period following the first great schism of the Christian Church.

In what follows, we shall outline several salient points of Hermes' vision of human activity and human discourse in the light of the relationship between man and God. The author of the 'Definitions' distinguishes five gifts with which, in their various combinations, the different kinds of living beings are endowed: life,

---

[28] After more than a century of debates and confrontations in the Near East resulting from the teaching of Eutyches and the ensuing council of Chalcedon, the Armenian Church rejected both the extreme monophysitism and the imperial doctrine at the council of Duin in 553–5. In the following centuries, Armenian divines elaborated an autonomous Christological theory along the lines of Cyril of Alexandria. The integral humanity of Christ was expressed by them in various ways, but the designation of Christ's divinity and humanity as *two* comparable entities belonging to one and the same abstract category of *nature* was avoided. On the schism provoked by the council of Chalcedon and on the formation of the autonomous Churches in the Near East, see the contributions of P. Maraval, N. Garsoïan and J.-P. Mahé in *Histoire du Christianisme*, ed. J.-M. Mayeur et al. (14 vols, Paris 1990–2001), vol. 3, pp. 457–81, 1125–67; ibid., vol. 4, pp. 457–548.

[29] Claudio Moreschini, *Storia dell'ermetismo cristiano* (Brescia, 2000), pp. 94–101.

[30] The most important manuscript of the 'Definitions' is a florilegium composed in 1282 by the learned Məxit'ar of Ayrivank' († c.1290), prior of the Monastery of the Cavern which had been carved between the middle of the twelfth century and the second half of the thirteenth within the rock in the gorge of the river Azat in North-Eastern Armenia; see Mahé, *Hermès en Haute Egypte*, vol. 2, pp. 320–27.

[31] Cf. Mahé, *Hermès en Haute Égypte*, vol. 2, pp. 333–54; M. Van Esbroeck, 'J.-P. Mahé, *Hermès en Haute-Égypte*', *REArm*, XVII (1983): 692–3.

breath, soul, intellect and discourse. Man is the only being endowed with both intellect[32] and discourse.[33] The intellect is the highest gift, which is superior to the natural world, the world of physical bodies, and is capable of supernatural and unlimited sight and thought ('Definitions' IV.2; V.1–3; X.5). It enables man to accomplish himself: 'The perfection of the soul is the knowledge of beings' (VI.3); 'Man's plenitude is the knowledge of God' (VII.5); 'Each man, insofar as he conceives of God, is a man' (IX.1). Man, for Hermes, is therefore a dynamic being who is realized in continuous becoming[34] and is ordained to the knowledge of the world and of God through the exercise of his intellect.

The intellect acquires knowledge[35] and understanding[36] in silence and expresses them in 'intelligent', or 'meditative',[37] 'discourse' which, according to Hermes, is its 'servant' interpreting the intellect's designs. Only the intellect is able to *conceive*[38] and to comprehend 'discourse' (V.1–3). Such discourse, proceeding from the intellect as its direct function inherits its qualities: since the intellect is infinite in its cognitive capacity, discourse is infinite in its capacity for articulating the wisdom acquired by the former. Therefore, meditative discourse, which through the intermediary of the intellect ascends to silence, becomes the image of silence; it links human existence to infinity and brings salvation to men: 'Man has become mortal because of his body, but because of discourse [he] is immortal' (V.2).

Meditative discourse is, similarly to James 1:21–2, at once man's creation and God's salvific gift. It is distinguished from the 'discourse of the crowd' (V.3; X.7) which necessarily proceeds from some other discourse – the crowd being deprived of intellect – and therefore does not establish any bond with the higher level of reality, i.e. does not represent a channel of the transcendent. The latter kind of discourse, which is merely 'man's invention', generates a vicious circle between

---

[32] 'Intellect': *mitk'* in the Armenian version. It corresponds to νοῦς in the surviving Greek fragments and evokes the 'heart' of the ancient Egyptian wisdom texts; see Mahé, *Hermès en Haute Egypte*, vol. 2, p. 297.

[33] 'Discourse': *ban* in the Armenian version, which corresponds to λόγος in the surviving Greek fragment.

[34] Similarly in the Epistle of James; cf. Frankemölle, *Der Brief des Jakobus*, vol. 1, p. 341; with respect to *James* 1.25ᵈ, H. Frankemölle underlines: 'Der Mensch sein Glück nicht (instrumental) "durch sein Tun" erlangt, sondern (modal, durativ) "in seinem Tun" und "während des Tuns"' (ibid.).

[35] 'to know': *gitem* ← οἶδα; 'knowledge': *gitut'iwn* ← γνῶσις.

[36] 'to understand': *imanam* ← νοέω.

[37] 'Discourse' is once called *mtawor* (V.3), 'intelligent' (a term elsewhere also qualifying the 'soul'), and once *par-imac'akan* (X.7), 'meditative'. The latter term appears only once in the text. The Greek fragment does not contain the parallel verses, but we may presume that the second term could be the calque of περινοηματικός. These terms should be distinguished from 'intelligible' (qualifying 'world', 'things', 'good' and 'substance'), *imanali* ← νοητός.

[38] 'conceive': *yłanam*, the same lexeme which describes the germination of embryos.

the bodies of this world and thus brings forth perdition (V.2–3).[39] Similarly to Hermes, James – as Ward notices – distinguishes between true and false wisdom, between the wisdom which 'descends from above' and brings good fruits and that which is 'earthly, animal and demoniac' (Jas 3:14–18).

In spite of the place reserved by Hermes for silence in the cognitive process and of his condemnation of the 'discourses of the crowd', the author does not confine his hearers to interior and abstract meditation. Although he contemplates beauty and harmony (II.1; IX.4; X.1,7), he is also concerned with the concrete setting of human life in the world and with man's responsibility with regard to everything his senses perceive. In Hermes's view, man is endowed with free will; he creates salvific discourse and is divinized through his active acquaintance and his engagement with the world: 'Will, comprehend, believe, love!' (VIII.7). Work is connatural to men, so that 'men working the earth' are likened by him to 'the stars adorning heaven' (IX.7).

The world exists for the sake of man, just as man for the sake of God, and man is a 'free living being' in the world, the only being which has 'dominion over good and bad' (VI.1; VIII.6; IX.1). Man's senses, by which he perceives and apprehends the world, testify that man and the world are ordained to each other as the Lord to his dominion: 'If there were no seer [of the world], there would certainly be neither he himself, nor that what is seen [by him]' (VI.1). Man therefore exercises his dominion over the world also through being its observer and interpreter. He thus occupies the key position in the universe wherein he plays the role of mediator between God and the natural world entrusted to him.

Man's attentive reflection on the world has liberating effect: 'If nothing seems to you an insignificant fact, you will discover both the fact and its artificer; if everything seems to you a joke, you will be made a joke yourself' (VIII.5); the world exists in order that through it man may know God (VIII.6); God is intelligible, he 'is invisible although observable in the things visible to us' (I.2); 'He who knows God, does not fear God; he who does not know God, fears God. He who knows nothing about the beings of this [world] fears everyone [of them], but he who knows all about these beings, fears no one … he who reflects by the means of the intellect on himself, knows himself' (IX.3–4). Through observation of the world, the intellect thus discovers its creator, and death is overcome through the understanding of the world: 'Death comprehended is immortality, uncomprehended is death' (VIII.5; IX.2,4; X.6).

---

[39]   Other Hermetic texts suggest that he who follows the instructions of meditative discourse is on the 'way of life'; see Mahé, *Hermès en Haute Egypte*, vol. 2, p. 298 ; Id., 'La voie d'immortalité', *Vigiliae Christianae* 45 (1991): 351–636. The accomplishment of God's commandments as the 'upright way' which gives life, as the image of the way from bondage to freedom and of the way to the promised Land, is also fundamental to several Biblical books (see above all Deut 5:32–3; 10:12–13; 11:22–8; 28:11–14; 31:29) whence it has been inherited by ecclesiastical writers for the definition of orthodoxy, the 'upright teaching', that is the 'upright way' which deviates neither to the right nor to the left which are associated with different heresies.

The natural world is 'the mirror of truth', the embodiment of bodiless reality, as meditative discourse is the image of silence. Only the intellect, however, is able to look into this mirror. The intellect is also called by Hermes 'light', because it illuminates, by means of the discourse it creates, visible things in such a way as to see through them the invisible things. The relationship of discourse to silence is parallel to the relationship of the world to truth: in both cases, the latter is the image of the former. Moreover, whilst nature is 'the light of non-manifest [things]' (VIII.5), the intellect is the 'light' which enables the one who possesses it to see the 'interior things' (IX.2).

The parallelism between discourse and the world – as well as between their prototypes, truth and silence – could probably be extended further. Above we observed that meditative discourse is, for Hermes, at once a gift and man's creation. We may consequently assume that the 'Definitions' implicitly allot a similar intermediate position also to the natural world. Indeed, we find there the following symmetrical statement in which the world occupies the central position between God and man: 'God is in himself; the world is in God; man is in the world' (VII.5). Hermes also seems to suggest that the world at once illuminates man and is the object of man's enlightened action: on the one hand, nature is called 'generous' because it 'teaches everybody' the truth (VIII.5); on the other hand, 'everything [exists] for the sake of man', and man, who exists for the sake of God, is called to act in the world, thus transforming it by his action and conferring on it a new meaning by his interpretation. Only through this twofold activity does man attain to salvation. This *coincidentia oppositorum* in the definitions of the world and of discourse – comparable to that observed by Ward in the Epistle of James – can, according to J-P. Mahé, be traced back to the procedures of the mythical thought of ancient Egypt.[40]

We may, therefore, observe a similarity between James and Hermes both in their anthropology and in their speculative methods. However, whilst in James' view (in accord with the idea dominant in the Bible and rabbinic literature) the Christian achieves perfection through the accomplishment of God's commandments,[41] for the author of the 'Definitions' man primarily expresses himself in cognition, thereby attaining to salvation. Nevertheless, Hermes' perspective cannot hereby be associated with Gnosticism. The author of the 'Definitions' implies no split within the intellect;[42] in sharp opposition to Gnostic perception, he implies monistic cognition and contemplates an optimistic anthropology in which all human faculties deliberately operate in the world in the effort to attain the knowledge of God.[43] Moreover, as we have seen, Hermes also envisages a piety enlightened by knowledge and implying

---

[40] Mahé, *Hermès en Haute Egypte*, vol. 2, pp. 290–91.

[41] Cf. Frankemölle, *Der Brief des Jakobus*, vol. 1, pp. 318, 337–8.

[42] Cf. Andreas Löw, *Hermes Trismegistos als Zeuge der Wahrheit. Die christliche Hermetikrezeption von Athenagoras bis Laktanz* (Berlin, 2002), p. 17, note 60.

[43] Mahé sees in the Trismegistus' optimistic view of life the spiritual legacy of the pharaohs' Egypt; cf. Mahé, *Hermès en Haute Egypte*, vol. 2, p. 454.

faith and love (VIII.7). Indeed, in his view, man's relation to God is not merely that of cognition, but also involves companionship, affinity and reciprocal longing: 'Where man is, [there is] also God ... God is man's friend, man is God's friend. [There is] a kinship between God and man ... Man is desirable for God, and God for man' (IX.6); 'What[ever] God makes, he makes for the sake of man' (VIII.2); it is solely man to whom 'God manifests himself' and 'to whom he listens' and, in order to talk to him, changes his form and 'becomes man' (IX.6).[44]

In what direction do the 'Definitions' orient theological thought? Hermes suggests that man's discourse must always proceed from a personal spiritual experience which implies the engagement with both silence and the world; otherwise discourse risks degenerating into chatter. This intuition warns the theologian concerning two options, the excessive institutionalization of theology and the overproduction of theological texts, especially in times of diminishing religious life. In both these cases the source of supernatural knowledge, the encounter with the divine occurring in silence, is interposed, in the one case by an impersonal structure and in the other by the infinite chains of derivative commentaries or by invented meanings.

The special veneration accorded the fathers by the Armenian and other Eastern Churches does not seem to be extraneous to Hermes' intuition. In the consciousness of these Churches, the fathers are the spiritual athletes whose theology is particularly precious, not on account of the fathers' formal ministerial office, but rather because of the conviction that it sprang from singular encounters with the divine. To refer to their heritage is therefore to maintain a living bond with the privileged moments of human history. This special position allotted the fathers has safeguarded the Eastern Churches from an excessive dilation of their dogmatic corpora. To return to the fathers is to return to the essential verities over the centuries of religious writing (and, also, of religious chatter).

The Armenians, the guardians of Hermes' 'Definitions', like other miaphysites, were indeed 'radical' in their attachment to the founding events, figures and texts of their Church: even the Byzantine tradition was in their eyes excessive in its centuries-old development of dogma. To cite but one example: the ninth-century Armenian divine Isaac Mṙut, a contemporary of Photius the Great, referring to the dogmas endorsed by the imperial Church since the council of Ephesus (431, the last Ecumenical council recognized by the Armenians), reproached

---

[44] In order to render our presentation less cumbersome, we have ignored all those concepts present in the 'Definitions' which do not directly relate to our topic: we have not spoken of the 'derivative' gods, nor of the distinctions between mortal and immortal beings, between the sensible and the intelligible worlds, between elements, substances and natures constituting the world. We have also ignored the qualities of genders and of souls and bodies. There are, however, passages in the 'Definitions' that complicate the picture of man we have drawn here. Thus, in VIII.4, the author affirms that there are in fact two intellects, one with which every man is endowed (in the Greek version called 'divine') and that 'pertaining to the soul' which, however, is not present in every human soul.

the Byzantines that their 'synods of all colours convoked here and there' drove them ever farther from the 'orders and the definitions of the faith which had been established by the power of the Holy Ghost'.[45] Therefore, although the Armenians continued along the centuries to seek further definitions for their pre-Chalcedonian orthodoxy, they have never attached to the results of these attempts an absolutely binding character.

To return to our main subject, Hermes' awareness of the danger of interposition between the voice sounding in silence and the receptive ear can probably also explain the 'incomplete' and 'moving' character of the Hermetic texts.[46] Since the word that breaks its bond with silence loses its meaning, every thought that pretends to the position of a rigid and accomplished system is distrusted. At each moment the word ought to spring anew, it can never get hardened, being otherwise unable to represent the image of the one who inspires it.

Could such a thought find room in Christian theology? This question merits a whole series of studies. One of the possible directions of such research would be the investigation of the impact of Hermes' ideas upon theological writing in Armenia and the consequent reception (and rejection) of post-Ephesian texts by the Armenian Church. But the Hermetic writings may also be of interest to contemporary Western religious thought. In this respect, we cannot but limit ourselves to a brief final remark. Dwelling on the fact that Hermetic literature, in J.-P. Mahé's words, 'puts itself continuously into question', we in fact approach – by a different route – what Gianni Vattimo has called *il Pensiero debole*, 'Weak Thought', a thought which avoids metaphysical categories, peremptory affirmations and closed systems. Vattimo's starting point is not, however, the encounter with silence, but rather God's *kenosis*: if the Creator of heaven and earth 'emptied himself taking the form of a slave' (Phil 2:7), then every systematic thought and every 'natural law' ought to be put into question.[47] He suggests that the thought which continuously overcomes itself derives from the very shape of Christianity: 'Revelation does not reveal a "truth-object"; it speaks of a salvation

---

[45]   Igor Dorfmann-Lazarev, *Arméniens et Byzantins à l'époque de Photius: Deux débats théologiques après le Triomphe de l'orthodoxie* (Leuven, 2004), pp. 50, 427–8.

[46]   Cf. the striking description given to Hermetic literature by J.-P. Mahé: '*C'est une littérature qui, par son essence même, refuse la perfection écrite et cherche systématiquement ce qu'il y a d'incomplet, de mouvant*' ; '*la véritable prière ... ne cherche pas à accumuler litanie sur litanie, et louange sur louange; elle tend, au contraire, à un approfondissement progressif ; elle ne cesse de se remettre en cause pour chercher, insatiablement, un contact plus vrai, plus direct avec Dieu. Aucun terme ne lui suffit, aucun dépassement ne la satisfait, elle finit toujours par constater son impuissance*', in Mahé, *Hermès en Haute Egypte*, vol. 2, pp. 437, 455.

[47]   Gianni Vattimo, *Credere di credere* (Milan, 1996), pp. 31, 35; *Dopo la cristianità: per un cristianesimo non religioso* (Milan, 2002), pp. 24–6, 63–73; These points of Vattimo's conception of Christianity are discussed in Igor Dorfmann-Lazarev, 'La découverte de la kénose de Dieu par la "Pensée faible": La religion dans l'œuvre de G. Vattimo', *Istina*, 49/4 (2004): 361–77.

in process … Christ presents himself as the authentic interpreter of the prophets, but at the moment of parting from his disciples, he promises to send them the Spirit of truth which will continue to teach and will therefore pursue the history of salvation.'[48]

---

[48]   Vattimo, *Credere di credere*, p. 43; cf. also *Dopo la cristianità*, pp. 29–43, 90, 131–3.

Chapter 7
The Beatific Vision of St Thomas Aquinas[1]

Phillip Blond

The theology surrounding the beatific vision is highly contentious. For both philosophy and theology, most of the problems of the beatific vision derive from a fundamental dualism. Classically, the situation is set up where the happiness attainable in this life is contrasted with a Christian beatitude achievable in the next. This situation is further complicated by Holy Scripture which seems to promise both some form of beatific appearance in this life, as well as a vision of that image which will await us in paradise, 'we see now through a glass in a dark manner; but then face to face' (1 Cor 13:12). In accordance with such injunctions Christians believe that they must rank the two realms of happiness (that achieved here below and that attained in heaven) in order to demonstrate that any happiness reached in this life cannot be the ultimate end of man.

Yet this supervening of beatitude upon quotidian *eudaimonia* produces another layer of interpretative difficulty. For Christians must now link desire in this life to a supernatural end in the next. But then natural man (as the Aristotelians might put it) would already be super-naturalized, for he would have a natural desire for the supernatural. And if one can have such an orientation, how does this non-natural desire relate to natural nature itself? How can natural man fulfil such a teleology? Does natural man achieve his aim by his own power or good works, or alternatively does the supernatural end itself intervene in natural life to enable itself to be attained? If the former, then man has no need of a divine beatitude and pagan virtues are requisite ends in themselves, if the latter then the former is again doubly confirmed. For it follows that man must not have been made in the divine image as God in a second act of making makes good a creation rendered as

---

[1]   Much of the most recent scholarship on the beatific vision has been French. The longest and most sustained treatment is that given by Christian Trottman, *La Vision Béatifique, des disputes scholastiques à sa définition par Benoît XII* (Rome, 1995). See also his *Théologie et Noétique au XIII Siècle* (Paris, 1999). Important works also include Pierre-Yves Maillard, *La Vision de Dieu Chez Thomas D'Aquin* (Paris, 2001). Jean-Pierre Torrell, *Recherches Thomasiennes* (Paris, 2000) especially chapter V. See also *Aletheia*, the special issue on *Nature et Grâce*, 19, June (2001). And also Otto-Hermann Pesch and Jean-Marie Van Cangh, *Béatitude eschatologique et bonheur humain* (Paris, 2005). In English see also Anna N. Williams, *The Ground of Union: Deification in Aquinas and Palmas* (Oxford, 1999).

initially deficient since he must still add something to humanity to enable man to achieve his promised and already desired end: the vision of God.[2]

However, I do not want to enter the whole debate between grace and nature, between Aquinas' attempts to construct an essentially complementary harmony between the two, the innovations of Cajetan in dividing them so fatally, and the purported recovery of their concordance by de Lubac. Thus, I want to sidestep the traditional debate concerning the beatific vision which concentrates on God's sovereignty and our possible infringement of it via the reception of grace through the expectation of nature. For my purposes, it suffices to say that I believe that nature is *already* in the order of grace. This means that I do *not* believe that God enacts a second creation to give to mankind a grace that he had initially refused. Yes, of course, God could have created rational creatures that would not enjoy the beatific vision, but this would be a world unlike ours. And if God has promised this vision to us by giving us a natural desire for it, then in some sense it must have *already* been given. Either we already have the beatific vision (in some as yet undetermined manner or degree), or we will never attain it. Not least because the means by which God grants us such a vision are as open to him in this life as they are in the next, there being no sense in the accounts that Thomas gives of the beatific vision that the soul in the next life is able to overcome its own finitude and see God by virtue of its own powers. By this I mean that God must still displace our own cognitive function whether we are in this life or the next in order to introduce his likeness into the mind of the beatified. God actualizes the potentiality to see him by providing what the creature lacks: the intelligible species of God. God donates what no created intellect embodied or separate can manufacture, intuit or abstract: an intelligible likeness of himself. The name of this act is grace. Grace so understood is that of which created nature is incapable and yet that which it can fully desire, phenomenologically anticipate and faithfully expect.

What I would like to focus on is what we see when we see God. I would like to inquire as to whether this vision is a purely intellectual manifestation or an encounter that demands augmentation by the body and matter. However quite what we do see in the beatific vision is as controversial now as it was in the thirteenth century. As I have said, Scripture both prohibits and argues for the cognition of the divine essence. God is said to be that 'whom no man has seen and no man is able to see' (1 Tim 6:16). Whilst other passages promise that 'we shall be like him because we shall see him as he really is' (1 Jn 3:2). The oscillation between the two injunctions produced both Augustine's Latin insistence on the immediacy of our encounter with the divine essence and the Eastern tradition of Pseudo-Dionysius, John Damascene and Gregory Palamas (and for that matter the great Irish

---

[2]   De Lubac extends this point when he argues that dividing happiness in this life from my finality in the next means that 'I must, fatally, appear to precede my actual being and my being in turn appears to precede its own finality'. Henri de Lubac, *The Mystery Of The Supernatural*, trans. Rosemary Sheed (New York, 1998), p. 76. French edition, *Le mystère du surnaturel* (Paris, 1965), p. 106.

theologian John Scotus Eriugena[3]) which emphasized an infinite (and therefore invisible) fontal source, with a cognitive dynamic of emanationist overflow and participatory encounter.[4] Whether these traditions are actually opposed is a question to be addressed elsewhere – but needless to say I think an Augustinian distinction between God's manifestation and our receptive limitation is not foreign to Dionysius or Palamas. Nor indeed is the Eastern vision of a divinity inseparable from the exoteric manifestations of mediation foreign to Augustine or Aquinas.

But all of the above is not my immediate concern. As I said I propose to concentrate on the place of matter and the body in the beatific vision. Since this is a vast field, I propose to focus on Thomas Aquinas' account of beatitude. Why Aquinas? Because over the course of his work, Aquinas changed his account of the nature and character of the final beatitude, inverting the privilege initially accorded to the resurrected body. In the earlier work of Aquinas, the beatific vision accrues to the fully resurrected soul – in the *Commentary on the Sentences* composed sometime between 1252–56, the vision is both corporeal and intellectual; whereas in the *Summa Theologica*, especially in the *Secunda Pars* (1269–72), we find this logic and direction wholly reversed. Here an abstracted and disembodied account of the beatific vision is offered and the body is held to be an accidental extension to the intellective beatitude enjoyed by the saints. Indeed so stark is this reversal that Aquinas almost argues that the separated soul enjoys a greater degree of beatitude more than the fully resurrected soul in the newly spiritual body.

These concerns are echoed by other scholars. Christian Trottman speaks of Aquinas changing his opinion.[5] Whilst Oliver Boulnois asks why Thomas abandoned the embodied and resurrected beatitude of *the Sentences* for the intellective account of the beatific vision that Aquinas subsequently makes in the *Summa Theologia*.[6] Which is the true Aquinas? Is it the younger Thomas of the commentary on the *Sentences* who following Bonaventure, thought that the beatific vision also implied the resurrection of the body? A position which indicates that

---

[3]   Eriugena, born in Ireland around the first quarter of the ninth century is among the most significant Western thinkers between the time of Augustine and Aquinas. His particular strength lay in his mastery of both the Western and the Eastern tradition. At the court of Charles the Bald in the 840s he translated all the works of Pseudo-Dionysius into Latin, the *Quaestiones ad Thalassium* of Maximus the Confessor and part of the *Ambigua ad Iohannes* as well. As such, Eriugena represents a synthesis of Byzantine and Latin theology before their subsequent fatal division.

[4]   As William Hoye points out, for Byzantine theology 'the multifarious teachings on this side of the controversy can be best summed up in the term theophanies: not the invisible divine essence, but theophanies, emanating from the divine essence, are to manifest the invisible divinity to the divinized human creature'. William J. Hoye, *Actualitas Omnium Actum, Man's Beatific Vision of God as Apprehended by Thomas Aquinas* (Meisenheim am Glan, 1975), pp. 146–7.

[5]   Trottman, *La Vision Béatifique*, p. 422.

[6]   Olivier Boulnois, 'Les deux fins de l'homme l'impossible anthropologie et le repli de la théologie', *Les Etudes Philosophiques*, 2 (1995): 205–22.

in some manner such a vision is already in the substantial form of man, or is it the author of the *Summa Theologia*, for whom the body is no longer essential for beatitude? In order to answer these questions we had best begin with Thomas' understanding of beatitude and an account of its development.

Thomas' Account of the Beatific Vision

It is in Book III of the *Summa Contra Gentiles* from Chapters 24–64 that Aquinas gives the fullest account of his reading of the beatific vision. The vision is introduced by way of reflection on the proper end of all things.[7] As early as Chapter 16, Thomas tells us that the end of every being is a good and he quotes Aristotle when he tells us approvingly that the good is that 'which all things desire'.[8] Whilst each creature's end is its own perfection, this perfection is not an autonomous goal independent of other perfections and fulfilments. The good in respect of which all creatures are ordered, is not some intermediate good appropriate only for an individual creature or its station of being.

On the contrary – all beings for Thomas are ordered to the highest possible good – which is God and God alone. And God for Aquinas *is* an attainable end for he tells us as early as Chapter 2 of Book III that insofar as all things act for an end, they act for that beyond which they have no further desire. Otherwise as he says 'actions would tend to infinity which is impossible.'[9] So conceived all things act for an end. This *telos* perfects each creature and also relates it to that which is beyond itself. And God is the end of all goods because he is the creating cause of good. As such he is that beyond which one cannot go. There being no cause prior to the first.

---

[7]   All Latin quotations from the *Summa Theologia* and *Summa Contra Gentiles* are taken from Volume III of the Busa edition: *S. Thomae Aquinatis Opera omnia: ut sunt in indice thomistico additis 61 scriptis ex aliis medii aevi auctoribus*, ed. R. Busa (Stuttgart-Bad Cannstatt, 1980). English translations of the above are as follows: St Thomas Aquinas, *Summa Contra Gentiles* 3.1, trans. V.J. Bourke (Notre Dame, 1975). This English translation is the University of Notre Dame's 1975 reprint of the 1955–57 Doubleday & Company edition. All English translations are from this edition with all publishing details the same, except Book 1 trans. A.C. Pegis; Book 2, trans. J.F. Anderson; Book 3.1 and 3.2 trans. V.J. Bourke; Book 4 trans. C.J. O'Neil; St Thomas Aquinas, *Summa Theologica*, trans. in five volumes by the fathers of the English Dominican province (Westminster-Maryland, 1981). All English translations, unless indicated or amended, are from this edition.

[8]   *quod omnia appetunt* (*SCG* 3.1 c16, n2, cf. *Nicomachean Ethics* 1, 1 (1094a 2)).

[9]   I give the reference in full: '*Sed in actione cuiuslibet agentis est invenire aliquid ultra quod agens non quaerit aliquid: alias enim actiones in infinitum tenderent; quod quidem est impossibile, quia, cum infinita non sit pertransire, agens agere non inciperet; nihil enim movetur ad id ad quod impossibile est pervenire. Omne igitur agens agit propter finem*' (*SCG* III c.2, n3). Thomas quotes Aristotle in the *Posterior Analytics* 1, 22 (82b 38) 'It is impossible to proceed to infinity'.

Moreover as Etienne Gilson points out, the cosmos itself is moved (literally) to a vision of God, 'even those beings devoid of knowledge operate in view of an end, desire the good with a natural appetite and desire the divine resemblance and their own perfection'.[10] This is possible because anything that is a work or act of nature is a work of an intellectual substance '*quod quodlibet opus naturae est opus substantiae intelligentis*' (*SCG* 3.24 n5). Thus does intelligence and intention lie at the foundation of all of creation such that it finds its order, reason and direction in its participation in the divine vision. But in returning to God, creatures and the cosmos are not just returning to their own form of perfection, their own excellence in whatever degree participates in something greater than itself – each creaturely perfection being an imitation of God and thereby a relation to other creatures.

But what is this end to which all creatures (even those without knowledge) aim? For Aquinas as we know 'final and perfect happiness can consist in nothing but the vision of the divine essence' (*ultima et perfecta beatitudo non potest esse nisi in visione divinae essentiae*) (*ST* I–II, Q.3, a8).[11] But in what does this beatific vision consist? Thomas appears to believe that the beatific vision consists in an intellectual cognition of God himself. In this encounter we see nothing but God: '*Ipsa visio divinitatis ponitur tota substantia nostrae beatitudinis*' (I *Sent*. d1, q1, a1, ans).[12] He notes that though some have held 'that no created intellect can see the essence of God' this opinion 'is not tenable … as the ultimate beatitude of man consists in the use of his highest function, which is the operation of the intellect' (*ST* I Q. 12 a1. ans).[13] And the intellect operates to unite the rational creature with 'the principle of its being; since a thing is perfect so far as it attains to its principle' (*intantum enim unumquodque perfectum est, inquantum ad suum principium attingit*) (*ST* I Q.12 a1.ans.).

The question is how this can be achieved? For Aquinas given that the embodied intellect cannot understand separate substances (angels and departed souls) since it is united with the body, still less are we able to see God who transcends even

---

[10] Etienne Gilson, 'Sur La Problématique Thomiste De La Vision Béatifique', *Archives D'Histoire Doctrinale et Littéraire du Moyen-Âge*, 31 (1964): 68. Gilson notes the cosmological radicality of this thesis 'it applies to all nature as such even that which is devoid of knowledge' (ibid., p. 69).

[11] See also *Questiones Disputatae de Veritate*, Q. 8, a1; *SCG* III 54, 57 and IV *Sent.*, d.49, Q.2 a.1.

[12] Thomas Aquinas, *Scriptum super libros Sententiarum magistri Petri Lombardi episcopi parisiensis*, (eds) M.F. Moos and P. Mandonnet (4 books, Paris, 1929). This edition used for all future quotations unless otherwise indicated.

[13] I give here the fuller context for this quotation, square brackets mark the actual reference used. '*[Hoc igitur attendentes, quidam posuerunt quod nullus intellectus creatus essentiam Dei videre potest. Sed hoc inconvenienter dicitur. Cum enim ultima hominis beatitudo in altissima eius operatione consistat, quae est operatio intellectus,] si nunquam essentiam Dei videre potest intellectus creatus, vel nunquam beatitudinem obtinebit, vel in alio eius beatitudo consistet quam in Deo. Quod est alienum a fide.*'

separate spiritual substances (*SCG* 3.1 47.1). Since contemplation of spiritual things requires us to withdraw from sensible things Thomas says the mind which sees the divine substance in this life must be completely cut off from the bodily senses by either death or ecstasy (*SCG* 3.1 47.2). Or, in a negative echo of Romans 1:20, if we do see God in this life 'the knowledge of God which can be taken in by the human mind does not go beyond the type of knowledge that is derived from sensible things …' (*SCG* 3.1 47.9).[14]

However, there is a problem; man's ultimate felicity does not come in this life. In this life man's natural desire is not yet, nor can it ever be, at rest (*SCG* 3.1 48). 'Therefore he must attain it after this life' (*SCG* 3.1 48.10).[15] But at the same time 'it is impossible for natural desire to be unfulfilled since 'nature does nothing in vain'' (*SCG* 3.1 48.11).[16] Moreover, 'every intellect by nature desires the vision of the divine substance' (*Omnis intellectus naturaliter desiderat divinae substantiae visioem*) (*SCG* 3.1 57.4).

How then can this gap between a mind capable of cognizing only sensible species and that of the highest intelligible be bridged? How can a corporeal nature which knows only through the senses fulfil a natural desire for the highest non-corporeal? The problem is cognitive in nature, and for Thomas, God resolves it in a similar manner.

The divine essence compensates for the lack of sensible phantasms by raising up the finite intellect to strengthen its nature for the reception of the divine essence: 'it (the divine essence itself) perfects the intellect for the act of understanding and this is not incompatible with the perfection of the divine essence' (*SCG* 3.1 51.4).[17] After which the mind of God enters the created intellect and co-mingles with it producing a phantasm of itself such that humans share in divine mind: 'it is impossible for this essence to become the intelligible form of a created intellect unless by virtue of the fact that the created intellect participates in the divine likeness. Therefore, this participation in divine likeness is necessary so that the substance of God may be seen' (*SCG* 3.1 53.2).[18] Or again in the *Summa*, Thomas

---

[14] '… *tamen cognitio Dei quae ex mente humana accipi potest, non excedit illud genus cognitionis quod ex sensibilibus sumitur*' (*SCG* 3.1 47.8; NB it is paragraph 8 in the Latin text 9 in the English translation).

[15] '*Oportet ergo quod consequatur post hanc vitam*' (*SCG* 3.1 48.11; paragraph 10 in the English translation, 11 in the Latin).

[16] '*Adhuc. Impossibile est naturale desiderium esse inane: natura enim nihil facit frustra*' (*SCG* 3.1 48.12; paragraph 11 in the English translation, 12 in the Latin).

[17] I give the full sentence with the last two clauses being translated. '*Species autem intelligibilis, unita intellectui, non constituit aliquam naturam, sed perficit ipsum ad intelligendum: quod perfectioni divinae essentiae non repugnat*' (*SCG* 3.1 51.4).

[18] '*Impossibile est igitur quod ipsa essentia fiat intelligibilis forma alicuius intellectus creati, nisi per hoc quod aliquam divinam similitudinem intellectus creatus participat. Haec igitur divinae similitudinis participatio necessaria est ad hoc quod Dei substantia videatur*' (*SCG* 3.1 53.2).

suggests that since God *can* be seen by the intellect what is seen must be 'some kind of participated likeness of Him who is the first intellect' (*ST* 1.Q12 a2.ans).[19]

If however intellectual substances have the desire to see God that they are not capable of satisfying by natural means then we have a natural desire for the non-natural. As Gilson again points out – he speaks of it as the decisive step for the interpretation of the doctrine: because the vision of God 'will henceforth be located outside of the grasp of nature and therefore supernatural, several conclude that this object stops being one that is subject to a natural desire'.[20] But one cannot have a natural desire that is to no avail, as Gilson remarks in the light of Aristotle 'man cannot have the natural desire of knowing an object if he doesn't have the natural means of knowing it'.[21] Aquinas concurs 'since it is impossible for a natural desire to be incapable of fulfilment … we must say that it is possible for the substance of God to be seen intellectually both by separate intelligences and by our souls' (*SCG* 3.1 51.1).[22]

What are we to make of all of this? On the one hand beatitude is not attainable in this life, on the other it is a natural desire of the human creature. Does the soul then only attain the vision of God in the afterlife? Clearly in this life we are finite embodied minds and so cannot see in full measure the infinite divine intellect. However we do not lose our finitude in the next life even if we are no longer limited to knowledge from sensible phantasms. Thus we remain finite created beings on our way to God both before and after death. Separation from the body does not by itself grant us the vision of God. Presumably this is why even in the next life (and even if we are among the blessed), we see God only insofar as we are seen by him such that God must co-mingle with our mind, making for us his own image so that separated souls may know him.

Given that God bypasses our agent intellect in the next life with his own activity; surely reason would suggest such an action would be equally available to him here below. If the motive for the prohibition of the cognition of the divine essence in this life were that of our intelligence being wedded to sensible species, since God bypasses our epistemic structure in the next – then such a co-mingling would logically, be as open to him here below as hereafter. Now it is true that the separated soul can see what the soul in this life cannot (other souls and angels) – but it still cannot see God by its own power. Thus even in the next life it is necessary for God to make the intelligible species by which we see our final end.

---

[19]   '*Et cum ipsa intellectiva virtus creaturae non sit Dei essentia, relinquitur quod sit aliqua participata similitudo ipsius, qui est primus intellectus*' (Iª q. 12 a. 2 co).

[20]   Gilson, 'Sur La Problématique Thomiste De La Vision Béatifique', p. 72.

[21]   Ibid.

[22]   I give the whole quotation with my references between square brackets ['*Cum autem impossibile sit naturale desiderium esse inane,*] *quod quidem esset si non esset possibile pervenire ad divinam substantiam intelligendam, quod naturaliter omnes mentes desiderant;* [*necesse est dicere quod possibile sit substantiam Dei videri per intellectum, et a substantiis intellectualibus separatis, et ab animabus nostri*s'] (*SCG* 3.1 51.1).

In that sense the prohibition on seeing God in this life by virtue of being wedded to the intellectual abstraction of sensible images – is beside the point. Given that in the next life we cannot see him, even though we no longer see via the action of our mind on sensible phantasms. Thus Aquinas' real injunction against seeing God is that no created substance can by its own natural power attain to the vision of God (*SCG* 3.1.52) and this applies *equally* to this life and the next. Hence, the frequent protestations (*SCG* 3.1 47.9) that we cannot see God in this life because of a mind and cognitive structure wedded to sensible species is a superfluous proscription that blinds us to the continuity of created finitude between this life and the next. Correspondingly, the unnecessary implication that matter is a barrier to cognition of God forces Thomas into an ambiguity regarding the status of resurrected matter such that he concludes that the resurrected body is but an accidental addition to beatitude.

Let me elucidate – in the early work of Aquinas, the beatific vision accrues to the fully resurrected soul – in the *Sentences* composed somewhere between 1252–6 the vision is both corporeal and intellectual; the *Summa Contra Gentiles* 1259–65 occupies an interesting intermediate position; whereas in the *Summa*, in the *Secunda Pars* that concerns man's ultimate happiness, probably written around 1269–72, we find a curiously abstracted and disembodied account of the beatific vision. It is almost as if the separated soul can enjoy beatitude as much if not more than the fully resurrected soul in the newly spiritual body. We know that it was around this time that Thomas produced many of his commentaries on Aristotle and it is almost as if the Stagirite's emphasis on intellective contemplation displaces a resolutely embodied and therefore truly Christian beatitude.

Needless to say, for Aquinas eternal life actualizes and divinizes all the capacities of man (*De caritate* a.10 ad 5; IV *Sent*, d.44 q.2. a1, sol 3, ad 4). Beatitude must include the fulfilment of all of our intellectual *and* physical potentialities – as Hoye again notes, and I agree with him, the 'doctrine of the total actualization of the whole human person in heaven follows logically from the controversial Thomistic doctrine of the single substantial form in a human being'.[23] Moreover the beatitude of the soul demands the body as the soul is the form of the body and its full actuation demands material concretition: '*Et sic patet quod si in hac vita homo non potest esse beatus, necesse est resurrectionem ponere*' (IV *Sent*. d 43, q.1.a.1,sol.1).[24] None of this is questioned in the *Sentences*, for the idea of a beatified soul existing other than in its resurrected body is an anathema, indeed the soul requires the body as Gilson notes 'unless it animated a body, the soul itself could not exist as a spiritual substance'.[25] The *Sentences* give the governing

---

[23] Hoye, *Actualitas Omnium Actum. Man's Beatific vision of God as Apprehended by Thomas Aquina*, p. 193. I am also grateful to Hoyle's text for the extensive references to this discussion.

[24] Thomas Aquinas in IV *librum Sententiarum magistri petri Lombardi*, ed. J.L. Vives (Paris, 1876), vol. XI.

[25] Etienne Gilson, *Elements of Christian Philosophy* (New York, 1963) p. 244.

principle of the resurrection: '*quidquid pertinet ad integritatem humanae naturae, in resurgente hoc totum resurget*' (IV *Sent* d.44, q.1, a.2, sol.3.).[26] We can determine by a definitive statement from the *Sentences* that the soul alone is insufficient to merit beatitude: '*necessitas ponendi resurrectionem est ex hoc ut homo finem ultimum propter quem homo factus est, consequatur: quod in hac vita fieri non potest, nec in vita animae separatae, ut supra dictum est: alias vane esset homo constitutus, si ad finem ad quem factus est, pervenire non potest*' (IV *Sent* d.44, q1 a1, sol 2.).[27]

So then we can conclude for the Sentences at least that full beatitude requires the soul to resume its body and so fulfil its form in its fully resurrected state. Likewise in the *Summa Contra Gentiles* Aquinas believes that 'resurrection is natural if one considers its purpose, for it is natural that the soul be united to the body' (*SCG* IV 82. 15).

But we also know from Scripture that the blessed even as separated souls, enjoy a vision of God and so are infinitely happy. This leaves us with a quandary as to whether the resumption of the body by the soul represents an essential or an accidental beatitude – because in the *Summa theologiae* Thomas seems to assert that the addition of the body is an *accidental* augmentation to beatitude.

The famous section is taken from the *Secunda Pars* (*ST* I–II Q.4 Art 5), the question itself concerns those things that are required for happiness, and the fifth article asks whether the body is necessary for man's happiness? Interestingly all of the initial objections affirm that the body is required if the soul is to be happy: 'the soul cannot be happy without the body' (obj. 1) (*ergo beatitudo non potest esse in anima sine corpore*) or the soul is not happy while separated from the body (obj. 5) (*ergo anima separata a corpore non est beata*). Thomas quotes Augustine in objection four where the Bishop of Hippos argues that the Soul 'has a natural desire to rule the body' (*Gen ad lit xiii* 35). He acknowledges in objection five that Augustine argues that the separated soul desires to reunite with the body – as the soul is not happy while sundered from its embodied form.

In the *solutio* however the following is argued – Aquinas accepts that happiness in this life requires the operation of the intellect and that this in its turn requires a body as the intellect demands phantasms in order to think. But this is different in the afterlife. There Aquinas tells us that the idea that the saints whose souls are separated from their bodies do not attain the beatific vision until they receive their bodies back again on the day of judgement is a conception contrary to both authority and reason.[28]

---

26 Aquinas, *librum Sententiarum magistri petri Lombardi*, ed. J.L. Vives, IV *Sent*.

27 Ibid.

28 '*Sed circa beatitudinem perfectam, quae in Dei visione consistit, aliqui posuerunt quod non potest animae advenire sine corpore existenti; dicentes quod animae sanctorum a corporibus separatae, ad illam beatitudinem non perveniunt usque ad diem iudicii, quando corpora resument. Quod quidem apparet esse falsum et auctoritate, et ratione*' (*ST* I–II Q.4 Art 5).

In support of this contention he cites Paul's injunction in 2 Corinthians 5:6–7 'to live in the body means to be exiled from the Lord. Going as we do by faith and not by sight – we are full of confidence, I say, and actually want to be exiled from the body and make our home with the Lord'. Leaving aside the fact that Paul was really talking about leaving behind the despoliation of the body by sin and concupiscence and ignoring the other accounts that Paul gives of a new creation and a new spiritual body – it is a curious text for the advocate of substantial form and the consequent resurrection of particular bodies to extol. But he continues in the *corpus* to assert 'that the souls of the saints, separated from their bodies, *walk by sight*, (*ambulant per speciem*) seeing the essence of God, wherein is true happiness'. Thus does Thomas associate sight with the purely intellective and disembodied contemplation of the separated saintly soul. Reason he tells us also demands this conclusion, because since the body no longer depends on sensible phantasms and given that the divine essence cannot be seen via such phantasms, we should rejoice in our separated state as now we can see the divine essence without the impediment of the body: 'consequently without the body the soul can be happy.' (*Unde sine corpore potest anima esse beata*) (*ST* 1–11 Q4.a5, corpus; see also *SCG* 4.91.10).

Yet the peculiar nature of this conclusion must have struck Thomas immediately, for he then equivocates and divides ultimate happiness into two modes, the first is an abstracted ethereal contemplation which though it 'constitutes the essence thereof' (*ad constituendam essentiam rei*) of man's perfection, represents only the disembodied state of the separated soul. The second is a curious curtailed account that suggests an auxiliary accidental perfection where, yes it is admitted that 'the beauty of body and keenness of perfection belong to man's perfection.' But this is only 'as necessary for its [the soul's] well being.' Thus the body is not so much the *actus essendi* of the soul as it is now a kind of vehicle that sustains the soul as it moves beyond or through the body towards a purely intellective contemplation of God. Since the body is no longer of the essence of (*essentiam rei*) the soul, this suggests that there is some kind of cognitive fall when the soul enters the body, both in this life and the next. And if this were true then the beatitude due to a resurrected soul reunited with its body must be either an accidental perfection added onto an already perfect state (which sounds metaphysically awkward to say the least) or embodiment is not a perfection at all but a hindrance to beatitude. At the end of the *solutio* Thomas even quotes from Augustine (*Gen. ad lit* x11 35) who he acknowledges claims that the dead separated from their bodies cannot see the unchangeable substance as the angels do. But in the reply to objection six – he defends his conclusion – contra Augustine – by arguing that the blessed can see more than the angels as the separated state of the soul actually permits a higher cognition than the angelic mind of the divine substance.

It is hard not to avoid a gnostic conclusion when reading this *quaestio*, nor are these quandaries resolved by the replies to the objections. In the first reply happiness is now restricted to the intellect alone by defining happiness as 'the perfection of the soul on the part of the intellect' (*ex parte intellectus*), while Thomas admits that the soul 'does not retain that natural perfection in respect of which it is the form of the body'. He in no way appears to think that this compromises the beatitude of the separated soul.[29] In the second reply to the objection that a perfect happiness demands a perfect operation which itself requires a perfected being which thus obliges the soul to be united to the body, Aquinas opens up a peculiar distinction between a perfected being and a perfect specific nature. He argues that the soul can enjoy perfect being whilst being separated from the body though it has not the perfect specific nature appropriate to it. He acknowledges that 'the human soul retains the being of the composite after the destruction of the body' but then he argues not that there is a potentiality to be converted into an act which one would expect if the soul was the form of the body, *no*; now matter is reduced to mind such that for the separated soul 'the being of the form is the same as that of its matter and that is the being of the composite'.[30] Thus separated souls are not composite in the way that angels are – composed of form and being, they are a new composite composed of form and a purely formalized matter. And surely if the being of the form is that 'same' as its matter (which I of course agree with) it though is still in potency to the actualization of that form – otherwise matter is not real and *it* does not matter.

In which case given the Christian accounts of resurrection which envisaged a new form of corporeality, is Aquinas arguing for an identity between the state of separated souls and that of the condition that pertains to souls reunited with their bodies on the last day? Is there then a kind of virtual resurrection before the actual reunification with the body? This must be so if resurrection adds nothing essential to the beatitude of the separated soul. The reply to Objection 4 though equivocates on the original equivocation, now Aquinas seems to indicate that although the separated soul is at rest in its appetite – it would still wish the body to obtain its share. Again we see yet another strange duality fracturing the body soul composite such that each part now has its own requisite desires and though the soul is fully satisfied for itself it still experiences a lack in its other half. However the soul is either satisfied or it is not. Self-evidently Aquinas concedes that it is not – yet he still argues that the separated soul is at rest, replete in its contemplation. This situation repeats itself in the reply to objection 5. Once again an unresolved dualism expresses itself, and the reply is instructive enough to bear repetition in full:

> The desire of the separated soul is entirely at rest as regards the thing desired; since to wit, it has that which suffices its appetite. But it is not wholly at rest as regards the desirer, since it does not possess that good in every way that it would

---

[29] '*Ad primum ergo dicendum quod beatitudo est perfectio animae ex parte intellectus, secundum quem anima transcendit corporis organa, non autem secundum quod est forma naturalis corporis. Et ideo illa naturae perfectio manet secundum quam ei beatitudo debetur, licet non maneat illa naturae perfectio secundum quam est corporis forma*' (*ST* I^a–IIae q. 4 a. 5 ad 1).

[30] '*Sed animae humanae remanet esse compositi post corporis destructionem, et hoc ideo, quia idem est esse formae et materia, et hoc est esse compositi*' (*ST* I^a–IIae q. 4 a. 5 ad 2).

wish to possess it. Consequently, after the body has been resumed, Happiness increases not in intensity, but in extent (*ST* I–11 Q4 A6 a5).[31]

Again after having achieved a presumably full beatitude (and what else can it be if Aquinas' main point is that the separated soul can see the vision of God) without the body, the soul experiences something almost like regret. But if the soul does not have the good in all ways that it would want then it is not and *cannot be* a full beatitude – why then does Aquinas argue the contrary by saying that the resumption of the bodily is not an intensive augmentation but only an extensive increase in happiness? These remarks have provoked much debate. In the *Commentary on The Sentences*, Aquinas argued that there is a real increase in beatitude with the resumption of the body: '*etiam ipsius animae beatitude augebitur extensive ... Potest etiam dici quod ipsius animae beatitude intensive augebitur*' (IV *Sent* d 49, q.1. a4, sol 1).

In respect of *ST* I-11 Q4 A6 a5, P. Glorieux has maintained that the *Summa*'s text is corrupted at this point and that it ought to read '*non solum intensive sed etiam extensive*' instead of '*non intensive, sed extensive*'.[32] I doubt very much if this can be maintained as the *Summa*'s text seems to accord with the general metaphysical thrust of the question. Again this is an innovation in the theory of the beatific vision, both Albert the Great and Bonaventure argue for an intensive augmentation of the beatific vision on the resumption of the body.[33] It is difficult to fully grasp a determinate meaning of intensive *esse* in Aquinas, if we however understand intensive *esse* as a qualitative mode and extensive *esse* as quantitative which I think is the meaning closest to Aquinas, then following the tradition that preceded Thomas which included all the existential requirements of existence as *qualitatively* distinctive then the body must be thought of as an essentially intensive act of *esse*. Quite how it could be thought of as adding no difference to the union with God such that it is only an extensive augmentation escapes me,

---

[31] '*Ad quintum dicendum quod desiderium animae separatae totaliter quiescit ex parte appetibilis, quia scilicet habet id quod suo appetitui sufficit. Sed non totaliter requiescit ex parte appetentis, quia illud bonum non possidet secundum omnem modum quo possidere vellet. Et ideo, corpore resumpto, beatitudo crescit non intensive, sed extensive*' (*ST* Iª–IIae q. 4 a. 5 ad 5).

[32] See footnote 18 for the requite text and see also P.Glorieux, 'Saint Thomas et L'accroissement de le béatitude', *Recherche de Théologie ancienne et médiévale*, 17 (1950): 125. Hoyle also refers to this debate see *Actualitas Omnium Actum*, pp. 206–7.

[33] See Bonaventure's Commentary on the Sentences In IV Sent, d.49, p.2, s.1.a1. q1 (ed. Quaracchi, IV 1012). Both Albert the Great and Bonaventure were monists who predicated their philosophies on light – while this has the advantage of avoiding a Thomist dualism it reintroduces Neoplatonic assimilation as the mode of beatitude. Ascending to the intensity of light means that beatitude risks assimilation thus though the body and all of creation are understood intensively their distinction is not thought integral enough so as to maintain its difference in the face of divine illumination and assimilation.

unless of course that one thinks the hypostatic union of the spiritual and material natures in Christ is of no account.

Moreover, the shift from the anthropology of the *Sentences* to that of the *Summa* is revealed by the *Summa* itself, or rather by its *Supplementum*. The Supplement was compiled by his followers (most probably Fra Rainaldo da Piperno) after Thomas' death in 1274. It derives from various commentaries on the fourth book of the *Sentences* by Lombard and thus it represents a much earlier phase of Thomas' work. These writings were probably completed in the early 1250s, if so then this text is indeed contemporaneous with the work on the *Sentences* and precedes the *Secunda Pars* by some 15–20 years. And here we find expressed the earlier concern with a beatitude augmented by bodily resurrection. He quotes approvingly, in *ST* Suppl, Q.69 art 2, rep 4, *Gregory's Dialogues* (*Dial*.iv.1c.) where Gregory accepts that after death the souls of the just are in heaven but 'surely it will be a gain to them at the judgement, that whereas now they enjoy only the happiness of the soul, afterwards they will enjoy also that of the body, so as to rejoice also in the flesh wherein they bore sorrow and torments for the lord'.[34]

Later in the *Supplementum* in Question 75 on the Resurrection we find a further account of the intensive augmentation of the soul by the body. In the first article in the *corpus* we find the following denunciation of those who argued for the superfluousness of the body in beatitude.

> Others have said that the entire nature of man is seated in the soul, so that the soul makes use of the body as an instrument, or as a sailor uses his ship: wherefore according to this opinion it follows that if happiness is attained by the soul alone, man would not be balked in his natural desire for happiness, and so there is no need to hold the resurrection. But the Philosopher sufficiently destroys this foundation (*De Anima, ii.2*) where he shows that the soul is united to the body as form to matter. Hence it is clear that if man cannot be happy in this life, we must of necessity hold the resurrection (*ST* Suppl. 75.a1.corpus.).[35]

One need only compare this passage with that of the *Secunda Pars*, to note the extraordinary shift in Aquinas' account of the nature and character of beatitude.

---

[34] '*Hoc eis nimirum crescit in iudicio, quod nunc animae sola singulari retributione laetantur; postmodum vero etiam corporum beatitudine perfruentur ut in ipsa quoque carne gaudeant, in qua dolores pro Domino cruciatusque pertulerunt*' (*ST* Sup Q.69. a2. rep 4).

[35] '*Quidam vero posuerunt totam hominis naturam in anima constare, ita ut anima corpore uteretur sicut instrumento aut sicut nauta navi. Unde secundum hanc opinionem sequitur quod, sila anima beatificata, homo naturali desiderio beatitudinis non frustraretur. Et sic no oportet pnere resurrectionem. – Sed hoc fundamentum sufficienter philosophus*', *In II De anima*, '*desrruit ostendens animam corpori sicut formam materiae uniri. et sic patet quod, si in hac vita homo non potest esse beatus, necesse est resurrectionem ponere*' (*ST* suppl. q75 a1 corpus).

According to Olivier Boulnois, this difference between the two texts is accounted for by Aquinas' study of Aristotle and his theory of the intellective soul.[36] Again Trottmann agrees and they both locate Aquinas' intellectual shift in his commentary on *De Anima*.[37] In one regard – I agree, it *is* the Aristotelian account of the intellective soul and its treatment of matter that leads to the body being excluded from the intensive augmentation of beatitude. It is Aristotelian noetics and their treatment of matter that divides the Thomistic vision of beatitude in two. Yet paradoxically, I would argue that it is in his commentary on *De Anima* – that Aquinas outlines an entirely unified alternative to the theory of beatitude that he subsequently employs. Thus whilst agreeing with Trottman and Boulnois that Aquinas is ultimately persuaded in this instance by an Aristotelian noetics. I think, and hopefully I will show, that a properly figured Thomism which is present in Thomas' *Commentary on De Anima* upholds the fundamental unity of body and soul in the final vision of God.

Matter and the Beatific Vision

However, to fully address the foundational division between matter and form and to challenge its received understanding in Aquinas is beyond the limits of this chapter. I have attended to the issues of matter and form at length elsewhere and indeed there I have argued for a new understanding of Thomistic individuation in respect of the claims that I make regarding the question of matter in Aquinas.[38]

In my mind matter is no bar to beatitude. This is not to say that the beatific vision is granted to us in this life – but it is to say that flesh or matter is traditionally understood to be a very real prohibition on the cognition of the divine essence. In respect of Thomas this position derives from the Aristotelian cognitive legacy, where the end of man is commonly taken to be a purely intellectual contemplation of the first cause. And since intellectual cognition is defined by the abstraction of universals from their individuation in matter it follows that cognition of universals cannot take place if universal forms remain enmeshed in material nature. And if this is true for any sensible form how much more true it is for God himself who as the form of all forms is the ultimate transcendent universal. Thus conceived, flesh as the bearer of individuation *par excellence* bars cognition of the transcendent and universal God.

But as a standard account of why we cannot see God in this life this reasoning appears deeply wrong. Matter is *not* the reason we cannot see God – since even

---

[36]   Boulnois, 'Les deux fins de l'homme l'impossible anthropologie et le repli de la théologie', p. 211.

[37]   See the reference above and also Christian Trottmann, 'Deux interprétations contradictoires de saint Bernard, Les sermons de Jean XXII et les traités inédits du cardinal fournier', *Mélanges de l'école française de Rome*, 105/1 (1993): 327–79.

[38]   See Phillip Blond, *The Eyes of Faith* (London, forthcoming).

when we are separated from matter as a soul we do not see God by virtue of our escape from material life. Indeed the *Summa Contra Gentiles* makes clear that no substance whether material or immaterial can see God through themselves or their own powers. On the contrary in order to obtain the beatific vision God must first elevate and strengthen a creature by the *lux gloriae* and then introduce his own substance into their mind. Given this there is no logical reason that such a displacement of finite knowing cannot take place in this life as indeed it does in certain mystical events. Furthermore, Thomas intuitively accepts Aristotle's greatest insight that universals occur in and through particular things not above or beyond them. This all suggests that matter occupies a radically different station in Aquinas' work than is commonly supposed.

For instance I propose that the early account of essence is still operative throughout the Thomistic corpus, the terminology may be discarded, but the dictates of *De ente et essentia* still apply: hylomorphism understood as substance dualism is utterly rejected. For Aquinas the true account of all natural creatures must include matter as well as form, the *forma totius*, and the 'essence' of natural beings forbids any description of matter as an accidental – and therefore dispensable – addition to substance.

In addition, I would argue that this post-hylomorphic notion of sensible form should be re-understood and re-ontologized. In this regard I contend that it was and *is* impossible to divide form and being. Yes of course, there is always more being than form, in the sense that there is no limit on being itself (God) or the beings it (he) can bring about, but being itself is never by itself. Being is never without a form and nor if it is ever actualized can it be without form. I maintain that the first effect of God is not common being (*esse commune*) but form and being (the intelligences), thus I argue that in Aquinas being *is* through form as form is *esse participans*. Taking this aspect seriously means that one must be serious about what exists. Now it is not the case that just genera and species exist. We do not live in a world with horses of all the same type nor are there just generic men and women. In this way only is nominalism correct: in some self-evident fashion we are all individuals and no one thing is ever quite the same as anything else. Leaving aside the universality that binds such creatures together in relation, we can say that the composition proper to sensible creatures is that specification of creatures granted by matter when it individuates form. Unless of course one thinks that that divine intention ends with the species but not the matter that individuates the human species into this man or that woman. Thus I argue that being as expressed in the form/matter compound is directed to just such an individuation by the divine mind. Accordingly, I suggest that the existential reading of Aquinas given by E. Gilson while correct in giving existence priority, failed to take this logic far enough – Gilson failed to give priority to what existence is for: the things *that* exist. Accordingly contra Gilson, Thomistic existential priority confers precedence on the particularized forms that exist not on existence itself. It follows then that in Aquinas the origin of diversity and individuation is to be found in divine intention (not in unwilled material placement or dimensional location).[39] God wills distinction or 'difference' within and across genus and species because it produces both singularity and relation. As such it expresses most supremely the ecstatic divine nature – and its intention that the world should more perfectly communicate divine goodness (*bonum diffusivum sui*) and divine creativity. As such form (and hence distinction) is the more perfect indication of God than existence itself, and the difference between forms (achieved by a divine idea as to what can more perfectly imitate him) and within forms (a material process achieved via matter as willed individuation) is a yet more mysterious and revealing demonstration of God. Why, because it is creation at its most particular that reveals God at his most universal – his ordering of the universe extends to the furthest reach of being and encompass all plurality and differentiation.

Thus my conclusions, albeit tentative and necessarily shortened are stark. Real things exist materially and spiritually – each material thing being a creation of non-material divine intention. When we see a material thing insofar as we see its form we do indeed see its divine idea – but this is an idea whose teleology is to become incarnational – it is destined to become matter – to put on sinew and bones (Ezek 37:1–14) and to live in the flesh. Moreover as Thomas in his *Commentary on Aristotle's De Anima*, makes clear 'the intellect's object is not the intelligible idea, but the essence of intelligible realities'.[40] As such the intention of a sensible form (*intentio formae sensibilis*) is never to be a mental proxy or a

---

[39]   The debate between Joseph Owens and John F. Wippel, over the precise nature of Thomistic individuation, is particularly instructive. For Wippel's work see *The Metaphysical Thought of Thomas Aquinas; from Finite Being to Uncreated Being* (Washington, 2000). See especially Chapter 9 section 4 of this text, and some of his earlier articles, especially 'Aquinas's Route to the Real distinction: A note on *De ente et essentia*, C.4.', *The Thomist*, 43 (1979): 693–707; 'Thomas Aquinas on Substance as a Cause of proper Accidents', in J.P. Beckmann, L. Honnefelder, G. Schrimpf, G.Wieland (eds), *Philosophie im Mittelalter. Entwicklungslinien und Paradigmen* (Hamburg, 1987), pp. 201–12. For Owens the two most appropriate papers to consider are Joseph Owens 'Thomas Aquinas: Dimensive quantity as Individuating Principle', *Mediaeval Studies*, 50 (1988): 279–310. And J. Owens, 'Thomas Aquinas', in Jorge J.E. Gracia (ed.), *Individuation in Scholasticism, the Later Middle Ages and the Counter-Reformation. 1150–1650* (New York, 1994), pp. 173–94. In the end I find Owens' account the more philosophically persuasive but Wippel's the more textually accurate. In short I think that only divine intention via the order of being can cause individuation but that Aquinas had great difficulty in squaring this with the insistence on matter being the prime individuator. Perhaps this is why after the Commentary on Boethius' *De Trinitate* 1255–1259 Aquinas seems to have quietly abandoned the notion of matter as being the principle of individuation.

[40]   *Sentencia De anima*, lib. 3 l. 8 n. 19. '*Unde manifestum est, quod species intelligibilis non est obiectum intellectus, sed quidditas rei intellectae*' (St Thomas Aquinas, Commentary on Aristotle's *De Anima*, trans. K. Foster and S. Humphries (Notre Dame, 1994), book 3, Lecture VIII, Note 718, p. 215).

spiritual abstraction but rather to convey a form's material nature in its universal and therefore relational aspect.

Accordingly when we see a form we do not see it abstracted from its material instantiation as standard accounts would insist, rather we see it in its spiritual or universal dimension. In such a manner we see into the mind of God as we see the thing's (*res*) relation to itself and to other things both like and unlike it – so we not only see the divine intention or idea made actual but we see its good order in relation to other creations and to God (*SCG* 1.78.7). Thus there is a kind of continuity between seeing the cause through its effect which is how we know God in this life (*SCG* 3.1.47.9) and seeing the effects through the cause which is how we know God in the next life.

So matter is indeed mysterious, in this life it is what we see first, in the next it is what we see last – so conceived matter offers a concretion of a divine idea and yet is held to be furthest from God. And since act is higher than potency, the completed or material fulfilled idea must have a higher status in being than the divine concept unfulfilled (not that there is any such temporal gap in God). As such a Christian intellective contemplation of the first cause leads not to a disembodied intellect contemplating ideas without matter – but rather its inverse: the concrete actualization of all particulars in being and the contemplation of this as somehow a more divine and ecstatic degree of beatitude.

Moreover, if divine intention is incompatible with hylomorphism understood as dualism (which it is) and if Aquinas fuses this distinction into one willed act of Christian Creation (which he does) – then matter is as ideal as form – since it comes from God and it is the means whereby species are made internally distinct so that they more perfectly demonstrate God. So if knowledge of the thing itself includes cognition of its specific material nature (and how can it not) then matter can only be a barrier to seeing God if matter is not of God and from God. Something that Aquinas wholly refutes: 'it is necessary to say that primary matter is created by the universal cause of things'.[41] So then the notion of an unbreachable material barrier to the vision of God seems metaphysically peculiar – unless that is Aquinas understands the beatific vision as purely universal abstract and wholly intellective intuition (which self evidently he does not though his account of full beatitude for the separated saintly soul risks just such an interpretation).

On the contrary matter exists for the sake of form (*ST* 1 Q.47 a1.corp) and all distinction comes from the forms which have as their origin ideas in the mind of God. And the divine ideas represent divine intention – which is nothing other than that which should be. And that which *is* – is a participated likeness of God – an amalgam of divine and sensible light, with revelation and beatitude being nothing but the realization that the natural is but the supernatural unrecognized as such.

And this perhaps takes us to the heart of the issue: the theological status of matter. Matter in this life does not recognize its supernatural status – it is fallen.

---

[41] '*Et sic oportet ponere etiam materiam primam creatam ab universali causa entium*' (*ST* I^a q. 44 a. 2 corp).

In this respect perhaps it is indeed true that the soul freed from fallen matter is indeed closer to God than the soul in this life. Yet if we are to avoid a Gnostic outcome we must read the message of the incarnation as the return of the soul to a glorified body and a recovered world. But this would only be true if the beatific vision as described delivered us to such a state.

All of which means that matter is not so much a barrier to the vision of God as it is – in part – the means by which we see him as he is, because – in part – that is how he sees himself.

The Vision of God

Let me give some textual justification for the preceding claims. Aquinas acknowledges in *SCG* 3.1 c 51.1, that it is only possible for the substance of God to be seen intellectually (*videri per intellectum*) by separate intellectual substances and by our souls.[42] We know that this cannot be achieved by the actions of man alone as no natural phantasms could correspond to the divine presence. Consequently – we must see him as he sees himself *through* himself such that God is both what we see (*quod*) and how we see (*quo*).[43] Thomas repeats the claim of 1 Jn 3:2 'we shall be like him because we shall see him as he really is'. Thus configured Aquinas concludes Chapter 51 of *Summa contra Gentiles* in paragraph 6 with the claim that the vision of God consists in 'seeing Him in the way that he sees Himself' (*videntes eum illo modo quo ipse videt seipsum*).

This requires a raising up of the intellect by the divine power. A process Aquinas describes as a making luminous of a diaphanous object (*SCG* 3.1 53.5) and in note 7 of the same chapter he quotes Ps 35:10 – 'In Thy light we shall see the light'. In this manner a created intellect is strengthened by the divine light in order to see the divine essence (*SCG* 3.1 54. 8). And since no one abstracted phantasm can stand for God – God introduces his own likeness or 'phantasm' into the mind of the graced intellect. The divine essence itself then becomes the intelligible species that introduces itself into the created intellect. As a consequence the divine essence is 'both what is seen (*quod videtur*) and that whereby it is seen (*quo videtur*)' (*SCG* 3.1 51.2).[44] This however does not mean that we see all that there is to be seen – we

---

[42] '... *necesse est dicere quod possibile sit substantiam Dei videri per intellectum, et a substantiis intellectualibus separatis, et ab animabus nostris*' (*SCG* 3i c 51).

[43] *SCG* 3 C51.2: '*Modus autem huius visionis satis iam ex dictis qualis esse debeat, apparet. Ostensum enim est supra quod divina substantia non potest videri per intellectum aliqua specie creata. Unde oportet, si Dei essentia videatur, quod per ipsammet essentiam divinam intellectus ipsam videat: ut sit in tali visione divina essentia et quod videtur, et quo videtur.*'

[44] I give the full sentence from which this quotation is taken: '*Unde oportet, si Dei essentia videatur, quod per ipsammet essentiam divinam intellectus ipsam videat: ut sit in tali visione divina essentia et quod videtur, et quo videtur*' (*SCG* 3.1 51.2).

see only to the perfect limits of our capacity – even though everything *is* available to be seen. Moreover, this is not a pantheistic union – we are not united with God in the act of being as a result of this cognition but only in the act of understanding (*SCG* 3.1 54.9) – since the intellect in principle *is* all things. Nor do we see God in the full proportion that God sees himself; if we did then the divine substance would not exceed the limits of the created intellect – which would be impossible.[45] However, even if God shows more than we have the capacity to comprehend, we see God in the way that he intends us to see himself.

What however do we see when we see God? On this point Aquinas is very clear – when we see God, we see *all* that he has made. When the intellect reaches its natural/supernatural end, it sees in God the principle of all things 'the natural appetite of the intellect is to know the genera and species and powers of all things, and the whole order of the universe ... each one who sees the divine substance knows all the aforementioned things' (*SCG* 3.1 59.1).[46] And why does God do this? Because since the intellect can in principle *be* all things, its perfection must consist in knowing all the things that it can be, thus its perfection consists in knowing the cause of how and why each thing is. Thus when we see God we see not God himself but his self-expression – we see *all* that he has made. Thus a purported intellective beatitude is perforce led to cognition of matter. If beatitude is the seeing of all things in all their genera, species, difference and matter then the beatified intellect – like God, must know matter. Not only is this true, but material singulars in this beatified state hold a higher estate than universals. For not only do self-subsistent universals not exist whereas participating singulars do – the existential priority confers on the latter a higher degree of divine regard: for after all individuals exist in the real order and universals do not (*SCG* 1. 65.2). Moreover, we have discursive knowledge (which in a way is saying that we do not know singulars enough) whereas God has 'practical knowledge' (*SCG* 1.65.7) which, since it is in act, demands operation which again is the domain of singulars. Indeed divine knowledge is the more perfect because it can know singulars whereas human knowledge cannot extend that far, since objects have to surrender their materiality to be known by the human intellect (*SCG* 1.65.9).

---

[45]   See *SCG* 3.1 55.5: '*Nullum comprehensum excedit terminos comprehendentis. Si igitur intellectus creatus divinam substantiam comprehenderet, divina substantia non excederet limites intellectus creati:quod est impossibile. Impossibile est igitur quod intellectus creatus divinam substantiam comprehendat.*'

[46]   English translation altered. Because of its importance I give the full Latin translation of the first section of Chapter 59; *SCG* 3.1, 59.1: '*Quia vero visio divinae substantiae est ultimus finis cuiuslibet intellectualis substantiae, ut patet ex dictis; omnis autem res cum pervenerit ad ultimum finem, quiescit appetitus eius naturalis: oportet quod appetitus naturalis substantiae intellectualis divinam substantiam videntis omnino quiescat. Est autem appetitus naturalis intellectus ut cognoscat omnium rerum genera et species et virtutes, et totum ordinem universi: quod demonstrat humanum studium circa singula praedictorum. Quilibet igitur divinam substantiam videntium cognoscet omnia supradicta.*'

Since however beatitude is sharing in God's cognition of himself – the world is indeed remade anew – we see what previously escaped our cognitive powers: the diversity and plurality and infinite riches of creation all under the auspices of the providential power. 'Therefore, God shows the intellect that is seeing Him all the things which he has produced for the perfection of the universe.'[47] This fulfils the promise made to Moses 'I will show thee all good' (Ex 33:19). So configured, this beatific perfection of the human intellect enables it to attain to an angelic understanding such that all the species, their requisite powers *and* their proper accidents are known and obtained through the final beatitude (*SCG* 3.1 59.6). Hence *even* the individuals existing under species are also known through the final beatitude. Here Aquinas argues that since individuals exist for the sake of species (which at first sight seems a retreat from particular to universal contemplation) this leads him to speak of proper accidents (*propria accidentia*) a move which divinizes the particular concreation of species in individuals since it suggests that accidents belong *per essentia* to substance. Thus Aristotelian substance itself is somehow itself already qualified by accidents such that what accidents were for Aristotle (a necessary though purely arbitrary addition to being) becomes for Thomas a direct and willed expression of God's love of particulars.[48] In this respect particulars or accidents have a certain priority over both substance and being since they are the individuated forms that being itself (as God) has chosen to make actual.

So beatitude is far from being an abstracted disembodied contemplation of the first cause conceived as universal static absolute, instead we see all things down to the most singular of distinctions; which again means that we see matter (resurrected in its unfallen form as spiritual body) and individuated form in the Thomistic account of beatitude in *Summa contra Gentiles*. But again we should not be surprised by the ecstatic and dynamic nature of God's essence and self-understanding. The Trinitarian self-differing God sets no limit (but he does imposes order) on the relations and distinction that he brings about. Moreover, nothing beside God is necessary – yet because he is good God still creates. So in that sense all creation and the means of its differentiation is accidental. All the substances being and essence – all the matter species and genera – all are accidental.[49]

---

[47]　*SCG* 3.1, 59.3: '*Omnia igitur quae Deus ad perfectionem universi produxit, intellectui se videnti manifestat.*'

[48]　Actually there is great debate in Aristotelian scholarship as to what constitutes the primary substance and thence the place of accidents. The Categories, now accepted as authentic, argue that concrete individuals are the primary substances whereas Metaphysics Zeta claims primacy for universal forms. See Michael V. Wedin's, *Aristotle's Theory of Substance* (Oxford, 2002) for a compatibilist account of these two seeming contradictions.

[49]　This point is partially recognized in contemporary phenomenology by Jean-Luc Marion when in *Étant donné. Essai d'une phénoménologie de la donation* (Paris, 1997), pp. 217–21, he writes of the *adveniens extra*, the being which comes to an essence (in this case a separate substance) from 'the outside' see *De ente et essentia* c4.6. Marion is right

So again a beatitude that shows the 'accidental' species and distinctions in God's essence shows all of God's love, goodness and perfection.

So again the question of matter must be reconfigured and rethought. For why is there matter? Matter does not vanish after the resurrection – it returns in its true nature as definitive of the very form of our eternal life. Both Aquinas, through his theory of substantial form, and the New Testament attest to bodily resurrection and the restoration in the next life of both heaven and earth. There is matter because it produces or helps to produce plurality – it does individuate – but this singularization is not a principle independent of God, it takes place within the order of being and divine intention. And why are there many things – well Aquinas tells us 'the reason for everything that has been made is derived from the end which its maker intended. But the end of all things made by God is divine goodness. Therefore, the reason for the things that have been made is so that the divine goodness might be diffused among things' (*SCG* 3.1 59.9).[50] And this act of creativity has no *a priori* limit, end or totality. There is always some new distinction and adumbration that can magnify God as no one thing can stand for God. 'For no one thing or any number of things copied from the divine essence can equal the perfection of their cause. There thus always remains a new way in which some copy is able to imitate the divine essence' (*SCG* 1.69.5).[51]

All things in both their distinction and relation are seen such that there is almost a visual language in Thomas' account of beatitude. One imagines a type of phenomenological inundation, where every visible/intellectual thing ever created is manifest to human sight – but the sheer saturation and flow exceeds our ability to encompass it in one sole gaze of intellection. But this is not the static positivism of a Levinas/Marion variety rather it would be closer to Merleau-Ponty's account of paradise in *Le Visible et l'Invisible*.[52] For here, vision and relation are encompassed in a recognition of my own subjectivity, that of others and the being of things

---

in suggesting that, as it were, all creation need not be but too Cartesian in suggesting that essences somehow remain essential or static whereas being is accidental and dynamic. In short he preserves a dialectic of rupture in appearance such that he claims there can be an appearing without being – but I think Merleau-Ponty is closer to the truth in his rendering of the entire phenomenal field as accidental and therefore all the more contingent, ecstatic and gifted.

[50] '*Ratio enim cuiuslibet rei factae sumitur ex fine quem faciens intendit. Finis autem omnium a Deo factorum divina bonitas est. Ratio igitur rerum factarum est ut divina bonitas diffundatur in rebus*' (*SCG*, 3. 59.7). Note the different section numbering between the Latin and English texts.

[51] '*... quia nec aliquod unum eorum, nec quotlibet plura exemplata perfectionem exemplaris adaequare possunt; et sic semper remanet novus modus quo aliquod exemplatum ipsam imitari possit. Nihil igitur prohibet ipsum per essentiam suam infinita cognoscere*' (*SCG* 1. 69.5).

[52] Maurice Merleau-Ponty, *Le Visible et l'Invisible* (Paris, 1964). Of course a Christian account of this work in our present existence would argue that it is a precipitate phenomenology in that it anticipates heaven before we are resurrected.

beyond my own immanence. Of course this double Thomistic logic of immediacy and mediation cancels and completes the opposition between the Eastern and the Western account of beatitude for there is both theophany and present propinquity.

Despite its seeming radicality surely such an account is not theologically surprising. Since God loves what he creates and given that *all* things are both universal *and* particular (even angels albeit that they possess this distinction in different manner) then it would be a strange reversal of creation if we were contemplated only in our universal aspect. In this sense in beatitude there is no necessary contradiction between universal and particular contemplation. Universal contemplation relates to the greatest good in caused things which is that which bonds and links all things which is the order of the universe (*SCG* 3.1 64.9) whereas singular or particular contemplation relates to the first perfection of a thing which is its form (*SCG* 3.1 64.11). Universal contemplation relates to the relations and orders of all particulars which is why Aquinas quotes from Genesis (1:31) 'God saw all the things he had made and they were very good' wheras scripture says that God said of the individual works that preceded this overarching recognition that they 'were good' (*SCG* 3.1 64.9 and *SCG* 1.78.7). Aquinas states that 'the greatest good in caused things is the order of the universe for it is most perfect (*Id autem quod est maxime bonum in rebus causatis, est bonum ordinis universi, quod est maxime perfectum*). But this ordering of the discrete parts of creation requires that there be singular works to put in relation – without distinction there can be no relation and no ordering of parts and hierarchies. And since Christian theology is not a meditation on henology – but rather a Trinitarian account of uniqueness and relation then singulars are as vital to beatitude as universals for without one there would be no other.

Matter, God and the Beatific Vision

But let me, in the light of all the aforementioned, re-address the questions that marked the outset of this chapter. The theory of the beatific vision is, as I have said, often marked by duality and opposition. Traditionally the beatitudes of this life and the next create a schism within human knowledge such that ordinary and elevated cognition are sequestered to their respective realms. So it is with Thomas, where we were at first sight presented with an opposition between illumination and knowledge by abstraction from phantasms. But this is a spurious opposition since even if in the next life we as separated souls know by likeness rather than abstraction we are still not capable of illumination by our own efforts. The true opposition is between finite knowing by both likeness and abstraction and illumination by God. We thus make a mistake if we think ourselves cursed by the limitations of sensible knowledge. The gap between God and ourselves can be bridged not by our death but only by God via an elevation of our nature, a disposition attained by the light of glory (*lumen gloria*), which then permits an introduction of the divine essence into the passive intellect.

Thus in some manner beatitude must confirm both forms of finite knowing. Discursivity and intuition occur in both this life and the next. Since the separated soul if it looks down at earth knows the discursive manner of knowing even if it exceeds it. Accordingly beatitude cannot be an exterior or extrinsic perfection added to the knowledge of man. Because if natural man (and we are still natural even if dead) receives an act which superimposes itself on mankind's first intellectual act (that by which the body subsists) then 'the subject receives as an accidental act that which gives to him his proper perfection'.[53] Since an accident cannot be definitive of a substance, the beatific vision is either added to man later as an accident, in which case natural man strictly speaking has no need of it, or this accident is in man's substantial form, in which case he possessed it from the beginning. And in this possession from the beginning we can find and recognize the beatitude we already had when we first opened our eyes and saw the work of creation. God does not operate differently in heaven than he does on earth.

Hence according to the principle that 'grace and glory perfect but do not destroy nature' must not the soul await reunion with its body before it partakes its full cognitive beatitude? If the soul which is last in the hierarchy of intelligences by nature needs a body to know, should not the true fullness of beatitude await the final resurrection? It surely cannot be that the beatitude of the separated soul differs from that of the soul re-united with its body only by an extensive magnitude – there must be a qualitative concretion of knowledge when the body free from corruption enters into the world for which it was truly destined. And there is a new material world after death as Scripture apply attests: 'then I saw a new heaven and a new earth' (Rev 21:1).

Of course as I have said it would be perfectly reasonable for God to create us and even if we remained innocent, never to offer us the beatific vision but then man if he was to be gifted with such a vision would have to be recast by a divine intention that was not present in the beginning. Something that Thomas denies throughout his corpus, since he always insists that we have a natural desire for the supernatural, but it is exactly this understanding that Thomas risks compromising with his later account of beatitude. It is little wonder then that subsequent Thomists did try to craft some continuity between this life and the next by producing a variant of obediential potency – a state Garrigou-Lagrange describes as 'not immediately and naturally ordained to any act or object, *but indicates an orientation toward an agent of higher nature, which it obeys*'.[54] Certainly, as de Lubac points out, Aquinas teaches that we cannot obtain the beatific vision on our own, but he does not deny that we desire it. Indeed it is only because our natural desire is directed

[53] Boulnois, 'Les deux fins de l'homme l'impossible anthropologie et le repli de la théologie', p. 211. In this regard see also E.H. Weber, *La personne humaine au XIII siècle, l'avènement chez les maîtres parisiens de la conception moderne de l'homme* (Paris, 1991), p. 249.

[54] Réginald Garrigou-Lagrange, *De revelatione per Ecclesiam catholicam proposita* (4th edn, Rome, 1945), p. 353.

to the beatific vision that we are capable of receiving grace and being fulfilled in that vision. Moreover if we only have obediential potency for fulfilment in the beatific vision we are only 'fitted to receive a supernatural finality *praeter naturam* (incidentally or beyond nature) or *contra naturam* (against nature)'.[55]

However this intellectual prejudice against nature and matter cannot survive theological or philosophical reflection. Taking the latter first, if there is an existential priority in Aquinas (which nobody really now denies), it cannot be a priority that accords to universals for universals do not exist by themselves. On the contrary universals only exist through singulars – without material singulars there could be no existent universals. 'Universals ... are not subsisting things, but rather have being only in singulars ...' (*SCG* 1.65.2).[56]

Since it is singularity (understood as that unique participation of form and matter as exemplified in an individual) that preserves or holds universality in being, it is individuals that prevent the real from becoming an abstraction. Otherwise universals would be more true of the real order of beings than the beings themselves – something that the purely intellective reading of beatitude suggests. To maintain the coherency of the position I am trying to articulate – I must argue that individuality is not caused by arbitrary dimensional location as Aquinas appears to suggest in his commentary on Boethius' *De Trinitate*.

On the contrary I argue there is an alternative source of individuation within Aquinas – the act of being – we know that God as being is the ultimate cause of individual unity – the problem stems from the principle of individuation (matter) being separated from the cause of individuation: being. Now being as God as the cause of each individual thing is not susceptible to a nominalist reading because God's will, love and intention stands behind every particular thing. In the order of being – being is the universal cause of individuation – it gives a unity to beings which perforce must be separated from being itself and all other beings. So if the act of being suffices for individuation – which I believe it does – then act and principle must coincide. Form then becomes both the cause and principle of individuation – which paradoxically does not cease to mean that matter individuates because now the cause (being), which wants individuals or singulars, realizes them via divine intention in matter – which means that being causes matter in order to have particular individuals within the same species. This means again that matter retains its crucial importance because it is the means by which (*id quo*) a certain desired form of individuality is realized in the actual order of existence.

If this was not the case, and if in some way it was argued that Aquinas preferred universal intuition to particular recognition then why would Aquinas in *Summa Contra Gentiles* claim the following? 'However to know the divine substance and to see its effects in it is a more perfect knowledge than to know the divine substance

---

[55]   De Lubac, *Mystery of the Supernatural*, p. 141.

[56]   '*universalia autem non sunt res subsistentes, sed habent esse solum in singularibus*' (*SCG* 1.65.2).

without seeing the effects in it.'[57] Of course universal and particular cognition in the beatified state coincide, so we see both God's providential ordering of the whole and the particular realization of the perfection proper to each part. But since his creatures exist in both universal and particular aspects the disinterested intellective contemplation of the first cause apart from its effects is replaced – as evinced by the preceding quotation – by a creative inversion of the traditional priority. Now the *intellectus* of higher reason sees the first cause contemplating not itself but its own particular creations. And God even knows virtually all the singular things that will participate him and his being (*SCG* 1.65.3) – for in the end the very designation of matter that produces an individual within a species is known and willed by God.

Only this reading can really explain why in Book I of the commentary on the *Sentences*, in q2 article 3 Aquinas maintains that God knows the proper natures of other things. Divine knowledge is not some vague awareness of individuals; as it would be if the dimensional account of individuality were to be maintained – if it were God would only know the universal rather than the singular aspects of creatures. On the contrary, God has proper and certain knowledge of individuals through his own single essence. He achieves this through knowledge of how all things and all natures can imitate his divine essence (*SCG* 1. 63–71). Moreover (*Dist* 36 q1, a1), since God knows other things through the way he brought them into being, he knows these things *precisely* in the way he gives being to them. In which case since God gives being through form, as form is the way one receives the limitation of being, form *is* definitive of a creatures' individuality. Indeed in *Sentences* I q2, a3 Thomas confirms that there are proper ideas in God's mind for individuals. That said the distinction between different species is held to be more perfect (in the sense that order is perceived more clearly in the whole than it is in the part) than that between individuals in the same species, since the former distinction is by form and the latter by matter. Of course since God produces both matter and form, he knows the individuals who are composed of both. He even in the *Sentences* defends the idea that there is an (albeit imperfect) idea of pure matter in God. Besides, in the *Summa Contra Gentiles*, separate substances are also deemed capable of knowing the material particularity that individuates sensible being. And it is the elevation by the divine light to this cognitive level that is defined as beatitude.

All of which tends to support that argument that I am wishing to make that matter over the course and trajectory of his work occupies an increasingly formal or ideal station in Thomas's metaphysics. This formality is not just because sensible being is included in a Thomistic account of the form of composite creatures. The very fact that both God and separate substances have an idea and thus cognition of matter suggests not just divine knowledge of this specificity but also a divine

---

[57] *SCG* 3.1 56,7: '*Perfectioris tamen cognitionis est cognoscere divinam substantiam et in ea eius effectus videre, quam cognoscere divinam substantiam sine hoc quod effectus videantur in ipsa*'.

will behind it. Of course there must be a divine will to bring composite creatures into being – but what is strange and what suggests that for God matter *matters*, he wills a sensible species in order to differentiate by matter those individuals within it. As such material existence must represent some particular intensification or perfection of being. If not why would there be a resurrection? We are promised that we shall be higher than the angels and that we shall sit on God's right hand and share in the full predication of Trinitarian deification. Why then do we not remain separated souls after death? Evidently we are not as equally beatified without our body as with it – reason can only conclude that we are resurrected back into the glorified composite in order to know the perfection that material existence represents.

Perhaps this is why Thomas was so insistent upon the soul being the form of the body, if man is substantially body *and* soul, any separated state of the soul is for him violence to an intended unity. The eschatology of humankind being that of resurrected flesh not separated intelligences.

More importantly however there is a more radical consequence; now flesh and intellect are one. If the principle and cause of material individuation is now the intellective willing and intentional being of God, then matter is an intellective outcome and a divine mental creation – in which case flesh can no longer be a barrier to intellectual contemplation of the divine. For if individuation is the end of universal divine activity (and how can it not be since the very priority of universal over particular has been inverted) – then should it not be the aim of intellective contemplation? This is exactly what Thomas argues beatitude consists of, since God must know both the universal and the singular perfectly if he is to know either at all (*SCG* 1.65.4). Thus God must perforce contemplate one while intuiting the other. All of which would make matter a diaphanous product within which the mental and material are both co-present and co-founding since it is the difference of matter that pluralizes the species and so allows universality to be incarnate. Thus the distinction between the vision of God in this life and the next should indeed be made – but only on the basis of the fall not on the basis of matter.

For example, the union of bodily resurrection and the vision of God are expressly foretold by Job. 'I know that my redeemer liveth and in the last day I shall rise out of the earth and shall be clothed again with my skin, and in my flesh I shall see my God' (Job 19:25–6). And again in *Summa Contra Gentiles* Aquinas acknowledges this arguing that nothing that is contrary to nature can be perpetual 'therefore man cannot achieve his ultimate happiness unless the soul once again united to the body' (*SCG* IV 79.11).[58]

Both Incarnation and resurrection suggest neither the ending of matter nor its conversion to the immaterial being that Angels possess. On the contrary, flesh and matter are rescued from death and saved from corruption. Matter is not so

---

[58] '*Non igitur potest homo ultimam felicitatem consequi nisi anima iterato corpori coniungatur*' (*SCG* 4.79. 11).

much changed as it is transfigured, glorified and restored to its original intention when we were made of matter but were not mortal. Perhaps this is why in the New Testament we can find the following injunction 'our present perishable nature must put on imperishability and this mortal nature must put on immortality' (1 Cor 15:50–53).

The restoration of immortality inspires the recognition 'Death where is your victory' but more than that it gives the destinal shape of the natural order. The restoration beyond death and sin and the descent of the heavenly city to earth such that there is as Revelations promises not an abolition of the created order but a re-making anew (Rev 21:5).

Why then did Aquinas articulate an account of beatitude that excluded the body? In part, one could argue that he was lead to this conclusion by Scripture in his reading of 2 Cor 5:5–6 when Paul pleads to be exiled from the body to make his home with the lord. Or in Aquinas' claim that the separated souls of the saints enjoy a full beatitude without the body (*SCG* IV, 91). Yet even his reading of Scripture can be questioned as Paul earlier says of the earthly world that he does not want to strip it off but put another garment over it – transfiguring rather than repudiating the earthly body (2 Cor 4–5). Moreover Aquinas' philosophical denial that we can see God in this life rests *only* on the claim that no created species can deliver the cognition of the divine essence (*SCG* 3.1 5.1.2). Hence the cognitive need for a divine elevation of the human intellect and the donation of a divine species by the divine mind. Presumably however, this is the case for the intellective soul both before *and* after death. For it is not the case that we have a different soul while we are living and then on death get a new soul that can see the divine without the aid of God. In which case there is no difference in terms of the cognitive structure of beatitude between seeing God in this life or the next. Our agent intellect is not more potent when we are dead such that it can by itself abstract the divine species from the divine mind unaided by the deity. Indeed the agent intellect and thus our agency plays no part in the cognitive structure of beatitude – the divine species is introduced immediately into the passive intellect bypassing entirely our normal cognitive processes. And again this ability of illumination and donation is as open to God to accomplish in this life just as much as the next.

So to conclude on both philosophical and theological grounds matter *per se* cannot be thought to be a barrier to seeing God. Quite why the later Aquinas adopted the position he did on beatitude is an open question – as elsewhere he increasingly incorporated matter into the order of being and divine intention. All we can say is that the Incarnation shows that nothing is more ideal and more real than flesh and matter. So much so that the resurrection deifies this state and inaugurates a new earth. As for this life we can conclude the following. Theologically and philosophically beatitude or anticipations of it thereof are as open to us in this life as the next – that the continuity of the supernatural and the fall of part of it into mere nature is a sin on our part passed to creation. That we can see beyond the fall in eschatological vision, aesthetic proclamation and mediated theophany is a self-evident Catholic and Orthodox teaching. Moreover seeing God in this life is an ontological stance that scripture itself call us to enact. 'Ever since God created the world his everlasting power and deity – however invisible – has been there for the mind to see in the things he has made' (Rom 1:20). As such Scripture outlines a noetics and a cognition that already unifies intellect and matter, visibility and invisibility and Creator and creature.

PART IV
Orthodoxy and Transfiguration

Chapter 8

Space, Time and the Liturgy

Andrew Louth

The Divine Liturgy takes place in space and time. Such an assertion seems obvious, but its very obviousness lays open the possibility – indeed, probability – of our misconceiving its significance, and consequently misunderstanding the classic Eastern Orthodox interpretation of the Liturgy from St John Chrysostom to Nicolas Kavasilas, by reading back into the liturgy our modern understandings of space and time which are thin and jejune compared with what would have been taken for granted by the Byzantine mind. The danger of such reading back is enhanced by the fact that in many respects the terms in which we understand space and time are apparently similar, so that ancient discussion of whether space is to be understood as a 'receptacle' – or a container, that in which things are – or as constituted by relationship, is very easily thought to be the same as the modern discussion as found for instance in the famous Clarke-Leibniz correspondence.[1] We then need to begin by exploring the ways in which the Byzantine mind understood space and time.[2]

The Byzantines were indebted to Plato, and especially to his famous discussion of the nature of the cosmos in the *Timaeus*. Plato's ideas had been subject to centuries of reflection, and the form in which the Byzantine fathers received them had been mediated by later thinkers, not least the Neoplatonists, whose ideas inform the influential conceptions of space and time implicit in Dionysius the Areopagite and discussed by St Maximus the Confessor. However, for the purpose of exposing our modern presuppositions about space and time and forming a general impression of classical and late antique conceptions, we can gain a great deal by discussing the twin pillars of virtually all patristic understanding of the cosmos: Plato's *Timaeus* and the account of the creation in six days, the *Hexaemeron*, in the first chapter of Genesis.

To begin with, let us sketch in our modern presuppositions. These are that space and time are principally matters of measurement. Space concerns the three dimensions of measurable physical existence, and time the measurement

---

[1] As Samuel Sambursky does: see his *The Concept of Space in Late Neoplatonism* (Jerusalem, 1982), p. 13. There is an English translation of the Clarke-Leibniz correspondence by H.G. Alexander (Manchester, 1956).

[2] I have not had the chance to see Simon Oliver, *Philosophy, God and Motion* (London, 2005), but to judge from David Bentley Hart's review in the *Times Literary Supplement*, 24 March 2006, p. 31, Oliver pursues somewhat similar ideas from what I have presented here, though with much greater erudition and covering a much broader span of intellectual history.

of duration. They are themselves quite inert; they constitute the framework within which measurability takes place. In this sense that they can be regarded as mechanistic, as opposed to organic. The changes in our understanding of space and time consequent on theories of relativity and quantum theory do not fundamentally alter the idea of a mechanistic notion of the universe, introduced by modern science from the seventeenth century onwards; they simply reveal some of the complications involved in such measurement. Relativity disposes of any absolute spatial framework, while our notion of the measurement of duration has been refined, so that instead of depending on the movement of the sun, moon and the stars, and the revolution of the earth, or the movement of a pendulum – all of which have been discovered to be insufficiently precise – we base our measurement of time on the vibrations of a quartz crystal, for example. If the beginnings of modern science produced mechanistic notions of space and time, the scientific revolutions of the last century have rendered our notions of space and time still more abstract and mathematical.[3]

Ancient Conceptions of Space and Time[4]

The discussions of space and time in Plato's *Timaeus* belong to a different, though overlapping, realm of discourse. Plato approaches his discussion of space in the *Timaeus* by way of his discussion of the 'receptacle, or as it were nurse, of all becoming' (πάσης ... γενέσεως ὑποδοχὴν ... οἷον τιθήνην: *Tim.* 49a). It is not just that in which things move, but that in which everything *becomes*. What takes place in the receptacle, which Plato will later identify with space (χώρα: 52a), is much more than the movement of material, physical bodies, it is nothing less than the change and becoming of everything subject to such change and becoming. To be in space is, then, not just to be geometrically located, as it were, but to belong to the realm of change and becoming: the ὑποδοχή is certainly a receptacle, but that means more than a container, something to put things in, rather it means that

---

[3]   I think this should probably be qualified, as the *Theory of General Relativity* envisages conceptions of space and time that are anything but inert; but these ideas have not percolated very deeply into the modern mind. In so far as they have they confirm something of the intuition of the ancients.

[4]   Two recently published books, which I read after writing this chapter, are relevant here and seem to me to confirm my approach, though with a degree of detail that would not be appropriate here. One is Pascal Mueller-Jordan, *Typologie spatio-temporelle de l'Ecclesia byzantine. La Mystagogie de Maxime le Confesseur dans la cutlure philosophique de l'Antiquité tardive*, Supplements of *Vigiliae Christianae* 74 (Leiden, 2005). This book reveals the lineaments of Maximus' debt to late ancient philosophy in his understanding of space and time, and shows how it informs his understanding of the liturgy. The other is Christian Moevs, *The Metaphysics of Dante's* Comedy (New York, 2005). Despite Moevs' somewhat advaitist interpretation of late medieval thought, he has some valuable things to say about concepts of time and space: see pp. 132–40, 140–46.

which receives, provides room for, everything that constitutes the cosmos – the product of reason and necessity. The cosmos for Plato is not something that can be considered in purely material terms. Before he comes to speak of the receptacle of becoming, he describes the cosmos as a living being having soul at the centre, with body wrapped round the outside, as it were, of soul (Plato clearly has in mind something like an armillary sphere) – it is for this reason that the cosmos and a human being can be seen as mutually reflecting one another, the human being, in the coinage of the Renaissance, being a *microcosm*, a little cosmos, μικρὸς κόσμος, an idea frequently found in the fathers.

Even a quick glance at the *Timaeus* reveals that the cosmos as a living being is not some sort of primaeval being, but is already instinct with principles of reason and proportion. Plato explains at some length how soul contains within itself complex and beautiful mathematical structures, and as he goes on to discuss what it is that is formed within the receptacle of becoming, we find a discussion that embraces everything that comes into being from the four elements of fire, earth, air and water, and how on this foundation we find the principles of pleasure and pain, tastes, odours, sounds, colours, and beyond that the emotional structure of the soul – its capacity for being aroused, ultimately to anger, and for experiencing desire and longing (its incensive and appetitive powers). The kinds of becoming envisaged within the receptacle of becoming go well beyond the movement of physical particles, and include what is perceived by the senses and the very process of sensation, the experience of pleasure and pain, and the complex reality of the soulful experience (to avoid the debased meaning attached to 'psychic' or 'psychological') of mortal beings.

Another dimension of space for the late antique mind – one only implicit in Plato – is bound up with the notion of relationship, and the experience of distance that makes relationship possible. The term used for what I have called distance is διάστημα, 'interval' or 'extension'.[5] This again is characteristic of everything that is subject to change and becoming: διάστημα separates one thing from another, but it refers to any distance or extension, including the capacity to move in an argument, say, from premises to a conclusion, or the 'distance' implicit in the notion of desire for something. The notion of multitude or the manifold is implicit in the realm of becoming and διάστημα is implicit in this. Everything that belongs to the realm of change and becoming is marked by διάστημα: it makes possible the 'space' required for relationship, in every sense, not just a geometrical sense, and so includes the 'space' that exists between human beings – the distance ('*die Weite*') that Rilke says we are to love, 'to give them the possibility of seeing one another in their complete form and against the greatness of heaven'[6] – and indeed

---

5   The term seems originally Aristotelian, but it became commonplace in discussion of space, and also time. There is a good discussion in Hans von Balthasar, *Présence et Pensée. Essai sur la philosophie religieuse de Grégoire de Nysse* (Paris, 1942), pp. 1–10.

6   Rilke, letter to Emanuel von Bodman, 17 August 1901, in Rainer Maria Rilke, *Briefe* (Franfurt am Main, 1950), p. 29.

the space that exists within a human being, giving the possibility of growth and development (as well as denying the realization of perfection).

This notion of διάστημα also characterizes time, but again does so in a multitude of ways. It certainly includes the time through which the sequence of the seasons pass, the succession of years, the movement from day to night and night to day, but it includes other experiences of time: the time through which human beings pass from birth, through infancy, and childhood, to maturity, and then on to death; the time through which our ideas, thoughts, feelings, relationships pass. These different modes of time all relate one to another, but the ticking of the clock, as it were, is not the proper meaning of time, in comparison with which psychological time, for example, has only metaphorical significance. And if it is true – as it is – that 'cosmic' time has some fundamental significance, as embracing and including all other experiences of time, then it needs to be remembered, that the 'cosmos' is more than a merely material reality; it is a 'living being with soul and intelligence' – ζῷον ἔμψυχον ἔννουν (*Tim.* 30b).

The centrality of the notion of διάστημα to ancient understanding of space and time has a further important consequence we should note. It does not mean that space and time are full of 'gaps', gulfs of unmeaning, as it were, dooming the world of becoming to ultimate meaninglessness. Even for Plato, for whom there can be no λόγος of anything in the realm of becoming (*Tim.* 29d), the truth is quite the contrary: the cosmos, existing in space, and time itself are creations of the gods; they have meaning that is revealed in their structures, constituted by relationship. Time is for Plato 'a moving image of eternity' (εἰκὼ ... κινητόν τινα αἰῶνος: *Tim.* 37d): it is ordered towards eternity; within the realm of becoming it represents eternity as its image. The sequence of time is not meaningless (though for Plato it is cyclic: it is a 'vulgar error', though popular among some theologians, that cyclic time spells meaninglessness, in contrast with the purposeful nature of linear time): it is ordered towards eternity. And space, too, has structures, relationships, that give it meaning, primary among which are the 'divisions of nature' (to use Eriugena's term): the distinctions between the spiritual world and the material, between the heavens and the earth – distinctions in which the lower (material, earth) is ordered towards the higher (spiritual, heaven) and embodies the higher within itself (so the material finds its meaning in relation to the spiritual, while at the same time manifesting the spiritual within the material) – exemplifying a principle expressed by Dionysius the Areopagite, who remarked, 'truly visible things are manifest images of invisible things'.[7]

It is with such notions of space and time that the Greek fathers read the Scriptures. As soon as these notions are transposed into a Christian context, there is a profound shift of meaning that, curiously, introduces into these notions a dramatic clarity. In my account I have been careful not to use the language of creation (such care is not always found in commentators on the classical

---

    [7]   Dionysius the Areopagite, *ep.* 10, ed. A.M. Ritter, *Corpus Dionysiacum* II, Patristische Texte und Studien 36 (Berlin, 1991), p. 208, ll. 9–10.

philosophers, not even Cornford, who is well aware of the problem[8]); instead I have spoken of the 'realm of becoming'. But for Christians the realm of becoming is identical with the created order. Everything created belongs to the realm of becoming; the very existence of created beings is based on becoming – on coming to be from nothing, *ex nihilo*; everything created has a beginning. For St Maximus, everything created is characterized by the triad: becoming – movement – rest.[9] Creatures 'become', through creation *ex nihilo* by God; they then exist in a state of movement or motion, in search of ultimate rest in God, to whom they owe their being. This 'movement', it hardly needs saying by now, does not simply mean physical movement, though it might involve this. It means the movement of change, a passage ideally from worse to better, the transformation of being (εἶναι) to well being (εὖ εἶναι), which God will finally crown with eternal well being (ἀεὶ εὖ εἶναι), to use the other triad St Maximos is so fond of in expounding his cosmology.[10] Διάστημα is, then, characteristic of *created being*; indeed to be created is to experience διάστημα, which is unknown to the eternal being of God.[11] Both space and time, equally characterized by διάστημα, are created realities, the created framework within which created beings exist.

With these preconceptions, the fathers read the account of creation in Genesis 1. The very first words of the Scriptures speak of the creation of space and time:

> In the beginning God created heaven and earth. The earth was invisible and unformed, and darkness was upon the abyss; and the Spirit of God was being borne over the water. And God said, Let there be light; and light came to be. And God saw the light that it was good; and God divided between light and darkness. And God called the light day, and the darkness he called night. And evening came to be, and morning, one day.[12]

The creation of heaven and earth *is* the creation of space, ordered between higher and lower. Earth, the lower, is without characteristics ('invisible and unformed'); with the creation of light, heaven becomes apparent to earth, and earth itself begins to receive form that orders it towards heaven. The first step in the forming or fashioning of earth is the creation of light, and the division of light from darkness.

---

[8]   See Francis M. Cornford, *Plato's Cosmology. The Timaeus of Plato* (London, 1937), pp. 34–5, where he criticizes A.E. Taylor, though Cornford uses the terms creature/creation regularly in his translation and commentary.

[9]   See my *Maximus the Confessor* (London, 1996), p. 67 (where there is an unfortunate mistake: the Origenist triad, which Maximus corrects, should be rest – movement – becoming).

[10]   See, for example, *Ambigua* 10. 3 (PG 91:1116A–D).

[11]   This means that there can be relationship in God without διάστημα, an idea finally expressed by means of the notion of περιχώρησις: see John Damascene, *Expositio fidei* 8, 223–85, ed. Kotter, Patristische Texte und Studien 12 (Berlin, 1973), pp. 28–30.

[12]   Genesis 1:1–5. My translation from the Septuagint.

With the division between light and darkness, there comes the sequence from darkness to light, from evening to morning – which constitutes day. Here we have the creation of time, not the coming into being of duration – the inexorable revolution of the heavens, or the ticking of the clock – but the sequence from evening to morning, from night to day. It is striking – and significant – that the sequence is this way round: from darkness to light, from evening to morning (a sequence that is repeated in this order for each day of creation: see Gen 1:8, 13, 19, 23, 31). For it means that time is ordered towards the light of the coming day. A day is, then, not just a period of time, of twenty-four hours, from midnight to midnight; it is a movement from darkness to light, from evening to morning, to daybreak, to the rising of the sun. This fundamental orientation of time is the orientation of life, as a passage from darkness to light, to the confession of the 'dayspring from on high', ἀνατολὴ ἐξ ὕψους, *oriens ex alto* (as the *Benedictus* has it: Lk 1:78) – Christ, to whom the whole created order is moving. This notion of time as moving from darkness to light is embedded in the liturgical notion of time, where the new day begins with vespers, and looks to the dawning of the new day, ultimately to the 'day without evening'– ἀνέσπερος ἡμέρα – of the Kingdom (something still fundamental to the concept of liturgical time in the Orthodox Church, though mostly abandoned in the liturgical office of the Western Church).

Space and time, and movement through space and time, are concepts in the patristic tradition that are freighted with meaning. They include the physical space and duration through which we move, but they include very much more. Space and time are ordered, structured, in the way just outlined. Furthermore, space and time are, so to speak, the coordinates of *all created existence*, not just physical existence, and the understanding of movement is consequently many layered. Physical movement is movement through physical space and duration, but there is cosmic movement concerned with the movement of the heavens, the sequence of the seasons, the passage from evening to morning. This cosmic movement is more than physical movement, for it has significance, meaning, bound up with the *quality* of time characteristic of the seasons – spring, summer, autumn, winter (vividly expressed in medieval calendars, not least those found (significantly) in books of hours) – and of the passage from evening, through night, to morning and the day. The creation in six days suggests a sequence of ages, prefigured in the successive days of creation, including the 'ages of the world', variously conceived. There are also the stages of human life, often modelled on the ages of the world: from birth, through the ages of man (variously divided, sometimes four – childhood, youth, maturity, old age – sometimes seven – as in Jaques' infant, student, lover, soldier, judge, declining into old age, and finally 'second childishness and mere oblivion')[13] to death.

Furthermore, there is the movement of the soul from its baptismal awakening by repentance, through growth in the image of God by ascetic struggle, and a

---

[13]   For some sense of the richness of the notion of the ages of man, see J.A. Burrow, *The Ages of Man* (Oxford, 1986).

deepening transfiguration through grace in which the life of God is manifest in the soul, to deification. All these experiences of movement suggest mutual analogies; it is not, as the modern mind is tempted to think, that physical space and duration are the 'real' meaning of space and time, the others being merely metaphorical. Rather all these experiences of movement in space and time are experiences of the modalities of creaturely being, characterized by διάστημα. Plato's conviction of the link, or harmony, between the soul and the cosmos is manifest in the closing paragraphs of the *Timaeus*, where he speaks of 'the most sovereign form of soul in us', which 'dwells in the summit of our body and lifts us from earth towards our celestial affinity, like a plant whose roots are not in earth, but in the heavens', and recommends that, because 'the motions akin to the divine part in us are the thoughts and revolutions of the universe', we should follow them, so that 'by learning to know the harmonies and revolutions of the world, [we] should bring the intelligent part, according to its pristine nature, into the likeness of that which intelligence discerns, and thereby win the fulfilment of the best life set by the gods before mankind both for this present time and for the time to come' (*Tim.* 90acd; Cornford's translation).

The Divine Liturgy

It is with such a sense of space and time that we can fruitfully approach the understanding of the Divine Liturgy in the Orthodox tradition. For the dimensions of space and time are integral to the celebration of the Divine Liturgy. It takes place in a space divided into the sanctuary and the nave (or 'temple', ναός), mirroring the division of the cosmos into heaven and earth, so that the whole church building is understood as symbolizing the cosmos. Nowadays this division is marked by an iconostasis, generally a wall of icons, pierced by the central doors, the 'holy' or 'beautiful' doors usually bearing icons of the Annunciation and the Evangelists, behind which is a curtain that can be drawn across or left open, as well as by other doors, north and south. The iconostasis is a late development, belonging to the second millennium, but the division that it marks is ancient. The cosmos reflected in the church building is a Christian cosmos: that is, heaven is not so much the place of the heavenly bodies – the stars and planets, with all the astrological associations that go with them – but of the heavenly beings, the celestial hierarchy of angelic beings.

Dionysius the Areopagite presented the ranks of celestial beings as three ranks of three: on the highest rank – Seraphim, Cherubim and Thrones, in the middle – Dominions, Authorities and Powers, on the lowest rank – Principalities, Archangels and Angels. The art historian, Thomas Mathews, has remarked how early this substitution of a pagan cosmos of heavenly bodies with a Christian cosmos of heavenly beings is found in the decoration of Christian churches.[14] But it is not the abandonment of cosmology that we see here, rather its transformation. It is in such a structured space, freighted with symbolism, that the Divine Liturgy takes place. And it is an action. Things take place – there is movement, there is encounter. It is not possible to understand the Divine Liturgy by treating it primarily as a literary text, as Western scholarship, even the best, has tended to do – in the last century among Anglicans, from Dom Gregory Dix to Catherine Pickstock – it is what takes place that matters: which is why Dionysius' explanation of various liturgical rites, including the Eucharistic liturgy itself, does no more than allude to the prayers that are said. The words of the prayers offered during the Divine Liturgy, not least the prayer of the Anaphora, the equivalent of the Roman *canon missae*, are important, but they cannot be understand without grasping their place in the Eucharistic action.

The Orthodox Church has never lost the sense that the liturgical worship of the Church takes place in a building designed for the purpose by a community of people all of whom have their specific tasks – and their own books. Fr Alexander Schmemann remarks somewhere that Orthodox worship requires a virtual library of books: a book for the priest, another for the deacon, a Gospel book, the book of the Apostle (containing the liturgical texts from the Acts of the Apostles and the apostolic epistles), a book for the reader, books for the choir, the twelve volumes of the Menaion, the *Pentekostarion* (containing the liturgical hymns for the season of Pascha and Pentecost), the *Triodion* (containing those for Lent and Holy Week), and the *Paraklitiki* (for the rest of the year), not to mention the books containing the rites for the other sacraments than the Eucharist, funeral services and a host of blessings. The Orthodox Church has never followed the way of the West in reducing this library to a few convenient volumes, handy and portable – the missal or the breviary – and that is not because we are stuck in some pre-modern time warp. For the production of the missal and the breviary corresponded to a privatization (and clericalization) of liturgical worship, a sense that liturgical space was secondary (all that was needed was an altar-stone and a missal, and a few sacred vessels), with the result that the essentially communal nature of liturgical worship, which could not be reduced to a text (not least, because the different activities of the different ministers often overlap), was precisely reduced to a text, recited by the priest from the one book he required, which could be supplemented by choir, congregation, etc., but did not strictly need them.[15] Nothing like this has ever taken place in the Orthodox Church, and this needs to be remembered if Orthodox worship is to be properly understood.

---

[14]   Thomas F. Mathews, *The Clash of Gods. A Reinterpretation of Early Christian Art* (Princeton, 1993), pp. 148 ff.

[15]   For something of the history of this development in the West, closely bound up with the emergence of the mendicant orders with their inherent individualism, see Stephen J.P. van Dijk OFM and Joan H. Walker, *The Origins of the Modern Roman Liturgy* (London, 1960).

Dionysius the Areopagite's discussion is mostly to be found in his work, the *Ecclesiastical Hierarchy*, which presents his view of the earthly Church ('our hierarchy', as he calls it) through the exposition of a series of liturgical rites: baptism, Eucharist, the consecration of *myron*, or chrism, priestly ordination, monastic consecration and the funeral service. He presents us, first of all, with a ceremony, or series of ceremonies. His account of the Eucharistic liturgy begins thus:

> The hierarch, having finished the sacred prayer at the divine altar, begins the censing from there and comes out, going round the entire area of the sacred place. Having finished, he goes back again to the divine altar and begins the sacred singing of the psalms, while the whole ecclesiastical array joins with him in the sacred psalmody.[16]

Prayers and psalms are mentioned, but not specified; what is central is the initial act of censing the church and congregation by the bishop. It is therefore the meaning of the act of censing that Dionysios expounds in the next chapter:

> For the thearchic blessedness that is beyond all, if in its divine goodness it proceeds into the communion of those who sacredly participate in it, does not come to be outside its essentially unmoved stillness and establishment, and irradiates all the God-formed in an appropriate degree, while remaining essentially in itself and in no way moved from its own identity. Just so the divine rite of *synaxis* ['gathering together': Dionysios' term for the eucharist], while possessing a unique, simple principle, folded in on itself, yet out of loving kindness is multiplied into the sacred variety of symbols and reaches throughout all hierarchical iconography, but draws all these back into unity within its own inherent singleness and makes one all those sacredly raised up to it. In the same God-formed way, the divine hierarch, if, formed by goodness, he hands on his unique knowledge of hierarchy to those lower down by making use of the multitude of sacred enigmas, but absolutely free and unaffected by anything less than him, he is restored without loss to his own beginning, and making his own intelligible entrance into the One he sees purely the unifying principles of what has been accomplished, making the goal of his loving procession to what is second the more divine return to what is first.[17]

The movement of the censing – out from the sanctuary to the furthest reaches of the church and back again – reflects God's movement out from himself in love for his creatures, and his return with them to himself: the divine love reaches out and enfolds creation in all its multiplicity, drawing it back into himself. As in the anaphora of the Divine Liturgy (especially the much fuller anaphora in the

---

[16] Dionysius the Areopagite, *Ecclesiastical Hierarchy* 3. 2, ed. A.M. Ritter, *Corpus Dionysiacum* II, p. 80, ll. 8–12.

[17] Ibid., p. 81, l. 17–p. 82, l. 10.

Liturgy of St Basil), God is seen manifesting this divine love for human kind, his φιλανθρωπία, 'loving kindness', both in creation, his care for creation, and preeminently in the Incarnation and the Cross:

> For you did not utterly turn away from your creature, O Good One, nor forget the work of your hands, but you visited us in divers manners through your compassionate mercy. You sent prophets, you performed deeds of power through your saints, who have been well-pleasing to you in every generation; you spoke to us through the mouth of your servants, the prophets, announcing to us beforehand the salvation that was to come; you gave the law as a help; you appointed angels as guardians. But when the fullness of time had come, you spoke to us through your Son, through whom you had also made the ages ... He appeared on earth and lived among men; and taking flesh of a holy Virgin, he emptied himself, taking the form of a servant, being made in the likeness of the body of our humiliation, so that he might make us in the likeness of the image of his glory (*Anaphora of St Basil*).

What the prayer of the anaphora represents in words, the movement of the liturgy represents in a gesture of embrace. As Plato saw the movements of the heavens restoring the true movement of the intellect, so Dionysius sees the movement of the liturgy drawing us back into a life focused on God, for which we were created. The ceremony, or gesture, described by Dionysius is able to effect this in a more universal way that through words and ideas, even those of a prayer.

The place of space and time in the liturgy can, however, be seen more fully in St Maximus the Confessor's reflections on the Divine Liturgy, especially in his short work, the *Mystagogia*.[18] This work is a commentary on the Divine Liturgy, presented as supplementary to Dionysius' *Ecclesiastical Hierarchy*, set in the context of reflections on various images of the Church, both as a community and as a building. In these initial chapters, which are recapitulated at the end of the treatise after the exposition of the events of the Liturgy, Maximus presents an understanding of the Church as the central element in a series of ways of understanding the relationship of God to the cosmos and to human kind. He begins by discussing in Chapter 1 how the Church is to be seen as 'an image and type of God' as it imitates and represents God's activity (ἐνέργεια). Evoking the idea we have just found in Dionysius of God's activity reaching out into the created order and enfolding it all in himself, Maximus sees God as the One who 'contains, gathers and limits them and in his providence binds both intelligible and sensible beings to himself and one another'.

---

[18]   For a critical text, see Ἡ Μυσταγωγία τοῦ Ἁγίου Μαξίμου τοῦ Ὁμολογητοῦ, ed. C.G. Sotiropoulos (rev. edn., Athens, 1993); English trans. (not always satisfactory) in *Maximus Confessor: Selected Writings*, trans. G.C. Berthold (London, 1985), pp. 181–225. And see the work by Mueller-Jordan, already mentioned.

It is in this way that the holy Church of God will be shown to be active among us in the same way as God, as an image reflects its archetype. For many and of nearly boundless number are the men, women and children who are distinct from one another and vastly different by birth and appearance, by race and language, by way of life and age, by opinions and skills, by manners and customs, by pursuits and studies, and still again by reputation, fortune, characteristics and habits: all are born into the Church and through it are reborn and recreated in the Spirit. To all in equal measures it gives and bestows one divine form and designation: to be Christ's and to carry his name. In accordance with faith it gives to all a single, simple, whole and indivisible condition which does not allow us to bring to mind the existence of the myriads of differences among them, even if they do exist, through the universal relationship and union of all things with it. It is through it that absolutely no one at all is in himself separated from the community since everyone converges with all the rest and joins together with them by the one, simple, and indivisible grace and power of faith. 'For all,' it is said, 'had but one heart and one mind.' Thus to be and to appear as one body formed of different members is really worthy of Christ himself, our true head, in whom says the divine Apostle, 'there is neither male nor female, neither Jew nor Greek, neither circumcision nor uncircumcision, neither barbarian nor Scythian, neither slave nor free, but he is all and in all'. It is he who encloses in himself all beings by the unique, simple and infinitely wise power of his goodness.[19]

This way of conceiving of God's activity, ἐνέργεια, as reaching out and drawing all into unity recalls the theme, common to the fathers, of the cosmic cross, rooted in the creative activity of the Word of God. As St Irenaeus put it:

And since He is the Word of God who invisibly pervades the whole creation, and encompasses its length, breadth, height and depth – for by the Word of God everything is administered – so too was the Son of God crucified in these fourfold dimensions, having been imprinted in the form of the cross in everything; for it was necessary for him, becoming visible, to make manifest his form of the cross in everything, that He might demonstrate, by His visible form on the cross, His activity which is on the invisible level, for it is He who illumines the 'heights', that is, the things in heaven, and holds the 'deeps', which is beneath the earth, and stretches the 'length' from the East to the West, and who navigates the 'breadth' of the northern and southern regions, inviting the dispersed from all sides to the knowledge of the Father.[20]

This notion of the Cross, through which Christ embraced and reconciled the whole human race, and indeed the whole cosmos, underlies Maximus' understanding of

---

[19]   *Mystagogia* 1, Sotiropoulos, pp. 152–4.

[20]   Irenaeus, *Demonstration* 34, in St Irenaeus of Lyons, *On the Apostolic Preaching*, trans. and ed. John Behr (Crestwood, NY, 1997), p. 62. Cf. Athanasius, *On the Incarnation* 16.

the Church and the Divine Liturgy.[21] This notion of an embracing radiance is further illustrated by the analogy of the radii of a circle converging on the centre applied to both God's relationship to the created order and the Church's relationship to its members; Maximus concludes that, in both cases, there is achieved a union that, though profound, does not confuse the beings joined, but preserves their integrity.

Maximus goes on in the succeeding chapters to show how the union of differences found in the Church is also reflected throughout the created order. To begin with, in Chapter 2, he suggests that the Church may be seen as an image of the cosmos, regarded as made up of visible and invisible beings. From this point on he thinks of the Church as a building, and more precisely as a building divided into two: the area for 'the priests and ministers alone', that is, the sanctuary (in Greek: ἱερατεῖον), and the area for the 'all the faithful people', which is called the nave (ναός).[22] This distinction he finds echoed in the cosmos, in the distinction there between the invisible part of the cosmos and the visible part. These two parts are closely related; indeed, Maximus says, the church is not properly speaking divided by the differences between the two parts, but rather by the relationship between the two parts, so that, 'the nave is potentially the sanctuary since it is a holy place by reason of its relationship to the goal of sacred initiation (or mystagogy), and the sanctuary is actually the nave, since it is there that the process of its own sacred initiation begins'.[23] So, too, with the cosmos: 'for the whole intelligible cosmos is imprinted in a hidden way on the whole sensible cosmos through the symbolic forms, while the whole sensible cosmos can be understood to be present to the intelligible cosmos through its principles (λόγοι) that reveal its simplicity to the intellect'.[24] We find here what we have already encountered: the notion of distinction as constituting space, an ordered structure. The distinction found in cosmos and Church that is the reason for one being an image of the other is a matter of relationship rather than separation; it is a matter of connexion, and not division, and it is an ordered connexion, the visible pointing to the invisible realm, so that the visible finds its meaning in the invisible, and the invisible finds its expression in the visible, and in this way reflecting the close relationship between sanctuary and nave in the church.

The following chapters suggest further images of the church: in the visible world itself, consisting as it does of heaven and earth (Chapter 3), and then in the

---

[21] For the beginnings of this idea, see Jean Daniélou, *The Theology of Jewish Christianity* (London, 1964), pp. 265–92. See also Alois Grillmeier, *Der Logos am Kreuz* (Munich, 1956).

[22] It is worth noting that, in speaking of the Church, first, Maximus does not use any technical term for the unordained laity (such as the already well-established term, λαϊκός), but instead refers to 'all the faithful people', and secondly, ναός means a temple, that is the whole building (and is still used in that sense), so that the distinction is really between the building as a whole and a special part of it, and analogously for the community.

[23] *Mystagogia* 2, Sotiropoulos, p. 156, ll. 16–19.

[24] Ibid., p. 158, ll. 8–11.

human person, consisting of body and soul (Chapter 4), and the soul, consisting of soul and intellect (Chapter 5).[25] Chapters 4 and 5 develop a fairly detailed understanding of the spiritual life, moving from the level of body, which is the level of ascetic struggle, in which we learn moral wisdom, to the level of soul, which is the level of natural contemplation, that is contemplation of the principles (λόγοι) of the cosmos, which are all summed up in the *Logos* himself, Christ, and finally to the level of intellect, the level of mystical theology, that is contemplation of God himself (Maximus, while still using the image of the twofold church to interpret the passage from one level to another, also combines them in a threefold image of the church with nave, sanctuary and altar, θυσιαστήριον). Chapter 6 introduces a further image of the Church:

> just as, in accordance with contemplation that brings about ascent, he [the 'old man', or *geronta*, to whom Maximus attributes his *Mystagogia*] called the Church a spiritual human being and human kind a mystical Church, so he said that the whole of holy Scripture is, in short, a human being, the Old Testament having the body, and the New Testament soul and spirit and intellect, or again, taking the whole of holy Scripture, both Old and New Testaments, its body is the historical letter, while the meaning of what is written and its purpose, towards which the intellect strives, is the soul.[26]

After what we have already said about the patristic conception of space, what might otherwise seem a series of rather far-fetched parallels should seem quite natural. What Maximus is doing is comparing the division of the Church, representing the cosmos, into sanctuary and nave to his biblically and classically derived notion of space as a structured reality between two parts (invisible and visible, heaven and earth, soul and body, intellect and soul). Because the notion of space is manifold, as we have seen, the parallels between the various forms of space characteristic of created reality are intrinsic, not arbitrary. Anything that takes place in one form of space has its counterpart in the rest, so that the meaning of each both borrows from and contributes to the others. There are then profound interconnections between Church, cosmos (understood both as embracing the spiritual and material realm and as embracing the visible heavens and the earth), the inward life of the human person, and even the Scriptures themselves, which again constitute a created cosmos. This means that the significance of what takes place in the Church building – pre-eminently the Divine Liturgy – has cosmic dimensions, but also has a meaning that reaches into the heart of each individual Christian and his or her own pilgrimage towards union with God. It also means that the Church, like

---

[25] This theme of what Eriugena was to call the 'divisions of nature' is found elsewhere in Maximus' writings, notably in *Ambiguum* 41 (PG 91:1304D–1316A), where Maximus produces a longer list of such divisions, which overlaps with those found in the *Mystagogia*.

[26] *Mystagogia* 6, Sotiropoulos, ll. 2–9.

Scripture, is a place where God has made himself known, and this being made known is not just, or even mainly, a matter of information, but rather a matter of participation in God himself through his activities or energies. Personal asceticism is therefore no mere *souci de soi* in a Foucaultian sense, but has ecclesial, indeed cosmic, implications, as Maximus makes clear in the following passage:

> The human is a mystical church, because through the nave which is his body he brightens by virtue the ascetic force of the soul by the observance of the commandments in moral wisdom. Through the sanctuary of his soul he conveys to God in natural contemplation through reason the principles of sense purely in spirit, cut off from matter. Finally, through the altar of the mind he summons the silence abounding in song in the innermost recesses of the unseen and unknown utterance of divinity by another silence, rich in speech and tone. And as far as is possible for humans, he dwells familiarly within mystical theology and becomes such as is fitting for one made worth of his indwelling and he is marked by dazzling splendour.[27]

Chapters 8 to 21 of the *Mystagogia* are devoted to explaining the meaning of the various ceremonies of the Divine Liturgy. These begin with the entrance of the bishop into the Church, accompanied by the people (in Maximus' day, the Sunday liturgy was evidently still preceded by a procession to the church). The entry of the bishop into the Church symbolizes Christ's first coming into the world in the Incarnation; the entry of the people symbolizes conversion – from unbelief to faith, from vice and ignorance to virtue and knowledge. In the readings, we encounter God's desires and intentions for us; the singing symbolizes the joy of our turning towards God; the bishop's acclamations of peace before the readings ('Peace to all' – 'And to your spirit') symbolize the help of the angels in our struggle to live a godlike life. Then comes the Gospel – and everything that follows it, for Chapter 13 discusses not just the meaning of the reading of the Gospel, but continues with a brief account of everything that succeeds it, even though Maximos is going to discuss these one by one in the next eight chapters. The gospel reading itself 'proposes to those who are zealous some suffering on behalf of the Word';[28] a true hearing of the Gospel always entails the bearing of the Cross in some practical way – as St Maximus' own life exemplified. The purpose of this suffering is to detach us from worldly matters and draw us more closely to participation in the secret wisdom of God.

All of this is brought out in the ceremonies that follow the Gospel reading: the closing of the doors, the exchange of the kiss of peace, the recitation of the symbol of faith, the creed, the singing of the thrice-holy hymn (the *sanctus*)[29] together with

---

[27]   *Mystagogia* 4, Sotiropoulos, p. 162; trans. Berthold, p. 190.

[28]   *Mystagogia* 13, Sotiropoulos, p. 200, ll. 5–6.

[29]   Berthold is mistaken is asserting (ibid., p. 222, note 107) that this means the *trisagion*, which is sung in the Byzantine rite before the readings.

the holy angels, the uttering with our lips the words of the *Our Father* in which we lay claim to communion with God, and then, beyond that, the chant *One is holy*, leading beyond knowledge to the unknowable unity, 'now that we are deified by grace, and assimilated to him by participation in an indivisible identity, so far as this is possible'.[30] However, the bishop's descent from his throne and dismissal of the catechumens, after the Gospel, symbolize the Second Coming of Christ and the final judgement. Everything that follows, therefore – the whole of the liturgy of the faithful – is understood by Maximus to take place *after the Second Coming*. The closing of the doors means our passing, after the judgement, into the nuptial chamber of Christ; the entrance into the mysteries our being admitted to the final revelation of the divine wisdom. The meaning of the kiss of peace, the recitation of the creed, the singing of the *sanctus*, the saying of the *Our Father*, the singing of the *One is Holy*, and communion itself in the divine gifts: all this Maximus has already explained, and all his further explanations underline their eschatological significance, with the coming together of heaven and earth, and the deification of the human as the fulfilment of the Incarnation of the Divine.

The proclamation of the Gospel is then, for Maximus, indeed the 'end of history'; to hear the Gospel is truly to pass into the *eschata*, the last times. This gives Maximus' understanding of liturgical time a highly distinctive twist. For Maximus, the biblical notion of time of progress from evening to morning, from darkness to light, implicit in the Genesis account, is fulfilled in the proclamation of the Gospel: as we listen to the Gospel, understand the teaching of the Cross, and draw close to Christ in the Eucharistic Liturgy, we pass into the 'day that knows no evening of your Kingdom' (τῇ ἀνεσπέρῳ ἡμέρᾳ τῆς βασιλείας σου: to quote from one of the prayers said immediately after communion by the priest in the Byzantine rite). The Byzantine prayer of the *anaphora* (in both the form attributed to St John Chrysostom and that attributed to St Basil) expresses this sense of passing into the *eschata*, when it recalls, 'remembers' (μεμνημένοι) 'our Saviour's command and all that has been done for us: the Cross, the Tomb, the Resurrection on the third day, the Ascension into heaven, the Sitting at the right hand' – 'and the Second and Glorious coming again'.[31] Maximus' understanding of the celebration of the Divine Liturgy is thoroughly eschatological; the ceremonies after the reading – the proclaiming – of the Gospel all take place in the age to come.

The way in which the early Church celebrated the Eucharist on the brink of the age to come (cf. the fragments of the Eucharistic anaphora of the *Didache*)[32] is fully preserved in Maximus' understanding of the Divine Liturgy. In fact, Maximus does not mention the Eucharistic anaphora; by his time it was probably said silently, and perhaps Maximus only commented on what he, not – it would seem – a priest, would have heard. Alain Riou, however, sees a deeper significance

---

[30]   *Mystagogia* 13, Sotiropoulos, p. 200, ll. 23–5.

[31]   The *Anaphora* of St John Chrysostom; the wording is only slightly different in the *Anaphora* of St Basil.

[32]   Cf. *Didache* 10.

in Maximus' omission of any mention of the Eucharistic anaphora, which is worth mention: 'The true anaphora (the configuring *anamnesis* and the eschatological *epiclesis*) of Christ is only consummated in the martyr himself: in that apophatic anaphora, the Christian and the Church receive in communion and consummate in silence their transparency to the paschal mystery.'[33] Riou's words recall the Eucharistic echoes of St Polycarp's prayer as the pyre was lit;[34] they also remind us that Maximus' words are the words of one who was to confess the faith to the point of death.

Maximus' understanding of the Eucharist is, then, eschatological. Liturgical time passes beyond any form of created time, and anticipates the fulfilment of life beyond death: the life of the resurrection. The full significance of the words quoted earlier from the first chapter of the *Mystagogia*, in which the Church was defined as an image of God, now become apparent: 'all are born into the Church and through it are reborn and recreated in the Spirit. To all in equal measures it gives and bestows one divine form and designation: to be Christ's and to carry his name. In accordance with faith it gives to all a single, simple, whole and indivisible condition ...' – which is ultimately that of the martyr, the witness for Christ, the witness to the truth about Christ. And this eschatological ecclesiology has ramifications – brought out in the multiple images of the Church drawn out by Maximus in his introductory chapters – for the cosmos, for the inner life of the soul, even for our understanding of Holy Scripture.

We can see something of what this means in a series of chapters from the *First Century on Theology and the Incarnate Dispensation*.[35] This group of chapters (51–70) form a series of meditations on the sixth, seventh and eighth days; Riou suggests, surely rightly, that they are a meditation on the Triduum – Good Friday, Holy Saturday and Easter Sunday. They provide a paschal interpretation of the Christian life, the three stages of which – ascetic struggle, natural contemplation, and mystical theology or deification – correspond to the sixth, seventh and eighth days, represented by the Paschal Triduum.[36] This rooting of the stages of the Christian life in the paschal mystery brings out what one might call the *ecclesial* dimension of asceticism. The *cosmic* dimension is manifest in the way the *transitus* through these days leads to, and beyond, knowledge of created things.[37] The different chapters illumine different aspects of this mystery, but characteristic is the sixty-seventh, which reads:

---

[33]   Alain Riou, *Le Monde et l'Église selon Maxime le Confesseur* (Paris, 1973), p. 165.

[34]   See *Martyrdom of Polycarp* 14, ed. J.B. Lightfood (London, 1930).

[35]   Maximus the Confessor, *Centuries on Theology and the Incarnate Dispensation* I.51–70 (PG 90:1101C–1109A); translation in *The Philokalia. The Complete Text*, trans. and ed. G.E.H. Palmer, Ph. Sherrard, K. Ware, (4 vols, London, 1979–95), vol. 2, pp. 124–8.

[36]   Cf. *Centuries* I. 55 (PG 90:1104BC; *Philokalia*, vol. 2, p. 125).

[37]   Cf. *Centuries* I. 66 (PG 90:1108AB; *Philokalia*, vol. 2, p. 127).

All visible realities need the cross, that is, the state in which they are cut off from things acting upon them through the senses. All intelligible realities need burial, that is, the total quiescence of the things which act upon them through the intellect. When all relationship with such things is severed, and their natural activity and stimulus is cut off, then the Logos, who exists alone in himself, appears as if risen from the dead. He encompasses all that comes from him, but nothing enjoys kinship with him by virtue of natural relationship. For the salvation of the saved is by grace and not by nature.[38]

The Paschal character of this ascetic realization of the life of the resurrection brings out the eschatological and cosmic nature of asceticism. In his understanding of the Divine Liturgy, all the central themes of Maximus' theology – cosmic, eschatological, Eucharistic, epicletic – are drawn together.

Central to all this is the Cross: the life-giving Cross of Christ, conceived of as a sign drawing everything together, the 'Cosmic Cross', the significance of which for Maximus we have already noted. But more than a sign: a reality, fulfilled in the death of Christ, set forth in the Eucharist, the meal through which the Lord interpreted his death and asked us to repeat 'in his memory' as a sacrifice 'in all and for all', and fulfilled again in the death of the martyr, the death that St Maximus himself was to suffer. This, for Maximus, was the axis on which the cosmos turned: something expressed in fine words in the lines with which David Jones closed his great poem, *The Anathemata*:

> He does what is done in many places
> what he does other
>   he does after the mode
> of what has always been done.
> What did he do other
>   recumbent at the garnished supper?
> What did he do yet other
>   riding the Axile Tree?[39]

---

[38]   *Centuries* I. 67 (PG 90:1108B; *Philokalia*, vol. 2, p. 127).
[39]   David Jones, *The Anathemata* (2nd edn, London, 1955), p. 243.

Liturgical Twilight – A Footnote to Andrew Louth

Catherine Pickstock

Andrew Louth's exposition examines ways in which Eastern Orthodox liturgical theology coincides with perspectives which Radical Orthodoxy has sought to emphasize. Indeed, RO regards itself as standing in the tradition of the Greek as well as the Latin fathers and seeks a richer ecclesiology informed by Orthodox and Catholic as well as Anglican traditions.

Several of Louth's emphases are akin to those of RO in general. First of all, he favours a participatory metaphysical framework to describe the relation between the creator and the creation, including the processes of redemption, which involves a constant outgoing and return. Secondly, this rhythm is seen as embodied in the three different orders of the cosmos, the soul and the Church as the true city or true human society.[40] There are isomorphisms between these three realities that are reflected in the liturgy. The latter renders at once a *synaxis*, or coming-together, a spiritual journey from sensation through cosmic contemplation to mystical union with the divine and a 'theurgic' process that contributes to the transformation of the cosmos itself by invoking the divine descent.

Thirdly, a true understanding of the liturgy is seen by Louth as involving a pre-modern account of space and time. Both realities concern the *diastema*, or stretching-out of becoming, which can be psychic or vital or qualitative as well as material and quantitative. Space, following Plato's *Timaeus,* is the *chora* or container of all changing things, while time is the mode of their diverse transformations. Neither exists in itself as abstract and neither is the most abstract aspect of the relation between things (to mention, with Louth, the two main modern alternatives). Rather, they are externality itself and becoming itself: they transcendentally coincide with all of finitude. One could add that Aquinas in the West referred to a 'time of the angels' and of angels being created within the refined space of the heavenly empyrean.[41] Louth mentions the similarity of this view with more ancient views of motion as explored by Simon Oliver. Up to and including Aquinas, 'motion' indicated the widest compass of transformations: physical, vital, psychic, intellectual.[42]

However, perhaps Louth would agree that one could say that the Orthodox liturgy only presupposes such an account of space, time and motion because it is in itself already a liturgical account. Physical distancing and transformation are to be

---

[40] This has frequently been an RO interest. See in particular the unpublished PhD dissertation of Matthew Bullimore (Cambridge, 2007).

[41] *ST* I Q 53 a 3; Q 61 aa 3–4.

[42] Simon Oliver, *Philosophy, God and Motion* (London, 2005).

understood as an approximation to, and motion towards psychic transformation, which is a motion back towards the divine and the eternal reality. As Louth implies, the doctrine of creation transformed the classical understanding of space and time. Once one has removed any notion of pre-existent chaos, finitude is itself a becoming, and it must be more emphatically a proceeding-forth from, and a returning-to, the Creator. The doctrine of deification gives a more radical meaning to return. Even the return of the created intellect to itself is not enough; it must ecstatically exceed the bounds of comprehension to return to a mysterious oneness with the Godhead. This radicalization was indeed accomplished by the Neoplatonic doctrine of *henosis*, but to this notion deification lends a more personalist aspect and allows that the human intellect fulfil itself by exceeding itself, since the personal God (unlike the Plotinian One) is eminently intellectual. But if all things return to God and point towards an intellectual and mystical return to God, then all motion is consummated as praise, as liturgical motion. Likewise all temporal and spatial *diastema* is a liturgical distancing.

For this reason it could be argued that the liturgy offers us the highest exposition of space, time and motion. Louth rightly emphasizes, following Maximus, the importance of the Church building in which the liturgical action takes place and Louth attacks a gradual tendency in the West to think that all one needs for worship is an officiant, an altar and a book. Rather, worship presupposes a sacred space which images the cosmos, allows for an ordered human foregathering, and physically maps our psychic journey. The whole church is a temple or *naos*, or nave, which is itself but a *pronaos*, or part of the whole church which leads up to the sanctuary. This leading-up echoes the way in which the visible cosmos (of physical time and space and movement) points to the invisible cosmos (of spiritual time and space and movement) and also the way in which the individual soul passes through ascesis towards contemplation and through this to mystical union. Likewise, for Maximus, this architectural passage repeats the historical movement from Old to New Testament and provides the right forum for the enacting of the liturgical movement past the reading of the gospel which concerns the first coming of Christ, into the second act of the liturgical drama which takes place as if already within the eschaton after the second coming.

In evoking the interplay between the nave and the sanctuary, Louth is close to a fourth RO theme, namely, the notion of perpetual liturgical recommencement, or non-identical repetition. As he says, the nave is *already* the sanctuary, while the sanctuary is also the 'nave' which is the whole church as the forecourt of the spiritual heaven. And following Maximus (who is emphatic on this point) he also emphasizes that while the lower leads us to the higher, the latter points back to and expresses itself in the lower, which never becomes redundant, but is gradually transfigured through this constant liturgical shuttle.[43]

---

[43]   Maximus the Confessor, 'The Church's Mystagogy', Chapter Two, in trans. G.C. Berthold, *Maximus the Confessor: Selected Writings* (New York, 1985), pp. 188–9.

Louth rightly argues that the central words of the liturgy are the *anaphora* (in the East) or the canon of the mass (in the West). These are the words which accompany the offering of the elements and therefore lie at the very centre of the shuttling movement, and which lead to our reception of the divine gift and return of this gift to God.

However, if Louth seems to part company with RO – or at least with my own arguments on certain related matters – this concerns the question of language. He argues that Dionysius the Areopagite only refers to prayers such as the *anaphora* because of their connection with the liturgical action. I would not want to contest this primacy of action, and in fact would suggest that this was insisted upon by Gregory Dix, who spoke much of the *Opus Dei*. I would also concur with the view that over time the liturgy itself became 'too textualized'.[44] Louth nonetheless provides valuable confirmation of this thesis; it is striking that the 'library' of books required by the many actors in the liturgical action was gradually reduced to one book that could in principle be carried by one man. But the library was found just as much in the Carolingian West as in the Byzantine East, and the real question is what happened in the course of time in the West, rather than describing a 'timeless' difference between West and East (which is not at all something which I think Louth would want to do).[45]

This is a difficult issue which I cannot adequately negotiate within the compass of this 'footnote'. For I do not think that one should denounce the 'movement into the open' of Western worship as in every way regrettable, especially if it does not lose the sense of the situation of worship within the cosmos, which the worship of the Franciscans initially most certainly preserved. Inversely, the greater physical confinement of Eastern worship within the ecclesial building (though this is qualified by the use of processions), it could be argued, is of a piece with a tendency of the church in the East to remain too aloof from the social and political domain, and to leave this to the secular arm, which was itself traditionally more sacral in character than in the West. The friars were moreover seeking to bring monastic rhythmic styles of liturgy and of preaching into everyone's lives and to this end they found a portable missal to be convenient, just as the use of missal books had already proven essential to the development of parish life.[46]

On the other hand, this tendency was first promoted by the Franciscans and only later spread to the Dominicans. Along with the new portability of the liturgical texts came also various measures towards streamlining and simplifying the liturgy which might be taken (as Louth perhaps implies) as remote anticipations of the reforms of Vatican II. There was also a new opposition to the idea that one requires many clerics to be present for the performance of liturgical activity. This initiated

---

[44]   Catherine Pickstock, *After Writing. On the liturgical consummation of philosophy* (Oxford, 1998), pp. 169–76.

[45]   See the book cited by Louth, Stephen J.P. van Dijk OFM and Joan H. Walker, *The Origins of the Modern Roman Liturgy* (Westminster, MD/London, 1960), pp. 15–45.

[46]   Ibid., pp. 57–67, 91–254.

a view that might appear to favour the needs of the laity, but which also tends to a weakening of the corporate aspect of the liturgy.[47] A further aspect of this shift was the Franciscan promotion of the normativity of the Roman rite (which eventually became the Tridentine rite, and which I chose to comment on in *After Writing*, as being the classic liturgical text of the West) again in the interests of communication. Elsewhere I have suggested that the loss of local liturgical diversity was something to be regretted and that it was an aspect of an unfortunate process of 'spatialization'.

On this point, however, there must be scope for further research (which I am grateful to Louth for opening up). In *After Writing* I suggested a continuity between the tendencies of some specifically Franciscan theology (eminently that of Duns Scotus) to embrace univocity, representation and the formal distinction with later early modern tendencies towards the flattening-out and abstraction of notions of time and space; I noted also a parallel shift from a predominance of speech to one of writing, accelerated by the invention of the printing press. I linked the latter with various early modern liturgical changes. So perhaps, indeed, the Franciscan (and to a lesser degree the Dominican – but what were the real Dominican attitudes here?) remoulding of the liturgy is a central aspect of this complex genealogy and this transformation does have a more ideological as well as pragmatic and egalitarian aspect. Perhaps the Franciscan re-shaping of the liturgy is the middle term between univocal theory and spatializing practice. But one cannot be dogmatic here without further inquiry and this is only a suggestion.

There is a more general issue on which I would like to comment with more surety. Louth criticizes the treatment of liturgy as text, but does not distinguish orality from writing, nor indicate the way in which any meaningful action is inevitably also symbolic and therefore in some sense also linguistic. One could take the case of the anaphoric action itself. The carrying up of bread and wine can be understood as an offering to God because of the accompanying words. Moreover, there is an homology between the action and the linguistic trope involved. 'Anaphora' in rhetoric means 'leading back' and especially the repetition of the same word at the beginning of subsequent sentences. The 'one' offering is itself a 'leading back', and it is a 'leading back' which will have to be done again and again. And it points forwards to the final eschatological leading back. This description is in line with Louth's own emphases.

In this way the reading of the action as offering and as an offering which is necessarily anticipated and then endlessly renewed, is possible because the action has a textual dimension, albeit that of a performed text. The written as well as the oral aspect of language is necessary here, and the two are held in balance. If the liturgical action is necessarily a repeated and renewed action, as Louth agrees, then it can only be a continuous action because it is textually located. Likewise, while one can say that the liturgy echoes the cosmic action, it is equally the case

---

[47]   Ibid., pp. 254–80.

that the cosmos as such is written in and constantly re-pronounces, a liturgical language. One can recall the mediaeval trope here that the world is also a text.

The world as a text is a liturgical text as well as a liturgical action. It is both a constant worship and an original renewal of that worship. Louth indicates two ways in which this might be the case. First, for Plato the cosmos is a living body. Various traditions within Eastern orthodoxy, from Gregory of Nyssa's 'eternal man' which traces its lineage back to Philo, to Sergii Bulgakov's variant of this theme and association of it with the created Sophia, suggest that if the creation is the receiving of a gift, then this requires an initial reflexivity (the giving of the gift one has received to oneself in order to be oneself); the alternative would be a mere causal action and not a gift at all.[48] It follows that the psychic and the intelligent must lie at the heart of creation and are not, as it were, afterthoughts. The first work of light in Genesis suggests the creation of intelligent being, and this text by no means implies that God, according to his *potentia absoluta*, might have created a merely mute and dumb nature, subservient to his purposes, as though he were an eternal Saruman.

Plato, however, expressed something of this notion (in relation to the sphere of becoming, not yet creation) though more extensively than Louth allows. In the *Timaeus*, Plato does not say that the cosmic body is wrapped around the soul, but the reverse, even though soul also lies at the heart of the cosmic body.[49] But this point confirms Louth's more general point about the strangeness of Platonic space, if material space could for him be situated 'within' the psychic. In contrast to Descartes (but perhaps anticipating Jean-Luc Nancy and Jacques Derrida),[50] the soul was for Plato 'para-extended' as well as non-extended. Without some kind of psychic extension, which is a response, an ecstatic yearning, a force and an ordered containment, there simply could not be for Plato any material space and time, nor, in consequence, any material cosmos. This view is remotely echoed by Aquinas when he says that angels 'virtually' contain the material places in which they elect to be and to appear to us.[51]

If we wish, like Maximus, to affirm that the cosmos is in fact a cosmic liturgy, then we need to regard space as psychic, because the soul is the mysterious outermost bound of space, not traceable within any space which we can inhabit. That this boundary is only 'thinkable' (though not in thought graspable) indicates that, indeed, only thought reaches a boundary that is itself a psychic and an intelligent reality, the *anima mundi* herself.

If we wish to affirm the cosmic liturgy, then we must also assert that time is the time of liturgical praise. Louth indicates the terms in which this is the case. *Genesis* does not speak of night, but of evening fading to morning. For this reason,

---

[48]	See Claude Bruaire, *L'être et l'esprit* (Paris, 1983), pp. 159–204.

[49]	Plato, *Timaeus*, 34, 44.

[50]	See Jacques Derrida, *On Touching – Jean-Luc Nancy*, trans. Ch. Irizarry (Chicago, 2005), pp. 11–20.

[51]	*ST* I Q. 5 a 2.

the Eastern liturgical tradition has continued to speak of the twilight not as the ending of the old day but as the commencement of the new one. The dawning of the light is most fundamentally the intelligent praise of God by angels and human beings. *Vesper in ambiguo est*, as I cited in *After Writing*, yet the balance tilts towards the dawn. It is for this reason, as I have argued, that all liturgy occupies the time of the evening. Hence the physical sun which shines back the divine light is situated within the Sun of the intelligible which is the Good, and for Christianity the light of offering, rather than vice versa.

This sense of time as intelligent worship was just as present within the Western as in the Eastern tradition. Indeed perhaps the finest expression of this trope is given by Augustine in the *Civitas Dei*:

> Now the knowledge of the creature is a kind of twilight, compared with the knowledge of the Creator; and then comes the daylight and the morning, when that knowledge is linked with the praise and love of the Creator; and it never declines into night, so long as the Creator is not deprived of his creature's love. And in fact Scripture never interposes the word 'night' in the enumeration of those days one after another. Scripture never says 'Night came'; but 'Evening came and morning came one day'. Similarly on the second day and all the rest. The creature's knowledge, left to itself, is, we might say, in faded colours, compared with the knowledge that comes when it is known in the Wisdom of God, in that art, as it were, by which it was created. For that reason it can more appropriately be described as evening than as night. And yet that evening turns again to morning, as I have said, when it is turned to the praise and love of the Creator.[52]

---

[52] Augustine, *The City of God*, trans. Henry Bettenson (London, 1972), XI:7, pp. 436–7.

Chapter 9

Wisdom in the Fathers:
An (Eastern) Orthodox Perspective

Marcus Plested

T.S. Eliot asked, 'Where is the wisdom we have lost in knowledge? Where is the knowledge we have lost in information?'[1] In our own age of the internet I believe we must now add, 'Where is the information we have lost in data?' Such 'lost wisdom' has emerged as a major theme of this volume. This is hardly surprising given that both our 'orthodoxies' are squarely set against the modern apotheosis of the independent reason which has largely displaced any notion of knowledge which is both revealed and lived. This process of displacement has had disastrous consequences in all spheres of human existence – consequences which I do not have to reiterate in this context. The theme of wisdom, properly understood, has the capacity to address constructively virtually all the major problems of our age. However, for it to do so effectively requires what I would term a 'creative affirmation' of the Christian wisdom tradition. In this chapter I intend to sketch the lineaments of this tradition, focusing on the patristic understanding but with some comments on modern Russian sophiology. Building on this Eastern Orthodox perspective I shall, in the last part of the chapter, attempt to tease out a more general comparison between Radical and Eastern Orthodox approaches with particular reference to the central problematic of tradition.

The theme of wisdom lies at the heart of the patristic theological enterprise. This is not to say that there is any single patristic voice or 'mind' as to the precise nature and character of wisdom any more than the Old or New Testaments provide us with a unitary account of wisdom. Rather, wisdom emerges in the fathers as a nexus of ideas exceptionally well suited to the expression of a particular and shared approach to and understanding of the nature and purposes of theology, theology itself being understood as nothing less than human life writ large – as St Irenaeus put it 'The life of man is the vision of God'.[2]

The study of the various ways in which the fathers reflect on the biblical figure of wisdom underlines what should be (but isn't) the most obvious feature of patristic theology: that it is above all a biblical theology. While the Harnackian approach is rarely found these days in its fully-fledged form, the idea that patristic theology is somehow accidental to or separable from biblical theology remains all

---

[1]   T.S. Eliot, *Choruses from 'The Rock'* (London, 1934).

[2]   Irenaeus of Lyons, *Against Heresies* 4.20.7 (SC 100, p. 649).

too common. The absolute centrality of Scripture in patristic theology also raises the problematic of tradition, tradition understood not as the dead weight of the past but as the living community of faith in which the gospel is both received and transmitted. This process of reception and transmission is pre-eminently one of education and formation – one of *paideia*. Patristic theology is best understood not as a series of more or less disconnected reflections upon discrete sub-disciplines – Christology, Trinitarian theology, cosmology, ecclesiology and so forth – but as an attempt to teach and communicate and inculcate the revelation of God in Christ, 'and him crucified' (1 Cor 2:22). Such doctrines and dogmas as are elaborated in the fathers are not the fruit of abstract speculation, or theological virtuosity, or a consuming interest in the difference between *hypostasis* and *ousia*, but as an attempt to witness faithfully to and transmit the apostolic teaching of the crucified and risen Christ.

At this point it may be helpful to say a very few words about what the Scriptures have to say on the theme of wisdom. The Old Testament uses and develops the theme of wisdom in a number of ways: as empirical knowledge and intuitive understanding, as formation or *paideia*, as cosmological principle and mediator, as active divine subject, and as a means of expressing God's transcendence and immanence. In looking at the patristic understanding of wisdom we also need to keep an eye on the classical hinterland. While far from being a univocal concept in classical antiquity, wisdom, with its cognate terms, rapidly emerged as one way of describing the character of the enquiry into the nature and meaning of things. The limits to this enquiry were soon recognized but this sense of the fallibility of human conclusions was to some degree balanced by an appeal to the divine source of such wisdom and knowledge as humans might possess. This explicitly theological approach was also not infrequently bound up with a mystical and moral/ascetic dimension, something that becomes perhaps most explicit in the Socratic dialogues.[3]

The New Testament stands as a meeting-point between the Jewish and Greco-Roman wisdom traditions with the emphasis very much on the former. Early Christian reflections on the person of Jesus Christ immediately and intuitively sought to locate this extraordinary figure within the wisdom tradition of Israel both as wisdom teacher and, evidently, something rather more than that. Matthew, in particular, gives us a clear portrayal of Jesus as the manifestation or embodiment of the Old Testament figure of wisdom. This is perhaps most obvious in the Lord's assertion that 'wisdom is justified by her deeds' (Mt 11:19), where the deeds in question are unambiguously those of Jesus himself (cf. Mt 11:2). The name 'Emmanuel' ('God with us') (Mt 1:23) resonates strongly with the Old Testament use of the category of wisdom as a way of articulating the divine immanence

---

[3]   In the succeeding generations, Aristotle's critique of the metaphysical source of wisdom and theory of its twofold nature (abstract and applied) gave way in its turn to a further process of reduction whereby wisdom was conceived of largely on the applied moral and ethical plane.

and presence. Matthew goes on to put great emphasis on Jesus' role as teacher. The community of the disciples is pre-eminently a learning community guided by Christ the archetypal teacher and master (Mt 23:8–10). Those who follow and act upon Jesus' teaching are pictured as scribes 'instructed (or 'discipled': μαθητευθεὶς) into the kingdom of heaven' (Mt 13:51–52; cf. Wisdom 6:20). This transformational process of discipleship and instruction is seen to give the apostles the capacity to transmit or 'tradition' their lived experience of wisdom.

The Gospel of John is, similarly, permeated with wisdom themes and imagery. The famous Word or *Logos* of the prologue is undoubtedly firmly rooted in the Old Testament figure of wisdom – the divine and pre-existent associate of God in his work of creation. Jesus is presented by John both as the means of approach and the goal of all human enquiry and endeavour: 'the way, the truth, and the life' (Jn 14:6). As locus and vehicle of divine revelation, Jesus both recapitulates and transcends Old Testament wisdom. All this is in turn summed up by St Paul in his confession of Christ as the 'wisdom and power of God' (1 Cor 1:24).

Following on directly for the New Testament, the theme of wisdom loomed large as the early Christians sought to articulate their faith in the Lordship of Christ and the divine ministry of the Spirit without compromising their inherited monotheism. This process of articulation (which tends to be resumed under the head of the doctrine of the Trinity) cannot be detached from the dimension of *paideia*. St Theophilus of Antioch, for example, having spoken of the triad of 'God, the word, and his wisdom' tells us that it is in the perception and acquisition of God's wisdom that we both see and image God.[4] St Irenaeus of Lyons, like Theophilus, consistently identifies God's word with the Son and his wisdom with the Spirit. These two are the vehicles of God's self-revelation, the means by which and in which he extrapolates himself and makes himself known. Tertullian develops an understanding of the word or wisdom of God as the vehicle of God's self-revelation, as the means by which the eternal ideas of the creation are brought into being.[5] This intuition of the extrapolation and realization of the divine plan for the creation in and through the word or wisdom of God is something we also find in Clement of Alexandria. Wisdom, for Clement, is saving knowledge and true philosophy. It has two aspects: eternal and temporal, the eternal aspect being identified with Christ, the human aspect the saving knowledge which unites the Christian gnostic to Christ. This duality is a theme – rooted in the Old Testament – that comes up again and again in patristic thinking on wisdom.

Origen, similarly, identifies wisdom with the Son, who alone is 'wisdom in itself' (*autosophia*).[6] In this wisdom, 'there was implicit every capacity and form of the creation that was to be' and when wisdom says that she was created as a 'beginning of the ways' of God, this means that 'she contains within herself both

---

[4]   Theophilus of Antioch, *Ad Autolycum* 1.7; 2.15 (SC 20, pp. 64–5; p. 97).

[5]   Tertullian, *Adversus Praxeam* 6–7 (PL 2 161A–162D). Tertullian uses the Greek term 'sophia'.

[6]   Origen, *Contra Celsum* 6.63 (SC 147, p. 336).

the beginnings and causes and species of the whole creation'.[7] Wisdom here, as in Tertullian and Clement, is presented as the divine plan for creation existing eternally *in potentia* in God *and* as the vehicle of God's self-revelation in and to that creation. Wisdom 'opens to all other beings, that is, to the whole creation, the meaning of the mysteries and the symbols that are contained within the wisdom of God'.[8] This is of course the principle that governs Origen's exegetical work: his chief concern is for Scripture to be approached and received pedagogically, as part of that educative and purificatory process whereby God unites the human being to himself. As he puts it elsewhere: 'each of the sages, in proportion as he embraces wisdom, partakes to that extent of Christ, in that he is wisdom'.[9]

For St Athanasius, when we speak of the Son as wisdom, we are speaking of the uncreated wisdom of God himself, eternally begotten of the Father (much as in Origen). When we speak of wisdom as created (as texts such as Proverbs 8:22 force us to do) we are speaking either of wisdom *qua* incarnate[10] or, in another interpretation, more generally of the impress of uncreated wisdom upon the creation:

> For as our word is an image of the Son of God considered as the word, so also the wisdom implanted in us is an image of the same Son considered as wisdom; and it is in our wisdom that we, having the power of knowledge and thought, become recipients of the all-framing wisdom.[11]

Wisdom is (again) seen here as the link-piece between the created and uncreated orders – a bridging function conceived in terms of *paideia*.

This is a theme we also find in that great ascetic teacher and disciple of Origen, Evagrius of Pontus. In his scriptural commentaries, it is clear that it is the gift of wisdom which allows us to perceive the truth in Scripture and the created world. This wisdom is also the 'Spirit of adoption' of Romans 8, incorporating us into the life of the Trinity. Wisdom is embodied in Christ and it is through him that 'the wisdom of the Lord' comes to rest 'in the heart of the wise man'. Wisdom in Evagrius is the gift of God communicated by Christ in the Spirit that nourishes and educates us so that we can perceive the wisdom of God in Scripture and the created order, coming finally to the summit of contemplation that is the vision of God. Note the element of formation: like the biblical Wisdom literature on which he models his work, Evagrius is concerned not with abstract concepts or dogmas but with the training of *paideia* through which the divine wisdom of God comes to dwell in man incorporating him into the life of God. Thus Evagrius very clearly reminds us of the holistic nature of patristic sophiology: it is not just an interesting

---

[7]   Origen, *De Principiis* 1.2.2 (SC 252, p. 114).
[8]   Ibid., 1.2.3 (SC 252, p.116).
[9]   Origen, *In Johannem* 1.34 (SC 120, §246).
[10]   Athanasius of Alexandria, *Contra Arianos* 2.46–7 (PG 26, pp. 245–8).
[11]   Ibid., 2.78 (PG 26, 312C).

way of talking about or defining God, or indeed a human attainment, rather patristic sophiology is concerned with the way in which God as wisdom trains, forms, and educates humanity such that we can begin to see and encounter God in Scripture and in the created world, and ultimately become ourselves dwelling places of divine wisdom.

Turning now to St Augustine, wisdom emerges, I think it fair to say, as the alpha and omega of his theology. His record of his conversion is structured around the pursuit of wisdom, a pursuit that was to govern the pattern of his life. The opening passage of *Confessions* glorifies the immeasurable wisdom of God.[12] His reading of Cicero's now lost *Hortensius* enflames him with a passionate love for wisdom, exhorting him 'to love and seek and pursue and hold fast and strongly embrace wisdom itself, wherever found'.[13] Augustine goes on, in the *Confessions*, to distinguish between that wisdom which is 'manifestly co-eternal and equal unto thee, our God, his Father, and by whom all things were created' and 'that wisdom which has been created, namely, the intellectual nature, which, in the contemplation of light, is light. For this, although created, is also called wisdom. But as great as is the difference between the light which enlightens and that which is enlightened, so great is the difference between the wisdom that creates and that which has been created'.[14]

Augustine defines this created wisdom as 'the contemplation of the truth, making the whole man peaceful and *bringing about the likeness of God*'.[15] The pursuit of this wisdom requires a long process of purification, being 'a kind of journey home to our native land'.[16] In this journey wisdom incarnate is our pattern, 'though wisdom was himself our home, he made himself the way by which we should reach our home'.[17] The divine Wisdom – Augustine continues in the *De Doctrina Christiana* – condescended to take on flesh in order to become not only the healer but also himself the medicine of mankind.[18] Here we see Christology not in abstract dogmatic terms but in terms of the single action of the divine wisdom incarnate, uniting man to God as pedagogue and physician, as teaching and medicine.

This sense of wisdom as the bridge or link-piece between God and the world that we have seen in a number of fathers so far is something that forms a central plank of the theological vision of St Maximus the Confessor. In him we have a fully developed vision of the world in God and God in the world – to borrow a formulation from later Russian sophiology. Much of this is summed up in Maximus' understanding of the divine *logoi*, the inner principles or ideas of creation

---

[12]   Augustine, *Confessions* 1.1.1 (CCSL 27, p. 1).

[13]   Ibid., 3.4.8 (CCSL 27, p. 30).

[14]   Ibid., 12.15.20 (CCSL 27, pp. 225–6).

[15]   Augustine, *De sermone Domini in monte* 1.3.10 (CCSL 35, pp. 8–9).

[16]   Augustine, *De Doctrina Christiana* 1.10.10 (CCSL 32, p. 12).

[17]   Ibid., 11.11.11 (CCSL 32, p. 12).

[18]   Ibid., 1.14.13 (CCSL 32, p. 13).

immanent within God from all eternity. Maximus identifies Christ as 'hypostatic wisdom and word'[19] – this having been established as the standard interpretation since the time of Origen. In this wisdom and word lie from all eternity the *logoi* of the whole creation, the ideas of God corresponding to every created thing brought into being in time and destined to be freely gathered and reunited to God on the last day. Here the *logoi* grounded in the divine *Logos* constitute the world in God and also represent God's self-revelation *ad extra*: in other words God in the world. It is chiefly by contemplation of these *logoi* and by configuring oneself to one's own *logos* that the human being is united to the *Logos* by the operation of the Holy Spirit. The Holy Spirit 'accords perfection through luminous, simple and complete wisdom to those found worthy of *theosis*, bringing them by all means and ways to the cause of beings ... It is in her and through God that they come to know both themselves and God through themselves, with no wall or some such thing being interposed. For there is *nothing interposed between wisdom and God*'.[20]

Wisdom here is the unifying action or *energeia* of God (i.e. not exclusively associated with the Son), the *single* operation of the Trinity in the world bringing the world into the divine life – no longer in potentiality but in actuality, through the free acceptance by the creation of the self-emptying of God in the incarnation and in the gift of the Spirit.

What I trust this whistle-stop tour leaves you with is sense of the scope and depth of the patristic interpretation of the figure of wisdom. We may now move on to a brief review of the claim of modern Russian sophiology to be rooted in the patristic tradition. Here we should note that Russian sophiology tended in practice to base itself rather more on the iconographic and liturgical traditions of the Church than on the patristic legacy. This is a curious fact given the wealth of the patristic teaching on the wisdom of God, some fragments of which I have highlighted in this chapter. However there are some attempts, most notably in Fr Sergius Bulgakov, to explore this rich theological inheritance more deeply.

Bulgakov claimed that his sophiology was essentially the product of a profound meditation upon the scriptural, liturgical, and patristic inheritance of the Orthodox Church – in other words an example of the kind of creative affirmation that must lie at the heart of any genuinely traditional theology. He very often points out parallels between his understanding of the divine wisdom and that of the fathers (demonstrating very wide reading in so doing). Equally, he often throws out comments that the theology of such and such a Church father is intrinsically sophiological and deserves further exploration – without ever undertaking that exploration. He could also, admittedly, sometimes be extremely dismissive and even cavalier in his treatment of the fathers.

Bulgakov's theological synthesis is a heady vision of the world in God and God in the world – a vision given spatial form in the church of Hagia Sophia in Constantinople. For Bulgakov, Wisdom becomes the link-piece of a vast theological

---

[19]   Maximus Confessor, *Quaestiones ad Thalassium* 63 (CCSG 22, p. 147).

[20]   Ibid. (CCSG 22, p. 159).

synthesis connecting Trinitarian theology, Christology, pneumatology, cosmology, ecclesiology and Mariology. Wisdom is understood as denoting the divine life, the unity of the triune deity. She is God's self-revelation both in and outside himself, a single principle capable of existing in both uncreated and created forms: God in the world and the world in God. She is the principle of the unity of the uncreated and the created, a unity manifested in and founded upon Christ. This mystery of union without confusion, of primordial Godmanhood, is poured out upon the whole created order by the Holy Spirit. Thus Wisdom is God's self-bestowal both within the Trinity and upon the world. She is the principle of unity and coinherence in God, and between God and the world – the very foundation of all that *is*.

This of course is only a very potted and simplified version of an immensely complex, often inconsistent and frequently problematic theological system. Bulgakov himself freely admitted that while much of his system was composed of solid rock, many parts were but *papier mâché*. But at any rate it allows us now to ask: How much of this is rooted in the patristic tradition?

It should, I think, be clear that there is much in Bulgakov's vision that emerges naturally from the patristic tradition. From the earliest figures looked at in this chapter we have noted a clear sense of wisdom as God revealed *ad extra*. God is made manifest as word and wisdom for the purposes of his dispensation, for creation and redemption. I have also picked up on a very widespread understanding of the eternity of the creation within God, of the pre-existence of the whole divine plan of creation *in potentia*. Where we have found a distinction between created and uncreated wisdom (as in Athanasius and Augustine, for example), these two aspects are united in the person of Christ. Moreover the fact that many of the earlier authors do not take a consistent line identifying wisdom with the word (as would later become the accepted pattern) stands in favour of Bulgakov's refusal to associate wisdom exclusively with any one of the divine hypostases.

The sophianic vision of the cosmos certainly forms an intrinsic part of the theological inheritance of the Church (particularly, but by no means exclusively, of the Eastern Church). But this is not to say that Bulgakov's theology is patristic in the sense of being a reiteration of patristic sources (a danger arguably implicit in the notion of a neo-patristic synthesis) – something which would in any case be foreign to the patristic conception of the nature of theology. Nor is it (quite) to say that his theology is unambiguously a creative affirmation of the living tradition of the Church: much of his system is problematic and often confused, it remains very much in the realm of *theologoumena*, submitted to the wider judgement of the Church.

Nonetheless there is enough in Bulgakov to show us that a recovery of a genuinely traditional, scriptural and ecclesial sophiology is possible and indeed perhaps necessary in order to respond to the needs of our age (and indeed of all ages) – a vision of the world in God and God in the world founded on the dogmas of the Trinity and the Incarnation, a vision of the eternal and creative self-giving and self-bestowal of God in the Son, through the Spirit. The way surely lies open for a creative and transformative theology based on this sophianic vision and which need not lag behind the world in a doomed attempt to be 'relevant' but which, rather, has the capacity to take the lead and transfigure the world.

This call for such a transformative theology is surely one that could be shared by Radical and Eastern Orthodoxy alike – and this leads me on to the last part of this chapter. The Eastern Orthodox perspective on the wisdom tradition I have attempted to outline today would certainly seem to offer a great deal to what I understand to be the Radical Orthodox programme. It furnishes a participatory ontology that rules out any separation of God from the world. It allows us to hold together God's immanence and transcendence in the person of the divine wisdom incarnate in whom all antinomies are abolished – between time and eternity, matter and spirit, reason and revelation.

Speaking more generally, it is clear that there is a vast deal of common ground between Radical Orthodoxy and the Orthodox Church – so much so that one has some right to be amazed that there has been comparatively little sustained contact between the two. If Radical Orthodoxy really seeks, as it puts it, to reaffirm 'a richer and more coherent Christianity which was gradually lost sight of after the late Middle Ages' and to do so in a way which avoids both Protestant biblicism and post-Tridentine Catholic authoritarianism, then surely (one might think) it *must* gravitate towards the tradition of the Orthodox East. It is precisely this tradition in which the 'late medieval collapse' did not happen, in which modernity was not spawned, Scripture not separated from tradition, nor God from the world, nor nature from grace. A tradition in which the creeds of the Ecumenical councils and the patristic matrix have remained entirely normative, in which Aristotle has never quite displaced Plato, and authority established in a manner which is hierarchical but not monarchical.

This is not, however, to be in any way triumphalist. There is certainly in the Orthodox Church more than a whiff of that mere nostalgia for the past of which the Radical Orthodox are rightly suspicious. There is a tendency towards self-satisfaction, towards being content, as Yeats's poem 'Sailing to Byzantium' put it, to study 'monuments of its own magnificence'. We remain excessively wary of anything that has even the slightest air of innovation – hence the fate of Bulgakov (widely dismissed or even condemned within the Orthodox Church) and, more generally, the rather sterile stand-off between the Neo-patristic and Russian religious schools in modern Orthodox thought. Equally, the socio-political dimension of Orthodox practice (if not theory) is unlikely to provide much to nourish Radical Orthodox thinking in that sphere. Moreover it may very plausibly be claimed that the problems of modernity need to be addressed from within that very tradition which produced these problems in the first place.

In this respect, the Orthodox have much to learn from the Radical Orthodox. The fathers spoke consummately the philosophical language of their day in articulating the unchanging truth of the Gospel. We must all do the same and here we must acknowledge the great success that Radical Orthodoxy has had in making the 'Christian *logos* sound again afresh' (to borrow a phrase from John Milbank). Here I am reminded of the lament of Julian the Apostate at the Christians' use of

Greek philosophy: 'we are stricken by our own arrows, for from our own writings they take the weapons wherewith they engage in the war against us'. This is surely precisely the kind of archery all Christians should be engaged in and I believe the Radical Orthodox can help us practise.

But all this brings me back to the central problematic of tradition. It seems that we have very substantial agreement on the content of the Christian tradition and its potentiality to address constructively the great problems of our age. Where I think we differ is on the way in which that tradition is to be mediated, received, and appropriated. Here we must remember that in the classical Christian conception, tradition is more verb than noun. It speaks more of the process of transmission than of the deposit of faith itself. This is made very clear in the opening of the first epistle of John:

> That which was from the beginning, which we have heard, which we have seen with our eyes, which we have looked upon and touched with our hands, concerning the word of life ... that which we have seen and heard we proclaim also to you, so that you may have fellowship with us; and our fellowship is with Father and with his Son Jesus Christ (1 Jn 1:1–3).

Thus it is in and through the tradition of the apostles that we are brought to share in that fellowship. In other words it is in and through the community of the Church that we come to share in communion with God. This sense of tradition as community and communion (*koinonia*) is, I think, a helpful one. It underlines the fact that tradition is not so much a thing which we receive as our reception into the divine life. Going further, we can say that the tradition is the work of God in the world, the life of the Spirit in the Church. This is an intuition picked up on by Vladimir Lossky:

> The pure notion of tradition can be defined by saying that it is the life of the Holy Spirit in the Church, communicating to each member of the Body of Christ the faculty of hearing, of receiving, of knowing the Truth in the light which belongs to it, and not according to the natural light of human reason.[21]

Tradition in this way of thinking is not what we perceive or know but that which makes it possible for us to perceive or know anything at all. It is – we might even say – the condition of the possibility of all meaning. In more biblical terms, it is the life of the Spirit in the Church, that which makes us sons in the Son and prays within us crying 'Abba Father' (Rom 8:15).

We know of course that the Spirit 'bloweth where it listeth' (Jn 3:8) and I would certainly not claim that the Orthodox Church has any sort of monopoly on the operation of the Spirit. Nonetheless it remains for me a real question (and I say *question* advisedly) whether the tradition can be realized in its fullness outside

---

[21]   Vladimir Lossky, *In the Image and Likeness of God* (London, 1975), p. 152.

of a living and unbroken continuum of faith. If something has gone wrong in the Western Christian tradition, as Radical Orthodoxy claims, then is it really possible to leap the intervening centuries to recapture the vision of pre-Scotist Christianity? Will that vision not be to some extent distorted and artificial? Will it not necessarily display an inbuilt eclecticism? Someone (I don't remember who) waggishly called Radical Orthodoxy a 'theology in search of an ecclesiology'. This is doubtless very unfair but it is worth asking whether Radical Orthodoxy might not find a home within the Orthodox Church. Whatever the answer to that particular question, it remains the case that tradition is most effectively mediated and communicated within the context of the *paideia* of the Church which in and through saving wisdom guides, trains, and forms us through liturgy and doxology, through Scripture, through prayer and asceticism, doctrine and ethics. There is a givenness in the ecclesial totality and historical continuity of the Orthodox Church (neither pre- nor post-modern) which – if we are able to receive it in all humility – provides us with a *specific* and *practical* basis on which to experience and appropriate this saving wisdom. Without this practical foundation I doubt very much that there can ever be more than a very partial restoration of the patristic and early medieval vision and any practical philosophy built on that partial restoration is likely to be to some extent skewed.

This is not to say that the Orthodox Church has perfect sight. In this fallen cosmos we all 'see through a glass darkly' and the practice of the Church inevitably and invariably falls sort of the theory. Equally, what I have said about Bulgakov will have made the point that we have no infallible criteria on which to distinguish that which is genuinely and creatively traditional from that which is merely novel. Nonetheless, I hope at the very least to have carried the point that the Orthodox tradition deserves a closer and more sustained examination on the part of Radical Orthodoxy and indeed to have indicated to some ways in which the reverse also holds true. Clearly we have much to learn from one another.

Here I will close with some lines of poetry which seem to me to say something useful about the nature of our shared theological enterprise. They are taken from Vernon Watkins' poem 'Taliesin and the Spring of Vision':

> In a time of darkness the pattern of life is restored
> By men who make all transience seem an illusion
> Through inward acts, acts corresponding to music.
> Their works of love leave words that do not end in the heart.[22]

---

[22]   This poem can now be found in Vernon Watkins, ed. R. Ramsbotham, foreword by Archbishop Rowan Williams, *New Selected Poems* (Manchester, 2006).

Chapter 10
The Theologico-Political Constitution of Monastic Liturgy

Mihail Neamţu

Introduction

In the Orthodox interpretation of Nicaea, Christ is the eternal Son in whom God has brought about 'the fullness of time ($τὸ πλήρομα τοῦ χρόνου$)' (Gal 4:4). Early Christian monasticism has offered one of the boldest theological articulation of this view of the Incarnation. Maybe Radical Orthodoxy and Eastern Orthodoxy most clearly part ways in their respective attitudes towards the desert fathers' manifesto. In this chapter I attempt to show how the individual or communal life of contemplation in the pursuit of the heavenly Kingdom can, and must be reconciled with the broken character of human history, culture and politeia.

More specifically, I shall inquire into the relationship between the public voice of the desert fathers and their private practice of asceticism. In what manner did the contemplative Christians from the Egyptian wilderness connect the universal language of love with the particular expression of truth? My argument in this chapter is that the personal praxis of renunciation and the ecclesial confession of Christ were part of the same theologico-political constitution of the Nicene faith. While the Church built itself up internally, it made public claims to truth.

This approach dismisses any 'esoteric' reading of Egyptian monasticism, without ever neglecting its 'mystagogical' character. To give only one example, the relationship between the spiritual father and his disciple has an immediate character ($μόνος πρὸς μόνος$).[1] It is wrapped into the mysteries of Christian initiation, without excluding the dialogue with the neighbour, who can happen to be both an 'affective friend' and 'theological enemy' (that is, heterodox). 'Do not be overbearing towards the image of God'[2] says Pachomius the Great in one of his instructions. The non-sectarian character of monastic liturgy is revealed by the capacity of Christian monastics to cope with the tension between their ecclesial identity and the religious 'Other' living next to their community. I call it the tension between 'truth' and 'love,' which enables silence and conversation to be integrated into the cosmic liturgy of the Church.

---

[1]   N 89. For a key to the abbreviations see p. 268.
[2]   Pachomius, *Instr.* 1.33 (Veilleux, 27).

In the *apophthegmata patrum* one finds the private realm and public sphere serving each other. The desert fathers spoke the 'offensive' language of 'orthodoxy' versus 'heresy,' just as they were aware of the distinction between 'friend' and 'enemy'. Far from overlapping, the parallel between the two sets of notions receive a non-ideological treatment. There is no full reconciliation of 'truth' with 'love', as there is no universal language of peace that Christians and non-Christians can inhabit together, speaking words that convey unbroken meaning or an original significance. However, the public critique of slander and the private culture of Christian compassion remain mandatory.

Only because it is liturgical does desert monasticism have a 'political constitution'.[3] Monastic liturgy builds the gathered people of the Christian Church and makes them mature individuals. This gradual transformation is the act of God in Christ 'for the life of the world' (Jn 6:51). Once the Nicene faith is located within the intermediary time between the Incarnation and the eschaton, no submission to earthly rule can be more than provisional. The final part of the chapter explains on what grounds the desert fathers offer their substantial critique of political idolatry.

The City and the Desert

The claim that monastic eschatology[4] leads to the proclamation of a theologico-political manifesto may seem an overstatement. The desert fathers feared 'worldly cares', knowing perhaps how easy public responsibilities can disturb prayer.[5] To rule a house (οἶκος), or to exercise power in the city (πόλις), can disturb inner 'rest (ἀνάπαυσις)', which is another variant of divine peace.[6] Apart from the daily disturbances caused by the distractions of life, the inevitability of coercion in economic matters and politics encouraged the monastics' scepticism towards 'all human' endeavour. Evagrius' warns against 'vainglory (κενοδοξία),' which tempts

---

[3]   E. Cattaneo, 'Il monaco come "uomo politico" secondo la *Vita Antonii* di Atanasio di Alessandria', in Cesare Giraudo (ed.), *Liturgia e spiritualita nell'Oriente cristiano. In dialogo con Miguel Aranz* (Turin, 1997), pp. 159–68.

[4]   Barbara Müller, *Der Weg des Weinens: die Tradition des 'Penthos' in den Apophthegmata* (Göttingen, 2000), p. 190, who speaks about the 'eschatologische Orientierung' of monastic practice.

[5]   N 266 (Ward, 39): 'One of the old men went to another old man one day, and while they were speaking, the first said, "I am dead to the world (ἀπέθανον τῷ κόσμῳ)." The other old man said, "Do not count on it (μή θαρσήσῃς ἑαυτῷ), brother, before you have left the body."'

[6]   N 283 (Ward, 42): 'A brother went to see an anchorite and as he was leaving said to him, "Forgive me, abba, for having taken you away from your rule." But the other answered him, "My rule (ἐμός κανών) is to refresh you (ἀναπαύσω) and send you away in peace."'

us to perform outward deeds.[7] The secular search for recognition leads to vanity, whereas holiness is achieved through an anonymous practice of virtue.[8] The world contains precisely the values that the desert fathers wanted to escape.

Their focus on doctrinal integrity, personal transformation and unity with the communion of saints established another model of life that was challenging for pagans and Christians alike.[9] In the hackneyed words of Peter Brown, 'The stance of the monks was a crushing rebuke to the religious style of the pagan world. A studied rejection of the usual manner of wielding power in society from supernatural sources completed the process of "anachoresis".'[10] Direct or indirect exchanges with their neighbouring cultures[11] helped the desert fathers remain different from any other sectarian religion of Late Antiquity.[12] They discovered a new way of dealing with power, which was different from the traditions established by imperial philosophers in the Roman world. They brought all secular authority under the kingship of Christ. Their separation from the world was paralleled by their integration into the ecclesial body. Hatred for sin did not exclude the art of compassion, extended to universal proportions.

The 'desert made city'[13] questioned the 'civil religion'[14] of the pagan Romans. The monastic communities also stood in contrast to the norms of imperial Christendom. The desert fathers could not avoid coming across the 'Other', seen either as bishop,[15]

---

[7]   Evagrius, *Praktikos* 12 (SC 171:528–30).

[8]   Abba Agathon (Ward, 24): 'Abba Agathon loved Abba Alexander because he was both ascetic and discreet'.

[9]   Jeremy Driscoll, *Steps to Spiritual Perfection: Studies on Spiritual Progress in Evagrius Pontus* (New York, 2005) on the relationship between lex orandi-lex credendi before Nicaea.

[10]   Peter Brown, *The Making of Late Antiquity* (Cambridge, MA, 1978), p. 93.

[11]   *SBo* 25 (Veilleux, 47).

[12]   *Pace* David Frankfurter, *Religion in Roman Egypt: Assimilation and Resistance* (Princeton, 1999), p. 31, who, as a historian of religion, stresses the similarities between Christian monastic movements and Egyptian 'millenarist sectarianism', documented by pre-Christian texts such as the Apocalypse of Elijah.

[13]   Athanasius, *Vita Antonii* 14.

[14]   On 'civil religion' during the Late Antiquity period see Ernest Fortin, 'Augustine and Roman Civil Religion: Some Critical Reflection', *Revue des études augustiniennes*, 26/3–4 (1980): 238–56, who refutes the view that the differences between Varro and Augustine are irrelevant. Robert Bellah, 'Civil Religion in America', *Daedalus*, 117/3 (1988): 97–118 reads the very distant echoes of this Christianized version of 'civil religion' in the post-war American politics.

[15]   John Cassian, *Inst.* 11.18.

Christian teacher, pagan priest,[16] Gnostic philosopher[17] or lukewarm believer.[18] In lieu of disdain, the architects of the Christian desert often expressed compassion for the one who was a stranger to their beliefs.[19] The encounter with the city was never fortuitous.[20] Mature monastics offered glimpses of the exceptional truth of Christ, proving their sovereignty over the worldly patterns of life.[21] Egyptian monastics did not set out to attack the political project of Constantine.[22] In his reign connections between the monastic enterprise and the ecclesial structures of the Roman cities became stronger. The public outworking of the monastic liturgy explains the role played by the first Roman Christian emperor, Constantine, in supporting the lifestyle of these monastic communities.

Liturgical Mystagogy

The eschatological awareness of the individual Christian emerged from their close interaction with the ecclesial body. Desert Christianity had an intrinsic element of 'mystagogy'. The classical form of address to God in terms of 'Father' showed that all other forms of 'fatherhood' had to derive their meaning and legitimacy from the divine source. Thus, the 'father' and 'son' relationship was part of the dialogue that constituted the core of the ecclesial tradition. This relationship first built the 'inner man' (Eph 3:16), by enriching the unique talents of every human person made in the image of God. The monastic ethics did not encourage the

---

[16]   Abba Macarius the Great 38 (Ward, 136–7) record the conversation with a pagan priest, who tells the Christian ascetic: 'it is not possible [*scil.* in hell] to see anyone face to face, but the face of one is fixed to the back of another; yet, when you [*scil.* Macarius] pray for us, each of us can see the other's face a little; such is our respite'.

[17]   Philip Rousseau, *Pachomius: The Making of a Community in Fourth-Century Egypt* (Berkeley, Calif., 1999), pp. 162–5.

[18]   Abba Bessarion 7 (Ward, 42), 'A brother who had sinned was turned out of the church by the priest. Abba Bessarion got up and went with him, saying, "I, too, am a sinner."'

[19]   As *SBo* 101 (Veilleux, 139) indicates, Pachomius prayed for the heathens; see also Abba Macarius the Great 39 (Ward, 137).

[20]   Antoine Guillaumont, *Aux origines du monachisme chrétien. Pour une phénoménologie du monachisme* (Bégrolles-en-Mauges, 1977), pp. 89–116.

[21]   Palladius, *Historia lausiaca* 26.1–4 tells the dramatic story of monk Heron, who because of disobedience ended up whoring and gambling in Alexandria.

[22]   This explains why John Howard Yoder, 'The Constantinian Sources of Western Social Ethics', *The Priestly Kingdom* (Notre Dame, Ind., 1984), pp. 135–47 falls short of the mark, when he is compared with the early Christian perception of the Constantinian revolution.

artificial creation of universal rules that would ignore the reality of each person, and their specific needs.[23] We are told that Abba Isaac

> lived with Abba Cronius. He would never tell me [*scil.* Abba Cronius] to do any work, although he was old and tremulous; but he himself got up and offered food to me and to everyone. Then I lived with Abba Theodore of Pherme and he did not tell me to do anything either, but he himself set the table and said to me, 'Brother, if you want, come and eat.' I replied, 'I have come to you to help you, why do you never tell me to do anything?' But the old man gave me no reply whatever.[24]

Repeatedly, 'speak to me a word' was the bold request made by young Christian novices in search of salvation.[25] The context for this type of dialogue was always personal, if not even intimate. The *apophthegmata patrum* suggest that experienced monks knew how to rekindle in others the virtues of Christian life, by adapting the wisdom of the Scriptures to their individual, personal circumstances. The seminal word offered by the spiritual father reflected the glory of the Word of God. The appropriation of that word, which was more than just advice, helped the initiation of the novice into the 'mystery of Christ' (Eph 3:4).

Before the 'translation' of the Gospel into the foreign idioms of the world, one's heart has to become first the invisible script, onto which the law of God is written. The 'heart' describes that realm of interiority where one single word can effect an extraordinary transformation. The mystagogical dimension reveals the core paradox of monasticism. The 'inner man' revolves around the passive experience of suffering in the Cross of Christ and the joyful celebration of the eternal Sabbath of God. These two tonalities, namely joy and suffering, characterize human participation in the divine life.[26] They express the eschatological paradox of charity and truth. Suffering cannot disappear given the brokenness of human language facing the revelation of God. Joy confirms the natural optimism of an heir of the Kingdom.

---

[23] Abba Nisterus 5 (Ward, 155), 'Do not impose rules on yourself'. Abba Hierax (Ward, 104): 'A brother questioned Abba Hierax saying, "Give me a word. How can I be saved"? The old man said to him, "Sit in your cell, and if you are hungry, eat, if you are thirsty, drink, only do not speak evil of anyone, and you will be saved".'

[24] Abba Isaac 2 (Ward, 99).

[25] Philip Rousseau, 'The Spiritual Authority of the "Monk-Bishop". Eastern Elements in some Western Hagiography of the Fourth and Fifth Centuries', *Journal of Theological Studies*, 22/2 (1971): 380–420, for an excellent discussion of this theme.

[26] G¹5 (Veilleux, 300), 'hearing of this great grace, his heart was set on fire with the fear of God and with joy'.

The eschatological self[27] supports more resolute deeds than doubtful thoughts.[28] The pursuit of truth does not resemble the Cartesian definition of method and scientific knowledge. The mystagogical condition of monastic life is expressed by brief, poem-like sentences or brilliant sayings, rather than by dry dialectics or lengthy pieces of rhetoric. Liturgical life builds spiritual charisma and not metaphysical scepticism. It nurtures straightforward Christian performances and less philosophical sophistication. It has much to offer in silence, when the world is floating over in shallow conversations.

In the sacrament of confession, in particular, the mystery of human personhood enters into dialogue with the 'mystery of Christ' (Eph 3:4). In order to acquire the gift of sonship, the monk has to relinquish the secular obsession with economic productivity. While it keeps the monk sober, active, and alert, the monastic liturgy chastizes the 'cost-benefit' calculus. Because it prepares for an encounter with the human heart, which is often beyond grasp, the monastic liturgy introduces no artificial rubrics in its temporal structures. The desert fathers, for example, never used a rule of prayer that measured the quality of Christian liturgy in seconds or minutes. The charitable labours in the desert did not have exact time-slots or predetermined rules of management.

---

[27]   In the words of Michel Henry, the birth of the eschatological self within the invisible sphere of the ecclesial life could be described as 'auto-affection'. Auto-affection translates in the jargon of Continental phenomenology the experience of conversion rendered by the Vulgate as 'in se autem reversus' (Lk 15:17). The term 'auto-affection' describes that particular event, which escapes the grasp of metaphysical thinking. Auto-affection suspends the appearance of the world, always dependent upon the ecstasy of human intentionality. As Michel Henry, trans. G. Etzkorn (The Hague, 1975), p. 219 put it, 'more original than the phenomenon of transcendence and so to speak prior to it is that of immanence'. The pre-linguistic or post-linguistic area of cognizance is the site where ultimate meanings occur. An 'arch-revelation' suddenly manifests itself in opposition to the discursive realm of debatable issues. Michel Henry, *Philosophy and Phenomenology of the Body*, 'Quatre principes de la phénoménologie', *Revue de Métaphysique et de Morale*, 96/1 (1991): 3–26 calls this the 'fourth principle of phenomenology', which operates the radical reduction of 'being' to 'donation'. The revelation of the donological and, thus, doxological character of being is rooted in what Michel Henry calls the 'transcendental body'. I have suggested elsewhere that, theologically speaking, among all the sacraments it is the Eucharist that can meet the roots of this purely transcendental body, within which divine Life irrupts. See Mihail Neamţu, *Gramatica Ortodoxiei. Tradiţia după modernitate* (Jassy, 2007), pp. 160–92, where I offer a critical comparison between Henry and Foucault's reading of the Christian body and of the Christian self.

[28]   Antoine Guillaumont, *Aux origines du monachisme chrétien. Pour une phénoménologie du monachisme* (Bégrolles-en-Mauges, 1977), pp. 117–28.

Public Witness

Christian *paideia* in the desert could not exclude the cultural outflow of the Gospel or the social interaction of Christian people with the outside world.[29] The 'birth from above' (Jn 3:5) was followed by the hermeneutics of the 'Other.'[30] If mystagogy framed the encounter with the 'inner man,' then the political aspect of the monastic liturgy was responsible for the dialogue with the neighbourhood. The liturgy, then, has a twofold character, reflecting thus the theologico-political constitution of the Church. On the one hand, there is the issue of true faith, while on the other, there is the task of infinite love. St Paul describes faith and love (1 Thess 1:3) in terms of 'works', which retain a liturgical connotation.

Liturgy is the divine service which orders the creation towards its final goal, thus putting secular history on hold (Gal 1:3–5). Alexander Schmemann pointed out that in the early Church the word liturgy had 'primarily ecclesiological and not cultic connotations'.[31] More recently, Catherine Pickstock reminded us that, when deciphered etymologically, liturgy can be seen as a 'political category'.[32] The experience of rituals, or the religious *rites de passages*, does not exhaust the theological meaning of Christian worship.[33] Nicene Christology compels one to see the Incarnation in terms that resist a sharp demarcation between the 'sacred' and the 'profane'. Here 'liturgical' refers to the encounter between monks living far from the city and the representatives of the non-Christian faith. We also call 'liturgical' the Eucharistic mass celebrated in the Christian villages of Egypt. However, liturgy does not comprise only the set of actions usually labelled 'rites'.[34] Especially in the case of the anchorites, the critique of ritualism was often

---

[29]   Louis Bouyer, *Mysterion. Du mystère à la mystique* (Paris, 1988) looks at how early Christianity surpassed the social patterns established by the pagan mystery cults.

[30]   Abba Matoes 13 (Ward, 145): 'He who dwells with the brethren must not be square, but round, so as to turn himself towards all'.

[31]   Alexander Schmemann, *Church, World, Mission* (Crestwood, NY, 1979), p. 136. Similar suggestions are to be found in the work of Jean-Yves Lacoste, *Le monde et l'absence d'œuvre* (Paris, 2000), commented by Joeri Schrijvers, 'Jean-Yves Lacoste: a Phenomenology of Liturgy', *Heythrop Journal*, 46/3 (2005): 314–33.

[32]   Catherine Pickstock, 'Liturgy, Art, and Politics', *Modern Theology*, 16/2 (2000): 160.

[33]   Elizabeth A. Clark, *Reading Renunciation: Asceticism and Scripture in early Christianity* (Princeton, 1999), pp. 204–32 prefers the category of 'ritual' in order to analyse the core of Christian asceticism. On Egyptian ritual see David Frankfurter, 'Ritual Expertise in Roman Egypt and the Problem of the Category – Magician', in Peter Schäfer and Hans G. Kippenberg (eds), *Envisioning Magic: A Princeton Seminar and Symposium* (Leiden, 1997).

[34]   Juan Mateos, 'L'office monastique à la fin du IVè siècle', *Oriens Christianus*, 47 (1963): 53–88; Henry Chadwick, 'Prayer at Midnight', in J. Fontaine and Charles Kannengiesser (eds), *Epektasis. Mélanges patristiques offerts au Cardinal J. Daniélou* (Paris, 1972), pp. 47–9.

done with reference to Jesus' negative remarks about Jewish legalism.[35] Monastic liturgy cannot simply be reduced to 'religious rites' since the latter often mark important class divisions.[36] Religious rites express in collective aggregations the piety of the body. They do not have to be connected to a set of doctrines or to any deep metaphysical convictions.[37] The liturgy of the desert fathers held together subtle ideas and basic performances. It abolished class divisions, while inventing an ecclesial type of sociality.

Often, liturgical performances have an obvious origin, but their purpose is less easy to grasp. Penance rites, such as confession, fasting, genuflexion, together with almsgiving, temple festivals, offerings, pilgrimages and relic worship are outward signs of the cosmic dimension of Christian worship. When understood in mystagogical terms, the monastic liturgy enables one to perceive the eschaton as the outcome of history, and yet as something prefigured from all eternity. The 'eighth day' is thus both the completion of the seven days of creation and the inauguration of 'new heavens and new earth' (Isa 65:17). The eschaton can be experienced in Christ as the 'fullness of time' prepared by the liturgy of the Church. Desert eschatology hosts the eruption of future totality and the retrospective reading of the sapiential past into the ever-expanding ecclesial present.

Liturgical acts are public in form, but their meaning has to be learned in secret. Historically, the significance of the monastic liturgy can be understood only indirectly, when theology receives the help of archaeology, epigraphy or literary analysis. Then, the holistic character of monastic liturgy can be contrasted with the fragmentary, and sometimes appears to be in contrast with the syncretistic character of urban religion. It is true that the inhabited world cannot hope to attain, by the same standards, the intensity of Christian life in the desert.

Monastic liturgy is both personal and ecclesial. It calls the beginner to participate in the *totus Christus* event. Church tradition is therefore the medium for the liturgical synthesis between mystagogical knowledge and political witness. Doctrine helps all individual or collective performances to be brought into one grand narrative. The sacraments graft the Christian ascetic unto the cosmic fabric of sanctification.[38] The Church helps the holy man confront the 'cosmic power brokers'

---

[35]   Lori Branch, 'The Desert in the Desert: Faith and the Aporias of Law and Knowledge in Derrida and the *Sayings of the Desert Fathers*', *Journal of the American Academy of Religion*, 71/4 (2003): 811–33. My disagreement with Branch is due precisely to her underestimation of the doctrinal orthodoxy of the Desert Fathers, in the context of the Arian polemics carried out during the fourth century.

[36]   Pierre Bourdieu, *Language and Symbolic Power*, trans. Gino Raymond and Matthew Adamson (Cambridge, Mass., 1999), pp. 168–9.

[37]   Robin Lane Fox, *Pagans and Christians* (New York, 1986), p. 31, 'pagans performed rites but professed no creed or doctrine'.

[38]   *Historia Monachorum*, pr. 9.

of pagan influence.[39] Monastic liturgy expands from the one-on-one confession into an outspoken intercourse with the Other. From reading practices and ritual performances to story-telling, hospitality, or medical care, the same monastic liturgy is built upon the private and public dialectic. It is based on the fusion of doctrine and prayer, of mind and body, of the inner self and political openness.

The dividedness of the human self requires that worship seeks the healing of the wounds that mark the human condition. Gradual instalments of ritualized gestures help the ascetic body become a microcosm. To give only one example, the lifting up of hands (Ps 134:2) in prayer cannot be understood without reference to the rich biblical narratives of salvation. 'When a monk stands in prayer, if he is alone, he does not pray at all.'[40] His arms in the air symbolize the Cross and the angels who are invisibly present at the time of prayer. For desert fathers, philosophical categories offered only general insights about the created order (e.g. the unity of the world, the natural difference between man and the animals, the basic divisions among ethical judgements, etc.). Concepts cannot purify us from passions. Dialectics cannot stop the human cravings from acting in support of greed, pride or concupiscence. This is why asceticism must be incorporated into the liturgical life of the ecclesial body.

Monastic liturgy plays a mediating role between the private and public dimension of the Christian faith, just as the tradition mediates between knowledge of the Scriptures and the life of the Church. It insures that there is always an element of continuity between the explicit creeds of the Church, the unknown mystery of Christ and the mystery of the human person. Theology, understood as the prayerful exercise of the Christian *coram Deo*, must be accompanied by public speech. Silence gives wings to persuasion. The eschatological self redeems the political subject. Monastic liturgy adopts the ecclesial system of 'checks-and-balances' that prevents the Church from collapsing into a liturgical ghetto, or into empty shouting at the world.

In that they follow the interpretation of divine *kenosis* in terms of *askesis*, monastic theologians do understand the open character of the Gospel. The monk avoids sin by withdrawing into the uninhabited territories of the earth. He interacts invisibly with the immediate environment. In accordance with the Nicene understanding of divine Incarnation, the Word seeks to find flesh in which to dwell.[41] The monks make the desert fertile and well-ordered. They break through the unknown and frightening territories of the earth, in the same way Christ harrowed hell. Then, the Gospel moves from the desert back to the city with the help of mature monastics, or ascetic bishops, who are able to offer an intelligible exegesis of the eschatological promise in Christ.

---

[39] Douglas R. Edwards, *Religion & Power: Pagans, Jews, and Christians in the Greek East* (Oxford, 1996), pp. 91–148.

[40] N 104 (Stewart, 37).

[41] Ewa Wipszycka, 'Le monachisme égyptiens et les villes', *Travaux et memoires*, 12 (1994): 11–14 claims that the echo of the Pachomian monasticism could be found in Alexandria, too, by the end of the fourth century.

In short, the Church is shaped by a theologico-political constitution. Renunciation of earthly goods, for example, is part of that wider range of practices which cannot hide their public dimension. To abandon the world, and then to convert it, are not two separate acts based upon the dialectical model 'either-or'. Similarly, the monastic liturgy recognizes the complementary character of productive labour and contemplation.[42] Before the eschaton one cannot give up the inner fight for faith and the persuasion of love. It is not the force of an external threat that makes one victorious, but the constant emanation of goodness, at the end of which Paschal joy makes death surrender.

Friends and Enemies

Christian life is the work of God, which requires the telling of truth apart from error. In the light of this statement, the political character of monastic liturgy accounts for the exclusive language used by the desert fathers. To discern 'truth' from 'error' meant to recognize who was the agent of 'orthodoxy' and 'heresy'.[43] It was not so for the Roman pagans, for whom 'the opposite of "heterodoxy" was not "orthodoxy", but "homodoxy," meaning agreement'.[44] 'Orthodox' versus 'heretic' represents, however, a second-order distinction pertaining to the self-understanding of the ecclesial order. It follows the primary epistemic division between 'friends' and 'enemies,' which helps one identify what is 'good' and what is 'bad'. The agile mind can tell apart orthodoxy from heresy, whereas the pure heart can decide what is friendly, and what is inimical to personal salvation. 'Say to your every thought which comes upon you, "Do you belong to us, or to our enemies?" and it will confess.'[45] In other words, along with the Pauline differentiation between the 'weak' and the 'strong', one has to internalize ascetically the Old Testament distinction between 'enemies' and 'friends'.

Often, the greatest enemy of ascetic Christians is the old Adam, who stands in direct contrast to the virtues of Christ. Monastic demonology plays an important part in the works of this noetic laboratory. We are told that 'the one who does not receive everybody as his brother ($\pi\acute{\alpha}\nu\tau\alpha\varsigma$ $\acute{\omega}\varsigma$ $\mathring{\alpha}\delta\epsilon\lambda\varphi\omicron\grave{\upsilon}\varsigma$), but makes distinctions

---

[42]   Abba Apollo (Ward, 36): 'There was in the Cells an old man called Apollo. If someone came to find him about doing a piece of work, he would set out joyfully, saying "I am going to work with Christ today, for the salvation of my soul, for that is the reward ($\acute{o}$ $\mu\iota\sigma\theta\acute{o}\varsigma$) he gives."'

[43]   Carl Schmitt, *The Concept of the Political*, trans. and intr. George Schwab, foreword by Tracy B. Strong, with notes by Leo Strauss (Chicago and London, 1996), p. 27. Abba Matoes 11 (Ward, 145): 'beware of your faults; do not judge others but put yourself below everyone; do not be friendly with a boy nor with an heretical friend'.

[44]   Robin Lane Fox, *Pagans and Christians* (New York, 1986), p. 31.

[45]   N 99 (Stewart, 36).

(ἀλλὰ διακρίνων) is not perfect (τέλειος)'.[46] The anonymous collection of *apophthegmata* informs us about a monk who learnt from a simple gardener that, above all ascetic efforts, a Christian should be ready to hope for the salvation of the whole world. Undisturbed by the noise coming from the streets, the layman constantly tells himself that 'all will enter the Kingdom (πάντως εἰς τὴν βασιλε ί αν ἀπέρχονται).' Humbled by this example, the monk acknowledges this virtue 'surpasses the toil of so many years (ὑπερβάσα τῶν τοσούτων ἐτῶν μου τὸν κόπον)'.[47]

On what basis is the paradox of monasticism founded, in that it can accommodate the idea of orthodox Christians having heretics as affective friends? If the 'enemies-versus-friends' distinction is mostly invisible, how can hypocrisy be avoided? Can this subtle distinction between the intimate language of love and the distant language of truth really operate in practice? Is the transfer from private friendship to the public sphere of ecclesial identity so easily made? Firstly, the fact that the desert fathers' writings contain numerous references to the demonic aspects of pagan practices,[48] just as much as harsh condemnations of heresy, is undeniable.[49] Secondly, there are many suggestions that the distinction 'private-versus-public' is abolished in the encounter of heresy or unbelief. We are told, for instance, that Abba Anthony never had 'friendly conversations with the Manichaeans', preferring instead 'to admonish them to convert to piety, for he thought and affirmed that friendship and association with them led to injury and destruction of the soul'.[50] Anthony's stance towards the initiators of schisms within the Church was no less severe. As an Orthodox ascetic, he never held communion with the representatives of Meletius, the schismatic bishop. Even more radical had been the approaches towards the Arian heresy. His biographer Athanasius describes Anthony's relationship with the collective identity of Arianism in terms of the rejection of an important error. How can one suggest, then, that there was room for drawing fine distinctions between 'affective friends' and 'theological heretics'?

First, it is not very clear in what manner the private encounters between Orthodox monastics and heretical Christians really took place. It is nonetheless certain that a theological 'enemy' did not have to be 'morally evil or aesthetically ugly' in order to be recognized as an outsider by the community of the elected ones.[51] 'Like a dead body, the humble [monk] cannot judge any person, and not even the one who

---

[46]   GCS 1.34 (Guy, SC 387).

[47]   N 67.

[48]   N 37.

[49]   *SBo* 103 (Veilleux, 144) suggests that there is no distinction between heretics and schismatics – 'each of which says, "Ours is the right opinion"' – and that hell may well be the posthumous destiny of each category.

[50]   Athanasius, *Vita Antonii* 68.

[51]   Carl Schmitt, *The Concept of the Political*, trans. and intr. by George Schwab, foreword by Tracy B. Strong, with notes by Leo Strauss (Chicago and London, 1996), p. 27.

worships the idols.'[52] The advice of Abba Poemen to Abba Joseph of Panephysis was: 'If you want to find rest here below, and hereafter, in all circumstances say "Who am I? and do not judge anyone."'[53] A non-judgemental take on personal relations does not contradict the theologico-political virtue of discernment. Even the most sincere commitments to doctrinal Orthodoxy are not sufficient for the eschatological immersion into the supreme good.[54] The reality of sin, and not just the spectres of heresy, had disruptive effects for the Church body, by and large.[55] For reasons related to this ontological confusion created by disobedience, one cannot always say who lies inside, and who lingers outside the ecclesial body.

Because of this subtle balance between the expression of truth and the practice of love, Christian monasticism in the Egyptian desert did not push for the dreadful ideological discriminations advanced by totalitarian regimes during the modern age.[56] The emphasis put on personal mystagogy may explain the paradoxes surrounding the 'friend' versus 'enemy' distinction. The relationship between the 'insider' and the 'outsider' was not based on that mechanistic causality that makes social fabric so prone to dictatorship.[57] Christians had to suspend the rule of reciprocity in hatred. The truth of revelation, in its turn, was not seen in propositional terms. The desert fathers were not ready to churn out 'list of errors', against which possible 'enemies of faith' would be publicly judged.[58] This is why Abba Theodore of Pherme says that 'there is no other virtue than that of not being scornful'[59]

---

[52]   N 559.

[53]   Abba Joseph of Panephysis 2 (Ward, 102).

[54]   Macarius the Great (Ward, 133): 'Do not sleep in the cell of a brother who has a bad reputation'.

[55]   Despite their harsh approach to heresy, the desert fathers often expressed themselves carefully in front of the heretics. Among the seven instructions sent by Abba Moses 1 (Ward, 141) to Abba Poemen, one reads the following advice, 'the monk must die to his neighbour and never judge him at all, in any way whatever'.

[56]   Not even the religious persecutions launched by archbishop Theophilus of Alexandria against the Origenist monks (399) could resemble the institutionalized violence of the revolutionary regimes, from France to Russia, during the modern age. For Theophilus, see Norman Russell, 'Bishops and Charismatics in Early Christian Egypt', in A. Louth, J. Behr, D. Conomos (eds), *Abba. Festschrift for Bishop Kallistos Ware* (Crestwood, NY, 2003), pp. 99–110. Cassius Dio, *Historiae romanae* 56.27.1 shows that book-burning and the repression of religious otherness took place also in the times of Augustus.

[57]   For I.V. Stalin (1879–1953) it was the factory, while for Mao Zedong (1893–1976) it was the furnace complex, which stood as the ideal picture of a thoroughly mobilized society, run under strict supervision and with rigid planning. See in particular Stalin, *Problems of Leninism* (Peking, 1976), p. 740.

[58]   As Tia Kolbaba, *The Byzantine Lists: Errors of the Latin* (Chicago, 2000) and Henry Chadwick, *East and West: The Making of a Rift in the Church* (Oxford, 2003) show, it was only a centralized understanding of ecclesiastical discipline that required the drafting of such 'lists of errors' later in Byzantium.

[59]   Theodore of Pherme 13 (Ward, 75).

and that 'monks have lost their manners' when they 'do not say "pardon"'.[60] The desert remained an open space, where forceful conversions were seen as nugatory. Echoing Lactantius' view on Roman policies,[61] early Christian hermits did not endorse the idea of compulsory religion. Only later, did the Christian Empire aim, perhaps, at homogenizing, top-to-bottom, the whole of society.[62] If modern historians felt inclined to accuse Constantine and his bishops of 'intolerance',[63] if not of 'Christian terrorism',[64] they spared the leading champions of the desert of such remarks.

Theological exclusiveness does not have to entail physical violence. A would-be 'enemy' in terms of metaphysical orientation can suddenly become a companion on the road to salvation. When the disciple of Abba Macarius approached an old pagan priest from the desert with the cruel shout of, 'Oh, devil, where are you off to?' the immediate response was brutal. Abba Macarius himself applied the rule of *politesse*, saying 'Greetings, greetings, you weary man'. The answer is revealing: 'I have been touched by your greeting and I realize that you are on God's side. But another wicked monk who met me insulted me and I have given him blows enough for him to die of them.'[65] In other words, good monks, who are perfectly aware of the doctrinal difference between heresy and orthodoxy, must also behave well in front of their theological adversaries. *Metanoia* takes place beyond any rigid planning and aside all military norms of conscription.[66]

---

[60]   Theodore of Pherme 6 (Ward, 74).

[61]   Elizabeth DePalma Digeser, *The Making of a Christian Empire: Lactantius and Rome* (Ithaca, 2000), pp. 40–45.

[62]   Andrew Louth, 'Introduction', in Andrew Louth and Augustine Casiday (eds), *Byzantine Orthodoxies. Papers from the Thirty-Sixth Spring Symposium of Byzantine Studies*, 23–5 March 2002 (Aldershot, 2006), p. 2, where the risky comparison with the Soviet system is made. However, the parallel with the Islamic type of religious imperialism might have perhaps been more apposite, as Garth Fowden, *Empire to Commonwealth. Consequences of Monotheism in Late Antiquity* (Princeton, 1993) seems to indicate. Ephraim Karsh, *Islamic Imperialism: A History* (New Haven, Conn., 2006) would disagree with this comparison.

[63]   Harold Allen Drake, *Constantine and the Bishops. The Politics of Intolerance* (Baltimore, Maryland, 1999).

[64]   Rodney Stark (2003), *For the Glory of God. How Monotheism let to Reformations, Science, Witch-Hunts, and the End of Slavery* (Princeton and Oxford, 2003), p. 35.

[65]   Abba Macarius the Great 39 (Ward, 137).

[66]   There is an important and painful exception to this rule. At the end of the fourth century and during the fourth century one notices the presence of the famous shock-troops, called *parabalani*, selected from among the Christian zealots (*philoponoi*). Ch. Haas, *Alexandria in Late Antiquity. Topography and Social Conflict*, Baltimore (Maryland, 1997), p. 67 notices that in official terms the *parabalani* 'appear to have had something to do with hospital organization in the city'. William Harmless, *Desert Christians. An Introduction to the Literature of Early Monasticism* (Oxford, 2004), p. 16 suggests these monastic 'stick-bearers' had been involved in the destruction of pagan temples (391), the murdering of

In sum, no straightforward demarcation should leave out the possibility of having 'affective friends' who happen to be, at least temporarily, 'moral strangers' or even 'theological enemies'. Such stark conceptual distinctions do not gainsay the possibility of converting a stranger into a friend. In the words of H. Tristram Engelhardt Jr., 'the term moral strangers recognizes that, in the absence of common moral premises or a common understanding of the moral life, individuals meet without the possibility of resolving important moral controversies'.[67] By swapping 'moral' with 'theological' or with 'political', one does not refute the political predicament of the ecclesial body, permanently nourished by monastic liturgy. The distinction between 'affective friend' and 'moral stranger' stems from the awareness that discursive minds and pure hearts are rarely united, and that only 'in one Spirit and one mind' (Phil 1:27) can such divisions be dissolved. If secular people may consider friendship naturally good, even in absence of this transcendental accord of values, the monastics have to purify every form of 'affection' bestowed upon others, whether they are villains, prostitutes or barbarians. In addition to that, the wise monastic does not cherish the illusion that one can adhere to the Gospel of Christ without fighting an inner battle. The monks and the nuns are precisely those who never bracket the search for the supreme good, in order to pursue instead the 'common good'.[68]

Heavenly Politeia

If 'politics are the process of moral discourse by which community is created and sustained',[69] then it becomes obvious why the desert fathers adopted a binary, and yet not dualistic, understanding of Christianity. Strict distinctions between visible and invisible 'friends' or 'enemies' are validated by personal discernment and then prolonged in the 'orthodoxy-versus-heresy' differentiation, operating at the ecclesial level. Without these classifications, the 'creation' and 'sustenance' of the monastic community in the wilderness would have not been faithful to the Creed of Nicaea, which speaks in mandatory terms about ecclesial catholicity. While they repudiated gullible mingling with those beyond the church frontiers, the desert fathers avoided any sectarian understanding of the Gospel. In the words of Evagrius of Pontus, 'if a solitary imagines himself entrusted with the spiritual rule of a city, he does not dwell on this thought for long because clearly it cannot

---

Hypatia the philosopher (415), or the violent demonstrations surrounding the Council of Ephesus (431).

[67] Tristram H. Engelhardt Jr., *The Foundations of Christian Bioethics* (Lisse, 2000), p. xxi.

[68] In the contemporary jargon of political science, one would term the political orientation of the Egyptian monastics as 'communitarian', with a strong 'libertarian' touch.

[69] Robert W. Jenson, *Systematic Theology* (2 vols, New York, 1999), vol. 2, p. 80.

be realized in practice. But if someone becomes the spiritual guide of a city and yet remains unaffected that means he is blessed with dispassion'.[70] Whether individual or communitarian, their asceticism does not bracket the catholic understanding of ecclesial politeia. Since God rules the earth by interventionist politics, the monastics prepare themselves for gently spreading the Word by word of mouth.

This explains why Pachomius the Great 'would pray for the whole world in kind',[71] with the monks and virgins 'in the first place', followed by 'those married in life' and then 'three classes of men'.[72] At this point, the saint prayed,

> first, for those who began to do what is good, but afterwards were unable to complete it because of the vain cares of the world which kept them from doing it; that the Lord may grand them means of doing what is good by freeing them from all concerns for this vain world – save solely for the needs the body imposes – and that thus they might do God's will, escape torments, and be heirs of the eternal kingdom. He would pray for those who cling fast to the works of the devil, for all the heathen and for those who without knowing it are deluded by heresies, having been led astray by others; that God may grant them understanding, that they might understand and bring forth worthy fruits of repentance, having in mind above all the good he always does them.[73]

Monastic liturgy can also be termed 'political' for intrinsic reasons. There is a plethora of references to the 'kingdom language' of the Scriptures in the writings of the desert fathers. There are numerous places where the monastics equate the 'kingdom' with the 'divine heavens'.[74] The 'kingdom of heaven' is seen as the crown of the monastic endeavour.[75] The King seated on the celestial throne is, of course, Christ. The chances to meet him in person are very good for those who take the Gospel to their heart. One of the most beautiful passages in the *Apophthegmata Patrum* bursts with evangelical optimism:

> Someone said to Abba John the Persian, 'We have borne great afflictions for the sake of the kingdom of heaven (διὰ τὴν βασιλείαν τῶν οὐρανῶν). Shall we inherit it?' The old man said, 'As for me, I am confident that we shall obtain the inheritance of Jerusalem on high, which is written in heaven. Why should

---

[70] Evagrius, *On Discrimination* (Palmer et al. 51).

[71] *SBo* 101 (Veilleux, 138).

[72] The modern editions and translations of the Life of St Pachomius (from Coptic) fail to divide the three classes, as Christoph Joest, 'Pachoms Gebet für Drei Menschengruppen und die Irrtümer Moderner Übersetzungen', *Le Muséon. Revue d'études orientales*, 118/3–4 (2005): 321–5 explains it very clearly: (a) the beginners in faith and good works; (b) the sinners tempted by the devil; (c) the gullible victims of heresy.

[73] *SBo* 101 (Veilleux, 138–9).

[74] N 67, N 390, N 490.

[75] N 53, N 211, N 614.

I not be confident? I have been hospitable like Abraham, meek like Moses, holy like Aaron, patient like Job, humble like David, a hermit like John, filled with compunction like Jeremiah, a master (διδάσκαλος) like Paul, full of faith like Peter, wise like Solomon. Like the thief, I trust that he who of his natural goodness (οἰκείαν ἀγαθότητα) has given me all that that, will also grant me the kindgom'.[76]

In other words, the kingdom is within reach. Monastic *paideia* is revealed at its best in this passage, which shows an impeccable appreciation of the covenantal theology displayed by the Old Testament, and the unmistakable Christian boldness in anticipation of the divine gifts. There is not only an exact portrait of each biblical character that matters in the redemptive narrative of the Bible, but also the exact rendering of New Testament vision of Messiah, and his renewal of creation. The comparison with the 'thief' (Lk 12:39–40) is not employed for rhetorical purposes, but it stems right from the central role played by the Cross in the ascetic theology of the desert fathers.[77] The way to that 'kingdom that cannot be shaken' (Heb 12:28) requires the encounter with the King himself. The goodness of Christ appears natural to his servants.

There are also echoes of the Pauline teaching on Christian citizenship (Phil 3:20), which suggest that the polity of the desert fathers was irksome for the secular habits of controlling the mores of the cities. Notwithstanding, the hermits did not have to behave like protean anarchists or self-appointed revolutionaries.[78] The flight to the wilderness does not abandon the hope of converting the secular polity to orthodoxy.[79] The monastics never agreed with civic lawlessness. The Pachomian constitution, to give here only one example, built itself around the same metaphor of the city.[80]

Without living in the blind present of history, the desert fathers deepened an eschatological vision already available in early Church times. The 'political' dimension of the monastic liturgy defines more than the visible sociality of their Christian existence.[81] The political sphere captures the totality of past, present, and future commitments to the promise made by God. Even when judged at the purely empirical level, acts of withdrawing and renunciation, or the pursuit

---

[76]   John the Persian 4 (Ward, 108).

[77]   M.G. Lefebvre, *Recueil des inscriptions grecques-chrétiennes d'Egypte* (Cairo, 1907), p. 112, where the French scholar transcribes the following Christian inscription identified at Philae (Upper Egypt): 'The cross has conquered. Victory forever!'

[78]   Athanasius, *De Incarnatione Verbi* (ed. R.W. Thomson) 55.4.

[79]   Eusebius, *h.e.* 10.4.7, who sees Constantinople as the recipient of God's blessings through the churches built by the emperor.

[80]   Pachomius the Great followed Clement of Alexandria, *Paedagogus* 2.93.4, and Origen, *Contra Celsus* 8.75 in construing the church as the alternative city of God.

[81]   This was not negligible, if one thinks that the name of Pachomius 'was heard even abroad and among the Romans', *SBo* 89 (Veilleux, 117).

of tranquility did not relinquish the shared virtues of attentiveness, generosity, and compassion.[82] In that it does not split 'practical' virtues from 'theoretical' commitments, monastic liturgy is 'political' and not ideological. There is a mutual correlation between what is liturgical and what is political within the monastic matrix of life, and this makes it strange to all the disturbing utopias nurtured by modern party-politics.[83]

Nicaea Against Self-Deification

Before the eschatological consummation of time, the theological reconciliation between 'friends' and 'enemies' seems implausible. On the one hand, Christian life must avoid any form of political utopia. On the other hand, it does not aim at establishing an esoteric tradition. The Gospel read by the early Christians called for the dissolution of political tyranny. The unruled ruler, symbolized by the Old Testament image of the Pharaoh, was called to obedience.[84] The Pharaoh is the icon of false deity, defined by the sheer exercise of will. For him, power, and not humility, represents the means to salvation. In the book of Revelation, the self-deified ruler emerges as an apostate. He rejects the lordship of Christ, taking pains to persecute the community of the faithful. He is reminded that the glory of the Son is not borrowed, but eternally shared with God the Father. Desert eschatology, in its turn, sees the coming Lord as that event by which the disobedient authorities in the secular sphere can be called to judgement. In this respect, the Egyptian monks walked in the footsteps of the Jewish prophets and early Christian martyrs.[85] Their manifesto was not deprived of political purport.

Christian martyrdom was generally caused by the rejection of the ruler-cult. The Gospel tells the rulers of world that they must be accountable both in heaven and on earth. As in the story of Herod and John the Baptist (Mt 14:1–11), God

---

[82] Heinrich Bacht, 'Antonius und Pachomius. Von der Anachorese zum Cöbobitismus', in Basilius Steidle (ed.), *Antonius Magna Eremita* (Rome, 1956), pp. 66–107; Pius Tamburrino, '*Koinonia.* Die Beziehung "Monasterium" – "Kirche" im frühen pachomianischen Mönchtum', *Erbe und Auftrag*, 43 (1967): 5–21 discusses the relationship between '*monasterium*' and the Church.

[83] Karl Mannheim, *Ideology and Utopia. An Introduction into the Sociology of Knowledge* (New York, 1985), pp. 55–108; Paul Ricoeur, *Hermeneutics and the Human Sciences: Essays on Language, Action and Interpretation*, trans. John B. Thompson (Cambridge, 1981), pp. 63–100; Gillian Clark, *Christianity and Roman Society* (Cambridge, 2004), pp. 110–45.

[84] The ruler in the ancient world was close to the priestly figure, as with Plato, *Republic* 290 d–e; see also J. Gwyn Griffiths, 'Plato on Priests and Kings in Egypt', *The Classical Review*, new. ser., 15/2 (1965): 156–7.

[85] Philip Rousseau, *Pachomius: The Making of a Community in Fourth-Century Egypt* (Berkeley, Calif., 1999), pp. 122–4.

denies the claims of any tyrant to have unchecked sovereignty. It censures their right to abuse public recognition, at the cost of neglecting public justice.[86] The Scriptures unmask the secret pact which the tyrants make with the history of their people, by rejecting the humility and love of Christ. Indeed, as the lives of the Roman autocrats shows, a despot compels his subjects to obey him for fear of punishment. This horizon of death introduces the cycle of violence, from which there is no escape. Even when his life is well spent, a Pharaoh-like individual begs posterity to offer him the honours of a posthumous deification.

Such dreams can be powerfully rebuffed on the basis of an orthodox Christology. Among other things, Nicaea lays down the Christian grammar of deification. It reminds us that only a deifying Christ, who dies on the Cross, and not a deified Jesus, who may have attained nothing more than moral perfection, can denounce the secret desire of all tyrants, who wish to become gods. The Nicene view of Christ seems therefore appropriate for a denunciation of political dictatorship. Tyrants prefer permanence, over change in office. This explains why Caesar was declared *dictator perpetuo* from 45 BC onwards, when he introduced his personal, namely the Julian calendar, according to which world time had to be measured. As with any other form of idolatry, political dictatorship is nurtured by defective pride, infectious hatred and mutual suspicion. The eschatological society of the monastics has at its centre the icon of Christ, who is both 'Lord and God', ready to sanctify his people, to make his people 'partakers of the divine nature' (2 Pet 1:4) and, by calling them 'gods' (Isa 81:6), to grant them the gift of immortality.

To say that humble Christians are the true companions of the eternal King is to make a political statement. Aware that martyrdom represents *via regia*, the eschatological community of the desert resists all pagan attempts to monumentalize earthly history.[87] They did not trust the Platonic ideal of having philosophers in the city as perfect rulers. The monks did not aim at such rewards. In their eyes, the polity of love obliterated the reign of terror by means of personal example

---

[86]   The philosophical dilemmas of tyranny have been explored in Xenophon's dialogue *Hiero*, commented by Leo Strauss, *On Tyranny*, ed. V. Gourevitch and Michael S. Roth (Chicago, 2001). For a complex mapping of the philosophical and theological issues raised by Strauss, see Robert B. Pippin, 'Being, Time, and Politics: The Strauss-Kojève Debate', *History and Theory*, 32/2 (1993): 138–61.

[87]   The bibliography on this subject is constantly growing, and includes G.W.H. Lampe, 'Early Patristic Eschatology', in W. Manson et al. (eds), *Eschatology* (Edinburgh and London, 1953), pp. 17–35; George Florovsky, 'Eschatology in the Patristic Age', *Greek Orthodox Theological Review*, 2 (1956): 27–40; F.F. Bruce, 'Eschatology in the Apostolic Fathers', in D. D. Nieman and M. Schatkin (eds.), *The Heritage of the Christian Church. Festschrift for G.V. Florovsky* (Rome, 1973), pp. 77–89 with reference to the apostolic fathers; Ian Gillman, 'Eschatology in the Reign of Constantine', *Reformed Theological Review*, 24 (1965): 40–51 discusses the eschatology in the reign of Constantine; Brian Daley, *The Hope of the Early Church: Eschatology in the Patristic Age* (Cambridge, 1991), pp. 69–92; Charles E. Hill, *Regnum Caelorum: Patterns of Future Hope in Early Christianity* (Grand Rapids Mi., 2001).

and, of God's natural emanation of goodness.[88] Their understanding of human relationship dissolved the 'master and slave' dialectic, by consecrating the 'father and son', or 'teacher and disciple' rapport. Only the latter paradigms, which put the self-emptying love of Christ against the vain attempts to self-deification, fitted with the spiritual charter of the city of God.[89]

The asceticism of the Cross is underwritten by the Nicene understanding of Christ's kenosis. Every ascetic self is not isolated, but entrenched by the life of the Church. In its radical interpretation, Nicene theology encouraged the implementation of an eschatological way of existence, bracketing the biological and social differences among people, who are called to worship the 'true God from true God' by facing death and putting to shame the evil powers. The desert fathers do not worship a crucifying god as king, but rather a crucified king as God. To serve Christ as 'Lord and God' means to boast only in his cross (Gal 6:14). This is the decisive mark of the monastic odyssey.

Conclusion

In what manner, then, is the relationship between the desert and the city imaginable? Where does the eschatological self take shape? How is the monastic Christian formed as a holy witness to God? How can one settle the monastic rejection of publicity[90] with the need for political witness? Did Constantine's appreciation of monasticism pervert it? Which were the specific elements that gave public voice to monastic liturgy, and how was the theological continuum between the desert and the city insured?

This chapter attempted to answer these questions in several ways. I have shown that without the balance existing between the empire and the desert, Christian eschatology would have been characterized as either 'realized' (in apocalyptic terms), or 'delayed' (in politically correct terms). Monastic liturgy was neither sectarian, nor fashionable. It constantly gathered the public and private, abrasive and compassionate, truthful and charitable, ecclesial and personal dimension of the Nicene faith. Thus, the Gospel of the desert fathers remained invisibly connected with the world, though its outspoken language (including the 'heresy' vs. 'orthodoxy' distinction) often seemed provocative.

The Nicene proclamation of the Incarnation legitimized political interaction with the pagan culture and the imperial internalization of Christian eschatology.[91]

---

[88] Plato, *Republic* 473d; Cicero, *Leg.* 3. 14; Marcus Aurelius, *Med.* 9. 29.

[89] Pachomius, *Instr.* 1.27 (Veilleux, 25): 'Again, get to know the city of Christ; give him glory, for he died for you.'

[90] *Historia Monachorum* 1.12 tells us that Abba John of Lycopolis despised publicity, just as Abba Anthony and Jesus himself tried to avoid the eyes of the multitude.

[91] Vigen Guroian, *Incarnate Love: Essays in Orthodox Ethics* (Notre Dame, Ind., 1987), p. 71: 'Christian ethics begins when the people of God gather to worship', and

The very reality of the desert comprised the theological paradox of the 'frontier', which suggests the complexity of the human confrontation with its own limits at the margins of the world. The contemplative oasis of the hermits was an immediate haven and a distant horizon for all uncompromising Christians during the fourth-century Egypt.

I have shown that monastic liturgy aimed at reflecting the wholeness of Christian life. The ultimate goal of the desert fathers was to acquire 'heavenly citizenship' (Phil 3:20). They contemplated 'Jerusalem from above', towards which the later representatives of the Christian empire were also drawn. Either through straightforward reclusion or by taking up the role of cultural *paideia*, the desert fathers had accomplishments in both spheres of Christian life.

Ancient Christian Authors

Athanasius the Great

inc.   *de incarnatione verbi*, ed. C. Kannengiesser, *Sur l'incarnation du verbe*
            SC 199 (Paris: Cerf, 1973); trans. R.W. Thomson (Oxford, 1971).

v. anton.   *vita antonii* (PG 26:835–976b), ed. and trans. G.J.M. Bartelink,
            Vie d'Antoine, SC 400 (Paris, 1994); trans. R. C. Gregg and intr. W.
            Clebsch, *The Life of Anthony and the Letter to Marcellinus* (New York,
            1980); *The Life of Antony. The Coptic Life and the Greek Life*, trans.
            Tim Vivian and Apostolos N. Athanassakis (Kalamazoo, Mich., 2003).

Clement of Alexandria

paed.   *Paedagogus*, ed. H.-I. Marrou, M. Harl, C. Mondesat and Ch. Matray,
            Le Pedagogue (3 vols, Paris, 1950–1960).

strom.   *Stromata*, ed. M. Caster, *Les stromates* (2 vols, Paris, 1951, 1954).

Desert Fathers

AP   *Apophthegmata Patrum* (collectio alphabetica graeca) (PG 65:72–440)
            ed. J.B. Cotelier, trans. Benedicta Ward, *The Sayings of the Desert
            Fathers: The Alphabetical Collection* CS 59 (Kalamazoo, Mich., 1984).

GCSF   French translation by L. Regnault in *Les Sentences des Pères du Désert:
            Troisième recueil et tables*, ed. L. Regnault (Solesmes, 1976); Jean-
            Claude Guy, ed., *Les Apophtegmes des Pères*, I–IX, SC 387 (Paris,
            1993).

---

the less eschatological commentary of Bernd Wannenwetsch, *Political Worship. Ethics for Christian Citizens* (London, 2004), pp. 32–88.

N   The Greek anonymous series of *Apophthegmata Patrum*; N 1–392, ed.
           F. Nau, 'Histoires des solitaires égyptiens,' *Revue d'Orient chrétien*,
           vol. 12 (1907), pp. 48–68, 171–81, 393–404; vol. 13 (1908), pp. 47–
           57, 266–83; vol. 14 (1909), pp. 357–79; vol. 17 (1912), pp. 204–11,
           294–301; vol. 18 (1913), 137–46; N 132 A–D were edited by F. Nau in
           Revue d'orient chrétien, 10 (1905), pp. 409–14. Unpublished material
           following N 392 available in *Les Sentences des Pères du désert: Série
           des anonymes*, trans. L. Regnault (Solesmes, 1985).

Evagrius of Pontus

pr.   *Praktikos*, ed. by Antoine and Claire Guillaumont: *Traité pratique, ou Le
           Moine*, SC 171 (Paris, 1971), trans. J. E. Bamberger CS 4 (Kalamazoo,
           Mich., 1981).

Eusebius

h.e.   *historia ecclesiastica*, ed. Theodor Mommsen, Eusebius Werke, vol. 2
           (GCS 1/1–2, Leipzig: 1903), trans. G.A. Williamson, *The History of
           the Church*, rev. with introduction by Andrew Louth (Harmondworth,
           1989).

John Cassian

Inst.   *Institutions cénobitiques*, ed. J.-C. Guy (SC 109, Paris, 1965).

Historia Monachorum

h.m.   *Historia Monachorum in Aegypto*, ed. A.J. Festugière (Subsidia
           Hagiographica 34, Brussels, 1961²); N. Russell (trans.), *The Lives of
           the Desert Fathers*, CS 34 (Kalamazoo, Mich., 1980).

Origen

cels.   *Against Celsus* (GCS 3), trans. H. Chadwick, Cambridge, 1953.

Pachomius

SBo   Sahidic-Bohairic *Life of Pachomius*, reconstructed by Armand Veilleux
           in *Pachomian Koinonia: The Lives, Rules and Other Writings of Saint
           Pachomius and his Disciples*, vol. i, *The Lives of Saint Pachomius and
           his Disciples*, trans. A. Veilleux, intr. A. de Vogüé, CS 45 (Kalamazoo,
           Mich., 1980)

G1   The first Greek version of Pachomius' life, ed. F. Halkin, *Vita Prima Graeca*, in *Sancti Pachomii vitae Graecae* (Brussels, 1932), p. 1–96, English translation A. Veilleux, *supra*.

Instr.   The Instructions of Pachomius, in Pachomian Koinonia, vol. iii, *Instructions, Letters, and Other Writings of Saint Pachomius and his Disciples*, trans. A. Veilleux CS 47 (Kalamazoo, Mich., 1982).

Palladius

h. laus. Lausiac history, modern edition (of the Greek text): Cuthbert Butler, *The Lausica History of Palladius: A Critical Discussion, together with Notes on Early Monasticism*, Cambridge, 1898–1904, trans. Robert T. Meyer, *The Lausiac History*, ACW 34. For the Greek version see also the critical edition of G.J.M. Bartelink, *Palladio: La storia Lausiaca* (Verona, 1974, pp. 4–292).

Chapter 11

The Transformation of Eros: Reflections on Desire in Jacques Lacan

Christoph Schneider

> How do you live and what do you radiate?
> Does Christ radiate in you?
> Elder Pophyrios (1906–91)

In this chapter I shall discuss aspects of the work of Jacques Lacan (1901–81) on desire – arguably the most important psychoanalyst after Sigmund Freud – from an Eastern Orthodox perspective. On the part of Eastern Orthodoxy I will primarily draw on St Maximus Confessor (580–662), whose work constitutes in many respects a synthesis of the Greek patristic era of the first centuries. I shall begin with a short outline of St Maximus' notion of desire and its transformation. Then I will reflect on Lacan's idea of the origin of desire. Finally, I shall discuss the issue of how desire is transmitted and shaped by a personal and impersonal mediator.

St Maximus the Confessor draws a distinction between a human being's *natural principle* (λόγος φύσεως)[1] and *mode of existence* (τρόπος ὑπάρξεως). Whereas the natural principle is fixed, inalterable, and pre-existing in God, the mode of existence constitutes the actual way of life adopted by a particular person, which may or may not correspond to his or her natural principle. The former term denotes human nature as it was intended by God – as his good creation – and comprises a protological and a teleological aspect: God is related to every human being as origin, middle (that is as sustainer) and end. In other words, the natural principle also determines the finality and goal of human nature, which is deification by grace. For it belongs to creatures to be moved towards their divine *telos*, which is itself without beginning and end. Their rational, irascible and concupisciple (ἐπιθυμία)

---

[1] According to St Maximus, each individual being that existed, exists or will exist possesses its own *logos*. There is also a *logos* that defines a being's essence or nature, one that situates it in a species and another one in a genus. Furthermore, there is a multitude of *logoi* which determine various qualities defining a being's essence. Thus an individual being corresponds not only to one *logos* but to a number of *logoi*, some of which also belong to other beings; see Jean-Claude Larchet, *La divinisation de l'homme selon saint Maxime le Confesseur* (Paris, 1996), p. 113, cf. pp. 125–51. Hans Urs von Balthasar, *Kosmische Liturgie. Das Weltbild Maximus' des Bekenners* (2nd edn, Einsiedeln, 1961), pp. 110–31.

powers unceasingly strive for God and come to rest in him as *true knowledge*, *peace* and *love* respectively (*Ep.* 31, PG 91:625A–B).[2]

But although this 'natural desire for God' (*Amb.* 48, PG 91:1364B) is ontologically grounded, postlapsarian human beings need to redirect their perverted desire towards God, so that their way of life corresponds to their natural principle. This process of redirection is mediated by the Incarnation and the Church and concerns a person's mode of existence, which entails volition and choice, leading to a particular comportment. The term *tropos* thus denotes the theologically good or bad use of a human being's natural powers and faculties. It reveals whether someone acts in accordance with or against his or her nature.

There is no dichotomy between nature and grace in St Maximus. Nature is always already shot through with grace and primordially designed to find completion and fulfilment in a perpetual striving and progress toward God (*Thal.* 60, CCSG 22:77, 70).[3] Thus Incarnation and its subsequent 'enacting' response on the part of human beings only alter the *tropos* but not the *logos*. The claim that human beings are endowed with an ontologically grounded desire for God need not exclude the insight that desire is linguistically and culturally mediated. It is precisely the interrelationship between *logos* and *tropos* which allows for a theory of desire that comprises both aspects. On the one hand the acquisition of an appropriate *tropos* – that is, the (re)shaping of human desire – is inconceivable without the mediation of the one *Logos*, Christ, and (linguistic and non-linguistic) creaturely signs whose meanings are derived from and point back towards this *Logos*. As will be shown in this chapter, it is primarily the liturgical symbols that fulfil this function. On the other hand the development of the *tropos* must be seen as the realization of a human being's natural principle (*logos*), which means that the former is not merely culturally conditioned.

1 Archē: Monism – From Nature to Culture

Jacques Lacan postulates a libidinal, prelinguistic unity between the child and the maternal body, which is subsequently disrupted through the intervention of the 'Name-of-the-Father'. The paternally imposed incest taboo is concomitant with the child's entrance into language (*E*, p. 278).[4] That is to say, the involvement of

---

[2]   I shall henceforth use the following abbreviations for the writings of St Maximus: *Ep.*: *Epistulae* I–XLV, ed. F. Combefis, *Patrologia Graeca* (= PG) (Paris, 1865), vol. 91, cols. 364–649; *Amb.*: *Liber ambiguorum,* ibid., cols. 1032A–1417C; *Myst.*: *Mystagogia*, ibid., cols. 357C–718D; *Thal.*: *Quaestiones ad Thalassium*, eds C. Laga and C. Steel, *Corpus Christianorum, Series Graeca* (= CCSG) (Turnhout, 1980, 1990), vols 7 and 22.

[3]   Cf. Von Balthasar, *Kosmische Liturgie*, pp. 121, 598.

[4]   The following abbreviations are used for Jacques Lacan's writings. *E*: *Écrits* (Paris, 1966); *Liv* I: *Le Séminaire. Livre I. Les écrits techniques de Freud* (1953–4), ed. J.-A. Miller (Paris, 1975); *Liv* III: *Le Séminaire. Livre III. Les psychoses* (1955–6), ed. J.-A. Miller (Paris,

the Name-of-the-Father is associated with the institution of the symbolic order; the infant is confronted with the Other[5] as language, as Lacan puts it. Through the symbolic order, the Name-of-the-Father represents a position of authority and the symbolic Law which bars the child's effortless pursuit of pleasure by clinging to the mother and forces it to seek satisfaction through alternative and socially more acceptable channels. Individuation is thus contingent upon the repression of pre-oedipal pleasure, which constitutes the child as a desiring subject. Accordingly, desire can be defined as the 'longing for the return to the origin that, if recoverable, would necessitate the dissolution of the subject itself'.[6] But since the child 'experiences' the object of the mother (for instance her breast) originally not as something separate from itself, it is only constituted *as* an object after it is lost. That is to say, the differentiation between subject and object results from the child's entrance into the symbolic order.

It would be nonsensical to believe that we can know about a presymbolic and prelinguistic realm – the *real* in Lacanian terminology – without relying on interpretive categories which are themselves derived from the symbolic order. However, the real does not just 'temporally' precede the symbolic order but is also that which cannot be (fully) symbolized, that which remains inassimilable, independent of whether the symbolic order is primarily associated with *logos* or *mythos* (cf. *E*, p. 388). Yet on a meta-level the Lacanian real (and its opposition to the symbolic order) is itself part of a *logos* or *mythos*.[7] In an early stage of his career we find a reference to Emile Meyerson (1859–1933), a chemist and philosopher of science, who used the term real in order to stress (against positivism) that Einstein's theory of relativity was to be interpreted in terms of a realist epistemology (*E*, p. 86).[8] Accordingly, at that time the real is considered by Lacan 'an invariant that subsists and resists; it is independent of the self and of consciousness, it is the *being* of all phenomena ...'.[9] Yet the meaning of this term undergoes various modifications throughout his career. Later on, under the

---

1981); *Sem VII: The Seminar. Book VII. The Ethics of Psychoanalysis* (1959–60), trans. D. Porter (London, 1992); *Liv XVII: Le Séminaire. Livre XVII. L'envers de la psychanalyse* (1969–70), ed. J.-A. Miller (Paris, 1991); *Liv XI: Le Séminaire. Livre XI. Les quatre concepts fondamentaux de la psychanalyse* (1964), ed. J.-A. Miller (Paris, 1973).

[5] The 'Other' in Lacan is both another subject as well as the symbolic order that mediates between me and the other subject. Yet the latter meaning is the primary one.

[6] Judith P. Butler, *Subjects of Desire. Hegelian Reflections in Twentieth-Century France* (New York, 1987), p. 187.

[7] About this question see François Roustang, *The Lacanian Delusion*, trans. Greg Sims (Oxford/New York, 1990), p. 89.

[8] Emile Meyerson, *La déduction relativiste* (Paris, 1925), p. 79: '[L]e réel de la théorie relativiste est, très certainement, un absolu ontologique, un véritable être-en-soi, plus absolu es plus ontologique encore que les choses de sens commun et de la physique pré-einsteinienne.'

[9] Roustang, *The Lacanian Delusion*, p. 61. Italics are mine.

influence of Martin Heidegger, being belongs to the symbolic order – and no longer to the real.[10] Furthermore, the real forms part of a *mythos* and does not have the structure of a *logos* anymore.

In a seminar taught in 1973, the real is the key idea in Lacan's 'myth of the lamella'. It stands for pre-sexual, immortal, libidinal life and the myth gives an account of the fall from this immortal state into mortality (*Liv* XI, pp. 220–23). On the one hand the real seems to be an ontogenetic category, yet it also figures as a cosmic principle: it is 'a sort of smooth, seamless surface or space which applies as much to a child's body as to the whole universe'.[11] Due to the many different connotations of this term, it is difficult to pin down its exact meaning.

Lacan's protology can be read as a kind of monism.[12] Difference, contrasting structures and distinguishable entities emerge out of the undifferentiated real but only by annihilating it through symbolization. The real is associated with the One and it is only by negating the One that difference, language and thought become possible, thus creating 'reality' – as opposed to the real (cf. *Liv* XVII, p. 148).

Lacan's monistic protology in some respects echoes the past heresy of Origenism (condemned at the Second Council of Constantinople 553AD), so that (aspects of) the Orthodox critique of the latter also applies to the former. According to St Maximus, the cosmological principle underlying Origenism is *rest* (στάσις) – *movement* (κίνησις) – *becoming* (γένεσις). In the beginning there was a primordial unity (ἑνάς) of rational beings and a state of satiety in which they were all connatural with God (rest). These pre-existing souls fell from their state of perfection which led to a great diversity of rational beings (movement) and were bound to physical bodies of varying material density (becoming).[13] If this principle is applied to Lacan, there is first *rest* since the real is One, that is, without differentiation, and because there is no desire, as all erogenous orifices are fully closed up and satisfied. This state is followed by *movement*, insofar as the instituting of the symbolic order differentiates the real and constitutes the child as a split and desiring subject. The quasi-religious character of this 'fall' from a pre-linguistic realm into language is evident in the aforementioned myth of the lamella.[14] Finally, there is *becoming*: The subject only acquires being and only emerges *as* a subject in the process of

---

[10]   Cf. Dylan Evans, *An Introductory Dictionary of Lacanian Psychoanalysis* (London/ New York, 1996), pp. 58–9, 16–17.

[11]   Bruce Fink, *The Lacanian Subject. Between Language and Jouissance* (Princeton, 1995), p. 24.

[12]   Cf. Connor Cunningham, 'Nothing Is, Something Must Be: Lacan and Creation from No One' in Creston Davis, John Milbank, Slavoj Žižek (eds), *Theology and the Political. The New Debate* (Durham/London, 2005), pp. 72–101.

[13]   See Polycarp Sherwood, *The Earlier Ambigua of Saint Maximus the Confessor and his Refutation of Origenism* (Rome, 1955), pp. 92–102.

[14]   Cf. Maire Jaanus, 'The Démontage of the Drive' in Richard Feldstein, Bruce Fink, Maire Jaanus (eds), *Reading Seminar XI. Lacan's Four Fundamental Concepts of Psychoanalysis* (New York, 1995), pp. 130–36.

symbolization, since being and the symbolic order are closely interconnected. And although the subject somehow already 'exists' in its bodily dimension 'before' it enters the symbolic order, human corporeality in its proper sense only results from the subject's being 'overwritten with signifiers'.

St Maximus replaces the formula *rest – movement – becoming* by the trias *becoming – movement – rest* (*Amb.* 15, PG 91:1216A–21B). According to him, all beings have been created out of nothing according to their *logos*, which denotes the principle of a creature's coming-to-be according to the divine will. Everything created is endowed with being and already participates in God (becoming). Nothing that has come into being is free of passion and no creature is by nature unmoved. Even prelapsarian Adam had a desire for God and possessed the capacity for spiritual pleasure, that is, he was constantly moving towards his divine *telos* (movement).[15] It is only after the Fall that deviant passions occurred. Finally, repose in God must be conceived of as the end state of this process, rather than the starting point (rest).

Yet the Lacanian protology can also be analyzed on the basis of a distinction between nature and culture. From this perspective, the Fall already is a Salvation, which is only misrecognized as a Fall, since what is left behind after the Fall is just 'stupid natural existence' (*E*, p. 277, cf. p. 518).[16] But this is not to say that there is a pregiven, natural desire, which is only subsequently moulded by the symbolic order and the Law. The Law is not just that which regulates desire; it first and foremost *creates* it. Desire is a reactionary force that rebels against the imposition of prohibitions and prescriptions (*E*, p. 787; *Sem* VII, p. 177).

Yet is it is questionable whether the transition from nature to culture, as envisaged by Lacan, can really be achieved. If the Name-of-the-Father is not instated properly and the subject fails to immerse itself into language, it becomes psychotic. If this process is successfully accomplished and the subject exposes itself – by indwelling language – to the Other's desire, it becomes neurotic. Yet Lacan knows of a further development, called *traversing of fantasy*, through which the subject newly positions itself in relation to the Other's desire by increasingly symbolizing it. But although the traversing of fantasy is supposed to overcome neurosis, very little can be said about this further process, for it leads 'into largely unexplored territory'.[17] I shall come back to this issue in the next section.

From a theological perspective, Lacan's view of the origin of desire is based on an immanentist differentiation between nature and culture. It is a differentiation that occurs *within* creation and which excludes the transcendent. For Orthodox

---

[15] For a more detailed discussion of this issue see Paul M. Blowers, 'Gentiles of the Soul: Maximus the Confessor on the Substructure and Transformation of the Human Passions', *Journal of Early Christian Studies*, 4/1 (1996): 57–85.

[16] Slavoj Žižek, *The Puppet and the Dwarf. The Perverse Core of Christianity* (Cambridge/London, 2003), p. 86.

[17] Bruce Fink, *A Clinical Introduction to Lacanian Psychoanalysis. Theory and Technique* (Cambridge/London, 1997), p. 195.

theology, by contrast, desire does not arise from the tension between nature and culture but is grounded *in* nature. It is co-primordial with being created and always already directed towards the divine.[18] Consequently, Christian culture is not opposed to nature but must be viewed as a realization of nature's original directedness and movement towards God (deification) in which human beings are actively involved. What resists the development of 'Christian culture' and the transfiguration of the world is not nature but evil, which St Maximus defines as 'an irrational movement of the natural faculties toward something else than their end …' (*Thal.* Prolog, CCSG, 7:29, 220–31, 223).

The way the Lacanian nature-culture distinction has replaced these fundamental Christian thought-categories can be exemplified by analysing the relationship between *eros* and *logos*, that is, between desire and reason (or language). According to Lacan, even if desire is manifest in and conveyed by speech, it is fundamentally unconscious and opposed to the subject as a conscious, rational and self-determining agent. It only becomes graspable in the fissures and gaps of speech, in that which is implicit rather than explicit in communication. *Eros* and *logos* are irreconcilable, or as Judith Butler puts it, desire is 'the precise moment of consciousness' opacity'.[19] There is an inherent antagonism between consciousness/ speech and desire that can never really be overcome.

In St Maximus, by contrast, in the state of love, the human powers, the rational, irascible, and concupiscible, are gathered (συναγωγή) and unified (ἕνωσις) in relation to their divine end (*Thal.* 49, CCSG 7: 353, 58–61).[20] This is not to uncritically maintain the Platonic, tripartite distinction of human faculties adopted and modified by the Church fathers. What solely matters here is that St Maximus' approach is based on the theologically fundamental distinction between creation and (its movement towards the) Creator and not on the immanentist differentiation between nature-culture, desire-reason, and real-symbolic (order). Christian theology knows of a more fundamental and genuinely theological distinction: Jean-Claude Larchet introduces the term *theophile unconscious* (*l'inconscient théophile*), which denotes a person's natural principle insofar as it is repressed because his or her mode of existence does not correspond to it.[21] The theophile unconscious is thus not a term for unconscious desire as opposed to conscious reason, but comprises all human powers insofar as they are not actualized in accordance with their natural principle.

---

[18]   The question of the origin of the passions in St Maximus is in fact much more complex; see Blowers, 'Gentiles of the Soul: Maximus the Confessor on the Substructure and Transformation of the Human Passions'.

[19]   Butler, *Subjects of Desire*, p. 186.

[20]   Cf. *Ep.* 2, *PG* 91:397A–B.

[21]   Jean-Claude Larchet, *L'inconscient spirituel* (Paris, 2005), pp. 111–38.

2 Mesotēs: The Mediation of Desire

2.1 Lacan's Antagonisms

Lacan's famous dictum that 'man's desire is the desire of the Other' (*le désir de l'homme est le désir de l'autre*), which has multiple meanings, leads directly to the question of how desire is interpersonally mediated (*Liv* I, p. 276). On the one hand this formula can be interpreted in the sense that the object of the child's desire is the (m)Other. On the other hand it can be taken to mean that the child's desire is to be desired by the (m)Other; to be her object of desire. But desire can also take on a mimetic and mediating function: the subject comes to desire from the viewpoint of another, that is, it desires a particular object not for its intrinsic value, which it might not be able to recognize, but because the Other desires it. That is to say, the desire of another person is converted into the subject's own desire (*E*, pp. 814–15). Finally, Lacan's dictum can be interpreted in terms of desire's insatiability. Unlike instinct, desire cannot be quenched by any specifiable object but rather moves from one object to the next: it is always '*desire for something else*' (*E*, p. 518).

Lacan rejects any atomistic view of the self and emphasizes that human beings are always already exposed to and influenced by the Other's desire. Yet despite 'the absolute ontological necessity of the Other for the making of the human subject, the relation with the Other does not cease being traumatic, difficult and dangerous …'.[22] According to Orthodox theology, however, interpersonal communion is considered a 'primary ontology', as something that corresponds to a human being's nature, even if under the conditions of the Fall, it can only be realized through the cross and asceticism. But let me first spell out the antagonistic character of interpersonality in Lacan.

The mother's desire for the child as well as the child's incestuous desire for the mother constitute a threat to the infant, since it stands in danger of becoming a mere extension of its mother, resulting in psychosis (cf. *Liv* III; *E*, pp. 531–83). Triangulation is achieved through the intervention of the Name-of-the-Father, which breaks up the mother-child unity by establishing the symbolic order and the Law. If this process is successfully accomplished, the infant comes to inhabit language, which enables it to bar the mother and to emerge as a separate subject. By indwelling language, the child is confronted with the Other's desire, which acts as the subject's object cause of desire (*objet petit a*). In the state of neurosis, the subject is entirely subjugated to the Other's desire.

In what follows, I shall first reflect on this 'violent' subjugation to the Other, which leads to neurosis (2.1.1). It has a different character, depending on whether the Other is primarily experienced as an impersonal Law (symbolic order), or as another subject. Secondly, I shall turn to the process of distantiation

---

[22] Nikolaos Loudovikos, *Psychoanalysis and Orthodox Theology. On Desire, Catholicity and Eschatology* (Athens, 2003), p. 107 (in Greek).

(*traversing of fantasy*) following this subjugation, which is part of the process of subjectification. It is equally 'violent', even if it takes on a different form in different phases of Lacan's work (2.1.2).

2.1.1 Subjugation to the Other   The idea of an aggressive subjugation of the self to the Other (as Law or symbolic order) reveals the correspondence between Nietzsche and Freudian/Lacanian psychoanalysis.[23] Nietzsche interprets man's forcible sundering from his animal past in terms of an internalization of instincts which cannot discharge themselves outwardly. Through the institution of the Law, a primordial aggression, which is innate to human beings and life itself, is turned inwards and precipitates an 'inner world': the soul, that is, bad conscious and reflexivity.[24] According to Lacan, the subject has to choose between some sort of primordial jouissance or language – but cannot have both. It is as if the subject were challenged by a robber: Your money or your life! If it chooses the money, it shall lose both its life and the money, if it chooses life, it shall be deprived of its money, but save its life (*Liv* XI, pp. 233–8; *Sem* VII, p. 43). Nietzsche similarly points out that the change from nature to culture and the emergence of the bad conscience was not a gradual or voluntary process, not 'an organic adaptation to new conditions but a break (*Bruch*), a leap (*Sprung*), a compulsion (*Zwang*), an ineluctable disaster ...'.[25] In striking parallel to Lacan, Nietzsche writes that human beings were faced with a forced choice: like sea animals that were compelled to either become land animals or perish – tertium non datur.[26] The instinct for freedom (the will to power) turned inward did not cease to make its usual demand but was rather forcibly made latent, inhibited and repressed. According to Lacan, neurosis is precisely defined in terms of repression and the return of the repressed in various symptoms.

Now the Lacanian neurotic to some extent accepts that he has no choice but to give up primordial *jouissance* and to internalize the Law unconditionally. But he adopts a resentful stance towards this loss and aims at receiving compensation for his sacrifice. This compensation the neurotic believes to find in object *a* – the remainder and reminder of his lost satisfaction. Prohibition eroticizes the pleasure the subject is forced to forego in the sense that its desire to commit a particular act is intensified. For this reason Lacan equates repressed desire with the Law (*E*, p. 782). In the words of St Paul, the Law causes its own transgression (cf. Rom 5:20; 7:5). It is particularly the unspecified Law that does not impose determinate prohibitions and injunctions, which triggers this destructive mechanism. It is the opacity and abstractness of the superego prohibition, devoid of any concrete

---

[23]   Cf. Ernest Jones, *Sigmund Freud. Life and Work* (3 vols, London, 1953–7), vol. 3, pp. 306–7.

[24]   Friedrich Nietzsche, *Zur Genealogie der Moral*. Kritische Studienausgabe, eds G. Colli und M. Montinari (2nd edn, 15 vols, Berlin, 1988), vol. 5, pp. 312, 321–4.

[25]   Ibid., p. 324; my translation.

[26]   Ibid., p. 322.

content, which generates a feeling of unbearable, infinite guilt. And this infinite guilt gives then rise to transgression.[27]

On an interpersonal level, the violent subjugation to the Other can be grasped in terms of the neurotic's fixation on the Other's desire.[28] That is to say the Other's desire acts as the subject's object cause of desire (*objet petit a*) and thus evokes as well as shapes the subject's desire. Even if the subject makes every possible effort to do exactly the opposite of that which it thinks the Other wants it to do, it remains entirely dependent on the Other. Lacan's dictum that 'man's desire is the desire of the Other' here means that the neurotic desires that object which the Other desires in order to be desired himself by the Other. Due to the subject's compulsive striving to adopt the Other's ego-ideal, it is unable to cope with the vague and enigmatic character of the Other's desire, that is, with the Other's own lack, and thus tries to convert it into *demand* (*E*, p. 823). The neurotic's constant 'demand to be demanded' is thus an attempt to overcome the anxiety-inducing intransparency of the Other's desire. The subject wishes to fulfil specific, clearly delineated wants, for it believes that only thus can the Other's attitude of approval towards itself be sustained.

2.1.2 Distantiation from the Other   Through the *traversing of fantasy* the subject repositions itself with respect to the Other as desire (*objet petit a*) in terms of a separation. In an early stage of his work Lacan conceived the way beyond neurosis as the development of the subject's own desire, which he regarded as opposed to that of the Other.[29] The analysand is advised 'not to cede on his desire', but to develop a decided and determined desire (*Sem* VII, p. 319). The subject only emerges as a subject if it manages to free itself from the weight of the Other; if it succeeds in holding at bay the latter's violent imposition. This view implies that the desire of the subject and the desire of the Other are intrinsically irreconcilable. Between the two, no harmony can be established. And because the subject is exposed to the Other's desire via language, it can only overcome neurosis and find access to 'its own desire' if it manages to separate itself (temporarily) from discourse. However, the freedom the subject gains vis-à-vis the Other through the

---

[27]   See Jacques Lacan, *Kant with Sade* (*E*, pp. 765–90). 'The decisive question is: is the Kantian moral Law translatable into the Freudian notion of the superego or not? If the answer is yes, then 'Kant with Sade' effectively means that Sade is the truth of Kantian ethics.' Slavoj Žižek, 'Kant with (or against) Sade', eds Elizabeth Wright and Edmond Wright, *The Žižek Reader* (Malden, MA/Oxford, 1999), p. 296.

[28]   It goes without saying that the relationship between subject and the Other (as another subject) is always mediated by the Other (as symbolic order and Law).

[29]   See Fink, *A Clinical Introduction to Lacanian Psychoanalysis*, pp. 205–7.

traversing of fantasy should not be confused with the freedom of the psychotic, which is a freedom 'before the letter'.[30]

At a later stage of his work, however, Lacan comes to the conclusion that desire is parasitic upon the Law and the Other who institutes it in the sense that desire merely seeks to realize that which the Law prohibits – as outlined above. Because there is no such thing as the subject's 'own' desire that would lead away from or beyond that of the Other, it is the subject's satisfaction that now takes centre stage.[31] The subject is no longer subjugated to the Other's demand or desire, but finds satisfaction in the partial object, 'object *a*', which 'belongs' to the Other. For the subject, 'object *a*' comes to represent the real and gives satisfaction because it fills the gap opened up by the primordial split. Whereas desire serves as a defence *against* satisfaction, it is the subject as *id* or as *drive*, which is now able to *find* satisfaction in 'object *a*' (see *Liv* XI, p. 304). 'Desire learns how to keep its mouth shut and let enjoyment prevail.'[32] However, this kind of satisfaction, based on 'object *a*', does neither have the character of a mimetic desire nor that of a *symphonia* between two different desires, since 'object *a*' needs to be detached from the Other in order to serve as the object of satisfaction for the subject. For it is precisely the Other's desire (or demand) which inhibits the subject's enjoyment. There is no room for alterity since the subject experiences *jouissance* by focusing on an isolated aspect of the Other; a partial object in Lacan's terminology.

Thus in both cases discussed in 2.1.2 the relationship between the subject and the Other remains antagonistic. If one follows Bruce Fink's interpretation of Lacan, it is difficult to see how far subjectification, relationality and interaction are mutually intertwined in the sense that the Other enables the subject's self-discovery and self-development. What remains unclear is in what way the 'freedom after the letter' differs from the 'freedom before the letter'.[33]

2.2 The Christian Other

In what follows I shall first reflect on the Christian 'Other' as divine Law (2.2.1) and then turn to the experience of the Other as 'another subject' (2.2.2).

---

[30]   Fink, *The Lacanian Subject*, p. 66.

[31]   Fink, *A Clinical Introduction to Lacanian Psychoanalysis*, pp. 207–17.

[32]   Ibid., p. 211. The difference between desire and drive is discussed in *E*, pp. 851–4 and Jacques-Alain Miller, 'Commentary on Lacan's Text' in eds Richard Feldenstein, Bruce Fink, Maire Jaanus, Reading Seminars I and II. *Lacan's Return to Freud*. Seminar I: *Freud's Papers on Technique*. Seminar II: *The Ego in Freud's Theory and in the Technique of Psychoanalysis* (Albany, 1996), pp. 422–7.

[33]   Although Lacan heavily draws on Hegel, he rejects the latter's *Aufhebung*. Eros and *logos* remain opposed to each other and the subject's alienation, caused the subjugation to the Other, is not followed by a reconstitution; see Butler, *Subjects of Desire*, pp. 186–92; Richard Boothby, *Death and Desire. Psychoanalytic Theory in Lacan's Return to Freud* (New York/London, 1991), p. 215.

2.2.1 The Other as divine Law From a Christian perspective, the relationship between the subject and the Other has a different character. Yet it is possible to return to the Lacanian school in order to overcome the problems outlined above. Žižek, elaborating on Lacan's thought, raises the question of whether there is love beyond the Law. In what way does the subject have to relate to the Law so as to avoid that the Law generates its own transgression? As long as the Law is experienced as something foreign and external, which imposes itself on the subject, erotization of prohibition and its concomitant, transgression, remain inevitable. Sin can be defined in terms of the subject's conviction that deep within itself, there is something which makes it infinitely lovable and which cannot be submitted to the Law. What leads beyond the Law to love is the renunciation of this attachment to a personality core that remains untouched by legal obligations, that is, the 'stance of total immersion in the Law'.[34] Neurosis is overcome if the subject's love for the divine Other is so unconditional that it relinquishes any wish for compensatory pleasure; if the fulfilment of the Law is itself the highest goal of its desire (cf. *Myst.* 24, PG 91:712A).

Within the liturgical world of the Orthodox tradition it is Matins of Holy Saturday which best expresses this truth. This service consists of a Christological interpretation of Ps 119, which praises the love for the Law of God and views Christ's death on the cross as the ultimate proof of his love for the divine will and as an act of pure obedience.[35] This is not at all to accept a disinterested sacrificial self-offering unto death, without expectation of a benefit in return, as the highest ethical ideal.[36] Such a view is excluded right from the beginning since Christ's assumption of fallen human nature and death in order to redeem us is inconceivable without his own victory over death in resurrection. Whereas the desperate yearning for compensatory pleasure and transgression caused by the superego injunction is a hindrance to the fulfilment of the divine will, hope for resurrection is itself an act of obedience (cf. Jn 10:17–18). What is at stake here is not the idea of a 'pure' unilateral gift, but the complete surrender to the divine will, which is only possible because of the certainty that thus alone real life can be (re)gained. Christ's sacrifice unto death cannot be separated from the conviction that by descending into Hades, sin, corruptibility and mortality are overcome.

The only way for us to accept the challenge of the Law, and to fulfil it – without unleashing a fatal counter-reaction – is to participate in the liturgically enacted (self-)sacrifice of Christ, which culminates in the Eucharist. Commenting on the first entrance[37] of the Divine Liturgy, which he associates with the Lord's

---

[34] Žižek, *The Puppet and the Dwarf*, 116–17.

[35] Alexander Schmemann, 'This is the Blessed Sabbath' in *Matins of Holy Saturday. With the Praises and Psalm 119* (New York, 1982), pp. 3–15.

[36] John Milbank, 'The Ethics of Self-Sacrifice', *First Things* 91/1 (1999): 33–8.

[37] At the time of St Maximus, the first or small entrance constituted the beginning of the Divine Liturgy and consisted of the bishop's entry into the Church. In Constantinople, Patriarch and Emperor entered the Church together, followed by the people; see Hugh

Incarnation, St Maximus points out that our destructive passions are healed by the live-giving Passion of Christ (*Myst.* 8, PG 91:688C–D). It is the beauty of the liturgy which evokes our desire to appropriate the salvific divine will as expressed in the life of Christ. Yet such an active involvement in the liturgical rites was not self-evident in pagan antiquity. For the Neoplatonist Iamblichus, for instance, the theurgic rites are self-efficacious and do not need to be interpreted by the participants. According to Pseudo-Dionysius, however, the Christian sacraments only have an anagogical, that is, 'uplifting' effect if they are actively interpreted and understood.[38] The endeavour to grasp the meaning of the liturgical symbols is an exercise for our desire and in the act of understanding we are drawn towards the divine mysteries.

It is thus the liturgical symbol which allows for an active appropriation of the divine 'Law' and which prevents the unleashing of destructive and reactionary human forces that oppose the divine will. The theological basis of this 'polysemy' is God's condescension in Jesus Christ, who takes upon himself our sufferings 'in proportion (κατὰ τὴν ἀναλογίαν) to each one's suffering ...' (*Myst.* 24, PG 91:713B). This allows for an analogical *appropriation* as well. On the diachronic level, the various interpretations which the different parts of the liturgy gave rise to in the history of the Church are well-documented.[39] On the synchronic level, St Maximus repeatedly points out that the understanding of the liturgical symbols and the transformation they bring about takes place in proportion (ἀναλόγως) to the capacity of the participants of the rite (*Myst.* 10, PG 91:689B–C; 24, PG 91:704A).[40]

However, it is important to keep in mind that Maximus' symbol is not that of the modern, secularized aesthetic experience in which the range of possible meanings is viewed as merely contextually and culturally conditioned.[41] Rather, the multiple meanings of the symbol fulfil a mystagogical function. Under the conditions of the Fall, God is no longer recognized as the centre and ultimate *telos* of all creation, so that creation has lost its original, unconfused unity. Through liturgy, the diachronically and synchronically fragmented creation is led (back) to the one truth of Christ. The relationship between the symbol and that which it

---

Wybrew, *The Orthodox Liturgy. The Development of the Eucharistic Liturgy in the Byzantine Rite* (Crestwood, NY, 1996), p. 76.

[38]   Andrew Louth, 'Pagan Theurgy and Christian Sacramentalism in Denys the Areopagite', *Journal of Theological Studies*, 37/2 (1986): 432–8; Paul Rorem, *Biblical and liturgical symbols within the Pseudo-Dionysian synthesis* (Toronto, 1984), pp. 99–116.

[39]   Wybrew, *The Orthodox Liturgy*, pp. 182–3.

[40]   On the 'special' level (as opposed to the 'general' level), each liturgical symbol (σύμβολον) has three different meanings, which correspond to the participants' different degrees of initiation. They are either believers, *praktikoi* or *gnostikoi*; see René Bornert, *Les commentaires byzantins de la divine liturgie du VIIe au XVe siècle* (Paris, 1966), pp. 121–3.

[41]   See Umberto Eco, *Semiotics and the Philosophy of Language* (Bloomington/ Indianapolis, 1984), pp. 162–3.

signifies is 'epiphanic', as the reality which it renders accessible is itself present in the symbol.[42] Consequently, semiotics and ontology are inextricably intertwined. To 'interpret' and 'understand' a liturgical symbol is not just a hermeneutic and cognitive activity. Rather, it enables the believer to *participate* in the divine mysteries, that is, in the salvific events of Christ's life, death and resurrection.

On the one hand, liturgy allows for an analogical appropriation of the divine Law which avoids any 'forced choice' and which cannot be grasped in terms of a break, leap or compulsion. Since there is no dichotomy between nature and grace, Christian culture is not opposed to nature, but the unfolding and actualization of the 'natural principle'. There is always already an *Anknüpfungspunkt* for human desire to be lured (back) to its divine *telos* and the addressee of the divine call is always already in a position to respond. It is 'the analogy between *grace* and *art*'[43] that pinpoints the nature of this divine-human synergy. Through the spiritual beauty of the Divine Liturgy God offers us challenging yet non-intrusive and life-enriching new possibilities, which must be freely grasped and actualized. In the words of St Maximus: the divine chants effect 'free consent (ἐκούσιον συγκατάθεσιν) of the soul to virtues' (*Myst.* 24, PG 91:704B).

Although the Divine Liturgy culminates in the Eucharist, there are no emotional or intellectual 'peaks', where we receive spiritual stimulation without being actively involved ourselves. Nor do we get instructions which we can follow blindly. Thus the neurotic's desperate demand 'to be demanded', to receive detailed directions as regards thinking and acting is not answered. Obedience to the divine will does not mean the mere carrying out of orders in analogy to human orders.[44] Rather, deification is to be conceived in terms of a radical transformation of the participant's desire, although the 'autonomy' and 'independence' we gain is – paradoxically – at once an ever greater dependence on God.[45] As long as the divine will remains something external and is experienced as imposed on us from outside, we are not yet Christians. As Lacan has shown, the neurotic's inability to cope with indeterminacy and his constant need for utterly unambiguous commands

---

[42]   See Bornert, *Les commentaires byzantins de la divine liturgie du VIIᵉ au XVᵉ siècle*, 113–14.

[43]   John Milbank, *The Suspended Middle. Henri de Lubac and the Debate concerning the Supernatural* (Grand Rapids/Cambridge, 2005), p. 53.

[44]   This is not to deny the importance of obedience as a spiritual discipline. But as Sergius Bulgakov points out, 'obedience is valuable only insofar as it is an act and a function of *freedom*. It is freely accepted and inwardly determined by freedom', Sergius Bulgakov, *The Comforter*, trans. Boris Jakim (Grand Rapids, MA/ Cambridge, 2004), p. 311.

[45]   On the basis of the above exposition of the relationship between the 'natural principle' and the 'mode of existence', it is clear that divinization does not mean *de*-humanization. Rather, as Grillmeier puts it: '*Je mehr der Mensch Gott geeint wird, desto mehr wird er selber Mensch*', Alois Grillmeier 'Die Wirkung des Heilshandelns Gottes in Christus' in eds Johannes Feiner and Magnus Löhrer, *Mysterium Salutis: Das Christusereignis* (5 vols, Einsiedeln/Zürich/Köln, 1969), vol. III/2, p. 382.

is closely linked up with his deep-seated reluctance to give up his primordial *jouissance*, to really follow the instructions unreservedly he so desperately asks for. In other words, there is a paradoxical relationship between his wish to follow concrete commands and his rebellion against such commands.

On the other hand, the objectivity of the Divine Liturgy needs to be emphasized. Liturgy does not allow for arbitrariness and amorphous participation and the encounter with the divine Other is experienced as being face-to-face with a reality that is completely and utterly uncompromising. Consequently, the appropriation of liturgy can be intersubjectively controlled insofar as continual participation in the liturgical rites initiates the believer into a Christian 'way of life'. The beauty of the liturgy transcends the dichotomy between indicative and imperative, for that which is freely and unconditionally given can nonetheless only be known and understood if it is actively received; if it is enacted (cf. *Thal.* 29, CCSG 7:211, 15–21). Thus liturgy always already points beyond itself towards the Church's mission in the world, to certain actions and deeds. Yet, as outlined above, the relationship between the divine will and human obedience should not be thought of in terms of carrying out individual orders which are presented to the recipient in the form of speech-acts.[46] According to St Maximus' understanding of deification, the 'mode of existence' is brought into conformity with the 'natural principle' by acquiring a particular *habitus* or *hexis* (ἕξις) – a stable disposition of our will.[47] The *habitus/hexis* denotes the *telos* of the human 'faculty of judging' (γνώμη) and deification takes place according to this faculty (κατὰ γνώμην) but through the habitus (ἕξει) (*Myst.* 24, PG 91:712A). We are here concerned with the middle phase of the trias *becoming – movement – rest*, with the ethical domain, where a particular person determines the 'how' (πῶς) of his or her natural movement (κίνησις) in cooperation with divine grace. Yet this process also reveals that in Maximus human freedom and deliberation are inextricably intertwined with the sheer givenness of human nature, since the meaning of *tropos* remains unclear without its correlate, the *logos*. The acquisition of a particular *habitus* and of particular virtues is dependent on the choices made by a human being using his or her faculty of judging. Insofar as every person is able to use this faculty appropriately or inappropriately, to adopt a good or bad *habitus*, both *gnomē* and *hexis* are associated with the *tropos*. Insofar as the term *hexis* is taken as the divine *telos* of *gnomē*, as that which qualifies the human faculty of judging theologically (and thus enables the believer to act in a Christian way), it belongs to the *logos*.

In spite of the importance of a free appropriation of the spiritual contents of the Divine Liturgy, the liturgical experience is objective and leads to the acquisition of specific and intersubjectively controllable habits, dispositions and virtues, which determine the participant's individual actions and deeds. Soteriological,

---

[46]   Cf. Nicholas Wolterstorff, *Divine Discourse: philosophical reflections on the claim that God speaks* (Cambridge, 1995).

[47]   Philipp Gabriel Renczes, *Agir de Dieu et liberté de l'homme. Recherches sur l'anthropologie théologique de saint Maxime le Confesseur* (Paris, 2003), pp. 267–372.

aesthetical, ontological and ethical aspects form a comprehensive whole (*Myst.* 24, PG 91:712A–13B). There is thus no unspecified Law, no opaque and abstract superego prohibition, which generates a feeling of equally abstract guilt, but fails to provide positive, life-giving orientation. For the semi-conscious conviction that I am literally answerable for everything and everybody, without knowing what concrete steps I could possibly take to do justice to this responsibility, can only elicit a feeling of infinite guilt, which will inevitably breed rebellion and transgression. As opposed to such destructive generality and indeterminacy, *gnomē* formed by a divine *hexis* mediates between the general and the specific.

2.2.2 The Other as another subject   On the interpersonal level, too, where the Other is experienced as another subject, Christian theology opens up new possibilities and allows for proper mimetic desire and love. Divine love, sacramentally embodied by a human (for instance parental) Other, as well as its reception, need be thought of in a way that overcomes the aforementioned impasses. In Lacan, there is an inherent antagonism insofar as his idea of intersubjectivity oscillates between a complete subjugation of the subject to the Other and an equally radical distantiation. Christian love, by contrast, does not know such an antagonism. Misdirected desire can be mimetically lured back to God by the desire of a virtuous Other (cf. *Amb.* 8, PG 91:1104C–105A). This presupposes that the redeemed human love of the Other can catalytically bring the subject's *tropos* into conformity with its *logos* – without constituting a threat. In what follows the emphasis will be placed on the mimetic character of desire and love rather than on reciprocity. Yet these two aspects need not be viewed as mutually exclusive.

The nature of Christian love transcends the dichotomy between sheer demand, requiring unquestioning obedience, and unconditional acceptance of all behaviour.[48] In the former case, the Other violates the subject's freedom and dignity and prevents it from establishing a relationship of mimetic desire through which the subject's very core of personality can be transformed (its *tropos*, but not its *logos*). In the latter case, the Other's attitude toward the subject is devoid of dynamism and directedness. It only manifests the Other's nihilistic and self-centred sentimentality, for the subject is narcissistically reduced to an extension of the Other. Human love, however, which participates in the Triune life, is inspired by an infinite source of divine creativity. It bears a sacramental character insofar as the loved one could not become what he or she should become without being loved in precisely such a way. That is to say, the loving Other unceasingly plays highly specific and highly personalized possibilities in the subject's way, which, if they are actively received and actualized, contribute to its flourishing and

---

[48]   Cf. Elder Porphyrios, *Wounded by Love. The Life and the Wisdom of Elder Porphyrios* (Limni, 2005), pp. 195–211.

spiritual well-being.[49] Love is directed and challenging insofar as the sequence of possibilities which the subject is presented with is governed by a divine *telos*; love is unconditional in the sense that even if the subject fails to respond, the Other perseveres in his or her attempt to lure the loved one into an eschatologically new existence, 'from glory to glory'.

The 'reception' of love, too, needs to be reconsidered. Neurosis consists in an obsession to completely and unquestioningly adopt the Other's ego-ideal, so that even the slightest ambiguity concerning the Other's desire causes confusion and stress. The neurotic thus desperately needs a despot deity which imposes his iron will on him. However, divine grace and love is not of this kind and can only be actively and creatively received. Thus the neurotic has to learn that the reception of divine love, mediated by a human Other, does not exclude but rather requires an act of self-making and self-crafting. The self is not sovereign and autonomous in the sense that it remains insusceptible to alterity and external forces; nor is it unilaterally and deterministically influenced by the Other.[50]

Subjectification should thus neither be viewed in terms of a violent subjugation to the Other nor as a development towards a solipsistic 'desirousness' that overcomes this radical subjugation. Rather, the subject's distantiation from the (parental) Other is inconceivable without the mediation of other mimetic models, so that the subject's desire is always determined by autonomy *and* heteronomy. Subjectification and mimetic desire thus remain inextricably intertwined.

3 The Uncreated Divine Energies and the Other

Independent of whether the divine Other is experienced in the liturgy or mediated by another person, it is the doctrine of the uncreated divine energies which constitutes the ontological basis of these encounters in the Eastern tradition. Yet it is important to notice that this doctrine in no way undermines or replaces the dogmas of Nicaea and Chalcedon, as is sometimes argued. Rather, it should be viewed as a development and refinement of Christology and Trinitarian theology, which tries to do justice to the specifically Christian understanding of relationality. There is neither space here to enter the ongoing debate about the historical, theological and philosophical problems associated with this doctrine, nor to give an account of its ecumenical significance.[51] The divine energies (ἐνέργειαι) are on the one hand acts

---

[49]   Cf. Ingolf U. Dalferth, *Becoming Present. An Inquiry into the Christian Sense of the Presence of God* (Leuven/Paris/Dudley, MA, 2006), pp. 82–3, 170–71. Dalferth restricts his considerations to divine love and does not discuss here the question of how divine love is mediated by human beings.

[50]   Calvin O. Schrag, *The Self after Postmodernity* (New Haven/London, 1997), p. 59.

[51]   For the significance of this doctrine in St Maximus see Vasilios Karayiannis, *Maxime Le Confesseur. Essence et Énergies de Dieu* (Paris, 1993); Renczes, *Agir de Dieu et liberté de l'homme*. For more general discussions see David Bradshaw, *Aristotle East and West*.

of *self-manifestation*, that is, acts of God's inner personal being (οὐσία), and on the other hand something that can be *shared* by created human beings.[52] Regarding the questions discussed in this chapter, two interrelated aspects of this doctrine are of particular relevance.

First, the doctrine of the divine energies plays a key role with respect to the ideas of analogy and participation, for it explains how the one simple God can be fully present in the wide variety of different creatures. Secondly, it is related to the idea of synergy and elucidates how we are to think of divine-human cooperation. Let me discuss these two issues in turn.

According to St Maximus, every creature – in being created – participates in God proportionally (ἀναλόγως) and is endowed with 'being' (*Amb.* 7, PG 91:1080B). However, God does not only infinitely transcend the participating beings (τὰ ὄντα μετέχοντα), that is, created beings, but also the participated beings (τὰ ὄντα μεθεκτά). Both types of beings are 'works of God', but the latter are uncreated, that is, they have no beginning in time. We can only participate in the 'things around God', as St Maximus also calls the participated beings;[53] in the divine energies/ activities, which must be distinguished from God's essence. With respect to the essence and unity of God, the divine energy is one. For God's power and action can only be one, even if he exits in three hypostases.[54] Regarding the world, the divine energy allows for divine presence to embrace creation in its spatio-temporal contingency; there is room for a multiplicity of coexistence (alterity) as well as for a multiplicity of succession (change, movement). Analogy means that the one God is present in different ways, first to different created beings, and secondly to the same created being in different states – although he is always present as a whole.

As far as movement and change is concerned, the divine energies actualize the potential residing in human beings and accomplish their divine *telos*.[55] They bring their *tropos* into conformity with their *logos*. This process has a synergistic character, for it can only take place with active human cooperation. A person receives the divine energies in proportion to (κατὰ τὴν ἀναλογίαν) his or her measure of faith and disposition of the soul (*Thal.* 29, CCSG 7:211, 15–21).

Metaphysics and the Division of Christendom (Cambridge, 2004); Anna N. Williams, *The Ground of Union: Deification in Aquinas and Palamas* (Oxford, 1999); Reinhard Flogaus, *Theosis bei Palamas und Luther. Ein Beitrag zum ökumenischen Gespräch* (Göttingen 1997); Dorothea Wendebourg, *Geist oder Energie. Zur Frage der innergöttlichen Verankerung des christlichen Lebens in der byzantinischen Theologie* (München, 1980).

[52] See the recent discussion by Bradshaw, *Aristotle East and West. Metaphysics and the Division of Christendom*, p. 266.

[53] *Chapters on Theology and Economy* I, 48–9 (PG 90:1100C–1101A).

[54] Cf. ibid., II, 1 (PG 90: 1125C); cf. Gregory of Nazianzus, *Theological Oration* 5, 14 (PG 36:149A).

[55] Renczes, *Agir de Dieu et liberté de l'homme*, pp. 139–42; see *Thal.* 2 (CCSG 7:51): God not only preserves creatures in their existence but also effects (κατ' ἐνέργειαν) their formation, progress and sustenance.

Through asceticism – understood positively as the Christologically, ecclesially and sacramentally mediated reorientation of a human being's powers towards God – 'being' (εἶναι) can be qualified as 'well-being' (εὖ εἶναι), and finally as 'eternal being' (ἀεὶ εἶναι).

In accordance with the above distinction, it is possible to differentiate between two different kinds of human receptivity or fitness. First, there is a creature's preordained 'essential fitness' (ἡ οὐσιώδης ἐπιτηδειότης), which delineates its capacity of receiving divine energy limited by its *logos* of being. Secondly, a creature possesses a 'habitual fitness' (ἡ ἑκτικὴ ἐπιτηδειότης). If a creature moves towards God according to its divine design, it becomes fit to receive the divine energy to a yet higher degree according to the *logoi* of 'well-being' and 'eternal well-being' (*Amb.* 7, PG 91:1080B–C).[56]

Synergism between God and man (on the level of 'well-being' and 'eternal well-being') is possible because of the ontological difference between Creator and creation. There is no dichotomy between divine action and human passivity and the reception of the divine energies does not destroy human self-determination. As Philipp Renczes has shown, it is the divine energies that *enable* the believer to shape his gnomic will (γνώμη) and to acquire a particular *habitus* (ἕξις).[57] In St Maximus' own words: 'As much as God is humanized to man through love for mankind, so much is man able to deify himself [ἑαυτὸν] to God through love' (*Amb.* 10, PG 91: 1113B).

To sum up: the idea of the divine energies allows for analogy and synergism and is thus one of the central doctrines regarding the question of otherness and alterity. It underlies St Maximus' hermeneutics of the liturgical symbol and is also indispensable for interpersonal love and mimetic desire. These considerations lead back to the 'phenomenological' level.

As regards the ideal of non-coercive but directive love outlined above, there is a close interrelationship between the doctrine of the divine energies and the charisma and beauty of the Christian saint. As Pavel Florensky points out, the saintly ascetic possess spiritual beauty, 'the blinding beauty of a radiant, light-bearing person …'.[58] He explains that 'to love visible creatures is to allow the received Divine energy to reveal itself – through the receiver, outside and around the receiver – in the same way that it acts in the Trihypostatic Divinity itself. *It is to allow this energy to go over to another, to a brother.*'[59] This is well exemplified by the following account:

---

[56] See Torstein Tollefsen, 'Did Maximus the Confessor have a Concept of Participation?', *Studia Patristica*, 37 (2001): 618–25, especially p. 623.

[57] Renczes, *Agir de Dieu et liberté de l'homme*, pp. 267–313; see also Lars Thunberg, 'Spirit, Grace and Human Receptivity in St. Maximus', *Studia Patristica*, 37 (2001): 605–17.

[58] Pavel Florensky, *The Pillar and Ground of the Truth. An Essay in Orthodox Theodicy in Twelfe Letters*, trans. B. Jakim, intro. R.F. Gustafson (Princeton/Oxford, 2004), p. 72. Italics are mine.

[59] Ibid., 62.

After a short time he [Old Dimas] fell into ecstasy. I cannot, I simply cannot describe to you his behaviour before God – motions of love and worship, motions of divine craving, of divine love and devotion ... He was bathed in grace. He shone in the light. That was it! Immediately his prayer was communicated to me. Immediately I entered into the atmosphere surrounding him ... He transmitted the grace of God to me. *The grace that that saint possessed radiated into my soul also.*[60]

As regards the encounter with the Other as divine Law, the divine energies are primarily experienced within the liturgical and sacramental life of the Church.[61] According to St Maximus, the invocation of the Lord's Prayer is a symbol for our subsistent (ἐνυπόστατος) and real adoption by the Father as his sons (υἱοθεσία) in and through Jesus Christ, which is effected by the grace of the Holy Spirit. Through worthy reception of the Eucharist we become gods by grace (*Myst.* 20–21, PG 91:696C–697A).

Filial adoption becomes manifest in the believers in a variety of different charismas, all of which are gifts of the one Holy Spirit. In order to explain this phenomenon, St Maximus resorts to the doctrine of the divine energies. The idea that different divine activities correspond to different charismas can already be found in St Paul: 'Now there are varieties of gifts (χαρισμάτων), but the same Spirit ... and there are varieties of activities (ἐνεργημάτων), but it is the same God who activates all of them in everyone' (1Cor 12:4–6). According to St Maximus' reading of this passage, the Holy Spirit is *fully* present in each energy (and thus in each charisma) – in an analogical way (*Thal.* 29, CCSG 7:211, 9–12). Accordingly, every believer posseses the *full* grace of Christ, although in a specific way, according to the measure of his or her faith. Furthermore, God *entirely* indwells them, that is, no part of them remains empty of his presence. This means that all human powers, the rational, irascible and concupisciple are transformed by divine grace.

---

[60] Porphyrios, *Wounded by Love*, 28. Italics are mine.
[61] Karayiannis, *Maxime Le Confesseur. Essence et Énergies de Dieu*, pp. 447–60.

Index

Adam-Kadmon, 49, 79, 82
Albert the Great, St, 196, 196n33
Alfred the Great, King, 112
Alvarez, Didacus, xiii
Ambrosius, 144
analogy, 54, 134, 144, 287–8
    of being, 115
anaphora, 222–4, 229–30, 234–5
Andia, Ysabel de, 72
Anglo-Catholic, 1
animism, 37
Anselm, St, 83, 113
anthropology, 4, 6, 11, 150–51, 177, 181,
    197
    theological, 166, 174
Anti-Christ, 33
Apocalypse, 36, 62, 100–101, 251n12
apophatic theology, 38
apophaticism, 43, 142, 154
Aquinas, St Thomas, 18, 20, 49, 51, 54,
    59, 62, 64, 64n49, 67, 67n61,
    72, 73, 75n81, 81, 84, 104, 109,
    113–14, 118n20, 121, 147, 149,
    155, 159–62, 185–9, 191–3, 195–9,
    200n39, 201–11, 232, 236
Armageddon, 17, 101
ascesis, 106, 161, 233, 257
asceticism, 7, 11, 22, 228, 230–31, 248, 249,
    255n33, 257, 263, 267, 277, 288
askesis, see ascesis
Athanasius the Great, St, 145, 165, 175,
    242, 245, 259,
Augustine, St, xi–xii, 18, 19n57, 20, 49,
    54, 63, 65, 67, 74n81, 78, 82, 86,
    111–12, 114, 117, 129–37, 144–6,
    149, 157–9, 162, 167, 175, 186–7,
    193–4, 237, 243, 245, 251n14
Austen, Jane, 56
Ayres, Lewis, 47n5

Bacon, Francis, 98, 124
Bakhtin, Mikhail, 43

Báñez, Domingo, xii
Basil, St, 165, 224, 229
Baudelaire, Charles, 67, 69
beatific vision, 71, 163, 185–9, 192–3, 196,
    198–9, 201–2, 206–8
beatitude 185, 187–9, 191–8, 201, 203–11
Belloc, Hilaire, 110
Benedict XVI, Pope, 24, 113n13
Berdyaev, Nicolai, 7, 30, 41
Bergson, Henri, 63
Berkeley, George, 124
Bernstein, Jay, 58
Bérulle, Pierre, 80
Blake, William, 80
Blondel, Maurice, 126
Blum, Antonie, 38
Boehme, Jacob, 46
Boethius, 113, 118, 121, 208
Bolshevism, 17, 23
Bonaventure, St, 75n81, 187, 196, 196n33
Boulatovitch, Antoni, 30
Boulnois, Olivier, 187, 198
Bouyer, Charles, 67
Bradshaw, David, 149, 160
Braudel, Fernand, 110
Brown, Peter, 251
Bruaire, Claude, 52n11, 61, 65
Bulgakov, Sergii, 4, 7–11, 13–14, 20–21,
    23–4, 29–43, 46, 48–55, 57, 59,
    61–7, 69–71, 78–84, 86–8, 105,
    106, 129, 161, 236, 244–6, 248,
    283n44
Bull, Malcolm, 96
Burckhardt, Jacob, 110
Butler, Judith, 276

Calvinism, xiii, 116
capitalism, 17, 23, 94, 96–8, 101, 105n39,
    106, 109–10
Chalcedon, dogmas of, 5, 8, 9, 11
    Council of, 15, 80, 129, 178, 183, 286
Charlemagne, 112

Chauvet, Louis-Marie, 38
chora, 232
Christendom, 23–5, 100, 109–16, 137, 156,
    163, 178, 251
Christian Neo-Platonism, 118n20, 119, 121
Christology, 5, 47n5, 49, 76, 78, 80, 130,
    166, 171, 174, 178, 240, 243, 245,
    255, 266, 286
Chrysostom, St John, 15, 111, 215, 229
Church Fathers, xi, 4, 8–9, 14, 21, 45, 84,
    111, 115, 175, 276
Church, 1–2, 6–9, 13, 21–3, 38, 47, 62,
    68n61, 81–7, 90, 100, 103, 105–6,
    110–11, 113–17, 120, 136, 154,
    156, 163–4, 178, 182, 221–8, 230,
    232, 244–5, 247–50, 255–60, 262,
    267, 272, 281n37, 282, 284, 289
    ancient, xi, 229, 255, 264
    Eastern Orthodox, xii–xiii, 3, 13–17,
        21–3, 30, 38, 112–13, 178, 182–3,
        220, 222, 234, 244–6, 248
    medieval, 15
    Roman Catholic, 20, 24, 49
    unity, 21–2, 24–5
    universal, 23, 113–14
    Western, 164, 220
civil society, 102, 105, 136
clash of civilizations, 109
Clauberg, Johannes, 19, 122
Clement of Alexandria, 165, 175, 241–2,
    264n80
Clement of Rome, 165n1
Clément, Olivier, 35, 38
clericalism, 136
Congar, Yves, 38
Constantinople, Council of, 111n4, 113
    Second, 274
Cornford, Francis M., 219
cosmology, 4, 134, 219, 222, 240, 245
cosmos, 4–5, 35, 45, 59, 64, 74, 75n81, 76,
    78–9, 85, 111, 117, 119, 128, 129,
    132, 134, 137, 142, 158, 162, 189,
    215, 217–18, 221, 224–7, 230–34,
    236, 245, 248
Creation, xii, 4–6, 8–9, 19–21, 34, 38, 42,
    45, 49, 62–5, 69–71, 74, 79–84,
    87–9, 98, 105–6, 115, 117, 119–20,
    127–9, 135–7, 146–51, 154, 159,
    161, 169, 171–2, 174, 166, 175,
    201, 204, 205n49, 206–7, 211, 215,
    219–20, 223–5, 232, 236, 241–5,
    255, 264, 271, 275–6, 282, 287,
    288
    doctrine of, 166, 175, 218, 233
    ex nihilo, 5, 159, 219
Cudworth, Ralph, 111
Cusanus, Nicholas, *see* Nicholas of Cusa
Cyril of Alexandria, St, 80, 165, 178,
    178n28

Damian, Peter, 118
Daniélou, Jean, 72
Dante, 93
Dawson, Christopher, 110, 156
de Lubac, Henri, 47, 61, 167–8, 174, 186,
    186n2, 207
deification, xi, 3–5, 15, 20, 45, 66, 70–71,
    78–9, 81, 83, 129–30, 157–8, 163,
    165, 174, 210, 221, 229–30, 233,
    244, 266, 271, 276, 283–4
    self-, 6, 265, 267
Deleuze, Gilles, 61, 123
Descartes, René, 48, 118n20, 121–4, 126,
    131, 150, 236
desert fathers, 249–51, 254, 256, 256n35,
    257–60, 262–4, 267–8,
desire, mimetic, 280, 285–6, 288
    natural, 122–3, 126–7, 133, 185–6,
        190–91, 193, 197, 207, 272, 275
    for the supernatural, 185, 207
Desmond, William, 49, 57
Dionysius the Areopagite, 19, 63, 66, 71–4,
    75n81, 77–8, 157–9, 186–7, 215,
    218, 221–4, 234, 282
disenchantment, 35
divine humanity, 62, 79, 127–8
divine impassability, 173
divine-human, liturgy, 13, 37
    relationship, 5–6, 283, 287
    unity, 81
Dix, Dom Gregory, 222, 234
Dominican order, xiii, 234–5
Dominican Thomists, xiii
Dostoevsky, Fyodor, 9, 11
Duncan, Peter, 17

ecclesiology, 16, 18, 21, 23, 81, 230, 232, 240, 245, 248
Eckhart, Meister, 20, 65, 113, 149
economy, 4, 18, 21, 24, 66, 69–70, 88–9, 93–4, 97, 100, 103–4, 106–7, 148, 171
    divine, 66, 104, 147, 170, 173
Einstein, Albert, 87, 273
Eliot, George, 56
Eliot, T.S., 236
energy, 8, 20, 30, 42, 70n67, 102, 126, 152, 160, 289
    distinction from essence, 14
    divine 32, 35–6, 70n67, 149, 287–8
Engelhardt Jr., H. Tristram, 262
Enlightenment, European, 17, 22, 98, 110, 113, 116, 152
Eriugena, John Scotus, 19, 63, 66, 113, 124, 187, 218, 227
eschatology, 9, 14, 100, 102, 155, 210, 250, 256, 265, 266n87, 267
esse, 65, 79, 146–9, 196, 199
essence-energy distinction, *see* energy, distinction from essence
Eucharist, 21, 32, 66, 83, 148, 161, 222–3, 229–31, 254, 281, 283, 289
Eugene IV, Pope, 114
Eusebius, 15, 165, 171
Evagrius of Pontus, 242, 250, 262
Evdokimov, Paul, 35

Ferry, Jean-Luc, 32
Ferry, Jean-Marc, 29, 32–41
Feuerbach, Ludwig, 9
Fichte, Johann Gottlieb, 46, 124
filioque, 54, 113
finitude, 57, 68, 123, 186, 191–2, 232–3
Fink, Bruce, 280
Florensky, Pavel, 14, 20, 22, 30, 42–3, 46–8, 50, 63–4, 129, 288
Florovsky, Georges, 2, 7, 12–13, 110
Foucault, Michel, 31, 228, 254n27
Franciscan order, 234–5
free-market, 89, 96, 109, 116–17, 136
freedom, xii, 6, 10–12, 24, 33, 35–6, 58–9, 84, 89, 96, 99–100, 116, 123, 126, 134–6, 172, 180n39, 278–80, 283n44, 284–5

Frere, Bishop Walter, 29
Freud, Sigmund, 271
Fukuyama, Francis, 116
fundamentalism, 24–5

Garrigou-Lagrange, Reginald Marie, 207
Gasper, Giles, 113
Gasperi, Aldo di, 90
Gelasius, Pope, 111
Germain V, Archbishop, 30
German idealism, 45–7, 130–31
gift exchange, 89, 105, 107, 154
Gilson, Etienne, 189, 191–2, 199
Glorieux, P., 196
Gnosticism, 48, 52, 69, 76, 165, 173, 181, 194, 202, 241, 252
Great Schism, the, 113–14, 178
Gregory of Nyssa, 57, 67n61, 72–4, 165, 236
Guillou, Marie-Joseph Le, 36

Habermas, Jürgen, 29, 41
Halifax, Lord, 29
Hamann, Johan Georg, 14, 47, 59
Hanby, Michael, 146
Hardt, Michael, 93–6, 98–9, 101–2, 106
Hauerwas, Stanley, 105
Hegel, Georg Wilhelm Friedrich, 31, 34, 46, 49, 52, 57–61, 65, 85, 110, 124, 126–7, 155, 159, 280n33
Heidegger, Martin, 19, 33, 87, 122, 125, 274
henosis, 158, 233
Henry, Michel, 254n27
Herder, Johann Gottfried von, 14
Hermes Trismegistos, 176–83
Hesychasts, 150–51
hierarchy, 49, 132–6, 207, 223
    celestial, 221
Hobbes, Thomas, 94, 96, 117, 124
Hosking, Geoffrey, 17
humanism, 97, 116
    atheist humanism, 9
    Christian humanism, 4, 13
    Renaissance, 116
Huntington, Samuel, 116
hylomorphism, 85, 199, 201

hypostasis, 5, 20, 31, 34–5, 40–41, 49, 51,
    55, 57, 61, 63, 65, 71, 79–81, 83–4,
    86, 145, 148, 150, 240

Iamblichus, 74–5, 76–7, 157, 282
Ibn 'Arabi, 68n61
icon, 14, 30–33, 36, 38, 83, 86, 164, 221,
    265–6
iconography, 86, 223, 244
Ignatius of Antioch, St, 38
Iljine, Vladimir, 87
illumination, 133, 152–4, 162–3, 196n33,
    206, 211
    doctrine of, 157
immanence, 93, 99, 117, 122, 126, 206,
    254n27
    divine, 240, 246
immortality, 123, 180, 211, 266
imperialism, 17, 261n62
Incarnation, 3, 5, 13–14, 32, 52, 66–7, 74,
    77–9, 81–5, 87, 103, 110, 127, 148,
    153–4, 165, 170, 200, 202, 210–11,
    224, 228, 244–5, 249–50, 255, 257,
    267, 272, 282
individuation, 119–200, 208, 210, 273
intellectus, 162, 209
Irenaeus, St, 225, 239, 241
Islam, 24, 57, 73, 261

Jacobi, Friedrich Heinrich, 45–7, 59
Jameson, Frederic, 100, 102
Jansenism, xiii
Jesus prayer, 157
Joachim III, Constantinople, 30
Job, 210, 264
John of Damascus, 15
John of Patmos, 100–102
John the Persian, Abba, 263
Jolivet, Jean, 118
Jones, David, 231
jouissance, 43, 278, 280, 284
Judaism, 24, 129–30
Julian the Apostate, 246

Kant, Immanuel, 31, 33, 40, 43, 45, 47–8,
    88, 110, 117, 121–4, 279n27
Kavasilas, Nicolas, 215

kenosis, 53, 71, 127, 165–6, 168–9, 173–4,
    183, 257, 267
Knox, Wilfred L., 167, 177
Knuuttila, Simo, 118
Kojève, Alexander, 58, 110

Lacan, Jacques, 152, 158, 271–81, 283, 285
Latin theology, xii, 45, 187
law, 11, 36, 68n61, 84, 89–90, 99, 104,
    111, 117, 126, 166, 171–2, 224,
    253, 279n27, 280–83, 285, 289
    Jewish, 166, 256
    Lacanian, 273, 275, 277–8, 279n28, 280
    natural, 88, 104, 111, 135, 183
Leibniz, Gottfried, 124, 130, 215
Levinas, Emmanuel, 125, 152, 205
liberal theology, 1
liberalism, 23–4, 105, 115, 118, 120, 124
    neo-, 102, 105
liturgical metaphysics, 104–5, 161
liturgy, 3, 37, 47, 75, 104, 106, 215, 216n4,
    221–9, 231–7, 248–50, 252, 254–8,
    262–5, 267–8, 281–4, 286
Locke, John, 94, 121, 124, 150
logos, 3–5, 22, 29, 34–7, 43, 46, 50, 62–3,
    65, 68, 71, 78–80, 83, 86–8, 103,
    120, 127–9, 134, 147–9, 160,
    167–71, 174, 176, 227, 231, 241,
    244, 246, 271n1, 272–80, 284–5,
    287, 288
Long, Stephen, 89, 98
Losev, Aleksei, 14, 42–3
Lossky, Vladimir, 7, 41, 247
Loudovikos, Nicholas, 114, 156–80
Louth, Andrew, 232–6
Luther, Martin, 72, 176
Lutheranism, xiii

Macarius, Abba, 261
MacIntyre, Alasdair, 21, 117
Mahé, Jean-Pierre, 177, 181n43
man-godhood, 9
Manichaeans, 259
Manicheanism, 14
Marion, Jean-Luc, 64n49, 87–8, 105, 122,
    152, 204n49, 205
Marsonet, Michele, 153
Marxism, 9, 24, 102

Mary, St Virgin, 62, 68n61, 82n106, 83, 153, 172
materialism, 84–5, 124
  economic, 9
matter, 35, 76–7, 84–5, 105, 124, 133, 144, 186–7, 192, 195, 197–212, 228, 246
Mauss, Marcel, 78
maximalism, 10
Maximus the Confessor, 4, 5n13, 15, 50, 66, 80n97, 85, 113, 147, 150–51, 155, 158–62, 165, 187n3, 215, 219, 224–31, 233, 236, 243–4, 271–2, 274–6, 281n37, 282–4, 287–9
mediation, 12–14, 20, 49–51, 55–62, 66, 70–71, 74, 77–81, 83, 94, 104, 116, 130–31, 157, 162, 187, 206, 272, 277, 286
Meeks, Douglas, 103
Men, Alexander, 87
Merleau-Ponty, Maurice, 205, 205n49
messianism, 17, 109
metaphysics, xi, 18–21, 23, 41, 103, 118–20, 122, 124–7, 130, 134–5, 142, 161, 204
  theological, 24, 124–7, 129, 136–7, 209
metaxu, 20–21, 49–50, 57, 71, 85, 87
Meyendorff, John, 15
Meyerson, Emile, 273
microcosm, 4, 37, 85, 217, 257
Milbank, John, 3, 14, 18–21, 29, 40–41, 86–90, 105, 110, 112n10, 135, 147, 149, 151, 154–5, 246
mimesis, 37, 56
mode of existence, 88, 148, 154, 271–2, 276, 283–4
monasticism, 249–50, 253, 257n41, 259–60, 267
monophysitism, 6, 9, 153, 178n28
Moses, 33, 72–3, 104, 204, 264
Mount Athos, 30
Mrut, Issac, 182
mystagogy, 226, 252, 254–5, 260
mysticism, 38, 72, 77, 144, 149–51, 153

Nagel, Thomas, 152
Name-of-the-Father, 272–3, 275, 277
nation-state, 16, 89, 89n125, 93–5, 99, 109

nationalism, 6, 16–17, 109
nature and grace, xi, xii, 2–3, 45, 119, 142, 186, 272, 283
Nazianzen, Gregory, *see* Nazianzus, Gregory
Nazianzus, Gregory, 70n68, 178
Negri, Antonio, 93–6, 98–102, 106
Nemesius of Emesa, 4
Nicaea, Christology of, 255, 257, 266–7
  Council of, 113
  faith of, 249–50, 267
Nicholas of Cusa, 20, 66, 113, 174,
Niebuhr, Reinhold, 98
Nietzsche, Friedrich, 110, 122, 125, 152, 278
nihilism, 45–6, 124, 142, 152, 165
Nikon, Bishop, 30
nominalism, xii, 30–31, 114–15, 118n20, 119, 124, 153, 199
nouvelle théologie, 18, 130, 156
Novak, Michael, 89, 96–102

Obolensky, Dimitri, 23, 112
Ockham, William of, 72, 115, 118n20, 119
Oliver, Simon, 215n2, 232
ontology, 13, 18–21, 33, 50, 62, 80, 83, 118, 120, 122–3, 135, 141–2, 144–5, 147–8, 150–51, 153–4, 158, 161, 165, 175, 246, 277, 283
organicism, 55, 109, 117, 135, 147, 216, 278
Other, the, 249, 251, 255, 257, 273, 275, 277–81, 284–9
ousia, 31, 41, 70, 143n11, 240

Pabst, Adrian, 1n1, 29, 86, 110n3, 117n19, 118n20, 120n25
Pachomius the Great, 249, 263, 264n80
paideia, 240–42, 248, 255, 264, 268
patristic theology, 4, 165, 239–40
Paul, St, xi, 60, 73, 78–9, 86, 111, 163, 165, 168, 172–3, 176, 194, 211, 241, 255, 258, 264, 278, 289
peace, 18, 58, 60–61, 89, 98, 111, 117, 122, 135–6, 172, 228–9, 243, 250, 272
  perpetual, 110
  ontology of, 19, 137
Pelagianism, 15, 78
  semi-, 78

personalism, 24, 145, 157
Peter the Great, 17
phenomenology, 19, 42, 122, 204n49,
        205n52, 254n27
Philo of Alexandria, 129
Pickstock, Catherine, 21, 29, 141, 146,
        222, 255
Plato, 20, 60, 112n7, 125, 133, 143, 155–6,
        167, 170, 215–18, 221, 224, 232,
        236, 246, 265n84
Platonism, xi–xii, 112, 118, 127, 142–4,
        153, 156–7
Plotinus, 74–5, 129, 143, 144–5, 150, 157
poetry, 168, 248
poiesis, 166–76
polis, 111, 119, 130–31, 137, 142, 154
politics, xii, 3–4, 17–18, 21, 23–4, 88, 109,
        111–13, 116–17, 118n20, 120–26,
        129, 131, 134–7, 250, 251n14,
        262–3, 265
Polycarp, St, 230
Porphyrius, 144
Porphyry, 144
Porreta, Gilbert, 117–18
Portal, Abbey, 29
positivism, 6, 9, 19, 24, 87, 122, 124–6,
        136, 205, 273
potency, 6, 121, 130, 133, 195, 201, 207–8
Prestige, G.L., 145
Proclus, 74, 77, 84, 157, 160
Pseudo-Dionysius, *see* Dionysius the
        Areopagite
psychoanalysis, 275, 278
pure nature, 117, 119, 122

quantum physics, 87–8
quantum theory, 216

rationalism, 17, 19, 43, 124
re-enchantment, 2–3
real relation, 119
realism, 19n57, 20–22, 114–16, 118, 124,
        127
Reformation, Protestant, 113, 115, 156
relationality, 21, 52, 56, 110, 120, 129, 131,
        135–7, 149, 158–9, 175, 280, 286
relativity, 13, 216, 273
Renaissance, 45, 48, 93–4, 116, 217

Renczes, Philipp, 288
revelation, 2, 5–6, 9, 13, 18, 33, 37, 42, 45,
        47, 59, 77, 115–16, 119, 128n39,
        129–30, 183, 240–42, 244–6, 253,
        254n27, 260
    Book of, 100–102, 265
revolution, 9–10, 95–6, 109, 114, 216,
        252n22, 260n56, 264
Ricœur, Paul, 32, 87
Rilke, Rainer Maria, 217
Rimbaud, Arthur, 155
Riou, Alain, 229–30
Roman Catholicism, 21, 24, 113, 156
    social teaching, 24
Romanides, John, 145
Rose, Gillian, 58
Rowland, Christopher, 100
Roy, Olivier du, 144
Russian Revolution, 114

sapientia, 129, 131–2, 134, 256
Schelling, Friedrich Wilhelm Joseph, 31,
        46, 48, 52, 58–60, 69, 88, 124,
        126, 130
Schmemann, Alexander, 2, 222, 255
Scotus, John Duns, 70n68, 80n97, 93, 98,
        115, 117, 118n20, 119, 122, 142,
        235
secular reason, 116, 164
secularism, 1–2, 7, 16–17, 25, 116
sin, xii, 8, 67, 69, 75n81, 81, 98, 102, 104,
        117, 170–71, 173–5, 194, 211, 251,
        257, 260, 281
    original, xii
Smith, Adam, 96, 98, 117
Sobornost, 22, 33
socialism, 9–10, 96, 109, 126, 135
Solovyov, Vladimir, 19, 23–4, 45–6, 58,
        63, 111–12, 121, 124–31, 133–7
Sophia, 4–5, 20–22, 36, 41, 50–52, 54, 57,
        60–66, 68n61, 69, 71, 77, 79, 82–6,
        88, 128–9, 134, 137, 161, 168–9
    created (fallen), 49, 63, 80–81, 236
    divine (uncreated, heavenly), 20, 63,
        78–9, 82, 106
sophiology, 20, 22, 45, 49–50, 71, 78, 83,
        86, 128n39, 161, 239, 242–5
Sorokin, Pitirim, 110

sovereignty, xii, 89, 94, 98–102, 115–16, 120, 186, 252, 266
space, 22, 47, 55, 64, 87, 104, 107, 115, 119, 132, 158, 215–22, 224, 226–7, 232–3, 235–6, 261, 274
Spaemann, Robert, 56n23, 162
Spengler, Oswald, 110
Spinoza, Benedict de, 93, 95, 98, 123–4
Suárez, Francisco, 20, 117, 119–20, 122
substance, 31, 33, 40–43, 55, 120, 123, 128, 128n39, 132, 143n11, 145, 179n37, 182n44, 189–92, 194, 199, 202–4, 207–9
Suger, Abbot, 73
supernatural, 20, 45, 83, 111, 115, 117, 119–20, 122, 127, 133, 162–3, 179, 182, 185, 191, 201, 203, 207–8, 211, 251
Swedenborg, Emanuel, 62, 80
Symeon the New Theologian, 150

Taylor, Charles, 35, 37, 149
telos, 6, 9, 78, 122, 172, 188, 271, 275, 282–4, 286–7
Tempier, Archbishop Stephen, 114
theandric mystery, 39, 85
theocracy, 23, 136
theodicy, 48
Theodore of Studite, St, 15
theosis, see deification
theurgy, 24, 66, 74–5, 87, 106
    Neoplatonic, 66
    pagan, 160
Thurén, Lauri, 169
Tikhon, Archbishop, 30
time, 22, 48–9, 52, 54, 64–5, 75n81, 78, 80–84, 87, 110–11, 128n39, 132, 142, 158, 163, 215–22, 224, 229–30, 232–7, 244
    liturgical, 220, 229, 230
Toynbee, Arnold, 110
transcendence, xii–xiii, 33–4, 66–7, 93, 117–18, 122, 126, 149, 240, 246, 254n27

self-, 88, 126–7
transcendental philosophy, 19, 24, 123
Trinity, 20, 36, 41, 47, 49–53, 56n23, 57, 61–2, 65, 77, 79, 81, 85–6, 104, 130–31, 134, 144, 154, 158, 160–61, 242, 244–5
    doctrine of the, 6, 13–14, 103, 241, 245
Trottman, Christian, 187, 198
Turner, Denys, 72

universalism, 2, 17, 110, 116, 124
    Christian, 126
universals, 115, 117, 119, 198–9, 203, 206, 208
univocity, 19, 49, 61, 115, 122, 235, 240
    of being, 64, 93, 119, 122
utopia, 10–11, 18, 22, 97, 110, 135, 265
utopianism, 6, 9–11, 102, 175

Venard, Olivier-Thomas, 29
veneration of the Name, 30
Vico, Giambattista, 14, 98
vitalism, 55, 62, 83
voluntarism, xii–xiii, 114–15, 118, 159
von Balthasar, Hans Urs, 47, 52–3, 67, 68n61, 72

wars of religion, 94, 109
West, the, xii, 2, 8, 15–17, 19, 47, 66, 73, 78, 109–10, 114–16, 136–7, 143–4, 147, 152, 154–7, 159–60, 163, 222, 233–5
Williams, Archbishop Rowan, 29, 51, 66, 77, 84, 134, 149, 158, 163
Williams, Charles, 164

Yannaras, Christos, 35, 41–2, 87–8, 145, 151

Zernov, Nicolas, 110
Žižek, Slavoj, 58, 80n97, 85, 281
Zizioulas, John, 19n57, 41, 145, 151